D0893247

Jeannette Rankin

"You are the best brother in the world."

Jeannette and Wellington Rankin in front of the family home, about 1914

Jeannette Rankin

A Political Woman

James J. Lopach
Jean A. Luckowski

UNIVERSITY PRESS OF COLORADO

© 2005 by the University Press of Colorado

Published by the University Press of Colorado
5589 Arapahoe Avenue, Suite 206C
Boulder, Colorado 80303

 The University Press of Colorado is a proud member of
the Association of American University Presses.

The University Press of Colorado is a cooperative publishing enterprise supported, in part, by Adams State College, Colorado State University, Fort Lewis College, Mesa State College, Metropolitan State College of Denver, University of Colorado, University of Northern Colorado, and Western State College of Colorado.

∞ The paper used in this publication meets the minimum requirements of the American National Standard for Information Sciences—Permanence of Paper for Printed Library Materials. ANSI Z39.48-1992

Library of Congress Cataloging-in-Publication Data

Lopach, James J.
 Jeannette Rankin : a political woman / James J. Lopach, Jean A. Luckowski.
  p. cm.
 Includes bibliographical references (p.   ) and index.
 ISBN 0-87081-812-0 (hardcover : alk. paper)
 1. Rankin, Jeannette, 1880–1973. 2. Women legislators—United States—Biography. 3. Legislators—United States—Biography. 4. United States. Congress. House—Biography. 5. Social reformers—United States—Biography. 6. Feminists—United States—Biography. I. Luckowski, Jean A., 1952– II. Title.
  E748.R223L67 2005
  328.73'092—dc22

                                                                    2005014129

Design by Daniel Pratt

14 13 12 11 10 09 08 07 06   10 9 8 7 6 5 4 3 2

Cover: photograph by Harris and Ewing, Washington, D.C., courtesy Montana Historical Society, Helena. PAC 74-57.4.

Frontispiece: Jeannette Rankin and brother Wellington D. Rankin in front of old Rankin home, Missoula, Montana, about 1914; photographer unidentified. Courtesy of Montana Historical Society, Helena. 9.44-477.

To our parents,
John and Alma Lopach
Jack and Teresa Luckowski

Contents

Preface

ORE THAN THIRTY YEARS AFTER HER DEATH, JEANNETTE RANKIN STILL CON-
fronts Montanans. Her likeness peers out from posters, her name
identifies buildings, her statue stands prominently in the state capitol, her deeds are dramatized on stage, and her memory is invoked
by politicians. Despite this recognition, this first woman of U.S. politics
remains a mystery, and attempts to dig deeper into the enigma of Jeannette
Rankin usually come to naught.

This book was born out of such frustration. Why was Jeannette Rankin
the first woman elected to the U.S. Congress, what did she accomplish during her historic first congressional term, and why did she become renowned
as a pacifist and feminist? Earlier works depict Jeannette Rankin hero-
ically ("The Lady from Montana," *Flight of the Dove*, "The Woman Who
Said No to War," *America's Conscience*), but original sources reveal that our
subject was more human than mythic. Rather than simply celebrating
Jeannette Rankin as a young woman from the West, imbued with democracy and peace, heading east to conquer Washington, we examined her

family relationships, friendships, political activities, and personality to answer our questions.

Our research revealed a complex person. As a pioneering political woman, Jeannette Rankin had a distinctive personality—energetic, driven, tough, and controlling—but as a member of the Rankin family she was subject most of her life to the will of her wealthy and powerful brother, Wellington Rankin. Montana claims Jeannette Rankin as its first daughter, but New York more than any other place inspired and sustained her. Jeannette Rankin achieved notoriety for voting in the U.S. Congress against two wars, but her notable strengths lay in her campaigning and not her ability to govern. She served only two terms in Congress, but for the rest of her life she strove to recapture her lost fame. She was feisty, but she was a pacifist. She lived as if she were poor, but she was financially well off. Jeannette Rankin, however, was not without constitution. Throughout her life, she remained unchanging and unbending in one respect: her belief in the superiority of women.

Because Jeannette Rankin's long life was paradoxical and because her periods of public activity were intermittent, a straightforward chronological telling of her story seemed inappropriate. A better framework, we concluded, would be a biographic overview followed by chapters probing the following major themes and influences: how her family roots and relationships de-fined, enabled, and limited her; how her woman-centered personal world paralleled her woman-based politics; how her coming of age politically and personally was facilitated by woman suffrage; how her strong personality blossomed into her indomitable campaign style; how her political impatience compromised the accomplishments of her first congressional term; how her feminism and failures forged the hard-edged pacifism of her second con-gressional term; how her political and personal inconsistencies cloud her legacy; and how her successes and flaws can be explained by the fact that she was a Rankin first and a radical second.

The portrait of Jeannette Rankin that emerges is not, with one excep-tion, "touched up." Always in a rush, she left mistakes in her letters and notes. For the reader's sake, we have corrected frequent but minor gram-matical and spelling errors (e.g., we have changed "thot" to "thought," "struggel" to "struggle," "Im" to "I'm," and "Ill" to "I'll"). Otherwise, we have allowed the record to speak for itself. We carefully identified our sources throughout the narrative. But here, too, there is an exception. Two of Jeannette

Rankin's relatives requested that their recollections not be attributed. Honoring this wish, we used these sources and cited them as "confidential interview" because we did not want to leave out this important information. Without it, Jeannette Rankin's story would have been much less interesting.

JAMES J. LOPACH

JEAN A. LUCKOWSKI

Jeannette Rankin

Prologue

Possessed by Politics

EANNETTE RANKIN, THE FIRST WOMAN TO GO TO CONGRESS, WAS "DRIVEN BY A demon." She was clearly restless, never staying anywhere for very long. Montana, her native state, became a political stage and summer retreat for its runaway daughter. Equally weak was the hold of Georgia, her adopted state, and New York, her spiritual home. For Jeannette Rankin, places were not for putting down roots—she lived everywhere, she said—but for giving speeches, organizing, and resting a bit before hurrying on. Her life was no more grounded personally. Although it was filled with people, many captivated by her, she enjoyed an abiding intimacy with no man or woman. Like many political women who came after her, she thought that a close relationship would consume the energy she needed to fight for her causes. The demon that possessed Jeannette Rankin, turning her personal life out and her public life in, was her desire for fame and influence. For more than sixty years, it propelled her through a seemingly endless series of suffrage, political, and peace campaigns. The story of Jeannette Rankin that emerges is less the tale of a western pioneering spirit and more the chronicle of a woman driven to find identity and fulfillment in politics.

Jeannette Rankin's parents, John Rankin and Olive Pickering, influenced her high-energy approach to life, but in different ways. John Rankin was a true pioneer. He arrived in Montana from Ontario, Canada, in 1869, coming up the Missouri River by boat to Fort Benton and then over land by oxcart to Helena. He worked as a carpenter in mining camps and then settled in western Montana. Olive Pickering, no less adventurous, came to Montana in 1878, traveling from New Hampshire to Salt Lake City by train and then north by stagecoach to become the second schoolteacher in Missoula. John Rankin, Jeannette said, loved each of his seven children, but he especially encouraged her, the eldest (born in 1880), because she showed a keen interest in his public activities: his ranch, lumber mill, and political and business affairs. Olive Rankin reserved her special affection for Wellington Rankin, the family's second child and only boy. As John Rankin's dutiful wife, Olive ruled the family's domestic affairs and viewed her outwardly looking oldest daughter as an "unresponsive 'problem' child." The "problem" was Jeannette's increasing dislike of Montana's isolation and the traditional housekeeping and maternal duties her mother imposed on her after her father's untimely death.

False starts and frustrations marked Jeannette Rankin's flight from surrogate motherhood and rural life. Probably more because of her parents' urging than love of formal education, she attended local schools and the new state university. Immediately after graduation, she taught at a rural school near the family ranch but concluded that she "didn't like it." She crossed the Continental Divide to teach fourth, fifth, and sixth graders in the small town of Whitehall. But she left the school after failing the state certification examination and becoming involved in an embarrassing event, "probably of a sexual nature." Back in Missoula after her father's death, she resumed the traditional duties of an oldest daughter, managing the family household, assisting a milliner at a department store, and studying furniture-making by correspondence.

Little by little, Jeannette Rankin became aware of other possibilities as her brother set out on a prestigious career path. After graduating from the local university, Wellington Rankin attended Harvard, Oxford, and then Harvard Law School. Jeannette saw firsthand the excitement of a big city and the challenge of a first-class education when she visited Wellington in

Boston. A world of alternative womanhood and female possibility opened up to her when she read Jane Addams and stayed for a time, during a period of convalescence, at a San Francisco settlement house. Her experience of a life beyond Montana's box canyons and one-room schoolhouses fueled her desire to escape. Her pent-up frustration was expressed in a cri de coeur she entered in her personal journal: "Go! Go! Go! It makes no difference where just so you go! go! go! Remember at the first opportunity go!"

In her desolation, Jeannette Rankin became inflamed by the person of Jane Addams, a place like Hull House, and Addams's idea that women's maternal instincts could have application outside the home. Her cry was answered by a calling, and in 1908 she entered the nation's motherhouse of social work, the pioneering New York School of Philanthropy. She left the New York School the next year with a graduate certificate in Social Economy and the belief that a better society could be achieved through social science investigation and fair economic policies. She returned to Montana with her sophisticated education, enhanced social conscience, and plans for a public bathhouse and single-sex jails. Wellington Rankin came home the same year with his Harvard law degree, Progressive Party ideas, and plans to enter politics.

The Rankin household had been too small for the childhood rivalries of Jeannette Rankin and Wellington Rankin, and soon Montana would not be able to accommodate their energy and ambitions. While Wellington was settling into a politically active law firm that included future U.S. senator Thomas J. Walsh, Jeannette, supported by a $75-per-month allowance (about $1,300 today) from her father's estate, traveled west to Spokane to work in a children's home. Finding the duties of institutional work "suffocating," she continued west to Seattle where she worked at another orphanage, this time placing abandoned children with foster families. Such proximity to the intractableness of human suffering proved to be dispiriting for the young social worker. "I couldn't take it," she said, and she turned her back on social work and volunteered with the Washington campaign for woman suffrage. To build on the forensic promise she had shown at the New York School and to prepare herself for the campaign work ahead, she enrolled in Oral Expression at the University of Washington. Speaking on street corners as a suffragist, she began to develop a distinctive political presence, one that raised her above the traditional woman's "self-denying, domestic, subservient" voice.

Jeannette Rankin's six years in suffrage work, beginning in Seattle, were politically formative. The lessons in organizing remained at the core of her political creed until her death. Minnie J. Reynolds, Rankin's mentor in Washington, reinforced her maternalist antiwar sentiments—that peace was peculiarly a woman's issue—that she had learned from Jane Addams. Reynolds was so impressed with Rankin's public speaking and hard work that she recommended her for more demanding political duties to Harriet Laidlaw, who, with her husband James Laidlaw, was a leader and patron in the New York suffrage movement. On her way to suffrage's front line, Rankin stopped in Montana to urge the state's political establishment, which now included her brother, to authorize a suffrage referendum. In February 1911, she became the third suffragist in the state's history to address the Montana legislature.

Beyond Jeannette Rankin's speech in the Montana statehouse lay the challenges, opportunities, and excitement of New York. For three years she worked for the New York Woman Suffrage Party as a sidewalk campaigner, lobbyist, and field organizer. Under the direction of Harriet Laidlaw, she campaigned with Mary Beard and Cornelia Swinnerton, later a close friend. Then, as national field secretary for the National American Woman Suffrage Association (NAWSA), she organized and lobbied in North Dakota, South Dakota, Missouri, Nebraska, Michigan, Ohio, Pennsylvania, Delaware, Tennessee, Alabama, and Florida. Working in pressure-cooker conditions state after state, Rankin continued to strengthen her political skills.

While based in New York, Jeannette Rankin's personal life became centered in Greenwich Village. There she met a group of educated and professional women who had the common bond of membership in the Heterodoxy club. These women were both politically radical and personally daring. Feminism, lesbianism, direct labor action, pacifism, and socialism ran through their lives. Their "erotic experimentation" was "an essential, innovative component of revolutionary struggle." Some of these women played recurring parts in Rankin's life, and some of her longest relationships stemmed from this period. Her friendships with lifelong partners, educator Elisabeth Irwin and author Katharine Anthony and later, after Irwin's death, with Anthony alone, provide some of the rare tender moments of Jeannette Rankin's story.

Jeannette Rankin's dedicated service to national suffrage groups did not prevent her from playing a central role in her home state's suffrage movement. Building on others' prior work, she took over the Montana Equal Suffrage Association in 1913 and through this association got a suffrage amendment on the ballot. After the legislature authorized the referendum, she resigned from NAWSA to direct full-time Montana's 1914 campaign to get the measure adopted. Her own assessment was that she excelled in her leadership role: "[T]he women did it. . . . [T]hey all did as I said." Others agreed that her contribution to the campaign's success was "remarkable."

NAWSA leaders, too, attributed Montana's suffrage success to Jeannette Rankin and gave her a "tumultuous welcome" at their 1914 Nashville convention. Needing her talents in the field, NAWSA president Carrie Chapman Catt sent Rankin to campaign in Pennsylvania and New Hampshire and lobby in Washington, D.C. But, unhappy with her lack of influence in the national headquarters and weighing a campaign for Congress, she again resigned from NAWSA and returned to Montana in 1915. Before shouldering the burdens of her congressional race, Rankin went to New Zealand to rest and study that country's social and political reforms. There she impressed those she met. Once home she received letters from a New Zealand women's organization that regretted it had not taken more advantage of her speaking ability. She heard complaints from Montanans, however, when she trespassed on "a man's world" by announcing her campaign for the U.S. House of Representatives.

Running as a Republican in 1916, Jeannette Rankin captured one of Montana's two at-large congressional seats by receiving 6,354 more votes than the third-place candidate. Her campaign was marked by the same skill, commitment, and energy she had shown in the Montana suffrage effort. She portrayed the essential but conflicting images of "altruism" and "toughness": a "perfect little lad[y]" with community officials and "brazen" and "unladylike" in the streets and at public meetings. She endured day after day of "hot dirty trains" and "inconvenient hotel rooms." She "'ran as a woman,' emphasizing her gender and the issues that had been developed by women's groups," compared with her pacifism platform in her 1940 campaign. "[T]he first time it was suffrage," she later said, "the second time it was peace." Her winning can be attributed to her aggressive campaigning; the at-large congressional district that allowed "multiple winners," especially an outsider like a woman; the support of newly enfranchised women; and Wellington Rankin's money, political savvy, and, it is rumored, chicanery.

Jeannette Rankin's stunning achievement—the first woman in the world to be elected to a national legislative body—incited the imagination of the press and public. Admirers referred to her as a western heroine, a Florence Nightingale, and the soon-to-be first woman president. From Delaware, Virginia, Pennsylvania, Ohio, and Wisconsin came poems celebrating her heroism. A Wisconsin woman enthused:

> She will win for us the fight
> She will win for us the battle
> Johnny Booze be put to flight
> Long will ring her praise and glory
> As she takes her welcomed stand
> Just as did the good St. Patrick
> Banish toads in Ireland.

Two NAWSA presidents, Anna Howard Shaw and Carrie Chapman Catt, saw her as the savior of suffrage and put aside their pre-election reservations. Shaw had thought Jeannette Rankin's campaign rash and Catt had thought Rankin not sufficiently "intellectual." In the post-election glow Catt exclaimed, "The day of our deliverance is . . . to be at the hands of a woman." Rankin knew that woman reformers were looking to her. She told the *New York Times,* "I am going to Washington to represent the women and children of the West, to work for an eight hour day for women, and for laws providing that women shall receive the same wages as men for equal amounts of work."

A messianic interpretation of Jeannette Rankin's victory came from Mary O'Neill of Butte, Montana, a journalist, radical suffragist, and Rankin's political ally and soul mate. Similar to feminist Charlotte Perkins Gilman's essentialist and evolutionist call to "mothers of the world to utilize their special 'transcendent power to remake humanity,'" O'Neill celebrated Rankin's election as messianic maternalism: "Your election means a recognition of the ideals for which Womanhood stands. You are the instrument used by a Higher Power through which to disseminate the spiritual force so necessary to the illumination of these ideals. . . . [M]y heart is with you in this great Hour of history; this Hour is read by the common people as a 'recognition of women,' but it is read by those who do understand as the Hour when the hands on the face of Time turn upward for the new Race being founded in this country. You shall be the one about whom the storm shall break during the next two years. Because of this you must conserve your energies, your force, your nerves, your beautiful body that you can be strong enough to stand the strain and discriminating enough to respond only to the very highest and best for Humanity."

Jeannette Rankin's mission began with a railroad journey to New York where she inaugurated a series of twenty lectures, the first at Carnegie Hall. Wellington Rankin's continuing involvement shielded Jeannette from the "sexual innuendo or hints of impropriety" that were certain to come from disapproving men and women. He negotiated the contract with the speakers' bureau, drafted her lecture remarks, and accompanied her on the trip east. On the last day of March 1917, Jeannette and Wellington arrived in the nation's capital, despite her telling a friend that it "is doubtful if I shall go to Washington until next winter."

President Woodrow Wilson had called a special session of Congress. The war Jeannette Rankin had ignored in her lectures now stared her in the face. At the roll call on the early morning of April 7, 1917, her vote against war was one of fifty-seven, but in her judgment she alone suffered retribution. Years later she told a biographer that for her World War I "came and destroyed everything." Although it is true that Congress's war agenda sidetracked her domestic reform plans, her antiwar vote did not cause her election defeat in 1918. She immediately backpedaled from her vote and was able to repair its political damage. What prevented her reelection was the way she resolved two conflicting roles: radical womanhood's representative-at-large and conservative womanhood's "deliverance" for the limited goal of suffrage. These two roles weighed on Rankin during her first term, and to the chagrin of too many Montanans she often chose a radical identity.

It was Jeannette Rankin's position on labor that especially alienated voters. Work conditions had figured in her 1916 campaign, and two opportunities to do something arose early in her term. The first, at the federal Bureau of Engraving and Printing, aroused little opposition but emboldened her to take on the second challenge. A constituent, whose sister worked at the bureau, had relayed stories to the congresswoman about workplace abuse. Rankin's inquiry exposed sexual harassment and brought an end to fifteen-hour workdays and forced resignations. The second opportunity arose in Butte. On June 9, 1917, a mining disaster killed 164 workers. A bitter strike and impasse between Industrial Workers of the World–inspired miners and the Anaconda Copper Mining Company ensued. With rhetoric reminiscent of her "great Hour of history" letter, Mary O'Neill urged Rankin to come to Butte and mediate a settlement.

Before departing Washington, Jeannette Rankin sought her brother's advice and found herself caught between his pragmatism and Mary O'Neill's radicalism. This time O'Neill won out. Jeannette Rankin's acts of patriotism—selling war bonds and raising Red Cross funds—had defused the war issue, but Montanans did not overlook her sympathies for the Butte Wobblies. A Montana newspaper that enjoyed the reputation of being "in the best tradition of American journalism" editorialized, "We heartily wish that some of the excellent things that [Jeannette Rankin] has done might balance her single mistake of lending her support to the I.W.W. leaders at Butte, but we cannot bring ourselves to that state of mind." Rankin's reelection was further poisoned by gerrymandering, "a ploy that has been used on more than one occasion since to oust a woman from office." The Montana legislature split the state's at-large congressional district in two, leaving her with the choice of running in the western district or in the eastern district. Her congressional colleague warned her that the western district was his turf, and she decided against carpetbagging in eastern Montana. What was left was a race against incumbent U.S. senator Thomas J. Walsh, Wellington Rankin's former law partner and a staunch supporter of woman suffrage.

After losing the 1918 Republican U.S. Senate primary, Jeannette Rankin stayed in the race as a National Party candidate. She lost in the general election, trailing, with 23 percent of the vote, Democrat Thomas Walsh and the Republican candidate. Wellington Rankin's campaign strategy of forging a coalition of labor, agriculture, and women could not overcome the serious obstacles of Jeannette Rankin's third-party candidacy. NAWSA president Carrie Chapman Catt endorsed Senator Walsh and asked Harriet Laidlaw to persuade Rankin to withdraw from the race. In a public statement Catt praised Walsh ("We have never had a better friend") and criticized Rankin ("Every time she answers the roll call she loses us a million votes"). Jeannette Rankin's repudiation by her suffrage colleagues colored her remarks when she departed Washington: "I was just the most awful person that ever was."

With NAWSA shutting out its once star campaigner, few career choices remained. For Jeannette Rankin and for women who lost elections years later, a problem was not having a career, such as law or business, "to fall back on." Knowing that "to be a . . . social worker–politician [would be] too much of a clash for employers," she observed, "no social worker would have anything to do with me." In the years ahead, defeated political women frequently had "no place to go but home," but even that door was closed to Jeannette Rankin. For the next twenty-two years, until her 1940 election to the U.S. House of Representatives, Wellington Rankin occupied the Montana political stage through five statewide elections. The practical choices remaining to Jeannette Rankin were working for NAWSA's rival, the National Woman's Party; the League of Women Voters; the Democratic or Republican Party; or new social reform and peace organizations. But she had learned from her suffrage campaigning that she detested battling bureaucracy and working under the direction of a supervisor. In contrast, Belle Moskowitz and Molly Dewson, "essentialists" like Jeannette Rankin, were women who wielded substantial organizational power in the 1920s and 1930s. Moskowitz "served as the right-hand woman of Governor Al Smith of New York," and Dewson became an influential New Deal insider by learning "to play the game by the men's rules." With her congressional experience as a credential, Rankin drifted for two decades through a series of lobbying positions, mainly concerning peace.

In 1919, as a Women's Peace Party delegate and in the company of Jane Addams and social reformer Florence Kelley, Jeannette Rankin attended the Women's International Conference for Permanent Peace in Zurich that established the Women's International League for Peace and Freedom. After Addams's Women's Peace Party became the U.S. branch of the Women's International League, Rankin served on its executive board and as an employee. The organization's agenda included establishing anti-hunger programs; releasing war and political prisoners, including "Wobblies"; ending profit-driven diplomacy; and outlawing war—goals that "fitted nicely" with Jeannette Rankin's views. In 1920 she lobbied Congress for the Women's International League, and in 1925 she worked as the organization's field secretary. Her speechmaking and willingness to endure arduous travel impressed her colleagues. But increasingly, she became dissatisfied with itinerant speaking and fund-raising. These assignments, in her judgment, were at odds with the lessons she had taken away from her suffrage and congressional campaigns. She left the Women's International League in late 1925 because, unlike her employer, she "wanted to do grassroots organizing."

While on the governing council of the Women's International League, Jeannette Rankin worked with Florence Kelley's National Consumers' League. Kelley, with her "deep capacity for affection [hidden] behind a gruff and demanding exterior," had impressed Rankin as a lecturer at the New York School of Philanthropy. The two women shared a capacity for hard work, socialist leanings, an interest in legislation to protect mothers and infants, and a friendship with Jane Addams. Kelley had asked Rankin as a congresswoman to introduce a bill to improve maternity and infant hygiene. The Sheppard-Towner Maternity Act, which Congress finally passed in 1921, was thought by Kelley to be the most important work of her own career. They collaborated again when Rankin served as a National Consumers' League lobbyist and fieldworker from 1921 to 1924.

For the National Consumers' League, Jeannette Rankin traveled to six midwestern states to champion the cause of minimum-wage and maximum-hour legislation. Her base was Jane Addams's Hull House in Chicago, "a colony of efficient and intelligent women" who "applied social science techniques to social problems." Florence Kelley had resided at Hull House in the 1890s where, in the upstairs rooms of the large old residence, women lived "as if [they] were back in college again, . . . transforming spinsterhood into a splendid self-sufficiency." Traveling at times with Rankin were Addams, Kelley, and Julia Lathrop, head of the federal Children's Bureau and one of Hull House's "core" residents. They would "take a 'drummers' room,' one with several beds, in a hotel in a state capital where they were lobbying." In 1924 Rankin left the National Consumers' League and returned to Montana to help in Wellington Rankin's unsuccessful U.S. Senate primary campaign. Then she went to Bogart, Georgia, to build a house on sixty-four acres she had bought. Reflecting on her work with Florence Kelley, Rankin said that she had "piddled around with this thing and then that thing, child labor and things of that kind." She was beginning to think that only peace work mattered.

Jeannette Rankin's living in Georgia made sense because of its mild climate, low cost of living, and proximity to New York friends and Washington politics. Montana was not an option because of its isolation, cold winters, and Wellington Rankin's unfulfilled political ambitions. During this period he called on his supposedly idle sister for several favors. In 1928 she dutifully returned to Montana to help him during his unsuccessful campaign for governor. Earlier, in 1925, she drove his new car from

Detroit to Montana. On his Montana attorney general stationery, Wellington Rankin had instructed his sister: "I am enclosing two checks, each for $50.00 for you to use when you need them. Yesterday I mailed $150.00 to Bogart. . . . [The] car will be ready for you at the Cadillac factory. . . . It is a closed five passenger sedan—four doors . . . a wonderful car. Have them explain all to you before you start. It doesn't require the changing of oil as often as it used to. I think it will go 2,000 miles. . . . The first thousand miles it must be run slowly as you know. . . . I can meet you in eastern Montana or western Dakota."

Jeannette Rankin did not need her brother's errands to keep her busy. She was engaged in remodeling her house and building up, "single-handedly," the Georgia Peace Society—as she described it, a "'center of infection' of peace sentiment." Her plan was to spread her message first locally—to business owners, government officials, ministers, fairgoers—and then move outward to neighboring counties. Through the mid-1930s she recruited members, organized parades and conferences, and campaigned against war-minded politicians. Sustained initially by her drive and sacrifices, the society went into decline when she grew bored, and the membership, upset about her solitary tactics, began referring to her as a "renegade."

In 1929 the Women's Peace Union invited Jeannette Rankin to return to the national stage. Peace work in Georgia was becoming stale, as she wrote to her new employer: "I have been in the country long enough to be quite thrilled with the idea of getting into the fight again." But organizational life once again frustrated Rankin. She continued to insist on working the grassroots rather than speaking and lobbying as her employer preferred. Before a year had gone by, officials of the Women's Peace Union censored a press release that contained her ideas and let her contract expire.

Out of work, Jeannette Rankin contacted Frederick Libby, who directed the nation's largest antiwar group, the Quaker-based National Council for the Prevention of War (NCPW). Although Rankin worked for the NCPW until late 1939, eventually as associate legislative secretary, the initial conditions of her employment—part-time lecturing and lobbying for expenses only—foreshadowed failure. Libby noted in his diary that Rankin expressed her dissatisfaction: "Nobody wants me. . . . I hate day-to-day jobs and have had them all my life." But the provisional and poorly paid position gave her flexibility to do other things that interested her. With Libby's permission and limited financial support and Wellington Rankin's ample resources, she traveled in Europe during several summers in the 1930s. Besides getting "a rested point of view," she visited cooperatives in Sweden, attended a disarmament debate at the League of Nations, and witnessed the rise of Nazism in Germany. One summer her way was paid by a wealthy admirer she had met on a previous trip. Mary Huntington Williams enticed Rankin: "There is a possibility of my going to Geneva about the 18th of August. Would you be my guest over and back and while there for about six weeks? Can you get permission before leaving Washington to loaf with me? . . . Of course you would be free to play with all your friends as well as me. Affectionately."

Toward the end of 1939, Jeannette Rankin's job with the National Council for the Prevention of War sputtered to a stop. An incident gave both Rankin and the NCPW an excuse to terminate their relationship. A speech written for her by the council's staff contained a sentence she wanted removed. When the council refused, she "gave the speech and left out the sentence." Frederick Libby dropped her from his budget, and she said, "I wasn't going to be under his direction." Other political women in the 1920s and 1930s "learned the lessons of networking and cooperation," but Jeannette Rankin could not or would not. Ever prizing her autonomy, she thought more than ever about her term in Congress, the one time in her life when she had been in charge and well compensated.

Many barriers lay in the way of Jeannette Rankin's return to Congress. Her long absence from Montana, except for summers at Wellington Rankin's ranch, her age (sixty in 1940), and her twenty years out of office opened her to charges of being old, a has-been, and a carpetbagger. To her advantage were her toughness and near-limitless energy, her identification with pacifism as the nation faced another war, and Wellington's wealth and connections. (Wellington Rankin was by then a leading lawyer and the best-known Republican in Montana.) In 1938 Jeannette Rankin had listed for an NCPW colleague the qualities of a successful campaigner: "The most important thing about a candidate is his . . . real desire for peace. . . . Next is his industry, his willingness to work, his courage in a tight place." Believing she possessed all of them and hoping she could get her brother's blessing, she returned to Montana in 1939 under the cover of starting a peace society in the Bitterroot Valley south of Missoula.

With her brother's assistance and her own relentless campaigning, Jeannette Rankin prevailed in the 1940 primary and general election. She and Olive Rankin spent early November at Wellington's ranch in subzero weather and, after they thought the Arctic front had passed, the sixty-year-old daughter and the eighty-seven-year-old mother set out by automobile for Washington and met "every night . . . a fresh snowstorm." Frustrated by their slow progress, Rankin "shipped the car from Minneapolis to Pittsburgh" by rail and arrived in Washington with "a cold in [her] eyes and nose." Ill, frustrated by the unavailability of office space, and knowing that the experience would "not be thrilling like the last time," Rankin, now an absolute pacifist, confronted the growing war movement.

Jeannette Rankin's 1941–1943 term in Congress was devoted almost totally to war. The declaration against Japan came quickly, just as the war vote in her first term had, but this time she did not hesitate or weigh options. "I learned from the first [vote]," she said. "I knew what I was going to do." She isolated herself from all pressure, including her brother, and cast the sole antiwar vote in Congress. She said later that her "second term ended for all practical purposes the day the Japanese bombed Pearl Harbor." Clearly her vote made her a reviled figure and ended any hope of legislative success. Her stock reply to her detractors included a feeble attempt at realpolitik: "We are in the war and we must insist upon a victory. . . . [T]he military policy and its activities come first and everything in life must be adjusted to that." But the war activity depressed her, and she stayed away from Washington, visiting friends in New York and Georgia and caring for her mother in Montana.

Jeannette Rankin did not so much leave Congress in December 1942 as drop from sight. She was supposed to be driving herself to Montana, but her friends lost track of her. "Where are you," Nina Swinnerton wrote. "I keep thinking of you on that long, long trail—the cold weather, the gas shortage." Mary O'Neill echoed, "Where in the world are you? . . . Wellington said you were on your way. . . . I am waiting patiently for your arrival." Rankin had gone to New York to be with Katharine Anthony whose partner, Elisabeth Irwin, had died in November. She stayed in New York until after the first of the year before obeying her brother's command to come to Montana and take care of their ailing mother.

Jeannette Rankin had made a "bargain" with Wellington Rankin. She would care for their mother and receive in exchange money for her "travel and needs." Many political women since have experienced conflicts because of their elderly parents, but for Wellington Rankin and other male politicians the tradition has been "the precise opposite: One of the women in his family will no doubt take care of the nurturing." Jeannette Rankin must have felt that her brother kept his part of the arrangement as she said that he "did everything he could to make me feel I had money of my own." On occasion, however, the burden became so onerous that she schemed "how to get out of it" and arranged escapes to Georgia, New York, Mexico, Turkey, and India. She remained Olive Rankin's principal caregiver until 1947, when Olive died in a "gruesome apartment" across the street from Wellington Rankin's law office.

After her mother's death, Jeannette Rankin was liberated from family and financial constraints. Wellington, grateful for the peace and freedom his bargain gave him, provided financially for Jeannette the rest of her life. He bought her a ranch, stocked it with cattle, and ran it with employees from his nearby ranch. He also bought her an annuity that paid $500 a month. To the time of his death in 1966, he purchased cars for her domestic travel and passage and letters of credit for her international trips. He regularly gave Jeannette and his other sisters corporate stock, financial advice, and legal assistance, and his estate left each of his three surviving sisters, including Jeannette, $75,000.

So provided for, Jeannette Rankin was constantly on the go. She summered in Montana, wintered in Georgia, and journeyed to foreign countries. In 1961 she joined her sister Edna at her birth-control assignment in Asia and, "chipper as a lark," enjoyed parties and fine hotels. Jeannette is living "just the sort of life she loves," Edna wrote to their sisters Mary and Harriet. In 1962 Rankin toured Europe by herself and the Soviet Union with a study group. When she visited Edna in Asia in 1963, Edna wrote to their sister Mary that Jeannette would stay "as long as she is happy." They lodged in Jakarta at the Hotel Indonesia, which, Edna told Mary, was "about the finest hotel service and comforts I have ever had, any place in the world." In Kashmir, Jeannette lived "in idle splendor on a houseboat afloat in the exquisite Wular Lake."

Both Edna's and Jeannette's letters suggested that travel helped Jeannette forget her political exile and facial neuralgia, which had plagued her since her youth. Writing from Chicago, Edna told Wellington that "Jeannette seemed to have a good time here for a week . . . but she was impatient to get on." From her retreat in northern India with a view of the Himalayas, Jeannette wrote to Edna, "I'm getting too bored and the result is I'm not so well . . . so believe I'll have to leave here." In a letter to Katharine Anthony, Rankin implied that she was "a solitary woman" ailing and slipping into depression. Anthony replied: "I am not going to allow you to say that you are a futile person. . . . With all that you have accomplished in life you should never let such a thought enter your mind. . . . I hope you are getting along without having to take so much of that aspirin that you buy by the tons." Rankin also had to cope with the death of friends and family, especially her sister Grace; Mary Weible, a North Dakota friend of "fifty years" whose home had been a frequent stopover during cross-country trips; Katharine Anthony, with whom she had enjoyed an "intimate relationship" extending back to 1912; and Wellington Rankin, her surrogate father, political mentor, economic provider, and closest male friend. For years Jeannette Rankin felt that she was outrunning death, at seventy-nine copying into a notebook another person's bargain with growing old: "He had a tacit understanding with age—he paid no attention to it and hoped maybe it would go away." But in 1968, after her facial pain became unbearable, she had an operation to sever a nerve that ended the pain but left her looking for the first time "like an old woman." She could no longer deny that death's footsteps were coming closer.

Jeannette Rankin's greatest fear was that she would be denied a final opportunity to make her mark politically. Occasionally her spirits were raised by a reassuring word or event. In 1958 U.S. senator John F. Kennedy, as an afterthought to his *Profiles in Courage,* praised Rankin in *McCall's Magazine* for her historic votes against war. She thanked Kennedy for the "cheering effect which your kind article gave to me personally." Then she appeared on national television and was delighted when fans sent mail to her, a "dimly remembered figure." She was buoyed again when the U.S. House of Representatives observed the fiftieth anniversary of her first congressional term. At the ceremony she challenged her new entourage of feminists and antiwar groups to protest the Vietnam War all the way to jail. Antiwar leaders asked her to lead the "Jeannette Rankin Brigade," a Washington protest march. Heartened by the acclaim and enabled by Wellington Rankin's estate, Jeannette Rankin at age eighty-eight flirted with fully emerging from political exile and running again for Congress. But convalescing from surgery and dreading poverty, she limited her political activity to not paying her telephone tax and not shopping on Tuesdays.

Not surprisingly, however, Jeannette Rankin did campaign furiously during her few remaining years. In 1971 and 1972, a law-student aide led her willingly on a political odyssey that would have daunted a young crusader but was astounding for a woman in her nineties recuperating from a broken hip. Her last hurrah was a blizzard of activities to sell the nation on two election reforms: multiple-member congressional districts and direct preferential election of the president. Since her at-large election to Congress in 1916, Rankin had praised the merits of electing several members of Congress from the same district. Her plan for direct preferential election of the president, which she had begun to formulate in India in 1952, would junk the Electoral College.

But by late 1972, little fuel remained in Jeannette Rankin's tank. Her demon spent, she could push herself no further. Having trouble swallowing and talking, and experiencing "dizzy spells," she began to turn down speaking invitations. With no family member to care for her, she moved from Georgia to a retirement apartment in Carmel, California. She sustained herself in her last days with hopes of being remembered. She inquired of little children, "Have you ever heard of Jeannette Rankin?" and she searched for her name in the "index pages of new reference, history and political books." A stroke weakened her, and her niece Dorothy, invoking memories of Olive Rankin, worried "about further cold nights on the floor in your own pee." After unsuccessfully begging her doctor to end her life, she stopped eating. Her final days were passed in the retirement home's infirmary watching the Watergate proceedings. The evening she died, a few weeks short of her ninety-third birthday, she left a note for her attendant: "I want to get back to my apartment before the 'garbage man' comes." Having given everything to politics, she believed nothing of value remained.

Family

In Her Brother's Shadow

J OHN RANKIN CAME TO MONTANA IN 1869, SEVEN YEARS BEFORE COLONEL
George Custer was defeated at the Battle of the Little Bighorn and
eight years before Chief Joseph and the Nez Perce fought the Battle of
the Big Hole and surrendered near the Bear Paw Mountains. The
Northern Pacific Railroad arrived in western Montana in 1883, and Montana received statehood in 1889. The births of Jeannette Rankin (1880) and
Wellington Rankin (1884) were on the cusp of Montana's transition from
Old West to settled land, but the two Rankin siblings could not as politicians credibly invoke log-cabin imagery. Even though Jeannette Rankin said
that she was aware of "many of the hardships" homesteaders faced, closer to
the mark was John Rankin providing his family not a sod hut on the prairie
but a gentleman's ranch in a mountain meadow and a modern mansion in
town. The Rankin family "lived an aristocratic lifestyle in a region still considered by many to be the frontier" and "thought themselves superior to others."

John Rankin was suited to the frontier. He was a large, strong, red-
bearded, and bullheaded man always ready to fight. He was a "rounder,

getting drunk with the boys and shooting off a cannon," and a "wonderful talker, able to spin anything into an engaging story." He became wealthy and influential as a rancher, builder, lumber mill operator, and proprietor of the Rankin Block and Rankin Hotel in town. He built the grandest house in Missoula, distinguished on the inside by its plumbing and central heating and on the outside by its mansard roof and Lombardy poplars. He volunteered for the army when there was an Indian uprising, and he served a term as a Republican county commissioner. With his engineering skills, he took flooded roads and washed-out bridges in stride. To a niece the busy John Rankin wrote in 1893: "[S]eems to me that I have too many irons in the fire. I am swamped with work all the time and have not time to call my life my own. There is no one that I can leave in charge to take care of any thing. I get nearly wild some times." By 1904 when he died of tick fever, he had become a pillar of the community. A picture of town fathers long hung in a downtown restaurant, John Rankin among them, his serious face with the long "Rankin nose" softened by a bushy mustache. His estate was valued at $150,000 (about $3 million today). Given his traits and accomplishments, it is not surprising that John Rankin's oldest daughter and only son, in their push to equal his success, exemplified historian Patricia Limerick's observation that "the West is a . . . place undergoing conquest and never fully escaping its consequences."

Olive Pickering's pioneering was not as dramatic as that of John Rankin. She taught in a one-room school, and married John Rankin in 1879. Jeannette was born a year later, and six other children followed: Philena, who died in early childhood, Harriet, Wellington, Mary, Edna, and Grace. Soon the family was spending summers at the Rankin ranch and winters in the town's finest residence. Olive challenged her children by inviting politicians and community leaders for dinner, filling the house with books, and hanging in the dining room a large map of the United States—the pull-down kind she had used with her pupils. After her husband's death, she increasingly surrendered household management to Jeannette and business affairs to Wellington. Plagued by a growing list of illnesses, Olive Rankin became "self-isolated" and took on the notions that her family should serve her and that visiting should be done in her home. She even instructed her married daughters that each grandchild should be born in the family residence. Increasingly inert but domineering, "always with something wrong" but tough, Olive Rankin "ruled" her children. Years later, sick and easily bored, she shuttled from daughter to daughter, but mainly to the unmarried Jeannette. Grace spoke for the others when she blurted out her frustration: "Do you forget how murderous one is after caring for her a few weeks."

When Olive Rankin was in charge, the family took on the traits of a tribe. They hung together and were not to be trifled with. Their first concern was their reputation. Olive once called her children together after a boy had declined to dance with one of the Rankin daughters. She told them that they were "cutting out" the other family. "From now on," Olive said, "we don't speak to them because he insulted your sister." Outsiders observed this family tightness. Jeannette's niece Dorothy reported that "B.J. Toole, Ross's wife, . . . saw them all in Helena and that it looked an enormous gang." Most importantly, the family's tribal spirit played a role in politics. A contemporary of Jeannette and Wellington said, "[O]nce you take on one of the Rankins, you have to whip the whole bunch. And they are formidable." When Jeannette or Wellington ran for office, the other set aside personal affairs and sibling rivalry to help in the campaign, just as all of the Rankins, nieces and nephews included, were expected to do their part.

Rivalry characterized not only interfamily but also Rankin family relations, especially between Jeannette and Wellington. They "were the most energetic ones . . . the kind of people that psychologically demanded more room." Seated across from each other at the dinner table and provoked by slights and jealousy, they were known to toss glasses and silverware at each other. Family gatherings continued to be arenas for family strife during adult years when the political ambitions of Jeannette and Wellington conflicted and their political views diverged. At Wellington's ranch the topic was usually politics, and discussion often turned to disagreement, "one knifing the other." Both thought that their own activities were of great importance, and both "were incapable of self deprecation." Both were "publicity hounds and each was slow to credit the other's accomplishments." None of the Rankin children was immune to such rivalry. Edna's daughter Dorothy once advised her mother: "I hope you warned Jeannette about your new car. I think more than anything I dread the expression on the Rankin faces when they see its magnificence."

Toward these vying Rankin siblings, John Rankin "was not a strict or harsh disciplinarian" and Olive Rankin became laissez-faire. But Jeannette Rankin, in fulfilling as eldest daughter "what Jane Addams called 'the family claim,'" was strict and harsh as a surrogate mother. She took charge of her sisters' meals, dress, disciplining, and schooling, especially for the youngest, Grace and Edna. Even though she later argued that peace begins in childhood and stems from democracy, Jeannette allowed her sisters "no choice." Regarding their health care, she was "dictatorial," to the degree of ordering Mary, Edna, and Grace to submit in their living room to a doctor's extraction of their tonsils. As adults, the sisters speculated that Jeannette was "irritable and domineering" because she was "restless and unhappy." But if so, Jeannette was not the only family member seeking greater autonomy. The year that Jeannette died, Edna told her own biographer, "I disliked my experience in Montana so much that I psychologically had buried all memory of it."

These harsh family relationships were not devoid of religious influence. Olive became a Christian Scientist after her cure from breast cancer. Wellington became a convert at Harvard because his Christian Science roommate, Ellis Sedman, pulled him through emotional depression after John Rankin's death. Olive's religious fervor infected Harriet, Mary, and Edna, but religion was not a priority for John Rankin and the other two daughters, Jeannette and Grace. Throughout her life, Jeannette Rankin did not believe in God or an afterlife, was "bitchy about Christians," and routinely called Christians "Christers." Her niece Dorothy referred to herself and Jeannette at Christmas as "infidels and anti-Christians." Before she died, Jeannette Rankin made it clear that she did not "want any goddamn Christian words spoken over [her] grave." Her deep dislike of Christianity— Saint Paul in particular—stemmed from its justifying war and making its believers "into sheep."

Whatever use Jeannette Rankin had for religion was purely practical. Missionaries gave her a place to stay during her travels, and churches provided her an audience for talking about peace. "I used to go to church meetings," she once said, but "I never go unless I can preach." As for Christian Science, it caused in her "a visceral, bitterly negative reaction." Even the intense facial pain from her lifelong neuralgia did not push her toward the religion, although Edna once tried. Writing to Mary, Edna described her attempt to proselytize Jeannette: "I hope your visit from Jeannette was not too difficult. . . . There is little one can do for her when she is seeming to experience her 'face pain.' When she had it in Jakarta I called Miss Blok, who is one of the most understanding practitioners I've ever known. Jeannette asked for help, but would *not* talk with her."

Two prominent Missoulians, Ruth and Edith Greenough, had carried Christian Science to the Rankin ranch in their horse-drawn buggy. They cured Olive of her cancer, and she became the Christian Science "mother superior of the family." Taken into the fold, Harriet, Mary, and Edna made Christian Science the center of their lives and a constant topic in their letters. Mary wrote to Wellington of the deep satisfaction her instruction and reading brought her, and Edna, from a birth-control posting, told her believing siblings how a Christian Science practitioner had saved her life: "When I returned from Bali, I lost my voice and even the ability to breathe, to the point that I thought I was passing on. She worked steadily until 3 A.M. . . . [The] next morning I was well." Explaining her religious regimen, Edna told Mary how having a roommate when traveling did not interfere with her Christian Science: "I usually read my lesson in the bathroom sometime during the night. I wonder sometimes just how I could cope . . . if it were not for my daily study of the lesson. . . . What a blessing we have." Suffering from a detached retina, Edna instructed Wellington in the "prayerful work" she wanted him to undertake: "[I]t will help if you can see me as young, vigorous and without physical handicap." Edna stressed with her biographer the importance of Christian Science in her life: "You have carefully refrained from indicating my most consuming interest and concern and study—My Religion. . . . [W]ithout my study and understanding of Christian Science, I could never have accomplished what I did—nor . . . withstood so many rebuffs."

Although Wellington Rankin adopted Christian Science too, it did not mean as much to him as it did to Edna. Those close to him said that, with respect to religion, he was more like Jeannette and Grace. He did not attend church, as Edna made clear when she campaigned for him in 1934: "I went to church this morning. And will go to a church recital tonight—what your sisters will do for you that you wouldn't do for yourself!" Instead of a comfort, Christian Science for Wellington Rankin was a "hatchet," a weapon to gain an advantage over an opponent, or a "gamble," something "to cover his butt." Like his habit of wagering on politics ("$200 that Japan surrenders within six months after Germany surrenders"), sports ("eight to five that Chicago Cubs beat the field for the pennant"), and the weather ("$10 that it will not hit zero in Helena by midnight November 30, 1945"), Christian Science accounted for part of his spending. From 1939 to 1941, he sent monthly checks totaling more than $5,000 to practitioner Ellis Sedman, his

Harvard roommate and in-law of his sister, Harriet Sedman. Between 1953 and 1964, he paid $50 to $100 a month to Maria Soubier for Christian Science services and, from 1957 to 1962, $50 to $90 a month to practitioner Paul Stark Seeley.

For his payments Wellington Rankin requested business and ranching prosperity and improved health for himself and his sisters. Ellis Sedman assured him that "the perfect law of God" took into consideration the welfare of "lower creatures," expressed his pleasure that "conditions are better with the cattle," and promised Rankin that he would not let up in his prayers: "[W]e will keep up the work through the calving season." Sedman also included Wellington Rankin's worsening hernia in his ministry: "I am working for you and we will put to rout all false symptoms." Maria Soubier assured Rankin that, as a "Child of God," the condition of his cattle and plans to buy the "Greenough Mansion" and a "new ranch" were "under the law of divine Mind." Her Christian Science also took notice of Jeannette Rankin's facial pain: "[Y]ou will soon be hearing that she is well and free of the claim." Paul Stark Seeley was bolder in his practice, warning Wellington Rankin that his "going it alone" and "personal interest in possessions" were not the way to "true humility. . . . God knows nothing about any of this." With his hernia still bothering him, Rankin absorbed the rebuke and two months later sent another plea to Seeley: "Still need help on old condition."

Wellington Rankin's hernia was a topic more of amusement than concern among the Rankin family. For years he was burdened by an "enormous bag of fluid drooping down his groin [that made] him seem in poor health whether he was or not." His cashmere suits from G. L. Dunne in New York—which complemented his Coes & Young dress shoes from Boston and his F. R. Tripler hats from New York—were tailored with "extra-wide left legs to accommodate the bulge." Rankin's personal adjustment was more difficult. He had to quit riding his stallion, White Man, and the mortality his condition conjured up frightened him. The medical profession bothered him, including a niece's husband who was a physician. During a dinner at his ranch, Rankin became incensed at the young man's unsolicited advice. Standing up from the table, Rankin shouted angrily at his guest, "Don't you realize you're arguing with a Child of God!" In a sense, Wellington Rankin's distrust of medicine was justified because he died at the Mayo Clinic in 1966 after undergoing abdominal surgery.

The Rankin family valued education more uniformly than religion. Olive, a teacher, and John, a self-taught engineer, made certain that their children had considerable educational opportunities. Jeannette, however, said that she had not enjoyed school or been well educated at the new state university from which she graduated in 1902 with a biology degree. Several contemporaries commented on what they described as her average performance. A professor recalled of the college student who became a congresswoman: "[S]he was an extremely timid girl and worked hard for what she got." A former classmate wrote to her after her 1916 election to Congress: "[I]t's hard for me to realize that you are the Jeannette Rankin I went to school with." Later, however, she rose to the challenge of the New York School of Philanthropy. Wellington graduated from the University of Montana and then Harvard College and Harvard Law School, after briefly attending Oxford University. Harriet attended normal school in Minnesota and worked fourteen years at the University of Montana, part of the time as Dean of Women. Mary received degrees from Wellesley and the University of Montana and taught English at the University of Montana and in California high schools. Edna attended Wellesley and the University of Wisconsin and graduated with a law degree from the University of Montana. Grace graduated from the University of Montana and devoted her adult years to her family and to caring for her mother in Idaho and Washington. Of these educated and talented Rankins, Wellington was unmistakably the power of the family. His superior education, money, influence, and worldliness made his sisters perpetually solicitous of him—although, at times, privately critical—and made him a constant force in their lives. Each lived her life in Wellington's shadow.

The Rankin sisters' dependency on their brother involved more than a little neurosis. Although he sent them money, bought them cars, gave them legal and investment advice, prepared their taxes, paid for their vacations and medical bills, and financed their annuities and children's educations, he also preempted their lives. His own needs and desires always came first, as when Jeannette was serving her second term in Congress. Early in 1942, he ordered her "to come out immediately"—"start any minute"—to care for their mother, and Jeannette obeyed even though it was "going to be a very hard week in Congress." Wellington also summoned Jeannette to Montana to discuss his 1942 Senate campaign. She wrote to friends in Georgia: "Wellington phoned me that he wants me in Montana so it looks as if I would leave this week." Even though he managed much of her life and "treated her like a turd"—criticizing "her morals" and "her lifestyle"—Jeannette still told him that he was "the best brother in the world," and said, "You are just too wonderful. . . . You give a lift to the spirit as no one else can."

Wellington Rankin treated Mary and Edna just as harshly. Although he called Mary "the only one of the girls that could make any claims of any beauty" and "the saint of the Rankin family" because she nursed for years her bedridden husband, he also criticized her because, as she admitted, she lacked Wellington's and Jeannette's energy and accomplishments. After Wellington visited her briefly in California, Mary wrote to him: "The money will help with the [children's] clothes problem. I wish it could do even more, but unfortunately money can not obliterate unhappy memories of the facts that you firmly impressed upon me—namely that I am the one whom Mother likes to visit the least; that I am your 'dumb' sister; that Grace, Edna, and Jeannette have told you that I am very hard to live with; that though you had not seen me for three years you had no time or desire to spend any of your second day here with me." But by letter's end, Mary had swallowed her anger and assured Wellington that she was a self-effacing daughter putting "her mother's welfare first": "I am sorry that I was worried about your not getting back last night. . . . The day mother arrived I was so ill that I didn't see how I could stay up. . . . Then the other night while we were playing five hundred I had such a spell with my eyes that I could scarcely see the numbers on the cards. However, I did not want to stop mother's fun so I said nothing and in time the spell stopped."

Wellington Rankin's hand in Edna's life was just as controlling. Edna, the youngest Rankin child, followed her brother's directives to study public speaking and, despite her opposition, attend law school. After becoming the first Montana-born woman to graduate from the state's law school, she worked for a time in Wellington's office. But Edna was "a more 'social' creature than either" Jeannette or Wellington, and Wellington became convinced "that [Edna] was more interested in talking with friends than practicing law." She was also "a pretty woman . . . the most feminine woman in the world." She "married for money" to impress her family, and, after her husband's business failure, son's death, divorce, and sending her daughter Dorothy to live with Jeannette, Edna's life came apart. In 1935 she described her condition to Wellington after going through the "analysis" he had paid for: "I know how difficult it must be to write a letter to any one who has 'cracked up' as I have. . . . But I'm really not that bad off. . . . I realize now that for years I have been existing under a very great strain of many conflicts. . . . I will for the first time in my life be able to live without dread—without an overpowering desire to die—and without a constant apology for my conduct and the way I will live."

Edna's declaration of autonomy soon ran into the realities of Rankin family life. In 1937 she began her birth-control career, first as a lobbyist for Margaret Sanger and then as a field representative for Clarence J. Gamble's Pathfinder Fund. Birth control, however, "was far more controversial than suffrage," and although Wellington eagerly supported woman suffrage and Jeannette's role in the movement, he vehemently opposed Edna's birth-control work. Even Carrie Chapman Catt told Sanger that birth-control reform was "too sordid." When Gamble asked Edna to explore the possibility of birth-control advocacy in Montana, Edna said that Wellington found the prospect "very distasteful. . . . [H]e didn't want me to do anything like this." His fear was that the ensuing ridicule would "wreck his prestige." He told Edna that "if she was going to work on birth control, she couldn't stay in Montana." When the Pathfinder Fund transferred her to Tennessee, Edna became the second sister Wellington Rankin had pressured out of Montana.

From the beginning of his life, Wellington Rankin was the center of attention. As the only son, he was his mother's pet—"The Boy"—and adored by his sisters. When he returned to Montana as a well-dressed lawyer, he was called "little Lord Fauntleroy" and "The Little Boy from Oxford." His appearance, however, if foppish, was certainly not boyish. Although not a tall man—about five feet, ten inches—his 190 pounds and natural aggressiveness left others with the impression that he was "huge in everything but height," a "damn big man" who "would roll over you." One of Wellington Rankin's critics, himself a "boxer and s.o.b. of formidable reputation," described the effect of Rankin's physical presence on others: "[Wellington Rankin is] strong, compact and heavy set. . . . [There are] some men who fear him for physical reasons." Rankin worked hard at creating this reputation. He was known as "the best 'Indian wrestler' in Montana" and, like his father, was "ready at any time to accept a physical challenge." He was "inordinately proud of being on the Harvard boxing club" and later gave his friend Gary Cooper boxing lessons in his law office before

Cooper became an actor. Even Jeannette flattered Wellington's prowess as a fighter, writing to him during her inquiry into the Bureau of Engraving and Printing scandal: "Several men need pasting. Wouldn't you like to attend to them?"

Wellington Rankin's first job upon returning to Montana was with a law firm that included the father of his first wife. Well educated and "very handsome," he undoubtedly had much to offer many women. But in 1913, three years after her marriage to Wellington Rankin, Elizabeth Wallace explained in a letter from Munich—in language reminiscent of Jeannette Rankin's cry for release from family life and Montana—why their marriage had failed. She had been trying, she told Wellington, "to analyze my feelings for you . . . because . . . your letters make that request." Her introspection had revealed, she wrote, "an active desire for greater development. . . . I am enjoying my freedom tremendously. I know I should feel suffocated if I found myself in . . . any definite marriage arrangement—I should scream for air. . . . I must have an absolute personal freedom." The escape Elizabeth Wallace desired was not only from Rankin but also from Montana's isolation: "I can not consider poverty. I love pretty things and enjoy the very best of life and I should never be able to live west. In fact I shall never be happy out of New York and I am sure I should love to live for a great part of the year over here. . . . If you had money and lived east or here we might be happy. . . . I loathe ugly commonplace people. . . . I hate crudeness more each day." Despite her appreciation of Wellington Rankin's "intellect . . . courage . . . [and] many other qualities that I have told you of," Elizabeth Wallace wrested herself free of his grasp. In the future, Rankin remedied his lack of money, but he could not give up his power base or respect another person's need for autonomy—whether that person was one of his sisters or his wife.

In her declaration of independence, Elizabeth Wallace told Rankin: "My sentimental idea of love is dead and now it must be one of a certain companionship." For the rest of his life, Rankin adopted his estranged wife's philosophy of relationships. For years he had a series of female companions, but he did not marry again until 1956, when he was seventy-two years old. During the years in between he was a "very vain" man who enjoyed the attention of women. An acquaintance remembered him in Harriet's house in Missoula in 1928: "He stood at the mantle and admired himself in the mirror. . . . I always thought of him as being more or less of a bachelor.

He was attracted to women. . . . There's all kinds of rumors that I wouldn't even want to comment on."

Innuendo suggests that Wellington Rankin became involved with numerous women soon after his separation from Elizabeth Wallace. In a 1917 letter to Jeannette Rankin, Nina Swinnerton, in discussing the recent behavior of "Deary Wellington," said, "He'll get over that 'red hood' infection." Some relationships were more than rumor, as in 1929 when Edna wrote to Wellington from Jerusalem about her traveling companion: "Sally is disappointed not to have had a letter. She talks about you incessantly. . . . She has every intention that you and she will come back over here next year." In 1935 a professional woman from New York wrote to Wellington Rankin that she had been "charmed" by her time with him and invited him to visit her. In 1941, after he took a woman friend to a political gathering, she thanked him for "letting me come and visit you—I loved every minute of it. . . . such a nice time playing with you." Nine years later the same woman expressed her indebtedness to Wellington Rankin for helping her find a job in Washington, D.C.: "I hope that business or pleasure will bring you back here soon so that I can tell you in person how very much I appreciate your kindness and in the meantime I am, dear Wellington, as always devotedly yours."

In 1931 a longer relationship began with a young woman who was attending school in New York and continued after she was married. She wrote to Wellington Rankin in 1946 from Los Angeles about investments, politics, and her passion for him: "You better get rid of that stuff you were talking about while things are still up; the Jews are making a mass appeal to their people to buy everything they can so as to entrench themselves in this country and there's lots of talk about that here. It seems Eddie Cantor is one of the ringleaders in it. That is why Hitler could arouse the German people about them—they did the same thing there. . . . It was wonderful talking to you last night, Angel. I get terribly lonesome for you but hearing your voice does help. . . . [You] sound as though you feel better. I was just sick the day I left as it made me feel as though I were responsible. I thought we would have to give up branding. . . . I love you Sweetheart with all my heart and can't wait to see you again." The next year, however, she admonished Wellington Rankin for sharing his favors with other women: "I hope you will forego exhibiting your physical prowess at least in taking them on in such numbers." In 1948 she decided that her relationship with Rankin had no future. "[It is] time for me to be on my way," she wrote. "You have too many interests to give me what I want in life. You are such a self sufficient person." Married in 1954, she nonetheless renewed her relationship with Rankin: "I'm driving over next week. . . . Will go directly to Clancy. . . . Will phone you and maybe you could come out there to see me so we would be away from prying eyes. . . . Heaps of love."

Wellington Rankin's relationship with the woman who became his second wife began in 1946, when he was sixty-two and she had recently graduated from law school. Despite Louise Replogle's many achievements—she had been a county attorney, prized associate in Rankin's law office, president of the Montana Young Republicans, one of *Mademoiselle*'s ten outstanding young women, and assistant secretary of a national Republican convention—Rankin family members became alarmed about Replogle's closeness to their wealthy benefactor and catty about her appearance. Rankin's niece Dorothy derisively described to her mother, Edna, "what Wellington's girl looks like": "[S]he has a pretty face, or rather a handsome one with very little expression, wears harlequin glasses which she snatches on and off. She has without doubt the worst body known to man—big in the shoulders and butt and none too small in the waist. . . . [She] wears clothes that were definitely bought in the matron department, sort of shapeless suits with three quarter coats, so that she looks a good thirty-five or well-preserved forty. . . . [She has] dreadful legs, which you notice because she sits badly. . . . [She] wears her hair up on top [and is] at least as tall as he. . . . [She is] awfully hard to talk to, and Wellington swears she is just plain dumb." Dorothy went on to tell her mother what was mostly on her mind—that Wellington's foot dragging about marriage gave the Rankin family some hope: "[T]he longer he puts it off the less apt he is."

Like her niece, Jeannette Rankin perceived "Wellington's girl" as a serious threat and hoped to derail the relationship. Three years before Wellington's marriage to Louise, Dorothy wrote to her mother, Edna, that Wellington was engaged and Louise "has a stunning ring on her finger, but Jeannette will not allow the subject to come up and will not mention the ring for fear of pushing Wellington into a corner." After the marriage, Jeannette's rivalry for her brother's attention and money continued. One of Jeannette's political associates gave her take on Jeannette's hostility toward the new Mrs. Wellington Rankin: "I always wondered what she thought about Wellington's wife because she never mentioned her. She talked so much about Wellington. In fact, for the first year or so I thought Wellington was a bachelor. . . . Maybe [Wellington Rankin's wife] was too powerful because Jeannette did not speak of her, never mentioned her at all." After Wellington's death, when Louise was seeing to the details of administering his multimillion-dollar estate, Jeannette and her sister Harriet threatened to sue their sister-in-law for not distributing the accumulated interest. Edna encouraged Jeannette: "I do want you to have the money which is right-fully YOURS from Wellington and you should have it now." Several weeks later the threat resulted in Louise sending Jeannette a $10,000 advance on Wellington's bequest. Not surprisingly, both women held Wellington in the highest regard. Louise "was totally taken by him, saw him as super human," while Jeannette "just loved Wellington. She thought he was the best and the smartest man."

Wellington Rankin's abilities and accomplishments were substantial. He was bright and "in some ways with a sharper intellect, a higher native intelligence" than possessed by his more famous sister. His presence and voice were so impressive that he had been "urged in his college years to become a dramatic actor." His speaking ability was "whiz like," both ex-temporaneous and oratorical. A Montana politician remembered an occa-sion when a scheduled speaker "didn't show up . . . Wellington got right up and made a speech there right now, just off the cuff." In the courtroom he was equally effective. After observing him at trial, Dorothy described the scene to her mother: "He is so wonderful in court you wouldn't believe it without seeing it. . . . He is the entire focus in the room, even when he isn't speaking." His reputation as "the most successful and widely known [law-yer] in the state" came from his advocacy skills. A Montana assistant attor-ney general recalled that "in court he was one of those lawyers who can always convince the judge of his idea of the case." His drive to succeed in law allowed little relaxation. Wellington Rankin's secretary once wrote to Jeannette Rankin in Mexico: "I wish you could get him down there, but no chance. Two days and he would be fed up."

Wellington Rankin's talent, aggressiveness, and ambition found an outlet first in law, then in politics, and during his later years in land. Two years after joining a law firm, he opened his own practice. By 1920, he was financially independent and "one of the top criminal lawyers" in Montana, with offices in Helena, Butte, and Havre. Benefiting from his skill and his determination to be "better prepared than anybody else" were the great and the small. One client identifying herself only as "Hazel"—probably the domestic partner of Rankin's secretary—honored him for saving her from a grievous wrong: "I appreciate your loyalty and sincerity expressed during the past rather rugged months. It makes living worthwhile to be able to establish faith in some of the humans that walk on this earth. I fully realize that you have not known me too well but fought for me because of the decent aspects involved and I admire you more than I have in the past because you have courage and few people today possess that rare virtue." Other beneficiaries were more prominent, including a police judge who failed to collect fines and the chief justice of the Montana Supreme Court charged under the state's corrupt practices act. Among Rankin's motives for defending the powerful was gaining "tentacles that reached everywhere" and "leverage he could use when needed."

As a lawyer, Wellington Rankin earned the reputation of being not only a masterful but also an "amoral" and "ruthless" tactician: "Any means to the end was alright." In 1948 when Rankin was running for the U.S. Senate, an opponent charged that he "glories in the trial of a case when he has a mortgage on the soul of the presiding judge." A former state attorney who frequently opposed Rankin said that he "had some kind of claim on two Supreme Court justices. . . . They were in his debt and he always had at least two votes on the Court." One of the two justices was rumored to have said, "Rankin once did something significant for me, and after that I always found great merit in his position before the Court." Rankin also sought special advantage with the lower courts. As the defendant's lawyer during a murder trial, he hosted a birthday party for the judge in the courthouse: "There was the judge, jury, defendant, and Wellington Rankin celebrating with cake and coffee Wellington had bought." He also was rumored to have the state's workers' compensation judge "in his pocket after he defended him before the Supreme Court and kept him in office."

Wellington Rankin relished having an advantage over other lawyers. Some opponents "fear[ed] him for physical reasons," and others regarded him as "the most selfish, inconsiderate and unreliable attorney" they knew. One critic told Rankin that his "word in regard to court appearances is never to be relied upon. A date will mutually be agreed to, only too often to be changed at the last minute." Lawyers learned to expect "calls from Rankin at 1:00 A.M. or 2:00 A.M. for a conference on legal points and a dawn call for a command breakfast conference before court." A more serious allegation was that "he'd tamper with witnesses." One Montana Supreme Court justice "was certain" that in a murder case Rankin "had the state's key witness holed up at one of his ranches. He made a deal with her, but you couldn't prove it, and she turned against the state." Undeniable was that Rankin's mode of operating was to "work below the surface." A former Montana attorney general used to advise members of the bar: "When going up against Wellington Rankin, you better have all your gun ports closed—you don't know where he'll attack you."

Wellington Rankin made his initial wealth through high-fee cases and maintained it through tight-fisted personal and business habits. His reputation as a lawyer was built on "big cases with big fees, and later on that's all he took." His bread-and-butter cases dealt with estates, personal injury, and criminal law. In civil matters, "he charged 40 to 45 percent of any sum recovered by settlement or suit." A newspaper reported a client saying that his "case was finally settled for $10,000 and the Rankin firm exacted a fee of $7,500." When asked about the size of the fee, the client said, "Rankin told you, you didn't tell Rankin." In his criminal law practice, the "story [was] that he had the standard fee of $5,000 for getting anybody off on a rape charge." Another rumor was that Rankin required defendants to sign over title to their property as payment. Such in-kind compensation was reportedly part of a high-profile extradition case. Rankin arrived at the hearing in a taxi and the defendant drove up in a Cadillac. After Rankin lost the case, the police took away his client in a squad car and Rankin kept the Cadillac as payment for his services.

Wellington Rankin ran his law office frugally and unfeelingly. He hired lawyers right out of law school but they didn't stay long because of the low salaries he paid. Research for the big cases he argued was done by two lawyers who wanted or needed to stay: the woman who became his second wife and a longtime employee who was "a good office lawyer but a hopeless alcoholic." After Rankin's death, his widow complained about her inability to get any work out of this associate, who had "gone off on some junket. . . . He is drinking again [and] needs Wellington's restraining hand." The office atmosphere was charged with Wellington Rankin's "fiery temper" and "dominating" ways. His workers "walked on eggshells." In a letter to Jeannette Rankin, Wellington Rankin's secretary told about his short Christmas trip to Spokane and said with regret, "It is a shame he does not care about getting away more, for his sake and also for ours." The office building he owned and occupied as sole tenant was known for its "creaky stairs . . . ancient cage-type elevator . . . [and] dimly-lighted hallways." After a fire, Rankin refused to repair the building and his safe fell through the floor of his third-floor office to the basement.

Wellington Rankin "flat didn't spend money. It killed him to spend." Those to whom he loaned money "had to pay off, and he was not a bit bashful" in his demands. But Rankin "avoided paying his debts. . . . [T]he only bills he repeatedly paid on time were for his custom clothing from New York, and his handmade shoes from Boston." His files were filled with overdue notices for law books, stationery, utilities, groceries, automobile repair, and veterinary services. A critic told Rankin in 1952 that he was a cheapskate: "[Y]ou never contribute a dime to charity or community betterment, never give a minute of your time to any public undertaking, never devote a thought to aught but Rankin." Rankin's papers indicate that he once sent a small donation to the Butte High School band, but an enclosed note suggests that he did not want the practice to become regular: "Please do not give any publicity to it." Because of Rankin's stinginess, few were close to him. A lawyer who practiced with Rankin said: "He didn't have friends, just acquaintances. No one I knew called him his friend. There was always an element of fear and awe, but never respect." His niece Dorothy observed in a letter to her mother that one of Rankin's former employees who had just died was "probably the only person this side of the divide with a good word to say for him." In 1948 a political associate used a Dickensian allusion to warn Rankin: "Some day, on the streets of your home city, your friends will pass and say, 'You heard about Wellington, too bad, what did he leave?' And the answer as always will be, 'He left it all.'"

Early on Wellington Rankin made his money in law, but he wanted to make his mark in politics. The abiding question was whether this Scrooge-like man could be elected. In nine outings, from 1914 to 1952, he won once— in 1920 as the Republican candidate for the office of Montana attorney general. In 1914, two years before Jeannette Rankin's historic victory, he ran unsuccessfully as a Progressive Party candidate for one of two at-large congressional seats under the slogan "Put the Anaconda Company out of Montana Politics." His other unsuccessful races were in the 1922, 1924, 1934, and 1948 Republican U.S. Senate primaries, the 1942 U.S. Senate general election, the 1928 general election for Montana governor, and the 1952 general election for Montana's western congressional seat. In 1924, to keep him from another U.S. Senate race, Montana governor Joseph Dixon appointed Wellington Rankin to fill the Montana Supreme Court seat vacated by the father of actor Gary Cooper. Finding the state supreme court to be "like a cemetery," he resigned from the position after one year. In 1928 he was appointed by President Coolidge and in 1930 reappointed by President Hoover to the office of U.S. District Attorney for Montana. And in 1932, he considered but decided against running for governor as an independent. The U.S. House of Representatives interested him very little (he "did not want to be one of 435 members"). The more prestigious U.S. Senate was the perennial office seeker's abiding passion, but an ambition he never realized. His failure haunted him but amused others. At the funeral of U.S. senator Thomas Walsh, a fellow pallbearer remarked to Rankin, "Hang on tight Wellington, this is as close as you will ever get to the U.S. Senate."

Wellington Rankin's quest for high office began in 1912 when he helped to organize the Montana Progressive Party. The new party opposed corporate and machine dominance of politics and supported direct democracy and woman suffrage. Prior to his Progressive Party candidacy for Congress, Rankin was chairman of the party's state executive committee. For a time he maintained his progressive credentials by supporting the causes of suffrage, agriculture, and labor both independently and as Jeannette Rankin's campaign manager in 1916 and 1918. In 1917 he cooperated with Butte unionists to establish a labor newspaper. One of his allies was Jeannette Rankin's friend, Mary O'Neill. In late 1917, O'Neill sent Wellington Rankin a status report on the project: "At a little conference this afternoon we took up the daily paper plan as outlined in your office. I presented it . . . and it met with the approval of the crowd. It has been decided to call a mass meeting for next Sunday afternoon to get everyone more enthusiastic over the idea of starting publication January 1, 1918. Can you come over and help us whoop up things? What do you think of getting a Non-Partisan 'big wig' here to help with a speech? [William F.] Dunne has just returned from the Coeur d'Alenes with a glowing report of progress made there. The miners are most anxious to get the paper on its feet and have contributed most liberally. . . . Our paper is now sure to be a go. . . . The men wanted to ask Jeannette to come, thinking she was in Missoula. . . . [T]hey will wait until later and give her a big ovation when she does come."

The newspaper cabal's membership made sense given the Rankins' political ambitions; Wellington Rankin's ownership of a newspaper in Havre, Montana; and Dunne's editing the *Miners' and Electrical Workers' Joint Strike Bulletin* during the 1917 Butte strike. When Jeannette Rankin spoke to the strikers in August 1917, Dunne was on the platform and asked the crowd to support a labor newspaper. As plans for the newspaper evolved, Mary O'Neill kept both Wellington Rankin and Jeannette Rankin informed: "[The] newspaper is now an assured fact, just getting details fixed up before we get started right. There is the possibility of a mistake being made right now, in the naming of two Socialists as directors, which I hope to get the men to see. Dorman of the Non-Partisan league is to be here Sunday and we will go over things." The labor and agriculture radicals wanted to counter the Anaconda Copper Mining Company's "complete control of . . . practically every paper throughout the state" and believed— mentioning U.S. congressman John M. Evans and U.S. senator Joseph M. Dixon but not Wellington Rankin—that successful Montana "politicians own newspapers." At the end of 1917, Dunne's *Strike Bulletin* became the *Butte Weekly Bulletin,* and in 1918 a daily. With Dunne, who later became coeditor of the *Daily Worker,* serving as the editorial writer, the new labor paper adopted a message that was "unabashedly revolutionary."

But compared with Jeannette Rankin, Wellington Rankin identified less consistently with radical causes. In his successful 1920 campaign for Montana attorney general, when he had "probably the widest acquaintance among lawyers and others enjoyed by any member of the state bar," voters saw him as "progressive and anti-company." After his election, he was "in league with the anti-progressive wing of the Republican party . . . perhaps to keep his senatorial ambitions alive." He opposed the plans of progressive governor Joseph Dixon, also a prospective U.S. Senate candidate, to raise the tax on metal mines and to investigate the warden of the state penitentiary for allowing the Anaconda Company "to use convicts as strike breakers in Butte and Anaconda." As attorney general he opposed charging the Anaconda Company president Cornelius Kelley and chairman of the board John D. Ryan for tax evasion, earning him the label "lackey" of the Anaconda Company. During the 1924 U.S. Senate primary, the now conservative Wellington Rankin asked Jeannette Rankin to help him not only with the "women's vote but also the miners" because she had not changed her spots. Unlike her brother, Jeannette Rankin never backed away from her 1917 populist condemnation of the Anaconda Company: "They own the state, they own the government."

Wellington Rankin switched his loyalty again in 1928 and once more in 1934. In his unsuccessful 1928 gubernatorial campaign, his opponent had the support of the Anaconda Company and he "aligned himself with the anti–Anaconda Company forces." The company's newspaper in Anaconda, Montana, attacked Wellington Rankin savagely: "[He] has all the dignity of a baboon, all the self restraint and poise of a tomcat, all the calm deliberation and judicial decision of a jackass, all the finer emotions and sentiments of a yellow dog, all the nobility and character of a snake." But by 1934, the sting of the company's criticism was assuaged by Wellington Rankin's senatorial ambition. In a campaign report from eastern Montana, Edna explained to her brother how his current accommodation with the Anaconda Company was helping his cause. The Prairie County clerk of court, she related, "says you'll carry the county if you don't fly off and stir up the company—says you stirred up all the fuss last time, and so I told him they (the company) had started it the other time but now they were not going to fight you and he was pleased." Twenty years later Katharine Anthony wondered in a letter to Jeannette Rankin what had "become of the old Anaconda that used to be out for Wellington's skin? Have they become reconciled?" Politics always dictated the timing and extent of the reconciliation. In 1955 the Anaconda Company chair of the board referred to Wellington Rankin as one of his "old and dear friends," but a longtime associate of the family said that the "Rankins always blamed the Company for any disappointments."

Wellington Rankin's political ambition might have fostered not only opportunism but also questionable campaign practices. In general, his political strategy was to determine the sources of power and how they could be manipulated. As for specific practices, a political opponent accused him of playing "cunning tricks upon the electorate" and a political ally lamented: "You had definitely made up your mind that you were going to be the next U.S. Senator from Montana and that nothing could stop you. You were ready to sell your own soul for this honor and never considered defeat." Edna Rankin, when advancing her brother's 1934 U.S. Senate primary campaign, reported a number of nefarious activities on his behalf. In Gallatin County, a state senator had "a good many men who will do as he says," and in Carbon County, Wellington's contact said that "he will have to handle

Red Lodge in his own way. The foreign vote will tell the tale. . . . [I]f you get one man, you get the precinct. . . . [The] bootleggers are all for you." Edna's report from Yellowstone County was even more sinister: "Mike Reynolds . . . wanted me to tell you confidentially that they have some pretty bad dope on Swords being connected with the dope ring. . . . Doesn't think he will do you any harm and may do you a lot of good in the underworld crowd. . . . Swords had a man named McCracken come up to his office to meet me—from the 'underworld' as Swords put it. McCracken says you will carry Billings if he had [sic] any thing to do with it. . . . I suppose he is a bootlegger for he's seen you in court and thinks you are marvelous." From the Crow Indian Reservation, Edna described other shenanigans: "Russell White Bear . . . offered to have me speak at a gathering and he would interpret. . . . (They say he is easily bought, however.) Robert Yellow Tail . . . had orders not to take part in politics but whispers behind his hand that he would have his family and relatives work for you. The advice is that if you come down the last week and have a barbecue you'll get the entire tribe."

Wellington Rankin might have used unethical tactics because it was the way elections were won. An analysis of Montana politics in the 1940s concluded that Rankin was one of three political powers in the state and that the "best understood" method of achieving political success was "to buy it." During Rankin's successful 1942 U.S. Senate primary campaign, Mary O'Neill feared election fraud. She wrote to Jeannette that Wellington's supporters needed "to save him" by stationing workers at the polls to "circumvent the election thieves." In that year's general election campaign against incumbent U.S. senator James E. Murray, another Butte ally warned Jeannette Rankin that "the Murrays will stop at nothing to elect their Dad." After the election, O'Neill told Jeannette that there was "no doubt in my mind that these precincts have been 'jokied.'" Later, Senator Murray's son said that Wellington Rankin "liked" him because Rankin "thought I was a crooked politician just like he was."

Dubious tactics also made up for what Wellington Rankin lost by being an unlikable person and a reluctant and poor campaigner. On the road for her brother in 1934, Edna reported opposition to his candidacy because he was seen as "too big a bully," having abused his opponent in 1928. He was criticized during his 1948 campaign as a politician with a "frustrated but relentless ambition [who] does the poorest and loses the worst where he is well known." In 1952 another critic blasted Rankin: "In the minds of the public it was not a congressional race, but a race between two sons-of-bitches. Unfortunately the public considered you the bigger of the two."

Ironically, Wellington Rankin's supporters urged him to do more personal campaigning despite his abrasive personality. In 1942 Jeannette Rankin advised him: "I am thoroughly convinced you cannot win unless you go out among the people yourself and find out how they feel. . . . If you lose . . . it is going to be because you do not campaign in the way the people want a campaign run. . . . Your aloofness is your greatest handicap." During his last campaign in 1952, an ally wrote to Wellington Rankin: "Above all Judge get out, hit the plowed ground, go in every nook and corner of the state, don't sit in your office and run up a big telephone bill, burn up tires and gas, we have to win this time, or there may not be the next time." To the end of his campaigning days, however, Wellington Rankin remained "almost to the point you might say arrogant," refusing to "talk to the man on the street [or] knock on people's doors." He seemed to realize and accept the difference between his and Jeannette's approaches to politics. After his last election, he told a political ally, "If I'd called Jeannette to come back and put her on the road, I'd have won." But both Jeannette and Edna had come up with reasons for dropping the curtain on their campaigning for their brother. Edna told him that her birth-control work would embarrass him when people asked "what I'd been doing all these years," and Jeannette, in India at the time, confided to her sister Grace that "Wellington offered to pay my way home and back to Africa and South America but I'd rather stay here."

Having succeeded in law and failed in politics, Wellington Rankin turned his attention to creating one of the largest ranching empires in the nation. On his "sixteen ranches . . . covering more than one million acres," he did not have to face a plebiscite. At the time of his death, he owned more than 629,000 acres and almost 27,000 cattle. His widow set the value of his estate at $9 million. It included cash and investments, hotels and oil-producing properties, and many of the Montana ranches with "historic names." The 150,000-acre Savage Brothers Ranch, when Rankin bought it in 1957, contained the largest herd of wild horses in Montana. The 300,000-acre Miller Brothers Ranch, bought in 1958, was the largest in the state and extended from the Canadian border to the Missouri River breaks. Other famous ranches were the Birch Creek, once owned by the Ringling brothers for wintering their circus stock, and Avalanche Ranch and 71 Ranch, which became summer retreats for the Rankin family. Overall, Rankin treated his ranches the same way he treated people and his other property: "He bled them white and ran them into the ground."

An appraisal prepared for Louise Rankin after Wellington's death on the condition of the ranches found that "every property he acquired, from the date of acquisition, immediately started to deteriorate. . . . [T]he annual death loss was high in all categories of cattle, reflecting a low level of nutrition and supervision." Unsubstantiated stories suggest the details: pastures unfenced, stock so weak they could be contained by bulldozed snow corrals, and properties demarcated in the spring by the smell of dead cattle. Attributed accounts make the same points. Rankin so disdained keeping up property that he boarded up the windows of a grand farm residence to turn it into a granary. Such meanness was not without payoff. Cattle buyers came from afar to buy his underfed calves because they paid according to weight. Ivan Doig's autobiography about growing up in a part of Montana owned largely by Wellington Rankin recalls the ranching practices of his notorious neighbor: "Rankin poured in cattle by the thousands. . . . [S]kinny creatures with a huge Double O Bar brand across their ribs . . . and then evidently skimped every expense he could think of."

Doig also described Rankin's pathetic ranch hands: "His cowboys were shabby stick figures on horseback. The perpetual rumor was that most of them were out on prison parole or other work release somehow arranged by Rankin; 'old Rankin's jailbirds,' the valley people called them." Wellington Rankin's papers contain letters from prisoners seeking jobs, and a relative who spent summers at his ranches said that the employees were convicts, whom the family called "the men," paroled to Rankin from the state prison. Rankin personally hired his "men," paid them a dollar a day, and promised to double their wages if they would stay on the ranch and away from liquor for sixty days. Their peonage included the requirement that, if they quit, they had to ask him in person for their back pay. They hitchhiked to Helena and sat in chairs outside his office, but "he wouldn't pay them. . . . [He] just let them hang there." One became so frustrated that he broke into Rankin's office with a gun and demanded, "pay me or I'll kill you." The low wages Rankin paid were not offset by good board and room. He kept storehouses of candy and cigarettes for his hires, but he deducted the price from their wages. The sleeping quarters were primitive and degrading. A ranch hand on the Miller Ranch complained of "a bare bedspring to sleep on at nite no mattress or bedding of any kind on it and a dirty filthy bunk shack not even fit for a dog." In Wellington Rankin's mind, making a profit made such grim conditions necessary. A Montana minimum-wage bill that applied to ranches, his wife wrote to Jeannette Rankin, "had us scared. . . . It sure would have put us out of the ranching business."

More idyllic for the Rankin family was Avalanche Ranch located on the Missouri River outside of Helena. Here Olive Rankin, her children, and grandchildren spent summer months as guests of Wellington, "the lord of the manor." The main residence was large with long hallways and many bedrooms. Surrounding the ranch house were haystacks, a horse barn, and an icehouse filled with blocks cut in the winter from the frozen river. The late-spring arrivals enjoyed free board and room at Wellington's Placer Hotel in Helena until the last snow melted and the cook and housekeeper were hired. But soon, Jeannette wrote to a friend, the Montana countryside became "unbelievably beautiful—white snow on the mountains, pussy willows along the roads and as warm and sunny as when I left Georgia." She further described the setting of Avalanche Ranch: "From our front window we can see thirty miles to the sunset, and on the north it is hard to see the top of the mountain from the window. On the south we slope down to Lake Sewell which is part of the Missouri River, where we have a darling cabin and lovely beach to swim. . . . [I]t is five miles from the house, all on the ranch, and we can coast most of the way down."

For the Rankin family, summers at Avalanche Ranch passed slowly and predictably. May saw the start of ranch activity, as Jeannette described to her friend: "[Y]esterday several hundred cows and their calves went up the gulch to the summer range . . . winding up the road with seven riders." She described how summer had not yet arrived by early June: "[We] still sleep with blankets and hot water bottles and have fires night and morning." Summer days, when they eventually came, were filled with fishing, croquet, checkers, the rivalries of cousins, and long horseback rides after dinner. The last activity of the summer season was canning, overseen by Jeannette and Olive. In a series of letters one fall, Jeannette described the scenery and chores to her friends: "The country is beautiful and the weather has been too gorgeous for words. . . . [T]he apple crop is short this year so we have been selling the good ones and putting up the windfalls. We have over 200 quarts of applesauce alone, besides several hundred glasses of jelly and apple butter and pickles. . . . [There are still] a hundred pounds of luscious, big tomatoes begging to be picked."

Avalanche summers were family affairs, and the dominant Rankins dominated life at the ranch. In the evenings everyone watched for the high cloud of dust thrown up by Wellington's speeding automobile. He presided at the dinner table, and after dinner he rode his white stallion in his tailored dark blue suit. Wanting his nieces and nephews to be proud of him, he dispensed money, candy from the ranch storehouse, and advice for success. Jeannette, the other dominant figure, carved out her own ranch role. Wellington always dressed formally, but Jeannette could appear "slovenly," at times "looking like a bag of potatoes." Close to the river she kept a little house, abandoned-looking from the outside, where she spent long periods by herself reading and thinking. Wellington was in charge of horseback rides, but Jeannette organized "shit kicking"—she and the children spreading the horses' manure on the front lawn. She emphasized thrift in her management of the household. At dinner, she gave a lesson of "waste not, want not" by eating whole a trout one of the cousins had caught, "putting the fish in her mouth and chewing and swallowing everything." She placed the household on a strict budget and limited long distance telephone calls.

Fundamentally, the two dominant Rankins were more alike than different, and in their similarities they were resented by their siblings. When Wellington gave his niece Dorothy hell over the wedding plans of one of her sons, her mother, Edna, sharply criticized her brother in a letter to the other family members: "[T]he poor old fool probably feels so frustrated over his own marital mistakes. . . . I hope that one day Wellington will learn to love his neighbor. . . . [N]o one ever knows what will set off his anger. . . . I shall not write further to Wellington because one never knows what a storm the most innocent letter will arouse. . . . Of course all the nieces and nephews think he is an 'old Fogy,' and why not. The poor dear has such a limited view toward life and toward people."

In letters to Wellington and their sister Mary, Edna similarly criticized Jeannette. When Jeannette refused to share her new car Wellington had bought, Edna told their brother: "[P]ast experience has shown repeatedly that one goes and comes when and if she is ready and willing. It is not that she wants to be unkind but she is so accustomed to having her own car that she would not be able to put herself in the other person's shoes." To Mary she wrote: "I feel that we must 'loose her—and let her go' and assume no responsibility for her. I feel sad that she has no interest in life but *herself*. . . . [S]he is grappling with the false sense of *self* which seems to have a tight grip on her. . . . [S]he didn't mention any rebuilding of her Georgia house but anything which takes her mind off *self* I'm in favor of, aren't you?" Another observer of the two dominant Rankins came to the same conclusion. They are "both alike," he said, "exceptionally ambitious [and] very self-centered people. . . . [They are] takers not givers." Jeannette Rankin seemed to recognize this trait in herself but not in her brother. Thanking him for his Christmastime offer to send her to South America, she replied, "I'm grateful but sorry I'm not big enough in spirit to give the same pleasure to others."

Friendships

A Woman-Centered Life

To call Jeannette Rankin a taker is harsh but perceptive. Although at age twenty-eight she was still managing the Rankin household, during the next eight years her life swung from caregiving to campaigning. By 1916, she had developed a political constituency that enabled her to become the first woman elected to the U.S. Congress and most likely the best-known woman in the world. Admirers thought that this onetime maternal surrogate might become the first woman president. For the rest of her life, however, Jeannette Rankin became identified more with a series of paradoxes than accomplishments. A reason for the less auspicious outcome is the person she was at the core. Her political obsessions that pushed her to cultivate political followers prevented her from sustaining intimacy in her personal life. In contrast, Molly Dewson, Rankin's contemporary, viewed her fifty-two-year partnership with Polly Porter as critical to her political success. Lacking a continuing intimate relationship with another adult, Jeannette Rankin was repeatedly beaten down by life's disappointments.

Jeannette Rankin's transition from the domestic to the political began with her escape from rural isolation. Early in the twentieth century, "the family became less central as an economic unit," and the work, social, and educational opportunities of big cities beckoned to many young men and women. Frustrated in Montana, and called a daydreamer by her mother and "restless and unhappy" by Edna, Jeannette Rankin confided to her diary in 1902 that she had grown weary of childhood things: "The kid crowd went sleighing. I went with them, but was real lonesome not to have anything to do." During the next six years her reading suggested another way of life. Orator and suffragist Anna Howard Shaw "quickened [Jeannette Rankin's] social sympathies," and Jane Addams described her own "long struggle, as a young woman, to find herself" and "the advantages of women studying social work." Addams was particularly impatient with the "stupid' . . . social arrangements in which young people were expected to grow up." Addams's rebellion struck a chord in Jeannette Rankin, hemmed in by her family-based life and traumatized by her sexual "slip" while teaching in a rural school. Tired of standing out like a tree on the prairie, she made the decision to attend the New York School of Philanthropy.

The New York School opened its doors in 1898 and quickly became the nation's premier graduate program in social work education. Its admissions process was competitive and attracted students from throughout the United States and foreign countries. During Jeannette Rankin's attendance in 1908 and 1909, women outnumbered men among the students, and the distinguished faculty, practitioners lecturing in their specialties, was increasingly composed of women. In this elite atmosphere, Rankin felt intimidated and challenged. Her undergraduate education "hadn't taught her to think," and now she felt in awe of her new peers, "such well-trained college girls." But she took away from the New York School both an excellent graduate education and the values of "the first generation of New Women." Rankin's settlement-house experience in San Francisco, her imaginative escape into Jane Addams's Hull House, and her experiences with her classmates and teachers at the New York School taught her that women would be "granted social license to arrange their lives as they pleased if they pursued an education and a profession." Clearly, the New Women had not prepared themselves to become "adequate wives." Their special female identity, they believed, opened up to them "love unimpaired by repressive male dominance."

Jeannette Rankin's grounding in early twentieth-century feminism deepened when she campaigned for suffrage in New York in 1911. She began what Edna Rankin called "our Greenwich Village days" and Katharine Anthony referred to as "[our] days . . . in the old Italian quarter of the Village." There Cornelia Swinnerton, Jeannette Rankin's suffrage colleague and friend, took her to a club at Patchin Place, probably Heterodoxy, a "luncheon club for 'unorthodox women.'" In its quaint atmosphere of iron gates, brownstone buildings, gaslights, and ailanthus trees, Jeannette Rankin dined and shared ideas with author Katharine Anthony, education reformer Elisabeth Irwin, editor and peace activist Mary L. Chamberlain, suffragist and lawyer Marion B. Cothren, birth-control leader Mary Ware Dennett, lawyer and political activist Crystal Eastman, utopian Charlotte Perkins Gilman, painter and writer Ami Mali Hicks, editor and suffragist Katherine Leckie, poet and journalist Ruth Pinchot Pickering, and union organizer and labor investigator Elizabeth Watson. In later years, all of these women played roles in Jeannette Rankin's life.

In Heterodoxy and throughout Greenwich Village, radicalism was "in the air": "It was the time of social change," and the environment of the "liberal/radical small town . . . encouraged a translation from personal experimentation to social activism." The sexual mores of Greenwich Village were free love—heterosexual, homosexual, and bisexual. The prevailing value system was feminism. The dominant political ideology was socialism. The 110 members of Heterodoxy included thirty-one known or probable lesbians, including Katharine Anthony and Elisabeth Irwin, for whom Greenwich Village's "new Bohemia" offered an escape from the "social pressures that family-centered and small-town lesbians had to face." It is not clear, however, if the politically radical Jeannette Rankin was a lesbian.

What is obvious is that Rankin's letters contain no hint of intimacy with a man and no references to men except in family, professional, and non-romantic contexts. To identify Heterodoxy lesbians, Judith Schwarz used many criteria, including looking at letters to see if "she never once mentions a male, except as a teacher or prospective employer." The Heterodoxy study also includes Schwarz's observation that "I have learned to regard friendship between a lesbian and a straight woman as a rare, fragile relationship." Jeannette Rankin's correspondence contains sexual overtures from women and her usually tepid but occasionally passionate responses. She maintained lifelong friendships with both individual lesbians and women partners, such as Katharine Anthony and Elisabeth Irwin and also Flora Belle Surles and Anne Gregorie. By associating with already partnered women, Rankin might have been protecting herself from the tangles of intimacy, viewing any intimate relationship as "a horrible alternative" to a single, unencumbered state. The judgment of one relative was that she was "tough as nails and couldn't love anyone, either a man or a woman." Another relative doubted that she was capable of "intimate adult relationships." Whether or not this was true, Rankin rejected personal partnerships and understood the ramifications of this choice.

Surrounding herself with people was another matter. A common observation was that Jeannette Rankin "did love to have company." Edna said that Jeannette could "be a charmer when she likes people." Another family member said that her laughter was sparkling; it infected people and drew them to her. A 1942 visitor to Washington, D.C., remembered her in her political mode, "hi-ing here and hi-ing there. And like this and that and the other thing, to everybody coming into the [Congressional] lunchroom." After a relative took her to the airport and arranged a bulkhead seat so she would be more comfortable, she moved "to sit in the middle of the plane so she could talk up everyone sitting around her." As an elderly woman she continued to crave the attention of others. In 1972 her friends contacted Ralph Nader and suggested that he interview her about her election reform proposals. She feared that Nader had never heard of her and would not contact her, but, nonetheless, she spent "whole days waiting by the phone for him to call."

Jeannette Rankin's sister Edna, in contrast, led an overtly sexual life. A family acquaintance said that she was "the most feminine woman in the world. . . . [She] had bleach blond hair until the day she died." She had an obvious interest in men, attracted men, and repeatedly mentioned male companions in her letters. While on a Mediterranean cruise she wrote to her sister "Gracie" about a dance to honor the ship's captain. The bandleader, after introducing the captain, "told [him] to choose his partner—and much to my delight and embarrassment he walked clear down the hall and chose me." She shared with Grace another story about a different captain: "a captain of a destroyer said that his ship was to be in England during the month of April and asked if he might come to the hotel and take me out to dance, etc. It will be fun. If he only remembers." Edna married and divorced a Harvard graduate and then had a love affair with a Yale graduate. Concerning the latter, Edna wrote to Jeannette: "[M]y Denver 'Experience' as you call it . . . has been lots of fun. There is nothing serious but it has given me quite a thrill." As the relationship headed toward marriage, Jeannette wrote Edna a note that probably revealed more of her loneliness than she intended: "I'm so happy over [your plans] for I know you will enjoy 'doing' for a man rather than a 'cause' for a 'cause' gets pretty tiresome at times."

Jeannette Rankin's well-dressed and handsome appearance created opportunities for her to "do for a man," even though some said "the Rankin nose" detracted from her prettiness. Journalists in 1916 focused "on what she looked like and wore," not what she thought or said, and made her "an object for the readers' gaze." The *Boston Traveler* noted her "feminine charm," the *Woman's Journal and Suffrage News* remarked upon her "striking personal appearance," and the *San Francisco Sunday Chronicle* portrayed her as "a slender creature with a wealth of soft, curly hair, a pair of wistful dark eyes and an expression that radiated the joy of living." Carving the stereotype deeper, *The Woman Citizen* gushed that she was "so good looking [and wore] such beautiful clothes." More restrained, the *New York Times* described her as "tall and slender, with hazel eyes, sandy hair, and energetic mouth . . . a pleasant-faced young woman," and the *Chicago Tribune* thought her to be "in her first thirties and looking as if she were in her last twenties." Rankin became "so disgusted" by the superficial coverage that she told a reporter "to go to hell" when he came to her congressional office for an interview.

Because of Jeannette Rankin's attractiveness and prominence, men took notice of her. As a young woman she had offers of marriage, and after her 1916 election she received bizarre inquiries from lonely soldiers and fortune hunters and romantic overtures some women would have welcomed. "Max" wrote to her immediately after her 1916 election: "To think you would have to fight it out for second place with a scrub like Mitchell makes me almost sick! But then, it is some accomplishment for a little girl to be the first woman [elected to Congress]. . . . [O]f course my ideal woman can do anything. Accept my congratulations and remember I am looking forward to the time when I may see you."

In Washington, D.C., an *Evening Star* reporter expressed more personal than professional interest in Jeannette Rankin: "Since having heard your little, impromptu speech . . . in the Park View school auditorium, I have been converted into an admirer of your charming self. You will remember, when it was my pleasure to be presented, I remarked I had seen you to advantage from the press gallery of the House. . . . I wonder if I may consider myself your friend [and] have the pleasure of receiving an (even brief) answer." Rankin's reply seemed to be premised on the advantage a politician might gain by having a friend in the press corps: "Your kind letter has been received and I cannot express what it has meant to me to know of your interest and kindness. . . . [It would be] indeed a source of encouragement and an inspiration to be able to consider you my friend and I am most grateful to you for writing as you did. If you care to come, I should greatly enjoy having you call upon me at my home" (which she shared with her mother and congressional aides). The reporter's reply, given Rankin's New Woman values, bordered on the delusional: "Your much-prized favor reached me [and] cultivation of your friendship surely will make me a superior young man, as I consider you the charming type of woman, dear Miss Rankin, that inspires and encourages the stronger sex to be bigger and truer men, bringing to the surface a better conception of the higher and purer things of life. Awaiting your pleasure." One suspects that his wait was long and futile.

Late in life, Jeannette Rankin still had male admirers. In India in 1952, she attracted the attention of Chester Van Allen, a fifty-six-year-old doctor. She used his hospitality and car, and he visited her at Snow View, her vacation house that looked onto the Himalayas. In his letters to Rankin while she was still in India, Allen struck a protective note and tried to impress her with his financial soundness. He wrote that he was "saving for the day when he could retire as a gentleman farmer to an estate he already owned by the sea." After she returned to the United States, his suit became more direct: "I want, too, a dear companion of similar tastes to share what remains of life and love." But Rankin's interest in him was not equally keen. To Wellington Rankin she mentioned, wedged between discussions of the recent Indian election and her travel budget, that Dr. Allen's borrowed car was "not very satisfactory." And after the doctor's visit to Snow View, she complained to Edna: "I asked Chester Van Allen out here but he got sick. . . . [H]e ought to be sick—he has such a nasty disposition." In 1972, when she was ninety-two years old, Rankin received a touching letter from a married male friend in Georgia. "For the past weeks," he wrote, "I have felt a growing sense of loneliness at not having been with you in such a long time. I love you dearly and my longing to see you is indescribable. I wish I could encourage you to come back and stay at your home. . . . [I]f you would come back for a visit I would devote my spare time to you and you could stay with us at the Wilkins House for a while, which would be wonderful!"

Jeannette Rankin had one special male companion, Fiorello LaGuardia, to whom some have tried to link her romantically. She and LaGuardia had similar backgrounds, and he was clearly interested in her. He grew up in Arizona and New Mexico, graduated from New York University's law school in 1910, was elected to Congress in 1916 as a Republican from the Democratic Greenwich Village district, was untraditional in his religious thinking, and was interested in social work and social policy. They entered Congress together and continued their friendship after she left Congress. From LaGuardia's perspective it could have been something more. With his arm around Jeannette's waist, he once told Edna, "You don't know how hard [I] tried to get this gal to marry me." As mayor of New York he wrote to Rankin at the end of her second term: "With all your faults, I love you still. Sorry I did not see you before you went home. . . . Write to me from time to time." Jeannette Rankin admitted to a relative, at the time of his marriage, that LaGuardia had proposed to her. She later described LaGuardia as her "close personal friend," but she used similar language when referring to another congressman who voted for suffrage: "He was my best friend from then on." Probably accurate was the judgment of Rankin's first-term secretary: "She had a number of men friends. . . . [LaGuardia] took her out to dinner and they discussed things . . . but there was nothing romantic. . . . I'm sure there wasn't."

What interest Jeannette Rankin had in men stemmed not from sexual attraction but from the advantages they had in business and politics. "She liked the company of men," Wellington Rankin's widow remembered, "because they were more interested in and could talk about public affairs, but men themselves never seemed to interest her." One of Jeannette's political contemporaries made the same point: "I don't think there was ever any man in her life. . . . She liked . . . to visit with and talk with them. . . . [M]en would . . . sort of pay court, like to a queen. . . . I didn't have any feeling that they wanted to make time with her . . . that they wanted to make a pass at her. . . . In fact, I never thought she had any particular sex appeal for men. . . . They just admired her and wanted to be around where she was, sort of like bask in her radiance." Jeannette seemed content to accept this attention, but at a man's desire to provide for her and use her strengths to buoy up his character and career, Rankin balked. As a young woman keeping house and caring for her siblings, she had come to despise her tethering. As a New Woman, she believed that "[i]t was the male-dominated . . . family that restricted women's full development." In 1943 she wrote to a friend that marriage for women meant a "parasitic life," and in 1969 to another: "You know I don't believe in marriage." Still a New Woman late in life, she said that "women are too dependent on men to realize their full potential." Wellington Rankin told his wife that Jeannette "scared off men because she . . . had to dominate everybody." But Wellington's widow said that Jeannette "did not want to be tied down again—to house, husband, family, or anything that interfered with her causes."

Unanswered is whether Jeannette Rankin would allow herself to be tied down to a woman. Clearly, many women admired her. After Rankin's return to Montana from New Zealand in 1915, a young woman, quite taken with her, thanked her for a "sweet little handkerchief": "I shall prize it very much knowing it is your own. . . . I should dearly love to go to America with you. . . . I miss you very much indeed and often regret not knowing you before." Helena Stellway, Wellington Rankin's secretary, responded gleefully to a 1917 Christmas present from Jeannette: "When your package came Sunday I was so happy I jumped up and down, for it didn't seem possible that you would remember about a little atom like me. And when I opened the package, you can imagine my delight over the dainty pink silk undergarments. They are adorable. And then the cute little 'garterettes' or whatever their name may be, with the cunning French bows. Indeed, your lovely gifts have made me very happy." Years later, as a footnote to Jeannette Rankin's gift of lingerie, Stellway shared with Rankin her happiness with another woman friend: "I only live for the day when Hazel and I can take up permanent residence in Mexico City. . . . I am delighted I never married."

Letters from women older than Jeannette Rankin expressed their attraction to what one associate felt to be her incomparable charm. Minnie J. Reynolds, Rankin's suffrage and peace mentor, chided her about campaigning for suffrage in Montana: "Your continued refusal to come to Jersey makes me feel bad. . . . I recognize Montana's first claim; but if you leave here again to go to some one else instead of us, as you did last year, I shan't like you any more." Mary O'Neill's correspondence revealed a personal infatuation with Jeannette Rankin. In a letter during the Montana suffrage campaign, O'Neill addressed Rankin as "Lively Maiden" and warned her, "with the sweetest love in my heart for you," that trying to "convert the multitude [might] rob you of your priceless winsomeness and beauty." Another Butte woman worried that her pre-Congress closeness with Jeannette Rankin had come to an end: "You don't know how jealous I am because you haven't written to me. . . . I certainly have thought of you often and I don't want to be forgotten. Don't you know how I used to pat your back in Butte when you had a serious attack of the blues." Maria Dean, a Montana suffrage leader and the first woman physician in Helena, lived her adult life with a female partner and became Rankin's campaign treasurer in her 1918 bid for reelection. Sending checks to Rankin's Washington, D.C., staff, she wrote: "I do hope she succeeds. I am very proud of her."

Younger women were more explicit in their desire to connect with the new congresswoman but wrote ambiguously or in code. Their language "suggests how closely the New Woman and the new possibilities of love between women might be aligned in women's minds everywhere by the turn of the century." A Montana suffrage colleague and New York law student wrote to Jeannette Rankin that she had "not recovered from the good news yet. Am sure that it will take me until I REALLY SEE YOU in Washington, D.C. . . . Please consider that one of my rooms is yours if you want to use it while you are in New York. . . . [J]ust think of me. . . . I am yours." Another Montana friend living in New York used the same "to see what I can see" motif in her letter to the congresswoman: "For a long time I've been wanting to see you for various reasons. First, of course, because I wanted to see you—by the very obvious bear-went-over-the mountain logic." A reporter for *Red Book Magazine* described in two 1917 letters Rankin's fund-raising success and the changed behavior of her "Japanese friend" during Jeannette Rankin's recent trip to Chicago. "You will be glad to hear," she told Rankin, "that the Chicago Woman's Club cleared expenses. . . . [Y]our coming was a blessing not in disguise but in pink chiffon and marabou. . . . So everybody is happy, and I, who have been eating and sleeping steadily ever since, am now clothed and in my right mind." But Jeannette Rankin had won the heart of her friend's companion, and the friend told Rankin that she was "quite jealous" that "Miss K. Tanaka" had sent Rankin a gift and become her "devoted Japanese admirer-ess." Closing her "purely personal and friendly" letter, she told Rankin that she understood her "never" writing and concluded, "I still like you." Another woman referenced a mutual acquaintance in making contact with Jeannette Rankin: "You are not absolutely unknown to me. . . . I feel an interest in you not wholly connected with your present political one. Trusting to hear from you." Rankin replied to this admirer: "[C]ome to see me soon, so that I may have the pleasure of meeting you and talking with you." A young woman from New York hinted at a special affinity when she asked to see Rankin after a 1917 Madison Square Garden speech: "I am proud to add that I belong to the Cult, and I shall have the pleasure of conveying your message at that meeting back to your unknown but interested Long Island friends." Another New Yorker confessed her total infatuation with Rankin: "I have longed to write you a hundred times and tell you I honor you and love you. . . . I have about made up my mind to picket at Washington." Rankin's reply did not demur or deter: "If you should decide to come to Washington please do not hesitate to call upon me."

Some of Jeannette Rankin's relationships with women that began during her early days in suffrage politics continued for years. When traveling state to state for the Women's International League in the 1920s, Rankin made the most of opportunities to see old friends. To Irma Hockstein, she sent an intimate note: "I am so pleased with the thought that I am going to see you next week. I am looking forward to it with great pleasure. I had a letter from May Murphy not long ago suggesting that we all start on a trip around the world in January. Will you be ready? Lovingly yours." To Wilma Ball she wrote: "I am going to be in Chicago a little earlier than I expected— so if you could come early to the conference, we could have more time together. Please write me at Hull House. Lovingly yours." And to Mary Weible, a lifelong friend in North Dakota, she wrote: "I felt very near you when I was in Minneapolis and frightfully disappointed not to see you. . . . Lovingly."

Jean Bishop was an especially close Montana friend and suffrage and Good Government colleague. After the 1916 election, she wrote to Jeannette Rankin: "You know you captured our hearts long before you did our ballots. . . . With warmest love." In 1961 Wellington Rankin's secretary was still recalling Jean Bishop to Jeannette Rankin as "such a lovely person." Bishop visited Rankin in Washington in 1917 and campaigned for her in 1940. Jeannette Rankin, in her first letter after the 1940 election, thanked Bishop for the "very good work you did in the campaign," was "disappointed that we did not have a chance to go to Mexico right after the election," and hoped Bishop would be "coming down here to see me." In 1955 Rankin and Bishop shared a "classy double room on the *S.S. Argentina*" while traveling to South America. Katharine Anthony, Jeannette Rankin's closest lifelong friend, wrote ambiguously but without jealousy to Rankin about her South America trip with Bishop: "Go on with your travel plans. I'll travel with you vicariously. . . . So awfully glad you have a traveling companion. It will be so much more fun. . . . Aren't there any witches or suffragettes in Argentina? You and Jean surely ought to be able to dig them out if there are any, and I'll bet there are. Lots of love, dear, dear Jeannette."

Another of Jeannette Rankin's longtime friends was Jane Thompson, their relationship going back to at least 1914 when Thompson succeeded Rankin as the field secretary for the National American Woman Suffrage Association. Thompson, assisting Rankin during the Montana suffrage campaign, gave the effort an East Coast flavor. Her New Woman argument was that a "homely woman," who was politically at a disadvantage and "just as much in earnest about getting through legislation as is the pretty woman," had special need of suffrage. Thompson visited Rankin during her first term in Congress, and one of their times together was described by a congressional staffer in a letter to Edna Rankin: "[I]t's nearly nine o'clock and I am getting sleepy. . . . [A]s soon as she gets her call [from New York] we are going home and she is going to dress and I am going to drive her to a suffragette reception at the Willard hotel." The next day the secretary continued her letter: "[A]s we were leaving [the reception] we ran into Jane Thompson and she insisted on taking us to her hotel where we had a nice lunch and danced and then went home." From New York, Thompson assisted with Rankin's 1918 reelection effort, suggesting to her campaign staff "a small dinner with certain selected people." After her 1940 election, Rankin wrote to Thompson who by then was married to an export company executive. Her quick transition from a personal message to political business was characteristic of her correspondence: "[It was] a joy to have your gift, which always keeps you close to me. . . . I wish you were coming down to see me seated. . . . In spite of [President Roosevelt's] blustery confidence I still feel sure that he can be bluffed out of going to war if the women will do their part."

By 1944 Jeannette Rankin—unlike Thompson—no longer viewed their relationship as intimate. Edna Rankin, in a series of letters to Jeannette, conveyed Thompson's continuing interest: "[Jane] asked me out [to Long Island] for next weekend. Wish you were to be there and so does Jane. She asked for you of course"; "Jane asks all about you and I constantly feel that she'd rather it was you that was with her"; "I had lunch with Jane and when I told her that you might go to Mexico her face dropped a mile—she was horribly disappointed"; "I told [Jane] that we would *both* have Christmas with her and she fairly shouted with joy. She is more than delighted that you are to be here." Although Jeannette Rankin's refusals of Thompson's invitations suggest the relationship had grown cold, another member of the Rankin family presumed that the two women continued to be close. In a letter urging Edna to "enjoy your new happiness to the fullest [with your] Yale man," sister Mary also expressed the wish that Edna's "friend Jane could do as well by Jeannette. She seems more alone than ever. I wish she might find a thoroughly congenial person to spend the rest of her life with."

One reason Jeannette Rankin refused Jane Thompson's invitations was that she had been enticed to Mexico by another old friend, Abbie Crawford Milton. Milton, a suffragist and pacifist, was married to the owner of three Tennessee newspapers, contributed to Rankin's first congressional campaign, and remained close to her after 1916. Rankin stayed with Milton in Chattanooga while campaigning for peace in a congressional district in 1936, and Milton visited Rankin in Washington during her "low" period after voting against World War II. In 1944 Milton's first pitch to her old friend to take a trip failed: "[L]et's go adventuring into Florida this winter . . . fish and loitering, mainly loiter—tourist class." Her argument for Mexico succeeded: "Enclosures make the trip seem realistic. . . . I shall expect you to look after the finances of the party—whether $25 or 25 cents per day is ok." Edna and Grace Rankin, however, could not envision their sister lying about with her friend. Edna implored Jeannette not to "rush through [Mexico] like a bat out of Hell," and Grace advised, "After you get through dashing around you should settle down to some regular living so you'll get the feel of the place."

As Jeannette Rankin's second congressional term was winding down in 1942, she visited Milton in Chattanooga and, after returning to Washington, wrote to Milton: "[A]rrived home last night. . . . [C]onnections were so poor. . . . [Y]ou are such a joy and inspiration to me. . . . I had such wonderful sleeps at your house and have been wakeful every night since." Summoned by Wellington to Montana to take care of their mother, Jeannette wrote to Milton before departing Washington: "I don't know how long I shall stay. . . . There will not be time for a good visit with you before I leave so please FINISH UP and be ready to make me a good long visit as soon as I return. I am disappointed that I have to go at this time. . . . If you can come right away, I may be able to postpone my trip. I enjoyed you very much indeed, and I do appreciate your giving me such a nice rest and so much pleasure. Devotedly yours." When Jeannette Rankin was leaving Congress for Montana at the end of 1942, Milton expressed her eagerness to continue the relationship: "Dearest Jeannette: And was your letter a welcome one to me!! I have longed so to hear from you. . . . You, darling, are an angel to want me around for a visit next summer. If there is any possibility of getting away you know I'd jump the first plane, train or ox cart. . . . I know you will enjoy life again after the bedlam of that war Congress. Peace to its ashes. Don't forget me in the frivolity of returning home. And let's stick together. Come and see me whenever you can. I can always make room and we'll move into a hotel if this house isn't big enough and rent a whole floor! Excuse my prosaic letter. It goes to you filled with love."

Another long-term relationship involved Cornelia Swinnerton, Jeannette Rankin's high-spirited suffrage and Greenwich Village companion. "Nina" Swinnerton's letters to Rankin during her first term in Congress hinted at a sexual relationship, but Rankin's replies were not reciprocating. Writing in 1917 to "Darling Jeannette!" Swinnerton consoled Rankin with the observation that "nobody believes" the "sobbing fiction"—the press's portrayal of Jeannette Rankin crying when she voted against World War I. Swinnerton urged Rankin to visit her in New York: "[C]ome up to town soon—the first Sunday you possibly can. Stay a weekend or longer. Your breakfast club is growing bigger—but before it gets any larger I want you to come up and talk to me. . . . [P]lease stay here with me when you come." Rankin responded with a "Dear Nina" letter that was typically more political than personal: "I was delighted with your lovely letter and am so pleased with the invitation to come to New York. I want to come straight to your house and stay with you. . . . Hope to arrive on Sunday morning. . . . I appreciated from the beginning what it meant to have a group of women ready to back me, but I appreciate it more now, when the necessity of having supporters appears. As you perhaps realize, all of this intense war feeling has grown since I left Montana and it has been very hard to be sure how the women stand. . . . I am getting out a letter to accompany some bulletins . . . to all the woman voters. This may help to get them in a better frame of mind. I shall be so anxious to hear the suggestions that you all make. It may be that this is not worth bothering about at all. With my best love."

Nina Swinnerton was obviously excited about Jeannette Rankin's decision to visit New York. In her "Dearest Jeannette" response she exclaimed: "It is perfectly grand that you are coming Sunday. I am bursting to hear your news always—and very, very keen to see your own dear self. I treated you to a horrid scullery floor—but this time everything will be in order and besides, I promise to protect you from callers better than I did before. We expect you and Miss Craft and your niece. . . . [T]elegraph or phone which [train] and what time so I can meet you or at least be dressed this time! There is room for two of you at Katharine Anthony's and room for one at my house—I hope that one will be you for I hate to have you anywhere but with me. I am forced into admitting, by the others, that their house is more remote and perhaps quieter. But— . . . With love to you, dear Jeannette. Always your old, Nina."

In Jeannette Rankin's personal relationships, the ardor of the other woman typically dissipated after being met by Rankin's coolness. Carroll Smith-Rosenberg's analysis of correspondence between American women lovers in the late nineteenth century and early twentieth century concluded that a good indicator of a relationship's warmth was the intimacy of the salutations and closings in letters exchanged. In one case, as the relationship blossomed the "tone in the letters . . . changed . . . from 'My dear Helena,' and signed 'your attached friend,' to 'My dearest Helena,' 'My Dearest,' 'My Beloved,' and signed 'Thine always' or 'thine Molly.'" The feeling in the relationship between Jeannette Rankin and Nina Swinnerton, as expressed in the rhetoric of the correspondence, evolved in the opposite direction. In July 1917, Swinnerton wrote to "Dearest Jeannette" and recounted the excitement of being together during the Bureau of Engraving and Printing investigation: "My but it was a wonderful—a marvelous experience to be with you that week! . . . Are you coming to New York Sunday the 29th[?] I haven't heard a word but tomorrow I am going back to New York for a few days and hope to see you at 4 Milligan then. Let me know your plans. Send my letter there or care of Elisabeth Irwin, 36 Grove Street. With dearest love." The same intense feeling comes through in a letter a month later: "Dearest Jeannette: Where are you going to speak Labor Day[?] . . . This house is lovely and clean, will you stay here? But I would rather have you come to see me at Mary Chamberlain's and Mrs. Cothren's house [Heterodoxy members], Monmouth Hills Club, Highlands, New Jersey. They are away and I am going there to stay tomorrow with Frances [Cothren] nine years old until Monday. Mrs. Cothren wants you to go there. It will be cool and restful high up in the woods above Sandy Hook and the New York bay. Will you come? . . . I'll be all alone if you don't come. . . . Faithfully & love."

Jeannette Rankin did not make the trip, and Swinnerton immediately conveyed to Rankin her dejection in another "Dearest Jeannette" letter: "I was frightfully disappointed not to see you Labor Day. . . . I shall see you at Misha Applebaum's concert September 27. Immediately after the performance, I'll slip out before the end so as to be in or near the dressing room when you come out. . . . [S]end special delivery letter if there is any chance of my meeting you at your train. . . . Always with love and affection." A more pronounced disappointment permeated Swinnerton's "Dearest Jeannette" letter a year later, when Swinnerton was conducting "mental tests" for the Manhattan "Children's Court" and, with Katharine Anthony and Elisabeth Irwin, writing postcards for Rankin's 1918 election campaign: "I am enclosing some postals which I hope tell the women of Montana how I feel about you. It is a rather limited space for such a large and splendid subject as your sweet self. . . . Couldn't you come up to New York some Saturday before August 10? No—it's too late now. I have to go home next Saturday the 10th! Elisabeth Irwin, Katharine Anthony and I often talk about you. . . . I don't write to you because I think you are too busy to be bothered with personal things; if I'm wrong you write and tell me. So Jeannette, bless you dearly. Faithfully."

At the end of her second congressional term, Jeannette Rankin was still corresponding with Nina Swinnerton. But, as happened other times, Rankin's friend, in an otherwise warm letter, expressed contentment in being with another woman. Swinnerton, in a 1942 Christmas greeting, wrote from Missouri that it "does seem good to have a family circle again . . . a cozy warm place. . . . Helen has just passed by and said, 'Give my best to Jeannette.' . . . I still think and talk about my grand visit with you in Washington—it was perfect—I wouldn't have changed any of it except the Montana election. . . . Much love darling. Affectionately." The next year Katharine Anthony wrote to Jeannette Rankin that Nina Swinnerton had suffered a heart attack and had requested Anthony to "let her do the calling up, as the telephone waked her too suddenly." Later that year, Anthony reported that "Swinnie has been a little ailing," and then, "Swinnie is all right and just as entertaining as ever. She reads such a lot and has her own individual interpretation of everything." Swinnerton maintained her own correspondence with Rankin. In 1943, when Jeannette was caring for Olive Rankin at Wellington Rankin's ranch, Swinnerton was still playful: "Darling your postal is better than a letter. Don't kill yourself writing letters. Tell Mother I behave terrible at night—make coffee 3 A.M. Read St. Augustine. . . . *The Red and the Black*. . . . [S]leep and get rested you darling child—get Wellington to take over Mother's bad nights." In 1945 Swinnerton continued to be engaged with life, buying an airplane and taking lessons from a "lady pilot." But in 1947 Anthony wrote to tell Rankin that the lively "Swinnie" had died: "[G]lad we had our little visit with her over the telephone last summer, for that seems to have been near the end."

An equally ambiguous relationship was with a mother and daughter, Millacent and Harriet Yarrow. Millacent was Jeannette Rankin's contemporary and Harriet, born in 1902, was Rankin's junior by twenty-two years. The lives of Jeannette Rankin and the elder Yarrow probably first crossed in Chicago at Hull House, to which both had an attachment. Millacent had been a teacher and, during Rankin's 1940 campaign, looked after subleasing Rankin's Washington apartment. After the election, she became a secretary in the congresswoman's office. Their correspondence during that period reveals Millacent's attachment to Jeannette. During Rankin's solo, cross-country automobile trip to Montana in January 1942, she sent daily letters to Yarrow, and Yarrow in reply tried to hearten Rankin with reports of approving mail and confessions of deep affection: "I hope [you have] read some of these fine letters that came in regarding the speech—real 'fan mail' again! You've been a dear to write me day by day. I leave day after tomorrow and shall be going toward you. . . . I do miss you so. . . . [I] wish I could look into your eyes." The next year Millacent Yarrow addressed Rankin in a letter as "You precious Jeannette" and urged her to run again for Congress in transcendent rhetoric reminiscent of Mary O'Neill: "You just can't have powers such as you've been given and not be seriously, inescapably responsible for their use. . . . I've let you rest these months . . . from the cruel battering through which you have lived since December 1941." The next month Yarrow concluded a letter to Rankin with "You don't know how this old Millacent loves you."

In her replies, Jeannette Rankin was not unresponsive. While caring for Olive Rankin at her brother's ranch in 1943, she conveyed a "daydream" of herself, Olive, Millacent, and Harriet Yarrow living together at her Georgia farm. Millacent replied, "I almost think I want to go to Georgia with you whether Harriet can go or not." Jeannette Rankin, however, was promiscuous with her fantasies and shared another version of her Georgia revel with Katharine Anthony. Anthony replied: "Jeannette dear, . . . I am interested in your daydreams. Your dreams of Georgia correspond with mine. I always have a picture of being there with you again. I don't know why but it is so. . . . Lots and lots of the most devoted and loyal love to you dear." Millacent Yarrow died in 1944, and to the end she expressed her deep affection for Rankin: "[H]ow I love and honor you, my great Jeannette Rankin."

Helena Stellway, Wellington Rankin's secretary, remembered Millacent Yarrow's daughter, Harriet, as Jeannette Rankin's "dear little friend." Harriet Yarrow graduated in history from Wellesley and worked as a teacher, social worker, and missionary. As a Quaker, she shared Jeannette Rankin's pacifism. In a 1940 letter to Rankin in Montana, Millacent wrote that she and Harriet were living in Washington "in a little apartment by ourselves and so happy . . . [n]ot far from you." In 1942 Harriet taught at a school in Turkey, and in 1943 she worked at the Tula Lake relocation camp for Japanese Americans and taught high school in Newell, California. There Millacent and Harriet shared a home with two other women, an arrangement Millacent explained to Rankin: "I've been having tea ready for the three when they come home from school: Harriet and the two who occupy the room which uses connecting bathroom with us. . . . [They are] fine young women, a missionary from Japan and a California Teachers College professor of biology. We have pleasant little times." Later that year Harriet visited Rankin in Montana on her way to work in another wartime project in the Midwest. In 1944 Harriet worked in the laundry of a Chicago school, and in 1946 she began a long commitment as a Quaker missionary in Turkey. In her later years Harriet Yarrow was attached to a Quaker house in Massachusetts and busied herself with volunteer teaching. In 1970 she attended Jeannette Rankin's ninetieth birthday celebration in Washington. Another in attendance described her in a letter to Rankin as "the delightful Miss Yarrow."

Jeannette Rankin and Harriet Yarrow did delight for a time in each other's company, although Millacent Yarrow acted more as acolyte in service of her hero, Jeannette. An early letter to Rankin from Harriet Yarrow revealed the younger Yarrow's boldness and familiarity; she both taunted Rankin and hinted at a love relationship with the older woman. Probably from Turkey in 1942, Yarrow wrote: "Dearest Jeannette, You could never guess where I am—on a boat in the Merain harbor! I left home last Friday [and went] to the Smiths' lovely mountain summer retreat. . . . Please do forgive me for entering into this subject . . . your financial dicker with Arthur Smith. . . . [H]e is of the opinion that nothing from you ever reached his bank. . . . [D]o forgive me for mixing." Besides daring to touch upon Jeannette Rankin's personal finances, Yarrow had fun with Rankin's jealousy in discussing how she was going to dress for a special occasion: "Your pink blouse will be the best (I've lengthened the black skirt, cheer up!). Your bubble bead dress, and Grace's napkin wrap the cheese!" At the end of the letter, Harriet Yarrow makes it clear that it is Jeannette Rankin's attention she prizes: "Would *you* were here! . . . I love you!"

While in Turkey, the pacifist Harriet Yarrow wrote to Jeannette Rankin about the encroachment of World War II on the school where she taught: "The army came out here to register all 'colonists' seventeen to thirty-seven for war combat or industry. . . . [O]fficers [were] rushing from block to block [and] terror reigns. . . . Two of us . . . resigned. . . . [T]he authorities decided they couldn't lose all their pacifists [because] school teachers are so scarce . . . [and they] agreed to give us leave—all who disliked the registering. . . . Another thing which may send me out at any time is cooperation with Junior Red Cross. . . . If it's organizing kids for war work, I can't. . . . Your letters mean much to me. . . . [W]here are you? (But don't come right now!) I love you!" Yarrow's letter coincided with Jeannette Rankin's depression over the nation's fierce opposition to her vote against entering World War II. In her anguish, Rankin had turned to her friends in New York, not to Yarrow in Turkey, for the solace she needed: "I had a very difficult time getting things straightened [out] from the time of the vote until I had a vacation with Katharine and Elisabeth."

A year later Harriet Yarrow was in California working with "evacuated American citizens" and teaching history and algebra, so busy she relied on her mother to convey her news to Jeannette Rankin. She did manage a tardy 1942 Christmas greeting to Rankin in which she said: "This is all that goes this year and it's late. But you know my love. Thank you for sweater which came via Mother. . . . Dearest love." The long-parted friends did have a rendezvous in Montana in summer 1943, and after their visit, on the train heading for Chicago, Yarrow wrote to Rankin of her satiation and happy memories: "The beast lacks nothing. . . . You are dear, dear. A big practical help, too!" In her reply to Yarrow from Wellington Rankin's ranch, Jeannette Rankin recalled their time together, her loneliness, the beautiful autumn weather, and her upcoming activities in Georgia: "You are such a joy in this world. . . . [The] weather is glorious and Pal and Blondy are in the orchard asking to be ridden. I wish you were here. . . . I plan now to fix up Shady Grove—that is the Negro house. . . . I think I can make a very sweet place to lite until the war is over. . . . Have you been to Hull House? Love to you dear."

During the next twenty years, as Jeannette Rankin and Harriet Yarrow lived increasingly separate lives and other friendships intruded, their correspondence still retained touches of intimacy, especially on Rankin's part. In a 1944 letter from Georgia, she struck an uncharacteristically cozy tone: "I had breakfast by the little stove in the bedroom and pretended you were with me. . . . I expected to spend all morning with you but some young girls came in so I'm getting them to mail this. Love always to you darling." A few weeks later she again used an affectionate voice: "If all the thoughts I've had of you since your sweet letter were on paper you would have to take a day off from the [school] laundry to read." The letter, however, also made reference to a new acquaintance of Yarrow's: "I'm anxious to meet Jean. She has very fine discrimination in her appreciation of you." During winter 1946, Rankin and Yarrow were again able to spend time together. Rankin escaped from caring for her mother, fought off rampant sickness on a converted troop ship, and endured the discomfort of overland travel from Egypt through Palestine to see Yarrow in Turkey. She stayed with Yarrow at a "school for girls [but] Harriet had to go away for a while and I was there alone." Seven years later, Yarrow's Christmas card reached Rankin in Kenya, and Rankin responded with hope for some future visit: "[S]o sorry not to be home when you came to Montana. . . . I shall try to be in Chicago some time between March and June—so shall look forward with joy to seeing you. . . . Love to you dear Harriet." Later that year Rankin spoke of another possible reunion: "Come to the ranch if you can—and remember that you are very precious and needed many places—you are a good girl. Lovingly." In 1956, when Yarrow was in Turkey, a letter from Rankin indicated a continuing relationship and desire for physical closeness: "If you could see the amount of work I've put in this house this fall you would not be concerned over the work I did for you—I have to keep working to prevent my being too sorry that you are not here. . . . [H]ope to hear your plans for next winter soon. It's too far ahead for me to be certain, except that Shady Grove cottage will be most anxious to have you, and so will I. Lovingly."

In 1961 Jeannette Rankin was eighty-one and Harriet Yarrow was fifty-nine. Increasingly, the longtime friends saw that a personal relationship was beside the point. Rankin wrote to Yarrow in Turkey: "It was such a joy to see your handwriting on the letter. . . . I keep seeing things you have given me . . . and I want to write but you know me. . . . I came home from India via the Pacific . . . on a cruise ship. . . . [It was the] best experience of any trip." Later that year Rankin planned more trips and told Yarrow that she might be included on an itinerary: "I'm thinking about a trip to Russia next summer and Turkey on the way to India next winter. . . . You know you have my love." Yarrow, too, came to see that their relationship had become an exchange of sweet words. Having returned from Turkey in late 1964, she sent Rankin a "blessing . . . for your dear one of December 13. It went right to the heart to know that you were thinking [of me] as I traveled over the miles. . . . I'll get a house whenever you are coming, cheer up. . . . With dear love." In 1970, when Jeannette was planning to be in New York before leaving for India, Harriet Yarrow expressed her expectation of a modest meeting: "If I could have an hour with you on the 24th, I'd come to New York. Grand that you are going to Delhi!" And at the end of 1971, Yarrow wrote perfunctorily about "Christmas . . . in Cambridge" and sent "high good wishes for 1972"and an apology: "[S]orry you didn't hear from me for so long."

The thirty-year relationship between Jeannette Rankin and Harriet Yarrow was sustained by more than memories of intimacies and hopes of future liaisons. Both women were politically aware pacifists and faced similar daily challenges. Employment and money were problems, and they exchanged advice on making their resources stretch and even shared clothes. Rankin once softened her counsel by saying: "I haven't taken the poverty oath for you. Just practice it for myself." Yet, she worried over the cost of the "jolly little presents" that Yarrow sent her: "I do feel very strongly that you should give great thought to keeping your money and make as much profit out of it as you can. Don't give it away but use it yourself as you think best. Of course I'm strong for pensions so get what you can." Yarrow expressed her gratitude for Rankin's recommending her for a teaching position at a California college: "I appreciate your taking time when you have so much to do! . . . [A]gain and always I say, Thank you, my dear." Rankin shared with Yarrow her frustration over being unemployed and working for a cause instead of money: "I'm coming home to settle down in Georgia (for winters) and stop rushing up blind alleys." Yarrow sought Rankin's assistance in helping her Turkish students gain admission to U.S. colleges. Rankin thanked Yarrow for keeping her informed about political developments in the Middle East: "I'm so happy you made it possible for me to have such a good background for all the goings on in your part of the world." In turn, Rankin recommended books to Yarrow that would help her understand developments in Asia: "I think you should read Edgar Snow's *Red Star over China* just to get an overall picture of the present situation and *America's Role in Asia* by H. P. Howard. . . . Am now reading Elspeth Huxley's *Red Strangers.*"

At times their correspondence turned more specifically to politics, ranging from international peace to Wellington Rankin's campaigns. About foreign affairs, Jeannette Rankin wrote as an anti-colonialist and isolationist: "When the Big Three take their hands off of Asia then we can contemplate a reign of peace but not until then. The Big Three are just as willing to sacrifice China as they are Japan and India. We must have Asia for the Asiatics. . . . I think you are right there is lots of peace sentiment, but [Americans] are fed up with all this bla about internationalism." In their presidential politics, the two pacifists were skeptical if not cynical. In 1944 Jeannette Rankin showed her hatred of Franklin Roosevelt: "The Dictator's majority was only half what it was in '40. The election means a continuation of war and deaths." In 1956 she held out some hope for Eisenhower: "Ike seems to be really in earnest about preventing war—it is the only way his name can live in history." Yarrow was equally critical of presidential candidates and compared Rankin's strengths to the inadequacies of the current field: "How do you explain Taft? He seemed to be 'very nice, just our kind' in pre–Pearl Harbor days. . . . How did you like the way Dewey won his nomination? Disgusting. . . . What is our remedy? More like you. . . . [G]o on with the speaking with all your mighty might!" Regarding Wellington Rankin's losing the 1948 Senate primary in Montana, allegedly because of election fraud, Harriet Yarrow seemed to be as depressed and angry as Jeannette: "I am just sick about your and Wellington's personal disappointment. . . . [T]hat it was not a fair fight makes it the more bitter!" In 1953 Wellington Rankin's fate and the women's reactions were no different. Jeannette Rankin wrote to Yarrow that "Wellington did not get in. The two Anaconda Company's counties were against him."

Yet another of Jeannette Rankin's woman-centered relationships was with the earthy Flora Belle Surles. Its roots ran back to 1917 and its close was marked by a short 1971 note from Rankin, busy planning another trip to India and promoting her election-reform ideas, to a relative of Surles's partner Anne Gregorie: "I know you are sad to have Flora Belle go. This is just a note to tell you that my love is with you. I am too saddened for more." Flora Belle Surles, seven years younger than Jeannette, was born in Alabama in 1887. She graduated from the Alabama Girls Technical College and worked as a lobbyist for the Southern Lumber Association. In her later years she remembered the day the famous congresswoman came into her life: "[W]hen I first saw you, in Birmingham, when you were first in Congress, I was impressed only by your daring, impudent womanly charm when you appeared as a 'suffragette' who should have been dressed in tight britches and carrying a walking cane and a derby hat." In the 1920s, Surles was drawn again to Rankin's appearance when they, as field secretary and office clerk, worked for the Women's International League: "There [was] something in the look of [your] . . . face . . . that attracted me." In correspondence with Rankin about her travel expenses and reports on "size of audiences," Surles hinted at an interest beyond business. She signed her letters "Affectionately yours" and wrote, when Rankin's work with the Women's International League was coming to an end in 1925, "I understand you will not be back here. I am sorry! . . . May I say that, personally, I am very glad you have had this little connection with us, and I'm hoping very much that after the summer vacation you'll be with us again. It always seems a privilege to me to work with one like you, and I assure you it is a personal pleasure to do so."

Flora Belle Surles did not have to wait long, because she soon joined Jeannette Rankin, Katharine Anthony, and Elisabeth Irwin for a summer retreat at Rankin's Georgia home. It was "the loveliest vacation I ever had," Surles recalled years later. The country sojourn also left a deep impression on Anthony, who chronicled the adventures of the four women in the *Woman's Home Companion*. There she describes "Florabel" as alien and lacking in beauty. Surles, Anthony wrote, "had the swarthy skin which marks so many daughters of the bayou states. She was thin, almost scrawny, and had dark circles below her eyes. Her head, with its heavy crown of long dark hair, seemed too massive for her body. In her jockey cap and tight riding breeches, she walked among the trees looking like a troll. There was something strange and wild about her. . . . Silent in ordinary society, she became vivid and expressive in the company of small boys and animals."

After the mid-1930s, Jeannette Rankin and Flora Belle Surles continued their visits in Georgia and in South Carolina, where Surles lived with Anne Gregorie, a historian, and, as Rankin called Gregorie, Surles's "old man." Surles occupied herself with helping Gregorie's brother in his general store, delivering mail, caring for children, tending her chickens and vegetable garden, and managing the house during Gregorie's research trips. Jeannette Rankin's life, in contrast, turned to political campaigns and international travel. In 1936 Rankin asked Surles and Gregorie to accompany her and Olive Rankin to Mexico or Canada in a new "Ford 60" Wellington had bought her. Visits and letters between the country woman and the national personage continued for years and provided both of them emotional sustenance.

The record of correspondence between Rankin and Surles goes back to 1935. Rankin invited Surles to visit her, Olive, and Edna in Georgia as soon as she, the peace lobbyist, returned from Washington where the "anti-peace Congress" had become "such a bore." In 1938 Rankin extended another invitation to Surles: "[I]f you and Anne want to come up [to Washington], we can take care of you if you don't mind living in a dormitory." Mostly on Rankin's mind, however, was Congress's opposition to the Ludlow Amendment that would have required a popular referendum on war. She urged Surles to write to President Roosevelt and ask him "why he distrusts the people." A 1941 letter to Surles described Olive's illness ("in bed for two months, most of the time with two nurses") and asked, "How do the people feel about saving the Red menace?" In a 1942 letter, as her congressional term was expiring, Rankin's spirits were even more on the wane: "Next winter I expect to spend in the South with mother. . . . I started a house in Georgia [and] hope some day to get on with the rest but when depends largely on whether all our men are killed or maimed and when the awful chaos really sets in. There is certainly not much to look forward to." After Rankin left behind the frustrations of Congress, Surles and

Gregorie repeatedly invited her to visit them. Surles wrote to Rankin in 1945, "[J]ust whenever it suits you hop a bus and come over, hear?" The same year Gregorie wrote to Rankin, "[C]ome at any moment that the impulse strikes." Rankin, too, asked her friends to visit her in Georgia: "I'm ready for you any time. . . . [S]tay a week and come as soon as Anne's work permits. Get that book out of the way." Jeannette implied, however, that Wellington was not equally open to the two women visiting his ranch: "I went out to the ranch with a woman to help clean. . . . [A]s soon as we can get a cook I'll go out to stay. . . . Wellington would love to see you and how."

Visits followed invitations, and letters recalled the pleasures of the visits. In her correspondence, Jeannette Rankin bared her feelings to a surprising degree. Returning from a visit to South Carolina in 1944, she confided to Flora Belle Surles a deep loneliness: "It was very hard to leave you—living in the glow of your love and care was a great joy. The rain expressed my feeling. The lunch was delightful and kept me knowing what I was missing." A month later, after Surles and Gregorie had visited her in Georgia, Rankin returned to a rain image to express her sadness: "We . . . have missed you so much that the heavens wept with us. . . . I planted the red berries where you suggested and thought of you." Late in 1944, after a visit to Surles in South Carolina, Rankin was even more revealing of her solitary life: "[I]t was very hard to give you up and come home alone. . . . [A] colored man [and I] built the corner cupboard. . . . [It was] some thing to do so I couldn't feel as lonely." In 1946, tied down in Georgia caring for her niece Dorothy's two sons, Rankin wrote movingly to Surles: "How I miss you!! . . . It seems almost like a dream that you were here. . . . such a joy to have you." And weighted with the care of her mother in her last months, she complained woefully to Surles, "I don't know when I'll ever see you but I shall love you just the same."

Jeannette Rankin was closer to Flora Belle Surles than to Anne Gregorie, but Surles and Gregorie's partnership created a complication. Rankin's sister Grace recognized the threesome when she said that she would rather be sending "your girls . . . a batch of fudge" than Jane Thompson. Glimmers of intimacy did appear in the letters between Rankin and Surles, but the presence of Gregorie at first and advancing age later on provided the check Rankin might have wanted on its fruition. A sexual interest between the two women was implied in Rankin's recurrent use of a suggestive metaphor. In 1962 she wrote to Surles: "It was so hard to leave you after such a lovely visit and such a gay one. The night before I returned to Shady Grove I found it very hard to sleep. Could it be I don't want to come back. . . . Thanks for your lovely hospitality and your good letter and for seeing you and taking such good care of the little red button." In another letter to Surles, Rankin wrote: "I think of you so much and wish I could drop in for a visit with my precious friend. Do continue to take good care of the little red button and your own dear self." Clothing was the context of other shared intimacies. In 1961 Rankin told Surles, "I'm wearing the fancy pretty nighty that you gave me." When Rankin was spending Christmas 1966 in New York, Surles told her: "I think of you every day in cool or cold weather. Remember that snuggy cut-away sweater you gave me long time ago? I keep it and wear it [to bed] . . . (and nothing with it [smile face])—it is such a treasure." Four years later Rankin discussed the subject of nightwear less playfully: "If you want to stay dressed all day in . . . the new pajamas I sent you, that's your business. Just spit . . . on anybody who says it ain't."

The correspondence between Jeannette Rankin and Flora Belle Surles provides a glimpse of not only emotional intimacy but also other aspects of Rankin's personal life. Her converted sharecropper shack in Georgia was uncomfortable during the winter months. In March 1944, she wrote to Surles: "Haven't been feeling any too pert. . . . I've spent so much time keeping warm in the day time." Caring for her mother in Montana, Rankin told Surles that she felt cut off from public events and exhausted: "[Y]our papers have given me a lot of information. . . . [I]t is difficult to judge situations from a distance. I miss getting gems from the Congressmen. . . . [W]e have no radio and few papers. . . . Edna is expected the last of the month—it will be grand to get a night's sleep." Jeannette's discussion of Olive's illness made it clear that Wellington was in charge: "Mother is still in town with Mary and three nurses. Expect to bring mother to the ranch. . . . Wellington seems to feel that mother is very low and that I should not go so far for they might need me." She also explained how Wellington compensated her. In 1950 she told Surles that her brother had given her a new Ford, and in 1955 she asked Surles, "Did I tell you that I'm buying a ranch," and then explained, "Wellington is going to run it and make the payments." Other references to cars made it clear how important mobility was to Jeannette Rankin. In 1938 she reported, "I have a new car"; in 1950 she was "for the first time in twenty-five years . . . without a car"; in 1955 she told Surles that "Wellington seemed to think I was driving too much"; but in

1965 she wrote that she was "sporting a beautiful '59 Ford." Rankin also mentioned her facial pain. In 1947 she complained, "Can't make my head work. I'm tired and there are so many distractions." In 1955 she told Surles, "I had an attack of pain but it's over now." And in 1962 she wrote, "I've had such a time with pain the time doesn't register." Several years later, just before her operation on a facial nerve, Rankin told Surles: "I have been in such pain I couldn't write. The same old trouble but more intense. It got so bad I went to Chicago to see Janet [Grace Rankin's daughter, a physician]."

In her letters, Flora Belle Surles recounts her own daily activities: feeding her eighteen chickens, planting onions, enjoying sandwiches at a sewing bee, and attending a Republican women's meeting. She also offered Rankin her opinion on urban riots: "I believe that the solution [for unrest] lies in . . . the differences in racial genes which have direct bearing in the thing that makes individuals of each race 'tick.'" She kidded Rankin about her unflagging travel: "I thought you were more or less joking about going anywhere beyond the borders of Georgia. Instead of putting Sam [Rankin's dachshund] on a leash maybe he'd best be putting one on you [smile face]!" Of greater interest were Surles's comments on Rankin's personal relationships as old age brought them to an end. At Katharine Anthony's death, Surles's condolences revealed insight about the closeness of Rankin and Anthony: "I know you will miss Katharine—though your times with her were few and far between and of short duration." At the time of the Jeannette Rankin Brigade, Surles expressed again her understanding of Rankin's relationship with Anthony: "I keep wishing you had Katharine Anthony to share your exciting adventures with for she seemed to share them more adequately than any I knew." Surles also understood the special role that Wellington played in Jeannette's life: "[S]o sorry that your beloved Wellington had to go before you—such a joy and comfort and pillar of strength he was for you! It was a great comfort to me to know that you had him!" Even more telling was Surles's end-of-life assessment of her own relationship with Jeannette Rankin. Thinking back to when she had been Rankin's office support at the Women's International League, Surles wrote: "[I]t was given to you to love all mankind. . . . And . . . as long as I live . . . I shall love you." But Flora Belle Surles's love for Jeannette Rankin was different from her love for Anne Gregorie. Surles's insight was that it was hard to deeply love the political Jeannette Rankin who had devoted herself to abstract humanity.

Jeannette Rankin's longest and most intriguing relationship was with Katharine Anthony, and for years it included Anthony's partner, Elisabeth Irwin. The Rankin-Anthony friendship resembled Rankin's relationship with Flora Belle Surles in that it was woman centered and complicated by the presence of a third person. Their relationship began in New York feminist circles, an intellectual and political network that provided educated and radical women "armor against a hostile environment." Katharine Susan Anthony, a relative of Susan B. Anthony's, was born in 1877 and educated in Tennessee and Germany before graduating from the University of Chicago. She taught English at Wellesley, worked as a researcher and editor, and from 1913 on wrote women's biographies and books on working women, labor law, and feminism. Elisabeth Irwin was no less accomplished and pioneering. She was born in 1880 and graduated from Smith, the New York School of Philanthropy, and Columbia University's Teachers College. In New York she worked in a settlement house and as an educational psychologist and became best known for her Little Red School House, a pedagogical experiment in Greenwich Village that grouped students according to their intelligence-test scores.

Jeannette Rankin's intellectual underpinnings were country cousins of the sophisticated theories of Katharine Anthony and Elisabeth Irwin, but an affinity developed among the three women because of their shared interests. Both Rankin and Anthony believed that women could make a critical contribution to society by being distinctively female. It was Anthony's systematic scholarship, however, that led her to assert that women would be freed from "economic dependency on husbands or the fathers of their children" only when "society recognized maternity 'as a service to the state' deserving of government support." Both Rankin and Irwin were skeptical of traditional approaches to teaching and believed that learning occurred best through practical experiences. But it was Irwin's empirically based psychology that allowed her to criticize with authority standard school practices because they "emphasized memorization rather than experience, abstraction and symbols rather than the realities of the child's life [and] disregarded the interests and capacities of children." Rankin's equal footing with the two scholars came from her election to Congress and her practical experience of what they were writing about. She had been bored by school and had learned best by doing. And she was undoubtedly ambivalent about her financial dependence on her brother. It was not surprising that a bond developed between the provincial politician and the urbane thinkers.

In this relationship, Jeannette Rankin benefited from Katharine Anthony's writing ability. Rankin found writing onerous and unproductive, yet as a politician she knew the importance of having her name in print. In 1917 Anthony became Rankin's ghostwriter. She stayed for several weeks in Rankin's Washington apartment and wrote an article for the *Ladies Home Journal*. "What We Women Should Do," published under Jeannette Rankin's name in August 1917, contained the two women's ideas about women's contribution to the war effort, labor conditions, and eugenics. It was the duty of American women, the collaborators argued, to answer the "cry for economy" by preparing and serving food in the manner of Europe's community kitchens. They used the Bolshevik revolution to argue against throwing out hard-won labor standards in the United States: "Recent events in Russia should be a warning to America that those who begin by forcing the workers to accept ten-hour and twelve-hour standards may, by so doing, finally be faced by the necessity of granting the six-hour day." They explained why wartime sacrifices should burden not the young but older Americans: "Life is sweet even to the oldest men and women, and that the hardships of war conditions may shorten their days is a prospect ineffably sad. . . . [But] any increase in infant mortality must and shall be prevented." They asserted that other tragedies of war—"the food speculator," "the great abyss of prostitution," "vast increases in juvenile delinquency"—could be prevented only by "the collective motherhood of America."

Katharine Anthony wrote not only about the ideas she shared with Jeannette Rankin but also about their personal relationship. Her three *Woman's Home Companion* articles idealized her and Elisabeth Irwin's stay at Rankin's Georgia home in 1925. Prior to the visit, Irwin wrote to Rankin: "Jeannette darling . . . I hope you won't mind our planning to spend the summer with you like this. If you want our room we will go off and let you entertain your friends while we joy ride around." At the end of the letter Anthony added a message: "Do come over and ride down with us, early in July, through the Shenandoah Valley and the Blue Ridge." After the visit, Anthony told the tale of two sophisticated and adventurous New York women on a country lark. They used their expert driving skills to avoid the crises of a thousand-mile motorcar trip and traded their accustomed pleasures of European travel for roadside camping. At Jeannette Rankin's farm Anthony and Irwin came upon "a low white house in a grove of young pines with a red chimney peeping out above the green tops." The clearing was carved from "sixty wild acres," a "cultivated district" of honeysuckle, peaches, pecans, and persimmon that overpowered the senses. The cottage's "screened-in . . . perfect porch," its most charming feature, "faced the west and looked into the tallest pines." There in the morning breakfast was taken and "at night, you fell asleep."

Katharine Anthony was enchanted by the country setting but even more taken by her hostess. In the *Woman's Home Companion* narrative, Jeannette Rankin became "Aspasia"—the clever and influential fifth-century B.C. figure who "stir[red] up the women of Athens to revolt." As a modern-day Aspasia, Rankin was "a pioneer" who devoted her winters to politics and her summers to rustic pursuits, but never laying aside her ideology and headship. "[B]orn to lead, not follow," Aspasia's "talent for organization came out" even in small things—"the way she handled her tea cart" and ran her household: "If anybody left the screen door open, Aspasia flew at him like a ruffled hen. On such a provocation, she could almost show temper." Rankin not only managed the house but also her three guests, Anthony, Irwin, and Surles: "When she led us forth to shop or call, the illusion was complete [of] our mother [and] three dutiful over-age daughters." In the city "for haircuts and manicures," she "dealt only with concerns which conformed with Fabian requirements." Anthony saved her most vivid imagery for Jeannette's physical appearance. Having "bought heavily" of grapes, "Aspasia squeezed with her own beautiful strong hands quarts of the thick sweet juice into bottles." And on the "perfect porch" when Aspasia "presided at breakfast in her apple-green dress with a coral-pink ribbon wound about her snow-white locks, she was like a summer morning in midwinter. . . . The premature silver of her hair made a piquant contrast with her vivid cheeks and soft dark eyes. Aspasia was beautiful."

Despite Katharine Anthony's attraction to Jeannette Rankin, their relationship remained incomplete. Their visits, complicated by caregiving responsibilities and distance, included Rankin's emotional convalescence at Anthony's Greenwich Village apartment after her World War II vote and at the end of her second term. Rankin and Anthony also visited in New York during 1942 (when Elisabeth Irwin was in a hospital), in New York in 1946 ("Was at Katharine's when the real cool spell came"), and in Georgia in

1948 ("I've just written to Katharine to come down"). But separated by accidents of life and temperamental differences, letters, not visits, ordinarily provided comfort, especially after Elisabeth Irwin's death when Jeannette Rankin was caring for her mother in Montana.

Late in 1942, Katharine Anthony wrote to Jeannette Rankin about Elisabeth Irwin's declining health, and Rankin relayed news of Irwin's condition to Flora Belle Surles: "Did you know that Elisabeth Irwin is ill in a New York hospital? She had an operation and had not been home long until she broke her leg. . . . Katharine goes back and forth to the hospital. . . . Elisabeth carries on her work in the Little Red School from the hospital. . . . She is very weak and I'm beginning to doubt she will ever leave the hospital. Katharine is standing up wonderfully well under the trying strain." Irwin was dying, and in the middle of her personal tragedy Anthony thanked Rankin for her letters: "Elisabeth has more pain. . . . I had [her] out on the porch this afternoon in the sun. . . . [Y]our letters are a big help. . . . Lots and lots of love." Irwin's death in late 1942 marked the beginning of a more intense personal relationship between Rankin and Anthony.

For many months after Elisabeth Irwin's death, Katharine Anthony's letters conveyed her hope that Jeannette Rankin would fill the emptiness in her life. Gloomy weather ("the days are all dark") and wartime deprivation ("food business is another strain . . . worrying here about coal") added to Anthony's despondency. Also weighing on Anthony was the burden of caring for her and Irwin's two adopted sons: "[With] no one to take the responsibility off me there has been no chance for a let-down. . . . After the children are in bed I am physically so tired that I'm not up to going out or really to having company. . . . When Elisabeth was with me I could just sit down in her presence and gain strength for the next day. . . . I don't know how long I can get by without more stimulation than I am getting. . . . I don't want to complain but I do feel the need to talk with you about everything. . . . Write me as often as you can, darling Jeannette. I look for your letters and lean on what you say."

At the time, Jeannette Rankin was caring for Olive Rankin, thousands of miles and weeks away from the turmoil of Washington and her post-term respite with Katharine Anthony. The separation bothered Anthony greatly, and she looked to letters to close the distance. "It gave me a thrill to get a letter from you that was written on January 19 and received on January 20," she wrote to Rankin in 1943. "If it were not for this war getting in the way there would be such wonderful adventures all around for us. Anyway, I'm appreciative of the pleasures that are left. One of them is that we're only twenty-four hours apart by air mail. . . . I hope you are coming back soon and certainly by next winter. I want you to be near. . . . Keep writing to me." A month later Anthony insisted again on the importance of frequent letters: "We must write to each other often. We have to annihilate the distance. Lots of devoted love to you." The separation seemed so great that Anthony was comforted when Rankin moved a few miles closer to New York, having brought her mother from Grace's home in Spokane to Wellington's Avalanche Ranch in Montana: "I'll be glad when you are there. It seems somewhat nearer." And after Jeannette Rankin scouted western Montana in preparation for a possible 1944 run for Congress, the uneasy Anthony felt relieved knowing that she was back at the ranch: "Somehow I feel better about you to have you tied to the ranch for present. I know how that hampers your real activities. . . . Write to me. . . . Just to feel that we are in touch is the thing. What I have to fight constantly is a kind of lost feeling."

Katharine Anthony's emotional need was great, and she confessed her dependency on Jeannette Rankin in a 1943 letter: "Here's all my love to you, darling Jeannette. I think of you every day and every night. I lean on you in my thoughts and you help to pull me out of depression when it falls on me. You are true and solid and enduring, and the part of me that is loyal to you just couldn't ever cave in. Ever yours." In 1946 Anthony was still using an intimate closing: "I think of you so often, and so lovingly." Rankin, however, was put on her guard by Anthony's plea for closeness and reminded Anthony of the obstacles to their being together: her duty to her mother, her bargain with Wellington, and her need to plan her next political move. Because Katharine Anthony desired so intensely to have Jeannette Rankin with her in New York (but "Washington or Georgia would do"), she rationalized why Rankin remained in Montana when she and the East beckoned: "In the mean time I don't think it is bad for you to spend some time in the Rockies and way stations. It is important for you to know the whole country. . . . I think it all right indeed for you to see a lot of Idaho and Montana. People who stay too much in the East don't know the country. But after all, the only work for you and me seems to be here. . . . Here's all my devotion and love to you." Throughout their relationship Anthony remained convinced that Rankin belonged with her in the East. Her letters constantly alluded to the attractions of New York that she knew Rankin enjoyed. In 1951 she seemed near desperation when her invitation to come to New York treated Rankin more like a tourist than a friend: "When you come up to New York, you will want to stay in the city and suck it dry. You have not been here for so long. There are people and things, organizations for world government . . . you would want to look into."

Katharine Anthony knew that it was impossible for the restless Jeannette Rankin to remain content for long with anyone. Soon after returning to Montana in 1943 to care for her mother, Rankin went to Butte to visit Mary O'Neill, and Anthony commented, "Hope you had a good visit in Butte and got a bit rested." Anthony knew about Rankin's plan to visit India ("I think your day dream about going to India is swell"), and in 1946, a year before Olive Rankin died, Anthony spoke of Rankin's return from Turkey and India: "I have been thinking about you. . . . Your mother must have been so delighted to see you." Jeannette Rankin, the on-the-go reformer, and Katharine Anthony, the place-bound scholar who had never flown in an airplane, were too different to be partnered for life. Anthony explained to Rankin that her own "restlessness seems to be satisfied by this twice a year upheaval of my daily life" when she traveled to and from her summer home in Connecticut. In 1943 Anthony refused an invitation to go to Mexico with Rankin and suggested a North Dakota acquaintance as a substitute: "I had been so tempted it was hard for me to write a refusal. . . . [W]ould Dr. Weible be available? She is alone now and foot-loose, I gather. And if she is available, would she be suitable? You know what I mean—have enough common interests with you, political, intellectual, etc. . . . I am ok and I love you." In 1949, when Rankin took her second trip to India, Anthony's writing was touched with sadness: "It makes me feel rather lonely to have you in India. . . . However, I am glad that my dear friends have the enterprise to explore the big world even though I have not." After Rankin's return from India, Anthony wanted to be reinserted into her life: "I would love to hear from you and have some general account of your trip." In 1955 Anthony was resigned to Rankin's traveling in South America with Jean Bishop: "Go on with your travel plans." Whether Rankin bestowed on her travel companions the intimacy Anthony was seeking is unknown. A 1961 letter from Jeannette to Edna about her cabin mates, when she was on a ship in the Pacific, obscures as much as it suggests: "Mrs. Miller has a bad cold but I think I've had mine. The new woman is kind and thoughtful—has lovely legs and almost black hair, is taller and weighs a pound or two more than I but I think her face looks very, very old. I think her name is Hyman. Hasn't offered to trade with me. Haven't offered my last present . . . but Miller wants her so I think I'm safe."

The visits of Jeannette Rankin and Katharine Anthony, Flora Belle Surles had observed, were "few and far between and of short duration." But Anthony always longed for the itinerant Rankin. She wrote in 1955: "[Y]ou will stay with me of course. . . . [L]ove til I see you." She expressed the same unconditional openness in 1956: "You know you have a home in New York." One of Anthony's invitations centered on her biography of Susan B. Anthony. She asked Rankin to join her on a research trip: "I have got to make her human and interesting. . . . Come spring, I must get around to the places where [she] used to live and have a good look at them. . . . How would you feel about coming up here and making the trip with me[?]" In July 1953, Anthony was "still hoping" that Rankin would spend part of a summer with her in Connecticut, and in winter 1954 Anthony was making plans to visit Rankin in her Georgia "hide-out" where she wanted to finish the Susan B. Anthony book. Anthony's trip to Georgia did happen, because a year later she wrote to Rankin: "I am so glad I snatched that visit with you last spring." In summer 1954, Anthony was again looking ahead, hoping that Rankin might spend part of summer 1955 with her: "I think you should come here next summer for the month of June. You always have to fill in time before Avalanche gets warm enough. . . . It will be something to look forward to all winter." Anthony's pleading in later correspondence, however, made it clear that Rankin had misgivings about the visit: "Have you forgotten that you once said you might [come to Connecticut in June]. . . . It would make me very happy if you would say yes. YES." Rankin did spend time in New York with Anthony in early 1955, and in 1958, waiting to hear whether her manuscript on Mercy Otis Warren had been accepted, Anthony was once again filled with joyful expectation of another visit from Rankin. Anthony wrote that she was "on tenter hooks till I hear from the publisher. Wish you were here to get me off the hooks! . . . Am looking forward to April 7 . . . with all my heart." But Rankin's arrival could never be taken for granted, as Anthony indicated in several letters the next month: "I can refer to your card saying 'I'll be up early' for reassurance. I am beginning to look for you all the time. . . . My social life is not so active as yours. . . . When will you come? Half of my little home is waiting and longing for you. My arms are always open."

The one-sided record of correspondence—which Katharine Anthony routinely closed with sentiments such as "I love you dearly," "I love you darling," "Love and devotion," "I love you and think of you all the time," and "All love for you darling"—indicates how keenly she anticipated Rankin's sporadic and short visits. She remembered with delight the small details of Rankin's Watkinsville cottage: "your sweet Georgia kitchen, every nook and corner of which I remember with love"; "your elegant pink boudoir with that wonderful kerosene heater going"; "all those Indian things [that] give it so much character"; the "daffodils and tulips—so much care you have put in them." In Anthony's recollection these incidentals symbolized Rankin, "so sweet and attractive . . . so expressive of yourself." Anthony also recalled the parts of Rankin's daily life she had shared: "I am thinking of you and wish with all my heart that I could see you and jump into the car and spin away to Athens or over to [Blanche Butler's] for a delicious lunch." Another time she pined, "How I wish I could come down and play around with you and sit by your fire and enjoy Wonder [Robinson] and the others." Nostalgia even overcame her with thoughts of Rankin's meal routine: "Come noon and lunch time I say to myself—time for Jeannette to set up."

But Jeannette Rankin's on-again, off-again commitments disappointed Katharine Anthony until her death in 1965. Early in 1959, Rankin's fickleness deflated Anthony's anticipation. The expectant Anthony wrote: "How lovely to hear your voice and to know that I will see you on February 10th. We must go to the theater and enjoy ourselves." But two weeks later a dejected Anthony wrote: "I have had the kitchen painted for you. . . . Maybe you will change your mind and still come. . . . I don't believe any of those expenses kept you from coming up. I guess you lost the impulse before you acted on it." Katharine Anthony's repeated disappointment, however, did not cause her to forsake Jeannette Rankin. In 1959 Anthony mustered enough courage for her first airplane trip and visited Rankin in Georgia. After the stay at Shady Grove, Anthony told Rankin, "I miss you a lot" and "Last night . . . I got homesick for you and I called your number on the telephone." But then Anthony's letters began to mention a new companion, "Viola." In May of the year she died, Anthony wrote to Rankin: "Viola is going to her Maine resort pretty soon where she always goes in the summer. I will sure miss her." Jeannette Rankin remained in touch through letters and gifts of pecans from her farm. In 1965, as part of a longer trip, she planned a stopover in New York to see her sister Harriet and the ailing Anthony. Harriet, living on Long Island, wrote to Jeannette that her daughter "Mary Elizabeth . . . will pick you up at Katharine Anthony's on Saturday October 30th and will bring you out here. She will take you to the airport Sunday evening." But on November 3, Anthony, still looking forward to Rankin's visit, wrote to her, "I am so anxious to see you." Katharine Anthony died several weeks later, and Rankin's niece Mary Elizabeth wrote to family members that "Jeannette was so undone at Katharine Anthony's death that she couldn't bear to come to New York this year and [has] taken off for Mexico." Jeannette Rankin had disappointed her closest friend once again.

Katharine Anthony probably knew Jeannette Rankin as well as anyone outside of the Rankin family. Like many others, Anthony was drawn to Rankin's charm, idealism, and energy. But also like many others, Anthony could not come truly close to the person she found so attractive. It was as if a window separated a bright lamp from the enchanted throng outside. As did Jeannette Rankin's sisters and other acquaintances, Katharine Anthony came to understand that Rankin's radiance was personal intensity more than personal warmth; the value that shaped Rankin's life was "doing for" humanity rather than loving an individual human being. Anthony hinted at Rankin's impatience and detachment from others when she cautioned her about her determination to set out on a winter trip: "[D]on't be rash just because you happen to be independent." She captured Rankin's incessant drive when she told her, "I often think of you and your brisk way." Jeannette Rankin's personality did not serve her well in her personal relationships, but it became a foundation of her political career.

Suffrage

A Glimpse of Self

eTWEEN 1910 AND 1915 JEANNETTE RANKIN TURNED INTO A POLITICAL DY-
namo. In the cause of suffrage, she traveled thousands of miles, spoke
on street corners and in meeting halls, and lobbied legislators. Role
models helped Rankin emerge from her domestic shell and become a
politician, "the most male of roles." Her father, as many politicians' parents since, modeled public life by serving as an elected official. A career in
politics seemed more attainable after John Rankin introduced her to a female candidate for superintendent of schools. The New York School of Philanthropy further encouraged her. There the "remarkable voice" of reformer
Florence Kelley inspired Rankin to perfect her own speaking ability.
Wellington Rankin stoked his sister's political fires when he helped to organize the Montana Progressive Party and campaigned as a Progressive
for the U.S. House of Representatives. Despite Jeannette Rankin's support
for the Progressive platform, particularly the planks on improving child
and maternal care and labor conditions for women, her political transfor-
mation became complete only after she became convinced that solving social

problems depended on women gaining the right to vote. Suffrage galvanized her political life. In state after state, she and her colleagues recognized that her intensity, appearance, voice, and organizing skills were rare political assets. She also learned that politics, far more than private life, challenged and gratified her.

After she completed the social work curriculum at the New York School of Philanthropy in 1909, Jeannette Rankin's brief experience in Spokane and Seattle convinced her that the hands-on part of solving society's problems was not for her. Frustrated by the bureaucratic details and interpersonal messiness of helping cast-off children, she volunteered to put up posters in neighborhoods surrounding the University of Washington. Her financial independence allowed her to work for free ("I paid my way," she said, "no salary"). Her father's estate provided $75 a month, and she sewed for a dressmaker to supplement her allowance. As a suffrage worker in Seattle and "nearly every county west of the Cascade mountains," she excelled in whatever tasks her superiors gave her. In NAWSA's *Woman's Journal*, Minnie Reynolds, a journalist and Jeannette Rankin's suffrage colleague, wrote: "No service was too commonplace, difficult, or disagreeable [for her]." Rankin's superiors noticed, in addition to her determination and energy, her "singularly sweet personality." The irony was that the harsh surrogate mother was becoming a beguiling politician. The drudgery of politics meant nothing to Rankin as she blossomed in the public eye.

On the suffrage stump, Jeannette Rankin's physical appearance attracted her audiences. She was "slim and slightly above medium height" with "straight posture," "abundant hair with its glint of red," "a fresh fair complexion," and "gray-green-blue" eyes. Wellington Rankin, already a politician, chose his attire to convey status and power and advised his sister to be similarly discerning. Early on, Rankin's skills as a seamstress and milliner abetted her brother's sartorial strategy. Later, Wellington Rankin's money kept her stunningly dressed. The effect was evident at two Montana suffrage events. At the 1911 Montana legislature, the floor and gallery "were helpless" before the earnest and expert presentation of the young suffragist clothed in a "long dress of green velvet." Addressing the Montana Federation of Women's Clubs at a critical point in the state's suffrage campaign, Jeannette Rankin wore "a gold colored velvet suit she had made herself and a big gold colored hat with plumes on it." A newspaper reported that she "looked just marvelous . . . the most thrilling looking person, full of energy and a kind of a luminous quality that just made the air electric when she started in." An editor said that she "looked like a young panther ready to spring." Suffrage opponents depicted suffragists "as either thin and lacking in the curvaceous form appropriate to femininity and motherhood—unmarriageable as it were—or as . . . fanatical, masculinized extremists . . . socially deviant and sexually suspect," but Rankin's "dashing and glowing" persona disarmed them. She was "simultaneously feminine and feminist."

Jeannette Rankin fully believed the suffrage philosophy that "women would become an important bloc of voters [and] bring their expertise into the legislative process." While staying at a San Francisco settlement house in 1908, she "attended meetings . . . on wage and hour legislation, factory working conditions, and child labor laws." Her course of study at the New York School of Philanthropy included the role of the state, care of needy families, treatment of criminals, social and race progress, and labor problems. Her reading of Jane Addams taught her that suffrage would allow women to address their traditional concerns about child labor and sweatshops. Minnie Reynolds counseled her that "pacifism should be a part of woman suffrage." At the inaugural event of the Montana suffrage campaign, Jeannette Rankin presented these positions forcefully to an overflowing Butte gathering: "men are doing their own work and doing it well, but . . . women cannot expect them to make laws to protect babies, to insure pure food, clean and sanitary conditions, to protect childhood from commercial greed."

A newspaper covering the Butte meeting called attention to Jeannette Rankin's speaking ability as well as her message. Her keynote address, the reporter wrote, was "convincing" and "straight from the shoulder." Acquaintances were amazed that the "timid and retiring girl" had evolved from elocutionary larva to butterfly. Inspired by the oratorical perfection of Florence Kelley, Jane Addams, and Anna Howard Shaw, Jeannette Rankin had striven to bring about the change. An instructor at the New York School of Philanthropy said that she "worked over her speeches, my how she worked. . . . Every invitation to make an address that Miss Rankin could find time for she accepted. [It was] not long before her exceptional ability to know persons enabled her to reach audiences of every kind." Her trademark no-text style was partly in place at her 1911 speech to the Montana legislature. To an interviewer she explained how she and Wellington Rankin had prepared for that coming-out address: "I didn't write it clear through. I wrote certain things and learned them and then we'd decide whether that was the way to present or not to present it." Encouraged by the responses she was getting, she continued to polish her speaking style. She wrote down and memorized the stump parts of her speeches and inserted other remarks extemporaneously, depending on the audience. Experimentation helped her to determine what "worked and what didn't work." Wellington's widow remembered Jeannette as a self-critical speaker with "the highest standards of grammar, diction, and enunciation." The ultimate aim of her striving, Jeannette said, was to achieve immediacy with her audience: "You can't get an audience reading. . . . I have to make them know that I'm talking to them."

Aides and journalists agreed that Jeannette Rankin was reaching her audiences. A colleague in the New Zealand Women's International League lamented they had lost her extraordinary skill: "We often speak of you and wish you had been able to stay here with us as we so badly need leaders who can speak in public, and we blame ourselves for not getting you some big meetings of women while you were here." Jeannette's secretary during her first term recalled, "It's an interesting thing, she never wrote a speech," and illustrated her point with a story. When a *New York Times* reporter requested the text of a speech the congresswoman was to deliver to the special committee on woman suffrage, Rankin told her secretary, "Well, you write something." The speech the secretary composed and gave the reporter appeared in the newspaper the next morning, but "when Jeannette got up to speak, something else had occurred in the mean time and she spoke on a completely different subject." The *Kansas City Independent* said that Jeannette Rankin had "an exquisite voice. . . . [O]ccasionally her enthusiasm gets away with her and she stops herself in her speech, goes back and tells the story in a different way [but] it forbids all notion of a set speech." A newspaper covering a first-term Fourth of July speech in Muncie, Indiana, wrote that "Miss Rankin . . . has the rare combination of femininity and force—a combination that is difficult to explain—but she talks convincingly and logically without at any time indulging in the peculiar noise-making tricks with which men orators so frequently seek to regale their audiences." As she campaigned for election reform in 1972, Rankin's voice and speaking style still served her well. Edna wrote to her about the impact she was having: "Everyone speaks of you. . . . The thing that impresses people the most is that you are so constructive in your thinking and yet you don't seem to want to pound home your ideas with a sledge hammer. You keep it light—even though what you say is dead serious." But several months later, the ninety-two -year-old Rankin's "exquisite" asset had become "almost mute."

In her suffrage career, Jeannette Rankin took advantage of another political asset, her skill for organizing. Olive Rankin became the first to capitalize on this strength when she, like many other mothers of the period, asked her "firstborn daughter to mother the lastborn children." Jeannette Rankin fled this "apprenticeship system [to her] mothers' world" and soon was organizing on the streets of New York. Her employer, the New York Woman Suffrage Party, had been founded in 1909 by Carrie Chapman Catt and followed the Tammany Hall model of organization. In the party's ranks, Rankin learned grassroots organization, saying later: "I think the old Tammany Hall organization is the most effective. Organize each county with a chairman and a central committee, and these in turn take charge of the precinct work and manage it according to the methods best suited for each particular location. The important thing is to have workers everywhere." Two years later, when she had returned to Montana to take charge of the state's suffrage campaign, Rankin explained the complex political structure she was building: "We are busily at work in this state getting our preliminary organization in shape. This means the precinct organizations and the training of a corps of efficient workers. . . . We want a capable, efficient woman in every precinct in the state. . . . These precinct captains will form in each county the county committee, and the county committees in turn will elect their chairmen, who will form the state committee and will elect the state organization." In her two congressional campaigns she applied the principles of precinct and county organization, and in her peace work she resisted her superiors because of their top-down philosophy. Her belief in sparing no effort in organizing voters never changed. A woman lawyer planning a California congressional race once worried in a letter to Rankin that she lacked sufficient campaign funds. Rankin responded that hard work and organization were more important than money: "At first glance it appears that money is a great essential, but the money is helpful only when it represents energy in disseminating ideas. If one had the energy to cover a district, it would not require money. No woman can be elected independently unless she has devoted at least two years on nothing else but working up an organization."

The Montana suffrage campaign eventually gave Jeannette Rankin complete freedom to apply her grassroots philosophy. Her first contact with its leaders came when she was campaigning for suffrage in Seattle. Seeing an opportunity to apply at home what she was learning in Washington, she sought an invitation to address Montana suffragists. Not receiving the reply she wanted, she nonetheless returned to Montana in 1911 and gave new life to Missoula's Political Equality Club. Her speech that February to the Montana legislature was delivered as a representative of the Missoula organization and in response to an invitation to all suffrage leaders to speak on the pending suffrage resolution. "[E]scorted to the reading desk by a number of old-time suffragists," including Dr. Maria M. Dean, the president of Montana's first suffrage organization, Rankin challenged the two chambers and a packed gallery with the ideas of Jane Addams. Addams saw suffrage as women "pursuing their traditional activities in a larger context." More concretely, Addams said that women "couldn't have a home if they had scarlet fever across the street; it would affect their home and they should have something to say about it." In her speech, Rankin interpreted Addams's insight: "Men want women in the home and they want them to make the home perfect, yet how can they make it so if they have no control of the influences of the home. It is beautiful and right that a mother should nurse her child through typhoid fever, but it is also beautiful and right that she should have a voice in regulating the milk supply from which the typhoid resulted." Despite Rankin's success in "bringing about [a] wonderful change of sentiment in favor of the bill," insufficient support stalled for a time the drive for suffrage in Montana. She then moved on to her next suffrage opportunity, campaigning for the New York Woman Suffrage Party at the invitation of one of its leaders, Harriet Laidlaw.

Jeannette Rankin toiled as a sidewalk campaigner in New York in 1911 and an Albany lobbyist in 1912 on behalf of the proposed suffrage amendment. State organizers told Harriet Laidlaw and her husband, James, that Jeannette Rankin "has worked day and night, heart and soul, for the measure, and always in such manner as to command the utmost respect of her opponents. . . . Her tact, her gentle feminine persuasion and her ever-ready logic have made many converts to Woman Suffrage." Her charisma, however, failed to move one New York legislator. State senator Franklin Delano Roosevelt told her that suffrage and labor reforms for women might make sense in the West but not in the East. "[H]e spent his summers in Maine,"

Rankin reported the East Coast aristocrat's words, "and . . . in that community the ships would come in with fish. They'd blow a horn and it was the signal for the women and children to go down and take care of the fish. If they had an eight-hour day or any restrictions, the fish might spoil." Rankin never forgave Roosevelt for his condescension and insensitivity to her cause.

Under the pressures of the New York suffrage campaign, Jeannette Rankin discovered that she was willing to let the importance of her cause excuse unethical tactics. When her superior criticized her for spending too much time trying to convert bystanders and too little time getting people to sign the New York suffrage petition, she resorted to a devious practice so she could show her supervisor "how quickly she could get signatures." She would "go into a saloon or anyplace," she said, and "say to the men, 'Did you vote for Delaney?'" If they answered yes, she would say: "Well I have a petition here for Delaney to do such and such. Will you sign it?" The result, Rankin said, was that she "came home with pages of signatures. The men who signed didn't know anything about what was in the petition." The incident demonstrated not only deviousness but also her less than absolute belief in the average citizen. This elitist approach to reform was reflected in an early journal entry: "All progressive movements were started by the few and no progress would ever be achieved if we had to wait for the will of the people."

In between her New York suffrage assignments as a street campaigner and a lobbyist, Jeannette Rankin campaigned for suffrage in California. She was disappointed when she was "sent into the country districts and especially into far off mining camps away from the picturesque activities in San Francisco." Because she had been frustrated by Montana legislators and successful on the streets of New York, she had assumed that the city vote—not the country vote—would be the critical factor in a California suffrage victory. Her reflections on the California campaign in a suffrage magazine included the admission: "We had entered—most of us who were sent out to help, at least—with the preconceived idea that the greatest liberalism, independence of thought and action, and equalitarian notions were in the great urban centers where experience and close intercommunication are teachers in themselves." But in California, as during other times in her life, Jeannette Rankin's experience taught her differently. She said that she and her colleagues had to "readjust many of our theories to suit the facts." The California campaign taught her that country folks were not always bumpkins. In California, she explained, there did not exist a distinction "between the people who use their minds and those who use their hands. . . . Apparently more educated people work and more working people are educated in California than in most States." In California she saw rural women and men working alongside each other. In the rhetoric of early twentieth-century feminist utopians, she explained that the "men of California are used to seeing women do things. . . . In the rural districts especially—where there are not so many idle parasites or shiftless and hopeless drudges—the women are respected more because they work and achieve things." Jeannette Rankin also took away from her California assignment the conviction that socialism was the ally of progressive politics. "I constantly came upon socialist groups in the country," she reported, "who planned suffrage meetings and invited me to speak, even if they could only gather a few around the car for a short stop. The socialists everywhere seemed to have permeated the out-of-the-way places with their doctrines, so that the idea of equal rights for women found fruitful soil."

After California and her second New York assignment, Harriet Laidlaw sent Jeannette Rankin to Ohio. There she continued her education in not only politics but also personal relationships. She discovered that she was vulnerable to the trauma of being separated from an intimate and that she had trouble submitting to a superior's directions. Prior to Rankin's arrival in Ohio, Harriet Upton, director of the Ohio suffrage campaign, told Harriet Laidlaw how excited she was that Rankin had been assigned to her. Any state would be enthusiastic about getting a campaign worker of her experience and reputation, Upton wrote to Laidlaw. The Ohio assignment, however, proved to be unsatisfactory for both women. Rankin became upset—so distraught that she told Upton she was going to leave the campaign—after she received "so many letters in one hand." Seeing that Rankin was "really sick and unhappy," Upton, as she told Laidlaw, "took [her] right home and she stayed all night because I thought she would be more rested." Alone with Upton, Rankin explained that her problem was "her family"—by which she meant Wellington Rankin—who "thought she ought to be earning something." Upton, though, said to her, "Now Miss Rankin, I believe you are going because of the beau." Jeannette Rankin's reply appeared to be dismissive not of Upton's assumption of a lover but of the lover's gender. "No! I am going the other way!" she corrected Upton.

Also depressing Jeannette Rankin was the Ohio assignment itself. The Ohio women frustrated her because they were "so untrained and held down by the church." Her relationship with Harriet Upton was also trying. Upton admitted "fearing I might have pushed her from town to town," and Rankin was quick to assure Upton that her fears were well founded. Writing to Upton after she left Ohio, Rankin said, "I'm sorry that my work was unsatisfactory but you must have known that a woman who likes to make her own plans and cannot work under orders is quite useless in a big organized campaign." Fearing Harriet Laidlaw's displeasure for alienating one of suffrage's top campaigners, Upton sent Laidlaw an explanation of her own actions. In her letter to Laidlaw, Upton attempted to work through the twists and turns of her relationship with both the suffrage leader and Rankin: "If I had felt helped by any one person more than another in this campaign it was you . . . and if there had been one worker in the field who had done her duty and pleased everywhere it was Miss Rankin. I got out my little file and read every word I had written her and do not see how she could have been hurt. The hurt was when I saw how nervous and tired she was. I felt as if I ought to have watched her and helped her more. . . . When she first came I tried to have her tell me a little more about her work than I knew but she did not seem to be able to talk to me. . . . I have had very few misunderstandings with people. . . . [T]here has been no campaign in my time when there has been so little friction. . . . I am awfully sorry . . . because I've done something to trouble you and [I've made] Miss Rankin think I did not like her personally or did not approve of her work."

In her response to Harriet Upton, Harriet Laidlaw gave her own understanding of "the strange complications about Miss Rankin," an interpretation that turned on Jeannette Rankin's financial dependency. "I can imagine," Laidlaw wrote, "that there is a possibility that Miss Rankin has overemphasized something you have written her, and that she is so nervously tried as to magnify things unduly. . . . As to whether Miss Rankin had a salary or not, is a matter of business entirely between her and me. . . . I wrote you not long ago to remind you that her volunteer work and her talk of going home might seem strange to you, and might be because her personal resources were low, and I added in that case Mr. Laidlaw and I would urge her to take some salary. . . . [T]he check which she speaks of is extra money which Mr. Laidlaw sent her for her to use aside from expenses. She has, however, some conscientious feeling about keeping it, so she has returned $100 to us. . . . Please let us drop the matter with this." Throughout the letter, Harriet Laidlaw indicated to the director of the Ohio suffrage campaign that she was taking the side of her star campaigner. And in a letter to Jeannette Rankin, Laidlaw made it even clearer that her contributions should eclipse the difficulties in Ohio. "Dearest Jeannette," Laidlaw wrote, "I hope you feel better. . . . I wish I could find a whacking good position for you in New York! Let me know what your plans are. Would you accept the legislative work again? . . . To me you stand out so much finer and dearer and bigger than most any of these other people."

As Harriet Laidlaw told Harriet Upton, Jeannette Rankin had been think-ing about returning to Montana. Her lovelorn condition, problems with money, and uneasiness about relying on her brother for support could be resolved by living at home and immersing herself in Montana's suffrage campaign. Wellington Rankin, now president of Montana's chapter of the National Men's Suffrage League, had been sending his oldest sister, be-sides her monthly allowance, suffrage news. He was also deep into orga-nizing the Montana Progressive Party, whose goals included women's right to vote. From his perspective, the presence in the state of his charismatic and hard-campaigning sister could help not only woman suffrage but also his own political career. Once back in Montana, Jeannette Rankin began to work with a suffrage steering committee to encourage the Progressive Party, the Democratic Party, and the Republican Party to endorse suffrage in their platforms. "We got every party," she said, to propose "strik[ing] out the word 'male'" in the state's law granting the right to vote. "[Then we] wrote to every candidate and asked him if he was going to stand by his party's platform. . . . [W]e used everything we could to make them know that we were in earnest." Doing "everything" meant, in addition to lobbying politi-cal conventions and sending letters to legislative candidates, traveling "county to county appointing chairmen," "urging the women to set up permanent local organizations," and talking to legislators at the state capi-tol about the merits of woman suffrage. The Montana suffrage campaign confirmed her belief in "the power of organization." In January 1913, the Montana legislature passed—with only two negative votes in each cham-ber—and the governor signed the bill proposing a suffrage amendment. After this victory, Jeannette Rankin and a friend from Whitehall began a three-week automobile trip east, politicking along the way and culminat-ing in a suffrage demonstration in Washington.

Because the Montana suffrage referendum did not take place until November 1914, Jeannette Rankin had time to devote herself to the suffrage campaigns of other states. In 1913, NAWSA hired her as its national field secretary. In that position she was given her head for about twelve months in at least ten states, "traveling wherever she was needed [and] making her own plans and running her own campaigns." In Florida, however, she was stymied when confronted with the argument that the combined vote of African American men and women would give them too much power. To refute this contention she asked NAWSA "for literature proving that woman suffrage would not create race suicide." Jeannette Rankin's thinking on the topic seemed to square with that of NAWSA, which was "often racist in nature as it tried to build support in the South." When Mary Church Terrell, the first president of the National Association of Colored Women, asked NAWSA to support "suitable accommodation" on trains for blacks, the objection of southern women caused Susan B. Anthony to declare that "it was beyond the scope of NAWSA's charge to pass 'resolutions against railroad corporations or anybody else.'"

Not only racial prejudice but also regional bias and sexual stereotyping stumped Jeannette Rankin in Florida. She became angered at society women posing as suffragists, referring to them as "perfect examples of Mrs. C. P. Gilman's sex women." Worse, the Florida women could not get beyond her "single blessedness." And the Florida men were "the worst liars [she] ever met" and were writing her off as a "northern woman." "[C]onfused" and "undecided" about how to proceed, she sought the advice of Mary Ware Dennett, a leading suffragist, pacifist, and sex education advocate. The whole Florida experience, she told Dennett, was enough to turn her "hair white," make her reject the state-by-state strategy, and drive her toward the more radical plan of going "thru congress." Although Jeannette Rankin's hair did turn white at a young age, Florida did not suffocate her suffrage fervor.

The depth of Jeannette Rankin's frustration came through in the conclusion of her letter to Dennett: "I never was in such a mess. . . . If you think it would be better for me to move on please telegraph and I'll obey orders." Because her energy was too valuable to leave untapped, NAWSA sent her to other venues. An especially satisfying experience was the National Woman Suffrage Pageant. Alice Paul, "who had worked with the more militant British suffragettes," had been appointed by NAWSA to its Congressional Committee and was organizing "more than five thousand women to parade through the streets of Washington, D.C., for suffrage the day before Woodrow Wilson's presidential inauguration." The parade was to move down Pennsylvania Avenue and a tableau was to be performed in front of the Treasury Building. Jeannette Rankin was at the head of Montana's contingent—which was made up of women, including Edna Rankin, dressed as American Indians. But the National Woman Suffrage Pageant was no pet-and-doll parade. It was a radical political innovation, as Sara Moore has observed, a more in-your-face demonstration than previously had been thought appropriate for women: "Daring to make a spectacle of themselves, the organizers . . . and participants . . . stood completely outside of conventional standards of feminine behavior and propriety." The male bystanders agreed, as NAWSA's publication, the *Journal*, reported that "women were spat upon, slapped in the face, tripped up, pelted with burning cigar stubs and insulted by jeers and obscene language." Because the pioneering event crossed cultural boundaries and received widespread notice, pageantry became, according to Moore, "a powerful tool in the political process." From then on, parades and displays became part of Jeannette Rankin's campaign repertoire.

Also in 1913, Jeannette Rankin joined a lobbying effort organized by her contemporary and friend Alice Paul. Her assignment for the Congressional Committee was to recruit U.S. senators from the South to the ranks of suffrage supporters. In an exchange with Senator John Sharp Williams of Mississippi, she demonstrated her willingness to use racist arguments to aid her cause. Senator Williams told Rankin: "[S]uffrage is all right for the women of the North. But the South can't have it on account of the colored women." Rankin's response, which invoked the legal roadblocks southern states had set up to discourage the vote of black men, reflected her at-any-cost attitude. "[C]an't you use the same laws against them that you do against the Negro, the men?" she asked the senator. Williams's reply showed him to be more respectful than Rankin. "You can't hit your baby's nurse over the head with a club," he told her. Although Jeannette Rankin and her suffrage sisters "exploit[ed] popular racist and nativist sentiments in their pro suffrage arguments," some of her admirers have tried to place her outside of this darker side of suffrage: "a white, middle-class, native movement which held to its bosom the worst elements of bourgeois sociality [and played] in the most tawdry fashion to the middle-class fears of the workers and immigrants." Racism and nativism, however, were not beneath Jeannette Rankin.

Jeannette Rankin's final period of NAWSA employment ran on for several months after Montana adopted suffrage in November 1914. Her assignments during this phase—serving as the organization's field secretary in Pennsylvania and New Hampshire and lobbying the U.S. House of Representatives under the direction of Alice Paul—brought her little satisfaction. Her time in Pennsylvania was one of several occasions when she had to deal with "libelous statements circulated about her." Their contents are not known, but men of the period commonly "condemn[ed] female friendships as lesbian and separate female institutions—whether educational or political—as breeding places for 'unnatural' sexual impulses." Impugning female relationships and associations as "morbid and pathological" was one way of "cast[ing] stones at women's aspirations for equality." Many politically active women, not just Jeannette Rankin, were labeled homosexuals, but most, "Jane Addams, for instance, shrugged it off." Jeannette Rankin "was never able to do so." She became so upset that she considered leaving her position and asked a NAWSA lawyer and her brother for advice. The NAWSA official did not want to lose Rankin's services, referring to her as "a very important spoke in the wheel." She tried to calm her with the argument that a suit against "the old man" would not be the best course of action: "This sort of thing is not as serious as it seems when it strikes people. . . . All you want to do is to keep these people quiet, keep them from circulating any libelous matter." Wellington Rankin similarly cautioned her not to go public. He called the smear "too contemptible to be worthy of notice" but told her that he would "take care of him later." In the meantime, she was to "be very careful." The NAWSA lawyer, Wellington Rankin, and Jeannette Rankin were looking to the future, but each with a different perspective. NAWSA wanted to preserve suffrage victory, and Wellington the Rankin name and his political opportunities. Jeannette Rankin, starting to think about running for office herself, was torn between litigating and avoiding the "punishment and social ostracism" a suit would cause.

Toward the end of her days with NAWSA, Jeannette Rankin was increasingly bothered by the organization's personal and political strife. She took offense at the "bossy ways" of its president, Carrie Chapman Catt, and became entangled in a "long-standing feud" with Mary Garrett Hay, Catt's loyal assistant. Rankin said that her problems with Catt stemmed from the sharp division within NAWSA between volunteer management and paid staff: "Volunteers set policies and staff did as it was told." Rankin regarded Catt and the other volunteer heads as "hoity-toity grand ladies. They were always telling people what they should do and telling me what I should do, and I felt as though I knew lots more than they did." After Rankin complained to Harriet Laidlaw about Mary Garret Hay, Laidlaw's reply—"all you can do is just to put her aside as a jealous 'brimstone heart'"—did little to lessen Rankin's resentment.

NAWSA was also fractured by two philosophies. Since 1912, Alice Paul and the Congressional Committee had opposed Carrie Chapman Catt's state-by-state strategy and advocated a national suffrage amendment. At its 1913 convention, NAWSA removed the dissident Paul as chair of its Congressional Committee, and Paul led her supporters into a new suffrage organization, the radical Congressional Union, later to become the Woman's Party. The Congressional Union pressured Congress for a suffrage amendment and criticized Democrats for not backing the measure. It was not until 1916, "[a]fter decisive state referenda defeats," that Catt changed her strategy and began to push her "Winning Plan" for a national amendment. Confronted with the split in NAWSA, Jeannette Rankin remained publicly noncommittal. She was personally closer to Paul, but she questioned the direct-action tactics the militant suffragists favored. In 1915 she resolved her ambivalence by leaving NAWSA and returning to Montana to begin her first congressional campaign. The foundation for Jeannette Rankin's congressional race had been laid the year before when she led her home state's final push to suffrage victory.

The Montana suffrage campaign had not been Jeannette Rankin's creation, and her involvement did not herald women's role in Montana politics. Many women had prepared the state's political soil for Rankin's suffrage leadership. By 1897 Montana had thirty-five suffrage clubs, whose 300 to 400 members "were generally among the better educated and propertied" women of the state. Dr. Maria M. Dean had been fighting for suffrage for fifteen years, and Mary O'Neill had been running suffrage's press campaign since 1903. For years, the Woman's Christian Temperance Union (WCTU) had been such an effective voice for prohibition and suffrage that it fused a link between suffrage and conservative values in voters' minds and made both causes "legitimate targets" of the liquor industry. One standout among the prohibitionists was Mary Long Alderson, who "gave the WCTU suffragists plucky leadership that matched Jeannette Rankin's forcefulness." Another political woman was Ella Knowles, the state's first woman lawyer and a candidate in 1892 for Montana attorney general. Alderson referred to Knowles in 1900 as "by far the most prominent woman in the political history of the state." In the 1894 drive to make Helena the state's capital, Knowles had "mounted a campaign that was energetic and efficient: door-to-door canvasses, a statewide network for correspondence and distribution of promotional literature, speeches in major cities, [and] appeals to isolated rural women and to the clergy." In 1897 members of the Montana House of Representatives invited Knowles and Sarepta Sanders to address them about suffrage, and in 1903 "suffragists gave testimony in both chambers." At the time of Jeannette Rankin's 1911 address, the "honor of floor privileges was not new." In 1902 Carrie Chapman Catt spoke and organized in Helena and Butte (the latter was then 36 percent foreign born) and "played to the nativism of [her] audience." Gail Laughlin, another national suffrage leader, visited by stagecoach "every town of importance, organizing more than thirty clubs and securing committees to circulate petitions where organization was impracticable."

This tradition of political women was one reason Montana welcomed Jeannette Rankin's claiming the suffrage banner. Another reason lay in economic, demographic, and political developments. In western Montana, Butte was becoming the "largest copper producing mine in the world," and the Anaconda Copper Mining Company was massing huge political influence in the state. Radical reformers rose up in response to the company's concentration of power. In 1912 supporters of "revolutionary industrial unionism," with ties to the Butte local of the Socialist Party, established a chapter of the Industrial Workers of the World Propaganda League. The Montana Socialist Party, which in 1914 surpassed the Montana Progressive Party in voting power, "included equal franchise in a large package of reforms by which they meant to break the alleged control of the privileged class." The Progressive Party, too, championed suffrage as a way to "broaden the base for reforms." In eastern Montana, homesteading provided another foundation for suffrage by altering political attitudes and increasing the number of reform voters. Harsh life on the prairie oriented homesteaders toward governmental solutions, and women's role in making homesteads work opened men's minds to the logic of suffrage. In 1900 the northern High Line and eastern plains portions of Montana held 38 percent of the state's population, but by 1910 their share had risen to 47 percent and by 1920 it was 57 percent. In 1912, two years before the suffrage referendum, a reform-minded electorate adopted by ballot measure the direct primary, popular election of U.S. senators, a presidential primary, and campaign finance regulations.

These reform precursors, however, do not detract from Jeannette Rankin's role in bringing about suffrage victory. When Montana became the eleventh state to adopt suffrage (the vote was 41,302 to 37,588), Rankin "earned the generous credit traditionally awarded her." Her title was chairman of the Montana Equal Suffrage State Central Committee; her contribution was her "dedication and remarkable leadership." At her side was Mary O'Neill, serving as assistant state chairman and press chairman and sending out "each week a letter of suffrage news . . . and occasionally some propaganda material." Another critical player was Maggie Smith Hathaway, an ardent prohibitionist, who drove 5,000 miles in suffrage's cause compared with Jeannette Rankin's 9,000 miles. What was distinctive about Rankin's contribution was her zeal and impatience. Mary O'Neill once locked Jeannette Rankin in a room at suffrage headquarters in Butte after she threw a "violent public temper tantrum." O'Neill later cautioned Rankin: "You have a great work to do—do not try to do it in thirty days. . . . Try and not be selfish in the work, leave a twig or two of laurel for someone else." Competitiveness and selfishness had undoubtedly crept into Rankin's approach because she was eyeing a congressional race. Maggie Hathaway, who was elected to the Montana House of Representatives in 1916, said that Jeannette Rankin "was afraid of my speaking ability and also aspired to political office."

But as the person in charge, Jeannette Rankin led the way with her bag of tried-and-true campaign tricks. She piggybacked suffrage onto activities of other groups. "I would go to the Union Hall night after night," she said, "because there'd be a different local meeting every night. . . . I would sit in the Union Hall until I had a chance to talk." She co-opted campaign appearances by asking a politician "to mention woman's suffrage" after she had stacked and primed the audience so that "there was all these claps" when suffrage was brought up. She debated anti-suffragists, "went to mines and talk[ed] to the men as they came off" shift, and "spoke at a three-county picnic on the Fourth of July [from] the back seat of a car." At the Montana state fair she organized a "Woman's Day and a Suffrage Pageant, the first parade in which women . . . ever marched in Montana." She later staged a "picturesque," "mile-long" parade that featured the Anaconda Company's band, NAWSA president Anna Howard Shaw "at the head, and next, carrying banners, . . . Dr. Dean, the past president, and [Jeannette Rankin, herself], the present State chairman." She brought to Montana the "great" Katherine Devereux Blake, a pioneering teacher and principal in the New York public school system who spent summers campaigning for suffrage across the country; Harriet Laidlaw, who "charmed [the local women] with her beauty and style"; James Laidlaw, who "surprised" Montanans "that a man of [his] standing should be at the head of a National Men's Suffrage League"; Jane Thompson, her friend and "successor as field secretary of the National Association"; and Ida Craft, East Coast labor organizer and political colleague. At campaign's end, Jeannette Rankin spoke to students, "at least one school in every county," hoping that they would go home and talk to their fathers about suffrage. On election day she enlisted children to wear yellow sashes that said, "I want my mother to vote."

Throughout the Montana suffrage campaign, Jeannette Rankin's principal asset was her total commitment. She personally "organized every county and . . . every ward in every county." So comprehensive was her method that she drove to out-of-the-way, hard-to-get-to farms so she could campaign in "kitchen[s] where the neighboring farm wives came and talked." Her web of proselytizers included a prostitute in Glendive. The "reason we found her," Rankin said, "was she used to . . . write letters to the *New Republic* . . . good letters on political issues. . . . She was a suffragist." After a bank failed in which the suffrage campaign had deposited $10,000, she encouraged suffrage opponents to believe "the money was totally lost and that the battle was hopeless" while at the same time making "representations to friends of suffrage as to prospects of victory that enabled the women's committee to get an abundance of money." Wary of the tricks of others, she stationed women to watch the polls on election day and alerted the nation through the Associated Press when it appeared that suffrage was "being counted out in Anaconda," purposefully confusing the town with "the company that controlled the state." So unstinting was Jeannette Rankin in her commitment that she disdained any effort that failed to meet her own exacting standard. In that frame of mind she sent a letter to national suffrage leader Margaret Foley in which she belittled the activities of Minnie Bronson, the executive secretary of the National Anti-Suffrage Association, saying that Bronson was behaving like a grasshopper, "jumping around throughout the state organizing a woman here and there and calling it an organization."

Jeannette Rankin's suffrage campaigning, never characterized by half measures, included deception, compromise, and extremism. When she "became confident of the 'dry' vote," she decided—despite her support of prohibition—that the suffrage campaign should "dissociate [itself] from temperance suffragists and invite support of the 'wets,'" and she ordered the WCTU leader, Mary Long Alderson, "not to dare to bring prohibition into the campaign." Repudiating principle even further, she and other Montana suffrage leaders "sweepingly declared that they were not interested in social reforms" in an attempt to win every possible vote. When the WCTU tried to "persuade the foreign-born that equal suffrage was in their interest" (20 to 25 percent of Montana's 1914 population), she replied that "effective participation by minority elements in the political process [would be drowned out] by a flood of traditional American votes from women." She argued eugenically that suffrage would mitigate one of war's evils because empowered women would "take the old men and leave the young men to propagate the race." And from the New York School of Philanthropy's perspective, she explained how enfranchised women would turn the state orphanage into a scientific laboratory where "we could see that these children were given intensive study . . . especially along the line of preventing disease and of keeping health and happiness curves about normal. . . . In time we could standardize motherhood, as all service to society must be standardized."

Despite Jeannette Rankin's ruses, the Montana suffrage campaign was characterized in the main by maternal arguments, which were at odds with the "natural rights and equal justice" goals of more radical feminists. Jeannette Rankin in Montana and many suffragists throughout the nation were willing to muzzle the cry of some of their sisters for "full citizenship." They argued, instead, that "women needed the vote to perform their traditional tasks—to protect themselves as mothers and to exert their moral force on society." Rankin's 1914 Woman's Day speech in Missoula included this kind of mainstream, conservative suffrage message. Here she sounded more like a protector of her mother's world than an advocate of the New Womanhood she had chosen for herself. "All over the country," she told her audience, "women are asking for the vote. . . . We are a force in life, a factor which must be considered in all problems. . . . While we Montana women have broader opportunities than the women of any other part of the world, we want the ballot in order to give opportunity to less fortunate women."

High on Rankin's list of women most needing suffrage and governmental assistance was "the woman in the home . . . who rises at six to cook her husband's breakfast, who gets the head of the house off to work, and then takes care of the baby, dresses and feeds the children and sends them to school; the woman who scrubs and cooks and irons and bakes and sweeps and mends until she has to cook dinner and get ready to entertain her husband all evening. . . . Votes for women bring happiness into the home."

Jeannette Rankin's Woman's Day remarks also focused on the plight of working women. "Census reports," she explained, "show that there are eight million women engaged in manual labor in this country. They are not there because they don't want to stay at home, but because they must work if they are to live." She gave poignancy to her message by telling the story of a young woman who worked in a Pittsburgh candy factory and lived with four roommates in a small room: "One night [she] came in, threw herself on the bed and cried from sheer exhaustion. . . . She had made candy from eight o'clock in the morning until six at night. After a few minutes for supper she had gone back to work, wrapped candy until four o'clock in the morning. From four until six she had slept on the floor, and got up and wrapped candy until six at night. The only extra pay she had received for this was her supper and her breakfast. When we asked her why she didn't complain the girl said, 'Aw, what's the use. I'd only lose my job.'" At the end of her speech, Rankin connected her story to suffrage: "Until [women workers] have the power to influence the laws which govern them their protests will be restricted by the fear of losing their jobs."

To some degree Jeannette Rankin's maternalism was tactical, as implied in a letter from Mary O'Neill, an Alice Paul supporter, after Rankin's speech to the Montana Federation of Women's Clubs. O'Neill urged Rankin to continue to include "all the dope you can about the influence of the women in behalf of the CHILDREN and appeal to the higher standard of MOTHERHOOD and truer home life . . . but even more so. That's the gush that gets the public. . . . That [kind of] speech . . . will do more to make suffragists than all the purely intellectual guff we might give them in a whole hundred years." Before that audience, Rankin had used maternalist "dope" and not egalitarian "guff." The women of the Montana club, part of more than two million organized nationally in 1910, were "fairly conservative [and] viewed . . . better governments as merely extensions of their traditional roles of wife and mother." It is clear that Jeannette Rankin and other

Montana suffrage leaders made a calculated decision to base their campaign on a "modified Victorian concept of women which was consonant with popular thought." But she probably had another reason, other than getting suffrage adopted, for playing down radical feminist themes. Her less apparent aim was to set the stage for a congressional campaign.

A campaign for Congress must have been constantly on Jeannette Rankin's mind as she talked about the reform legislation that would follow upon suffrage and as she thrilled to her home state's enthusiastic response to her speeches. Simultaneous with the Montana suffrage campaign, Wellington Rankin had been leading a group of prominent men in support of suffrage and running as a Progressive Party candidate for the U.S. House of Representatives. Because his share of votes cast was only 4 percent, Jeannette Rankin began to see herself and not her brother as the next Rankin to enter a congressional race. She had demonstrated to him that she was "the best single-handed campaigner" in Montana, and she had convinced herself that "I could be elected where other women couldn't be elected." Running for Congress became the natural extension of campaigning for suffrage. She told an interviewer: "[A]ll during the suffrage campaign, they had discussed what we could do to help the other women, because they'd helped us with money and workers. . . . [W]e decided that a woman in Congress would . . . make it very difficult for the man who was against woman's suffrage to vote against it." Even more succinctly, she expressed the connection she saw between campaigning for suffrage and running for Congress: "I didn't run for Congress. I ran for woman's suffrage and got elected to Congress."

Two explanations of Jeannette Rankin's first campaign for Congress can be set aside. She did not run in order to vote against war and she did not run as an anti-politician. During the initial phase of the Montana suffrage campaign, war was not even on her mind. She recalled not only where she was when World War I broke out ("I was sitting on your porch in Lewistown," she told a Montana suffrage ally) but also "the shock" she felt at the announcement of war: "I thought I was the only one that didn't know that it was coming." Afterward, the war figured in her suffrage message in Montana. She recalled that she had "mentioned this war a good many times and said that was one reason women should have the vote." She recalled more specifically her "speeches . . . on the streets of Butte against the war in Europe." But women's welfare and not war was the theme that carried over from her Montana suffrage campaign to her first campaign for Congress: "[I]t was entirely on suffrage and the idea that women should be represented and that women should have something to say about the laws that I ran and was elected on."

Jeannette Rankin's equation of suffrage politics and congressional politics shows that she was not a reluctant candidate for Congress. Some, however, prefer to portray her as a Cincinnatus, persuaded against her will to abandon rustic Montana to advocate the people's interests in far-off Washington. One longtime associate said, "I would never describe her as a politician." But during her six years of suffrage work Jeannette Rankin systematically perfected the skills of an expert campaigner. By the time of the Montana suffrage campaign, her political assets of appearance, speaking ability, and organizing were possibly unparalleled in the nation. She had learned to engage her audience from the stump and to silence her opponents with quick and sharp retorts. To the argument that a "woman's place is in the house, baking bread," she had replied: "I can make bread and will prove it by doing so and making you eat it." (Ironically, 1984 vice-presidential candidate Geraldine Ferraro years later responded to a heckler's put-down, "Can you make a blueberry muffin?" with "Sure can, can you?") She had put together parades and pageantry to inspire the imagination of voters. She had mastered the "staggering" campaign difficulties of "cars that broke down . . . in the middle of nowhere," "choosing the right towns [and] finding the right location for a meeting," and "arranging places to stay, and keeping . . . neat and clean and attractive in bedrooms where the only water for bathing was in a jug and basin on the washstand."

With the Montana suffrage victory in hand, Jeannette Rankin's political skills did not grow stale. In 1915 she organized "[m]any of the suffrage work-horses" into the Montana Good Government Association, ostensibly "for intelligent use of the ballot." Mary O'Neill, a Good Government insider, hinted at another purpose for the Good Government clubs when she wrote Rankin that "we have organizations now in nearly all the big towns" and, at a statewide meeting in June, "you will be the central figure around which the program will be built." Rankin's plan was to promote her candidacy for Congress by presenting "citizen lectures" to the Good Government clubs. She wrote to the National Voters League about using its publication, "The Search-Light on Congress," as part of this "course of civic study." The league's secretary responded: "The cause would surely profit by such a move on your part. Of course I am referring to your political plan. So far as I can see, there could be no objection to the kind of preliminary campaign about which you talked—one in which the work of the League might be placed before the people of Montana. That ought to be the most effective kind of a campaign measured in personal political results, and at the same time be not a campaign in the orthodox sense." Jeannette Rankin was turning suffrage into a Trojan horse for her congressional race.

Campaigning 5

What She Loved Most and Did Best

J EANNETTE RANKIN'S GROUNDBREAKING CONGRESSIONAL CAMPAIGN RAN INTO a series of barriers that have frustrated political women since. Voters saw the first woman of U.S. politics through a "perceptual screen of general female stereotypes." Not having a predecessor to learn from, she coped as best she could with "decidedly negative" attitudes. A newspaper said that a woman running for Congress would be a "freakish thing," and a friend conveyed another's belittling remark: "Tonight a hen will attempt to crow." Further, as a social worker, political neophyte, and reformer from the "tradition of principled, altruistic" service, Jeannette Rankin lacked the solid career and credible credentials of most male politicians. In contrast, her brother ran for the U.S. Senate in 1922 as a well-known lawyer and former state attorney general. Besides bias and disbelief, Jeannette Rankin was saddled with "family demands" to care for her mother. By having sisters, Wellington Rankin and other political men avoided political women's "double duty as caregivers." Jeannette Rankin also had to contend with the discriminatory attitudes of the "male party structure." She was literally "outmanned" in the Republican Party, while Wellington Rankin was a leader in a party "run by men." Finally, Jeannette Rankin lacked personal financial resources and the means of raising campaign funds. Her brother enjoyed both, and Jeannette Rankin ended up depending on him for political money. Given these barriers, to call Jeannette Rankin's run for office "anomalous" is an understatement.

Jeannette Rankin's surmounting these barriers in 1916 can be explained in two ways. Wellington Rankin served as her shield and sword, protecting her from attacks and providing strategy and money. Her part was doing what she loved most and did best, campaigning relentlessly. In politics she was ruled by her determination, not her head or heart, and her steely will could foster the unconventional. One spring when she and Wellington were inspecting cattle, their windshield became splattered. Stopping to clean it, Wellington found only a newspaper and set off to get some water. By the time he returned, Jeannette had urinated on the paper and cleaned off the mud. Given her impatience and disdain for propriety, the challenges of campaigning did not deter Jeannette. She was happiest when on the move, driving back roads in one of her Fords (from a robin's egg blue to a sleek red-and-cream). Her constant pushing made her an incomparable campaigner but worried her friends. When she was going nonstop for suffrage, Mary O'Neill cautioned her to conserve her energy: "[Y]ou are always on the jump and I presume usually worn to a frazzle. . . . I feel that I must help protect you against yourself in the intense and even reckless passion to turn the world over like a flapjack."

What Jeannette Rankin did on the campaign trail was as inevitable as her drive. She said that she used the same tactics in 1916 that had served her well from 1910 to 1915: "I did everything in the suffrage campaigns first, and then did it in my own campaign. . . . I had tried out everything; some things worked and some things didn't work." Montana newspapers reported what was working to generate "abounding enthusiasm throughout the state." "Brass bands and street parades and all the good old-fashioned fancy trimmings that used to go with significant political meetings," the papers explained, "are being revived in honor of Jeannette Rankin. . . . Open-air meetings are being held in every county, and Jeannette Rankin clubs are being organized all over the state." These bipartisan groups were the offspring of the post-suffrage Good Government clubs Jeannette Rankin had established. She was building, she said, on her earlier political work that had made her, except for the governor, "the best known person" in Montana.

Also in Jeannette Rankin's quiver were postcard mailings, telephone calling, personal campaigning, and speeches. Wellington Rankin's law office became her headquarters; "walls were hung with the maps of all the counties" and voters' names were spread out on tables. On penny postcards women volunteers wrote a clever note "to every woman on the polling lists": "We are in Helena and enjoying it very much. We're going to vote for Jeannette Rankin, and we hope you will." Each volunteer signed the postcards with her own initials. Campaign workers also made telephone calls from Wellington Rankin's office. Jeannette Rankin remembered that "[e]veryone who had a telephone was greeted the morning of the election with, 'Good morning! Have you voted for Jeannette Rankin?'" Not married or tied down by young children, she toiled outside headquarters, going house to house and giving street-corner talks. Her campaign communicated more than postcard messages and telephone reminders. Her slogan, "Let the People Know," came from her experience as a congressional lobbyist, as she explained: "[A]ll the rules of Congress . . . were made to keep [the members'] constituents from knowing what they did. . . . [E]very time a congressman engages in legislation, he loses votes. . . . [T]hey all work it so that the constituents do not know what they're doing." Her populist slogan also conveyed her hatred of Montana's being "controlled" by the Anaconda Copper Mining Company. Besides "Greater publicity in Congressional committees," her campaign flyer announced that she stood for "National Suffrage," "Child Welfare," "Tariff revision for protection of the worker," "State and National Prohibition," and a "Farm Loan law." The brochure boasted her modest family roots, despite the Rankins' prosperity and her East Coast education and national suffrage experience: "I was born on a Montana farm, and lived there long enough to learn and to sympathize with the problems." Absent was any mention of war, as the "war was not then a campaign issue." Looking back to 1916, Jeannette Rankin said: "I was running on issues and my reputation as a worker. . . . [Being antiwar] wasn't a thing we talked about." What she wanted to talk about, national suffrage and the reforms that would follow, she proclaimed everywhere. Her energy and boldness were not matched by her primary opponents: "seven mediocre men," she called them, "[who] had too much dignity [to] stand on the street corner and talk."

Jeannette Rankin bested her primary opponents both on the streets and at the polls, winning the 1916 Republican primary with a plurality of 22,549 votes, 26 percent of the total. One loser—rendered "less male, somehow unsexed," and vulnerable to the taunt "beaten by a woman"—committed suicide. In the six-candidate general election of Montana's two at-large U.S. representatives, Jeannette Rankin was elected with the second highest vote total (76,932). Democrat John M. Evans was the top vote getter (84,499). Finishing behind the two winners were a Republican, a Democrat, and two Socialists; the third-place runner-up had 6,354 fewer votes than Jeannette Rankin. Montana had not yet apportioned itself, and the election's at-large feature was decisive. But two months later, the legislature—with the backing of the Anaconda Company and the slogan "Do you want to keep a woman in Congress?"—divided the state into two districts. Jeannette Rankin, gerrymandered out of contention for the western district seat in 1918, had seen right away how the statewide election of two representatives favored her 1916 candidacy. "'I could be the first [woman to go to Congress],'" she said, "because we had two at-large districts in Montana. . . . [Each person] could vote for both a man and a woman. . . . [Y]ou could have two ideas represented, instead of one." During the campaign she exhorted her audiences: "[V]ote for your local candidate and Jeannette Rankin," and she usually "had the second vote."

Besides the at-large election and Jeannette Rankin's energy and tactics, other factors contributed to her victory. Critical was her support among women, especially those who advocated prohibition. Prohibition women had not given her their full support during the Montana suffrage campaign, but "they all got out and voted" for her in 1916. The prohibition referendum, which was a bigger draw than her candidacy, criminalized the manufacturing, giving, or selling of "intoxicating liquors of any kind." Allied on the dry side of this "big-gun war" were the Woman's Christian Temperance Union, the Anti-Saloon and Public Welfare League, the clergy, and the political parties. The wet argument was carried by "bankers, cattlemen, labor leaders and even Clarence Darrow, who was imported for the occasion." The Great Falls newspaper said that the prohibition campaign was "one of the bitterest political fights ever waged" and that it made women "the outstanding feature at the polls." Women, the paper reported, represented only 36 percent of the city's "total number [of] legal voters," but "the split on the day's vote was probably fifty-fifty for the sexes." Prohibition helped Rankin not only in Great Falls. Across the state the successful measure passed in thirty-eight of Montana's forty-one counties, and in thirty-three of these approving counties Rankin was either first or second among the four major candidates.

In addition to the woman vote, a "graveyard vote" aided both prohibition and Jeannette Rankin's election. The turnout for the prohibition measure, an impossible 100.2 percent of those registered, must have raised eyebrows. This shadow electorate was reflected in not only the 176,666 total votes on prohibition but also the 158,232 total votes in the at-large congressional election. Some have suggested that Wellington Rankin might have been behind the inflated vote. Politically scarred and cunning as a result, he had pledged to his sister that "he would elect her if she ran." He told her flatly, "I'll pay for your campaign, and I'll elect you." His confidence stemmed from both his political experience and his money. Jeannette Rankin officially spent little on the election. Federal law limited her to "half of the first salary [she] would earn if [she] got elected," which in 1917 was "$7,500 a year." She reported spending even less: $1,039.23 in the primary election and $687.80 in the general election. But rumored among Rankin family members was Wellington Rankin's boast that he had "spent $20,000 on buying the 1916 election at a dollar a vote." He was sufficiently confident at election time to assure Jeannette that eastern Montana returns would elect her even though state newspapers were reporting she had lost. Wellington Rankin might have compromised voters and election officials to offset the dirty tricks of his sister's opponents. After the 1916 election, a Montana politician told the congresswoman about "a trap that was set for you but which did not go off. It is not a nice thing to write about. You thought you were in the hands of your friends [but there were] base traitors in your meeting at Baker." Another ally wrote to her about a "rumor current in Butte that our voting machines can be manipulated to vote every fifteenth vote solidly Democratic."

As Jeannette Rankin's campaign manager, Wellington Rankin more definitely "outlined a plan for the campaign," placed himself at the center of its execution, paid the campaign bills, and exhorted campaign workers. His plan called for Jeannette and her sisters—but not himself, he "never traveled" during campaigns—to concentrate on the more populated eastern part of the state and emphasize agricultural issues and prohibition. Jeannette explained how Wellington ran things by telephone from his Helena office: "My brother was in touch with [people] all over the state. . . . Immediately they got word to him how I was doing. He knew . . . that [their election information] meant certain things." A campaign worker told her that, when the outcome was in doubt, Wellington Rankin rallied the dejected: "Twice you were posted here as lost, once heavily. . . . Mister Rankin's cheering words on the phone gave us new life." Wellington Rankin's second wife believed that he truly wanted his sister to go to Congress and saw "no conflict between his and Jeannette's political ambitions." Alternatively, he saw her as his stalking horse at a time he was sidelined, advancing the name they shared and cultivating the constituencies they had in common: women, farmers, and anti-corporation populists.

Three stories involving the Montana Republican Party illustrate the control Wellington Rankin exercised over Jeannette Rankin's 1916 congressional campaign. Despite the opposition of "Old line Republicans" to her candidacy, Jeannette Rankin ran for office as a Republican. Her choice of party was determined by Wellington Rankin's party affiliation, although at different times other explanations were given. To one biographer Wellington used a family rationale: "Our father was a Republican. Our mother was a conservative from New England, and it was always a family that was Republican." To another interviewer Jeannette gave a class-based explanation: "In the South, the aristocrats were Democrats, and in the North, the Irish and newcomers were Democrats. So we were Republican because it was the aristocratic thing to be." Belle Fligelman—Jeannette Rankin's suffrage colleague and campaign publicist "who helped put [Jeannette] on the map, who conducted her campaign bureau and made all the politicians of Montana sit up and take notice"—used the more credible "piggy-back" theory to explain Jeannette Rankin's partisanship: her "brother was a powerful Republican (that's why she ran on the Republican ticket)."

Early in the 1916 campaign, the Montana Republican Party tried to compromise Jeannette Rankin's candidacy. Party officials, she said, were "going to send me out with a young lawyer who was a good speaker." But Wellington Rankin saw through the ruse. His fear, Jeannette explained, was that the party hack would "stand on the platform and praise me and . . . then go into the saloon and laugh at me." She went along with her brother and not the Republican Party: "Wellington didn't let me go campaigning with him . . . [but] had me go with a wonderful man who was running for lieutenant governor, as dull as dishwater." At the end of the general election campaign, the Republican Party was still trying to undermine her candidacy. Her final speech brought out "more people than the Missoula theater could hold . . . [d]espite a wet and heavy snowstorm." When the party chairman introducing her droned on for two hours and refused to give way to the speaker the crowd had come to hear, the audience "interrupted with tremendous applause, which would not silence, and by cries of 'Rankin! Rankin!'" In the few minutes left her Jeannette Rankin acknowledged Wellington Rankin even though, she said, she "was not supposed to . . . because Wellington felt that it would make enemies or something. But I said, 'Now Wellington says that all I need is 50 percent of the vote and one more, and then I've won. You may be the one to make me win.'"

Jeannette Rankin's 1916 election sent her to the Sixty-fifth Congress, and her performance there became the backdrop of her 1918 reelection campaign. Three of her actions as a congresswoman created problems: her vote against entering World War I, her failure to get the national suffrage amendment through Congress, and her association with labor radicals when attempting to mediate the 1917 Butte copper strike. Her war vote at first appeared to compromise her reelection chances, but her coming around to support the war disarmed her opponents on that front. Although one Montana newspaper called her antiwar vote a "fit of female hysteria," another more characteristically said, "[W]e hold Miss Rankin wholly sincere in her vote and this should relieve her of any unnecessarily harsh criticism." A more serious problem was the split in the suffrage movement and lack of progress on the national suffrage amendment. Rankin's ambivalence toward radical suffrage tactics left her open to attack by national suffrage leaders. The vice president of the National American Woman Suffrage Association told Harriet Laidlaw that Jeannette Rankin "is putting the women of the country in the worst possible light" for her silence on "lawless" suffrage picketing in front of the White House. The greatest obstacle to reelection, however, was Rankin's association with the Industrial Workers of the World. For her radical labor sympathies, she was criticized unrelentingly in the press, one newspaper calling her "the Joan of Arc of the I.W.W." The widespread adulation that had greeted Jeannette Rankin at the start of her first term soured for many into disgust by the end of the term. The *New York World* assessed her reelection chances as almost nonexistent: "It would be a tremendous stretch of the political imagination to conceive Miss Rankin returned to the lower house next year, but as for the Senate—it is to laugh."

When gerrymandering was added to the three criticisms of Jeannette Rankin's performance in office, it became obvious that reelection would require once again all of her energy and skill and all of her brother's savvy and resources. The Montana legislature had apportioned the state into two congressional districts by the time she arrived in Washington. One of Wellington Rankin's political allies told him years later, "[O]pponents of your sister Gerrymandered the State in order to defeat her for re-election to Congress. There was a 10,000 normal Republican majority in the State in those days, but they divided the State in such a manner that there was a 20,000 Republican majority in the eastern part of the State, and a 10,000 normal Democratic majority in the western district." The nominally Republican Jeannette Rankin, who had grown up in western Montana, was left in 1918 with three political choices: run in the Democratic western district against the other incumbent congressman, Democrat John M. Evans, who also was from Missoula; run as a Republican in the heavily Republican but distant eastern congressional district; or win the Republican U.S. Senate primary and try to defeat the incumbent U.S. senator, Democrat Thomas J. Walsh.

Political realities eliminated the western district option. A newspaper reported that in the 1916 at-large congressional election, "Evans' vote in the geographical limitations now set by the Montana legislature in the district in which Miss Rankin and Representative Evans live was about 6,000 greater than Miss Rankin's vote." To further secure his hold on the western district, Evans "warned her that she had better make her attempt on the senate, because he purposed returning to the house." When Evans referred to Jeannette Rankin as "Little Mother Jones," echoing the charge of Montana newspapers that she was an IWW sympathizer, he further undermined her western district candidacy. Shut out in western Montana, she gave serious thought to running for Congress from the eastern Montana district. Its partisan split favored her, and some residents were urging an eastern district race because eastern Montana was home to radical agrarian groups that were in tune with her political bent. A farm woman wrote: "Of course you know the homesteaders had no crop whatever last year. . . . Socialism is increasing on a rapid rate (confidentially to you and can you blame them?)." That Jeannette Rankin gave serious consideration to the eastern district option was evident in her remarks to a Montana newspaper. She first said, "Yes, I will run in the eastern Montana district," but then she "quickly corrected herself and said that she did not know as yet." Because cries of carpetbagging would have sounded, the Rankins discarded an eastern district race.

Jeannette Rankin and Wellington Rankin ultimately settled on the U.S. Senate option for 1918. Reports of Jeannette Rankin running for the Senate began to appear in the Montana press in summer 1917, when she was contemplating coming home to mediate the copper mining strike. Later, newspapers commented on the labor ties that brought her to Butte. The *Butte Tribune-Review* asked, "[W]hy did Miss Rankin adopt a partial attitude in Butte's labor controversy, realizing that on the solution of the perplexing problem the future weal or woe of Butte depended?" The editor of the *Helena Independent* continued the speculation: "I cannot tell you how much I regret your coming to Montana. . . . There never was a possibility of your doing any good. . . . I am sorry that something has inspired you to do the things you have done." The explanation given for Jeannette Rankin's interference and partiality was campaign politics. Her surest way of returning to Washington as a member of Congress was winning the U.S. Senate race, and labor would have to be an important part of her electoral coalition. In September 1917, Wellington sent a cryptic telegram to Jeannette that probably alluded to the political decision that had been made: "Everything arranged and in my hands."

There were two ways that Jeannette Rankin could build up her labor constituency for her Senate campaign. She could take a middle ground and emphasize that moderation and cooperation were in the best interest of the unions, copper mining companies, and nation at war. Or she could attack the companies and win to her cause not only the radical elements in the unions but also farm radicals and socialists. Wellington Rankin was the author of the first approach, and Mary O'Neill advocated the second. Wellington's moderating influence was seen in September 1917 when Jeannette addressed the national meeting of the Nonpartisan League (NPL), a socialist-agrarian organization formed in North Dakota in 1915. He sent her a copy of her March 1917 Carnegie Hall speech, which he had written, to use at the NPL gathering in St. Paul. In that speech she had lamented poor labor conditions and the end of free western land and warned that prosperity for the many would not come from concentration of resources in the hands of the few. But she did not call for direct action by labor unions or for government ownership of mines. Similarly, her August 1917 address to the assembly of strikers in Butte bore Wellington Rankin's stamp. Like the Carnegie Hall address, it was moderate in tone, balanced in structure, and written out. In Butte, she—who had voted against war—called World War I the "great war," acknowledged the nation's need for copper, and argued: "Carried along on the waves of misguided patriotism have come subtle attempts to destroy the industrial standards of this country. . . . But it is also misguided patriotism that believes that direct action has a place in civilized society. . . . Let it be known that it is unpatriotic for capital to refuse the just demands of labor, and that it is unpatriotic for labor to refuse the just demands of capital."

Wellington Rankin's influence can be seen in another attempt by Jeannette Rankin to explain her views on labor. In October 1917, Oswald G. Villard, president of the *New York Evening Post,* asked her to send him "at once copies of your recent speeches out West. . . . It is being alleged here by persons inimical to you and your attitude on labor questions, that you endorsed and encouraged the I.W.W. and that you were guilty of other unpatriotic and seditious utterances." His aim, Villard said, was "to take up the matter fairly and squarely with . . . my fellow directors on the Associated Press . . . to produce [for you] a favorable impression." Jeannette Rankin replied to Villard, "I appreciate more than I can tell you your efforts to correct the impressions of the directors of the Associated Press and others." She asked him, however, to base his corrections not on her heated first letter, which was "cancelled" by her secretary in a telephone call to Villard, but on her second more moderate letter. In the cancelled letter, Jeannette Rankin had written that "the only violence that has occurred in all the months of the strike has been on the part of the soldiers who are in Butte presumably to keep order but who have told the strikers that they are only waiting for a chance to shoot them down." The parallel section in the "official" version played down her pro-labor sympathies: "The more radical of the [union membership] were not back of me, and objected to my helping the union, believing that I was too conservative." Addressing the issue of miners' wages in the first letter, she wrote: "The men do not want a sliding scale which slides very slowly in comparison to the price of copper and to the cost of living. They want a flat rate of pay. . . . The wages have never risen in proportion to this risk of injury and death which the continued development of the mines constantly enhances." In the second letter, she played down her pro-unionism: "As to the wage question, you have my speech in which my statement appeared." In that speech, the Wellington Rankin–crafted address to the Butte miners, Jeannette Rankin had stunned her audience with a compromise proposal: "I ask you again, will you be willing for the purpose of settling the troubled conditions, to accept the existing scale of wages and go back to work if the rustling card [a form of blacklisting] be abandoned?"

Mary O'Neill was the countervailing political influence on Jeannette Rankin. "[D]ynamic" and full of "new ideas," she had come to Butte from Missouri in 1902 as a journalist. She became "one of the so-called radicals" in Butte, once criticizing an officer of the League of Women Voters for calling league members agents of "socialism, bolshevism, and anarchism." O'Neill's interpretation of the accused league members' politics was that they were "simply progressive women who believe in the innate love of Justice within the heart of Woman." Jeannette Rankin, in O'Neill's mind, was the embodiment of women's inherent political virtue. O'Neill also believed that Rankin's political future was tied to such essentialist radicalism. She regularly sent her political advice and the union perspective on strike developments in Butte, and Rankin acted on O'Neill's counsel. Wellington Rankin, far more pragmatic than Mary O'Neill and politically to her right, dismissed her as a "visionary."

Early in the 1917 copper strike, Mary O'Neill sent Jeannette Rankin a series of telegrams urging her to accept the mediation role that fate and nature had intended for her: "[Y]our friends here believe that if personally present you can bring about a settlement of miners' troubles with companies"; "Miners and unions depend on your personal presence to get better terms"; "It all depends on you. . . . Give you greater power in future." The "future" O'Neill referred to was the 1918 election; she was trying to strengthen Rankin's labor constituency for her Senate campaign against Democratic incumbent Thomas J. Walsh, another advocate of labor and suffrage. In a letter to Rankin after the congresswoman had returned to Washington from Butte, O'Neill said that she had run into Senator Walsh and "could see that he had you in mind as a possible contestant. Had you not come out here he would have slid along in the easiest way possible to get into office of Senator again, but now he is right up against the miners and the large mass of people against the [Anaconda] Company on one side and the [company] with its trailers on the other side." To settle the Butte strike, Rankin had called for nationalization of the copper industry and accepted O'Neill's invitation to come to Butte. As a result, Walsh had two political options: to go to the left of Rankin or side with the Anaconda Company. O'Neill thought that Walsh would try to go to the left by seeking an investigation on behalf of the workers and that Rankin, if she followed her advice, would not be outmaneuvered: "Walsh just told me that an investigation was already arranged for on the recent fire in the mine. And that the 'government ownership of the mines' could not be effected, especially until after the 'investigation' took place. I see his scheme, I believe, to head you off in Congress before adjournment. . . . This is why I wired you to act at once and put one over on him [and keep] ahead of him. . . . [Y]ou have kept up the fight for the workers. He wants to get a so-called investigation of the recent fire—not of the strike and its causes and results. . . . It is another bit of camouflage. If you demand that the Bureau of Mines investigate the strike . . . and ask Congress to back you up on it . . . it will show up the deception—and you'll beat him to it again."

Montana newspapers lost no time in equating Jeannette Rankin's union leanings with labor radicalism. Early in August 1917, the *Helena Independent* speculated that she would "be a candidate for the U.S. Senate next year on a 'labor platform.'" The editorial went on to criticize Rankin for her political bedfellows: "The lineup will then be: I.W.W. Organizations, Miss Rankin, Radical Union Labor, Theoretical Mothers, Slackers and Traitors, Pacifists VERSUS Montana Farmers, Montana Mining Interests, Montana Lumber Industries, Montana Business, Legitimate Labor Unions, Real Mothers of Montana. Now Miss Rankin cannot disown the constituents she has chosen." On the same day, the *Great Falls Tribune* editorialized that the congresswoman "represents Montana, and more particularly the I.W.W. element in Montana." Another newspaper argued that Rankin's "association with the disloyal elements of the industrial life of Butte is alone enough to disqualify her as a representative at Washington of the loyal people of this state." These editorials were not the only indication Montana was turning against those who strayed from the mainstream. In 1918 the state's Council of Defense prohibited "use of the German language in public and private schools . . . and in the pulpit. Preachers using German must hereafter use English or remain silent. German books and histories must be thrown out of public and private school libraries."

Jeannette Rankin's compromises in Congress shielded her from criticism stemming from her war vote, but they did not deflect doubts about her foreign sympathies stemming from her Butte activity. A group of Deer Lodge citizens denied her permission to speak on behalf of the Liberty Loan program. A press report explained: "The attitude of the citizens who attended the meeting was that Miss Rankin cast reflections upon her loyalty by associating with the strike leaders who have been accused in Butte of I.W.W. affiliations." Some observers, however, approved of her association with radicals. The *Sanders County Signal* said that "Miss Rankin is on the right track. The Industrial Workers of the World . . . are just common laboring people trying to organize to meet the organized capitalists of the world. . . . When you read of threats to destroy by the I.W.W. . . . it is the hired press. . . . We are all I.W.W. or ought to be, if we are not capitalists." Jeannette Rankin's friend Nina Swinnerton, writing from New York, also commended her links to labor radicals: "As for your labor speech about the I.W.W. and other miners I think it was magnificent! You are the only bright thing in the landscape these dark days."

Montana newspapers commented, too, on Mary O'Neill's pushing Jeannette Rankin to the left. The Butte-based *Montana American* said that "she is in touch with a group of malcontents in this city who are pumping her full of brilliant ideas. Jeannette is going out to capture the 'roughneck' vote." The Lewistown *Democrat-News* twice editorialized on Rankin's associates who were promoting her ties to the IWW. "If she has been advised to champion the cause of the most lawless and dangerous set of men who ever infested this state in the hope of attracting to her support the organized labor forces of Montana," the first editorial ran, "we would suggest that she immediately change her staff of counselors for they are giving her a very inferior brand of political advice." Two days later the paper again took notice of Rankin's political plans and "the destructive and lawless activities of members of the I.W.W." and concluded, "[W]e humbly submit that her present campaign has been mapped out by some very ill-advised tacticians." Jeannette Rankin was undoubtedly baiting the labor vote by attacking mining companies, but Montana newspapers had no reason to identify Wellington Rankin with his sister's populist tactic of "seeking to play upon a prejudice which is always more or less strong in this state." The *Helena Independent*, a longtime antagonist of Wellington Rankin, understood that his "peculiar school of politics" was pragmatic and opportunistic, not ideological.

The two Rankins and Mary O'Neill did cooperate on one political strategy to win the 1918 election: converting the *Joint Strike Bulletin*, a publication

of the Metal Mine Workers' Union and the International Brotherhood of
Electrical Workers, into a weekly labor newspaper. Just before Jeannette
Rankin's August 1917 address to the Butte strikers, several union leaders
told the crowd "that there was emphatic need of a daily labor press in
Butte." O'Neill, a journalist, feared that strike news was being slanted by
the copper interests' ownership of the *Butte Miner* and *Anaconda Standard*.
"Press reports about Butte and Anaconda strike situation all bunkum,"
she told Jeannette Rankin in a telegram. Another Butte politico, Elizabeth
Kennedy, president of the Butte Housewives League and the Butte Good
Government club, told the congresswoman that the miners suspected the
local newspapers "of sending out 'doctored' reports to keep the government from interfering" and wanted "our press investigated for suppression of news [that hurt] the Mine Owners." For his part, Wellington Rankin
understood the advantages other Montana politicians had enjoyed from
controlling news publications. He already owned a paper in the High Line
town of Havre, where he ran an auxiliary law office, and he began cooper-
ating with Butte labor and Nonpartisan League leaders and O'Neill in
their project to start up a labor paper in western Montana. In November
1917, O'Neill told Wellington Rankin that she had contacted a press service, coordinated the new paper with his Havre paper, and secured contributions from miners in Idaho. The *Butte Miner* reported that Jeannette
Rankin, too, had contributed $500 to their new competitor, the *Butte Weekly
Bulletin*.

Involvement with the labor newspaper was part of Jeannette Rankin's
strategy to firm up a three-legged election base of workers, farmers, and
women. The paper advocated simultaneously the abolition of economic
classes, the Russian revolution, and Rankin's election and became a con-
duit to the Nonpartisan League, a key component of her farm constituency.
The socialistic Nonpartisan League in North Dakota had "called for state
ownership of grain elevators, mills, and packing houses; demanded the
establishment of a state bank that would advance credit at low interest
rates; and advocated a system of state hail insurance." The Montana chapter of the Nonpartisan League added planks urging confiscation of war
profits and "increased taxation of railroads, mines, and public utility corporations." Labor radicals and socialists in Butte saw the advantage of al-
lying with the Nonpartisan League. The "*Butte Bulletin* made contact with
the League in the spring of 1918," and William F. Dunne, the editor of the

Bulletin, became "an active player in the Nonpartisan Club's political drive." The new labor newspaper was located in a Butte hall that already head-quartered the Metal Mine Workers' Union, and soon the building became the "nest" of the Nonpartisan League.

The Montana branch of the Nonpartisan League immediately tied its populist hopes to Jeannette Rankin's candidacy. An organizer in western Montana informed her that "the farmers and their wives are unanimous for conscription of war profits to pay for the war." More importantly, he congratulated Rankin for the "vigorous manner in which you strike J. D. Ryan," the president of the Anaconda Copper Mining Company, and en-couraged her politically: "[T]he farmers of Flathead County are joining the Non-Partisan League in goodly numbers [and] among the farmers, your course is meeting with general approval." An organizer in eastern Mon-tana expressed his support more directly: "Dear Comrade. . . . We need you in [the U.S. Senate] as we know where your heart and your work lies." A Missoula lawyer allied with the Nonpartisan League reinforced Rankin's 1918 strategy: "I hope you will try for the Senate next year. . . . [T]he 20,000 members of the Non-Partisan League in this state will support you and that means nearly that many more of their wives. Unless some change comes . . . you will get the strongest Labor vote that any candidate ever got in Montana, and these two forces ought to elect you."

Like Jeannette, Wellington Rankin was aware of the political potential of farm populism. He provided legal counsel to the Society of Equity, an organization that shared the Nonpartisan League's interest in tax reform but did not agree with the league's call for an expanded government role in agriculture. Equitable tax policy, the society argued, would result in big mining companies having to pay their fair share of taxes. The Society of Equity increased its membership from 200 to 6,000 from 1914 to 1916, and, like the Nonpartisan League, attempted "to achieve a close working rela-tionship with organized labor." Wellington Rankin also had contact with the Nonpartisan League, discussing his sister's possible Senate candidacy with a league organizer at a Montana labor convention. By midsummer 1918 he had become sufficiently certain about her political chances to give her the green light. The Great Falls newspaper reported: "Jeannette Rankin announced today she will be a candidate for the senate to succeed Senator Walsh. The nominating primaries will be August 27. Miss Rankin said at present there is no other Republican candidate."

Jeannette Rankin's campaign for the U.S. Senate had two centers of operation: the East Coast effort run out of her congressional office and the Montana effort run by Wellington Rankin. The East Coast activities focused on securing support from women, her third core constituency. It was run initially by her friend and Montana suffrage colleague Mary Stewart, and later by her sister Harriet Rankin Sedman. Stewart and Sedman had good Montana connections, both having served as Dean of Women at the University of Montana. In late 1917 Stewart wrote to Rankin about getting work in Washington: "I have been in New York only a few weeks, too late [for] work at Columbia this semester. . . . Frankly I am trying to get something to do. . . . I am not bent at all on suffrage work—only I thought I know how to do that. I'd rather do some war work—if there are any paid positions. I can't give my services any more. I have to have a living salary. Please wire me not to come if my coming would be inconvenient for you now." Stewart ended up managing the Washington part of Rankin's campaign until a family emergency called her away. Her principal task, and later Sedman's, was to organize a "campaign stunt," mailing postcards from New York women to Montana women. The effort ran into the same problem that Jeannette Rankin faced within herself—how to bridge effectively those two very different worlds.

Two weeks after her announcement to run and five weeks before the primary, Jeannette Rankin's Washington campaign staff was still struggling with the text of the message that New York women would send to women voters in Montana. Margaret Dreier Robins in New York cautioned Mary Stewart: "I am earnestly hoping that the letter has not gone out. . . . It is always dangerous for outsiders to suggest to any group of voters what they ought not do, but it is very serious to intimate as this letter does that Montana voters may be guilty of carelessness [if they] permit local party politics to decide on what is really a great issue, the re-election of Miss Rankin. I think that every postcard or letter ought simply to state the fact that Miss Rankin has served the women of the country so effectively in Congress that we earnestly hope the Montana voters will re-elect her, and thus in their turn serve the American women, especially the working women." Another New York supporter, Marie Virginia Smith, sent a similar warning: "There is an enormous amount of cordial support for Miss Rankin on every hand among the women here but we are all painfully conscious that the advice of New York on any subject is not popular in the west." Jeannette Rankin responded by adopting Margaret Robins's recommended changes in the campaign letter.

Another challenge was organizing a committee of well-known women whose names would be used in campaign letters and fund-raising. Some whose support Jeannette Rankin sought agreed readily to be on the committee, but other women presented the campaign staff with a variety of difficulties. An update about campaign problems in New York came from Marie Virginia Smith: "I have talked with a few of Miss Rankin's friends and admirers, every one of whom is more than eager to do her bit in the line of postcards. The main point, however—the securing of Mrs. Beard or some one similar from the Committee of One Thousand Women—I have not been able to accomplish because Mrs. Beard herself has been out of the city. . . . Have Miss Shaw and Mrs. Laidlaw consented to act on such a committee or is the whole scheme developing differently in Miss Rankin's mind?" Harriet Laidlaw did agree to serve on the committee but expressed misgivings about Rankin's running for the Senate: "[O]f course I will go on Jeannette's committee and will do anything I can. . . . I do hope it will be all right for the senate. I just couldn't bear that Jeannette shouldn't be returned. She has meant much to so many of us, and she has been so fine and so dependable. If labor doesn't realize how wonderful she has been they would be ungrateful indeed." Jeannette Rankin's New York friend Jane Thompson was pessimistic about her ability to recruit "Mrs. Vanderlip" for the committee: "She doesn't love me—but I hope that will not interfere." Later Thompson reported, "Mrs. Vanderlip declines." Another New York refusal came from Helena Louise Johnson. To Harriet Sedman, Johnson wrote, "I am fond of your sister," but fondness could not overcome Johnson's reluctance to allow her name to be used as if she were speaking for the entire "Federation." Minnie Fisher Cunningham of Texas consented to be on the committee but worried about its effect on the national suffrage movement and reminded suffrage leaders that Jeannette Rankin was not their top priority: "Will he [Rankin's opponent, U.S. senator Thomas Walsh] stay put [as a suffrage supporter] if outside state presidents go into his district to help elect his opponent? . . . Just remember we are pledged to put the passage of the Federal Amendment ahead of every thing else, except loyalty to the National Government."

Jeannette Rankin's Washington office also was responsible for mailing out the postcards and raising money. The cards were written and signed by

New York women, most of them with a Heterodoxy connection: Elizabeth Watson, Katharine Anthony, Elisabeth Irwin, Katherine Leckie, Ami Hicks, Marion Cothren, and Ruth Pinchot Pickering. Then, just as Jeannette Rankin had gone to bat for the women employees of the Bureau of Engraving and Printing, they—as many as twenty-five at a time—volunteered to address the 75,000 postcards to Montana women. Harriet Sedman explained to labor organizer Ida Craft of Brooklyn the system that was being used: "The Bureau girls are working in the office addressing every afternoon and evening. . . . [G]et your friends to write as many as they can and send them to me. . . . I will have them addressed from our lists to the women where they will do the most good."

Fund-raising was a more difficult task. Harriet Sedman told supporters that the $1,100 Jeannette Rankin could legally spend of her own money would be inadequate "in a state the size of Montana. With the increased railroad and postal rates such an amount will not cover the state either by literature or speakers." Contributions were slow to arrive; an office report listed total receipts of only $258. When Dr. Maria Dean of Helena, the campaign treasurer, mailed just three checks to Mary Stewart, she speculated why support was so slow in coming: "[The average voter] jumps in line with prejudice and fear. There has been so much distortion of facts. So many women have been made afraid that Jeannette is not a patriot. The powers that be—meaning big machines and their interests and all men politicians—are opposed to Jeannette and to all women in any position of influence."

With a month left in the campaign, Harriet Sedman urged on Jeannette Rankin's New York friends: "The primaries will be August 27th, so that the time is short and money is even shorter." But the responses from New York were not encouraging. Jane Thompson replied that "a dinner here would be a good thing—a small dinner with certain selected people." Nina Swinnerton similarly wrote to Rankin that she, Katharine Anthony, and Elisabeth Irwin "long to have a luncheon for you. . . . I think you are just fitted for [the Senate] and I know you will be elected." Coming to naught a year before had been the New York women's more ambitious plan, described by Swinnerton: "[It will be] a huge working women's (professional & industrial) reception or supper . . . probably at Washington Irving High School. Give everybody baked beans & coffee. Then have you recount all your magnificent, unparalleled deeds for women & labor since you were seated. Do you like this idea Jeannette[?] No one is to speak but you—a one lady show and that the first lady in the world." Marie Virginia Smith used the dog days of summer as her excuse for not making any progress: "Such a really painful time of year to accomplish anything in this old town! Everyone is out of the city three-fourths of the time—including myself." Ida Craft explained that Jeannette Rankin was no longer the only item on women's political plate: "The women are all so busy in working and giving to war activities, it is hard to get money from them for anything else. . . . There are a number of New York state women running for office who hope to be elected this fall, and as they are like the women of other states when they get the vote they want the money for their own campaigns."

Campaigning in Montana, Jeannette Rankin could not help out in New York. She was stumping in her nonstop fashion against the four primary opponents who had come forward and trying, in Harriet Sedman's words, to "counteract much of the [IWW] poison which has been circulated by the newspapers." She told a Missoula audience: "I have been traveling 150 miles a day in a Ford car. . . . I have already talked to more people than I faced in my first campaign." In "daily letters," Wellington Rankin gave Harriet Sedman even more robust accounts that she used in her progress reports to supporters. Wellington Rankin put the total size of his sister's audiences at "five or six times as many people as she had the opportunity to speak to during the last campaign." He was especially encouraged because the Republican primary vote would be split among five candidates, and she would have the combined support of women, the "strong labor vote," and the "farmer vote." Harriet relayed Wellington's assessment to a New York union leader, "all of the politicians are admitting that she will win, even the *Butte Miner*," and to one of Jeannette Rankin's former aides, "Wellington writes that the women who worked for Jeannette are still for her, so if we can hold the women, it is all we need." There was no doubt that women had been with Jeannette Rankin. Their enthusiastic endorsements in 1916 included "your election . . . is signal victory for the cause of women"; "you will now be in a position to do the Suffrage Cause the most possible good"; and "we know you will stand for everything noble, true, and right." But now some women were beginning to waver. One pleaded with the congresswoman to do something about "the ill-advised course of some over-zealous [suffragists]. . . . I beg of you, do not allow woman suffrage to be killed." Another wrote after Rankin's involvement with the IWW that "some women think you have ruined suffrage in this state by the stand you have taken."

The distance Jeannette Rankin had fallen in the estimation of some women was illustrated by a letter Carrie Chapman Catt, NAWSA's president, wrote to NAWSA director Harriet Laidlaw and her husband, James Laidlaw, just before the 1918 election. For the sake of suffrage, Catt argued, the Laidlaws should persuade Rankin to drop her candidacy for the U.S. Senate. Catt was writing to the Laidlaws because she believed that they had "more influence with Jeannette Rankin than anybody else this side of Montana." Catt continued, "[N]either Miss [Anna Howard] Shaw or I approved of her [1916] candidacy and did not render any aid to it." During Rankin's term in Congress, the two conservative NAWSA leaders ended up on the outside with more radical women on the inside: "She was surrounded by Woman's Party people and consequently one could not see her without seeing them. . . . [W]e did not hang around her office as perhaps our workers would have done had it not been that Ida Craft was there all the time and she was a very ardent Woman's Party supporter." The crux of Catt's argument was that Rankin's candidacy, whether she won or lost, could mean suffrage's loss of their best ally, Senator Thomas Walsh: "We have never had a better friend, more willing to fight for us on all occasions than Senator Walsh. . . . [I]f we have to continue in Congress another session we could lose [his] cooperation. . . . As I am writing today, we feel assured that we have the necessary votes to put us through the Senate." Catt also argued that Rankin had much to lose personally by continuing her campaign. Because "the newspapers have criticized Miss Rankin with great and cruel severity," she stood to "lose what prestige she has remaining." "For her sake as well as ours," Catt concluded, "it is most advisable that she should quit at this stage and if you have any influence with her whatsoever, I hope you will bring it to bear."

Along with NAWSA, the Republican Party tried to remove Jeannette Rankin from the Senate race, but she ultimately came in second in the Republican primary with 17,091 votes. The winner, Oscar M. Lanstrum, had 18,805 votes, and the third-place candidate had 5,878 votes. In Jeannette Rankin's mind, her loss was the result of "a great epidemic of flu" and Lanstrum's ability as a medical doctor to "go into the home of people afflicted" while she faced called-off meetings and closed-down towns. A more significant factor than the flu, however, was the Republican Party. Wellington

Rankin's assertion that his sister would have won the primary if all of the candidates had remained active and split the vote had been correct. But Republicans recruited Lanstrum "to run against [Rankin] . . . to defeat her" and then, when three other candidates entered the race, argued that "all the candidates should retire [and the] Republican Committee should nominate a man to run against Miss Rankin." None of Rankin's primary opponents withdrew, but all except Lanstrum "stopped campaigning or at least lost time in their campaigns." Wellington Rankin viewed the primary election meddling as "contrary to the principles of the Republican party" and an affront to his own standing in the party. He "threatened" the national party committeeman seeking Jeannette Rankin's defeat that he would "have Jeannette run independently" in the general election if she lost the Republican primary. Word of his threat was more alarming to the Democrats than to the Republicans. The Democrats offered "to buy [his] Havre newspaper for 'an extravagant price'" in exchange for Jeannette Rankin's dropping out, but Wellington Rankin refused.

Jeannette Rankin ended her primary campaign in Missoula. The town's newspaper reported that a small crowd "composed largely of outspoken admirers stood in a drizzling rain [for ninety minutes] last night [before] the candidate drove up to the courthouse square in a muddy and somewhat elderly Ford car and descended to shake hands." In the light rain she spoke from her open car and "did not attempt to conceal her intimacy with . . . [the Nonpartisan] league." She pledged to continue fighting for national suffrage and national prohibition and reminded her audience of her successes regarding the Bureau of Engraving and Printing, maternity health, and irrigation on the Flathead Indian reservation. She said she had given "support [to] every war measure introduced since declaration of war"; she "spoke at length concerning her attempt to end the miners' strike in Butte"; and she gave support to taxing "99 percent" of the Anaconda Copper Mining Company's profits "to pay the costs of the war." Her populism was also displayed in her props. "If she was less natty than usual," the paper said, "it was because her hat and clothes looked a trifle weather-beaten. Indeed conservation was slightly expressed by the coat which the candidate dropped over the rear seat of her car with the worn-out lining in view of the audience."

Because neither Rankin was willing to give way after Jeannette Rankin's primary election defeat, she ran in the 1918 general election as the National

Party candidate for the U.S. Senate. Principally "a vehicle for her candidacy," the National Party was a loose organization of progressives, prohibitionists, farmers, and "pro-war Socialists." Her campaign slogan emphasized her backtracking from her 1917 vote against war: "Win the war, and make the world safe for humanity." She promised she "would support President Wilson in 'whatever measures he may recommend to more efficiently prosecute the war.'" She sought the vote of the Montana Nonpartisan League by stressing her support of public power projects, low-cost farm loans, government irrigation of reservation lands owned by white settlers, and flexibility for homesteaders in meeting their occupancy requirements. Responding favorably, the *Butte Weekly Bulletin* ran "full-page ads identifying her as a candidate of the 'toilers'" and editorializing, "Miss Rankin has constantly spoken for the lowly and the oppressed . . . trying to obtain some small measure of justice for the workers, and from them and them alone . . . must her support come." But the national Nonpartisan League, already "suspected of disloyalty," refused to support her out of fear that "alliance with Miss Rankin would confirm those suspicions."

Jeannette Rankin's radical positions had another implication. Democrats began to fear even more that she "would attract left-wing votes that might otherwise go to their candidate," Senator Thomas Walsh, and hand the election to Republican candidate Oscar Lanstrum. They responded to the threat by trying to terminate Jeannette Rankin's campaign. Three letters to Senator Walsh revealed their plan. Participating were not only Walsh and his former law partner, C. B. Nolan, but also Wellington Rankin, their former colleague. Also involved was a former Montana lieutenant governor and Democratic Party operative, Archibald Spriggs. Between the primary election and general election, Nolan recommended to Walsh that "every influence possible be brought to bear on Wellington not to have [Jeannette] run." During the same period, Spriggs explained Wellington's complicity in the plot in two letters to Walsh. Wellington had advised Senator Walsh to use his office to "help [Jeannette] get a position with the government, preferably overseas, that would allow her to retire from politics gracefully." The pragmatic Wellington viewed the arrangement as "politics." Jeannette saw the plan in a different light: "I was offered bribes not to run on the Independent ticket." The bribe, she said, was to "make it possible for me to do what I intended to do—going to Europe and things like that." Years later, when a doctoral student's research was about to expose the story, Jeannette asked

Wellington to sue to prevent its publication; Wellington responded, "No one will read his book." As an elderly woman Jeannette Rankin was still trying to ensure that history would interpret her career favorably. An aide, referring to a manuscript and a film, suggested to her: "You will certainly want to correct any mistakes, misunderstandings, and/or false impressions connected with these things." In 1918 Wellington Rankin's primary concern was getting his radical sister to "retire from politics." He was to run for state attorney general in 1920, and his first U.S. Senate campaign was just four years away.

Pushed by ethics or ego, Jeannette Rankin stayed in the race and came in third. Thomas Walsh won with 41 percent of the vote; Oscar Lanstrum received 36 percent and Jeannette Rankin 23 percent. Faced with losing the election unless he abandoned his progressive base, Walsh moved to the right; he "buckled, . . . bent with the wind and kept his [job]." He sought the aid of the Anaconda Copper Mining Company and received "more than ample financial and newspaper support for his campaign." Jeannette Rankin's radical strategy served her well as far as it could go. She lost Butte to Walsh by only 79 votes, and "Non-Partisan League support carried three northeastern counties for her." Because of her repudiation by Carrie Chapman Catt (Catt told a Montana newspaper, "every time she answers the roll call she loses us a million votes"), the women's vote probably swung to Walsh. In subsequent elections "separate [female] institutions did support women who were able to maintain formal political authority," but the first woman of U.S. politics was not able to hang on to that base. In two years Jeannette Rankin's star had shot across the sky and burnt out.

Jeannette Rankin did have a political future, but it was twenty-two years in the making. Coming together in 1940 were the country's isolationism and her absolute pacifism. Rankin told a friend that the second ingredient, which she described as "a real desire for peace," would be essential to a successful congressional campaign. She returned to Montana from Georgia in 1939, out of work and accompanied by her mother. Her stated purpose was to establish a replica of her Georgia Peace Society in the Bitterroot Valley south of Missoula. Unspoken was her plan to frame a campaign for Montana's western district congressional seat as a referendum on war. At first she did not level with Wellington Rankin: "I don't know whether I told Wellington or not. I think I did say I wanted to, but it was just very vague." She knew, however, that he would have to be the driving force of her campaign as its strategist and banker. Reflecting on her 1916 and 1940 victories, she admitted that "she could never have done it without him." Her own contribution would once again be campaigning as the little red hen, doing most things herself; a political contemporary remembered her as "one of the ablest campaigners that I ever saw."

After telling Wellington Rankin obliquely about her wish to run, Jeannette Rankin set out across western Montana to "feel out the situation." She visited precinct committeemen and high schools county by county. Personally and politically, her mission was daunting. She still shared responsibility for her mother, and after "starting on Monday morning and working continuously till Friday afternoon" she needed to "go back and try to help Grace take care of [Olive]." Republican officials were not enthusiastic about her running, and the district had recently favored Democrats by 12,000 votes. Accordingly, she presented herself as "an American first, a Progressive second, and a Republican somewhere down the line," despite her brother's position as chairman of the Montana Republican Party. Her nonpartisan plan meant speaking and canvassing as a pacifist and not attacking, as a Republican, her hated adversary President Roosevelt. To political activists she posed the question, "What do you think about my running?" To students at fifty-two high schools she "talked about . . . how stupid war was" but avoided mentioning Roosevelt. "[S]ome of the people," she said, "were afraid I was going to say something against Roosevelt . . . a god. . . . I never mentioned him." Her hope was that the students would tell their parents that she had "talked sense." She also hoped that she could inspire the girls, as she had been motivated by feminist role models, by predicting "some day we'll have a woman president."

Jeannette Rankin finally took the difficult step of telling her brother that she wanted to run. Wellington Rankin, in a political dry period between 1934 and 1942, replied that "he would back" her. Later Jeannette both downplayed and emphasized the importance of Wellington's support. She once said, "And of course I would not run without the consent . . . not consent, without the advice of my brother." But another time she said, "Then Wellington decided that it was all right to run; I wasn't going to run if he didn't think so, because he'd have to pay for it." Others did not understate Wellington's "tremendous influence with Jeannette." A local politician's insight was "I always thought he guided her. That she didn't move unless he made the decision—the command decision." In Jeannette Rankin's 1940 campaign, there were many decisions for Wellington Rankin to make. He sent his sister "to the best dress makers [to] get good clothes, and he would pay for it." He wrote her campaign brochure, which balanced isolationism and protecting the nation. In part it read: "I believe we should use every means that money, science and ingenuity can produce for the defense of our country; in fact we should prepare to the limit, but I also believe that we should keep our men out of Europe." From the flyer came her campaign slogan: "Prepare to the limit for defense; keep our men out of Europe." Wellington paid the campaign bills and approved political endorsements and even his sister's tactics involving women voters. Concerning "an appeal to women," Jeannette told her brother: "I'll submit [it] to you [and] find a place to make it, if you think it would be wise." He coordinated the campaign work of family members. Mary Rankin Bragg wrote to him about her participation and that of her two children, whose tuition at Harvard and Columbia was being paid by their uncle: "We all want to do whatever you think is best." The family ended up doing a lot in the campaign. A primary opponent said, "[E]very place I went the Rankin girls had been there. Every bypass, every station. . . . They were workers [and] very well known."

As chief strategist, Wellington Rankin charted out for Jeannette Rankin and campaign workers detailed itineraries: "Go see Harold K. Near at the Montana Power Company and he will take you by the hand and lead you to the right Honorable James H. Morrow. . . . See Ray Nixon who has a dairy near town—Bring me some cheese. See Phil Duncan and he will swing Louie Lepp to you who is a Democrat. . . . Ty Robinson and Les Colby will arrange for a committee to meet you at Darby and accompany you through the Bitterroot Valley. . . . We will be ahead of you on the phone in all spots and will keep you advised." Campaigners on the road reported back to Wellington Rankin: "Townsend Club at Eureka with 140 members is for Jeannette. . . . After a thorough canvass of business places and spots of habitation along the highway we are ready to bet that Jeannette will carry Lincoln County. . . . [The] impression all over is that the Catholic church is for Jeannette. . . . [The] consensus of opinion seems to be that Jeannette will run very strong in Flathead and that in general there will be a 20 percent switch from the Democratic vote based on last election. . . . [W]e will be here today and tomorrow and catch four union meetings and the Republican women. . . . [We have been] successful in placing hundreds of stickers in cars, shop windows and service stations." Wellington Rankin's control probably extended to choosing the "very glamorous picture" that was used in Jeannette Rankin's 1940 campaign brochure. A longtime acquaintance said about the photo, "She never really looked like that picture, but I'm sure it did a lot to elect her." And, during the campaign, Wellington Rankin was "on the telephone incessantly morning, day, and night."

While Wellington Rankin was in his office planning strategy, directing campaign workers, and paying the bills, Jeannette Rankin was contributing her sweat and shoe leather on the hustings. A contemporary said that she "was a tough person. . . . [N]othing phased her when she was after something. . . . She would go anywhere. Anywhere." Hungry for a win, the "anywhere" included "a house of prostitution—it didn't make any difference. . . . [She] would make herself at home." Anywhere included driving "a hundred miles up in the mountains . . . in some isolated canyon. . . . If she heard of a vote . . . she would go up and see them, drive up there and it didn't make any difference about the roads." It included streets and sidewalks: "She would . . . bump into everybody and solicit their votes. . . . [She would] rub elbows with the common herd." It included any place that would accommodate her speeches. She had the ability "to right now just start talking. . . . [S]he would get up and talk and talk." A newspaper in 1940 described her as "vivacious with a quick, nervous speech, adjusting and readjusting her horned-rimmed spectacles. . . . cram[ming] her conversation with statistics without sacrificing any of her feminine charm." Jeannette Rankin's incessant campaigning debunked the criticisms of age and carpetbagging. The "slogan my opponents planned to use was," she said, "'You aren't going to send an old woman to Congress.'" Also circulating was the complaint that she "hadn't been in the state for a long time." She said that she wanted people "to know I was in their district. . . . [S]ome were going to mention my age [but] those who had seen me said, 'Well, she came here driving her own car.'"

War was the central issue of the 1940 campaign for both Jeannette Rankin and the voters. Her most important constituency was women, who in her thinking had come to be linked inextricably with peace. Prior to taking her solitary tour of the district and announcing her candidacy, she "kept saying" to herself, "[I]f I don't run, the women [who] don't want war [will] have no one to vote for." She communicated her pacifist views by printing and distributing thousands of copies of two of her radio speeches that had been inserted in the *Congressional Record*. She told Wellington Rankin with some urgency: "I have 5,000 copies which I can send to friends and ask them to mail them to others. . . . More of the enclosed would cost $2.50 per thousand—this month." The radio speeches conveyed her distinctive isolationism and pacifism. In the earlier address, delivered in Helena on September 29, 1939, she flatly rejected "the argument that America was morally committed to aid the allies." She admitted that the United States has "a moral responsibility to help correct the unspeakable conditions that exist in the world," but not by going to war. For America to use force to stop Nazi atrocities would be to sink to Germany's level of immorality. "Our responsibility is to say," she explained, "We do not like your Hitler methods of violence; therefore we are not going to use violence." Instead of going to war, the United States should lead, she said, "by our example" of disarming unilaterally. She reassured Americans that they "need not fear— Germany will never be able to come over." She promised further that war could be "abolished," just as "for over 100 years, outlawed war [governed relations] between the United States and Canada." The nation's first step toward peace was to choose democracy, the "right method," and reject war, "a stupid, undemocratic method." At the core of her democratic philosophy were women: "Mothers alone can prevent our entering the war if they will express their opinions now." Rankin's second radio address, printed in the *Congressional Record* on August 7, 1940, gave the conclusion to her antiwar argument: "By voting for me . . . you can express your opposition to sending your son to foreign lands to fight in a foreign war." She tried to make herself a "symbol against war that they had an opportunity to vote for."

Jeannette Rankin's candidacy, however, was not a referendum on war. In both the primary and general elections, she had opponents to contend with. Contesting the Republican U.S. House primary, besides Jeannette Rankin, were three men, including incumbent Jacob Thorkelson, "an isolationist who had littered the *Congressional Record* with anti-British and anti-Semitic diatribes." Rankin referred to him as "a good man," "never said a word against him," and distinguished herself from him by her years of lobbying senators and representatives about peace. "I'd be better," she said, "because I know Congress better than he does." She drew other contrasts with her principal opponent: "He hadn't much personality. He couldn't meet people and talk to them." With 36 percent of the vote, she won the primary election; Thorkelson came in second. The total vote of the four Republican candidates was 29 percent of all votes cast in the primary election. The Republican vote in the three prior western district congressional primaries was 29 percent, 19 percent, and 21 percent. If Thorkelson could be elected congressman as a Republican in 1938, Rankin thought that she had a good chance in 1940.

Jeannette Rankin's Democratic opponent in the general election was a radical from Butte, Jerry J. O'Connell, who in his primary had defeated a more moderate and less acerbic candidate from Butte, Mike Mansfield. After graduating from college, O'Connell had gone to Washington to attend law school and work for the Democratic National Committee and U.S. senator Thomas Walsh. He subsequently served in the Montana legislature and on the Montana Public Service Commission, was elected to the U.S. House of Representatives in 1936, and lost his congressional seat to Thorkelson in 1938. He was well-known in Montana as a zealous anti-corporation reformer. Campaigning to be a utility regulator in 1934, he advocated public ownership of all utilities and natural resources, a hydroelectric tax, and a corporation license tax. After his election to the regulatory commission, he was unrelenting in his radicalism: "I want the power trust to know that I resent their efforts to defeat me. Henceforward, when utility companies spend the tremendous amount of money they employed to fight me, or spend any amount of money in an endeavor to defeat any progressive candidate for any office, it will always mean that their profits have been excessive, and a consequent reduction in their rates must follow." The state's principal utility, the Montana Power Company, and its longtime business partner and political ally, the Anaconda Copper Mining Company, had despised O'Connell in 1935, and the feeling continued in 1940.

Jerry O'Connell's candidacy posed a problem for Jeannette Rankin. The "records of the two were roughly similar." They both stood for reduction and reorganization of the military, a constitutional amendment requiring a referendum on declaring war, high taxes on war profits, and hatred of the Anaconda Company. Rankin tried to distinguish herself from O'Connell by using "red baiting" to position herself to his right. During the campaign "she endorsed a widely distributed radio script that implied that her opponent . . . was associated with the Communist Party." Ironically, the American Legion at the same time was circulating "in the interests of Americanism" a flyer to remind voters of Rankin's "radical" Georgia Peace Society.

But O'Connell's candidacy did present some advantages for Jeannette Rankin. Because the Anaconda Company could not decide which candidate they hated more, the company and its newspapers sat out the campaign. Rankin observed that it was fortunate "for me there was a very good enemy of the Anaconda Company nominated on the Democratic ticket. . . . Newspapers did not mention me, but they were equally reticent about mentioning my opponent." One result of the silence, a Helena businessman recalled, was "not . . . much interest" in the race among the electorate generally. Rankin agreed, as she said that her "greatest difficulty was getting the people to know that I was running." Not surprisingly, her solution came from "the women in all of these communities [who] thought of something to do." They "rented space in the papers" and "asked the radio stations to let them have time." She "drove around the district as much as [she] could [and] practically covered every part." When the November vote was tallied, Rankin had defeated O'Connell 56,616 to 47,352—even though he carried the labor strongholds of Butte and Anaconda.

Jeannette Rankin was sent to Congress in 1940 to vote against war, and her second congressional term effectively came to an end after she cast the lone dissent to America's entering World War II. That unpopular vote, however, did not precipitate her decision not to seek reelection. Months before Pearl Harbor, and possibly earlier, she had "stepped aside" to make room for Wellington Rankin's 1942 candidacy for the U.S. Senate. Her decision to abdicate in favor of her brother was known to a few of her intimates. Friends in Georgia wrote to her: "[Y]ou ought to be in Congress yourself, . . . but to plan future events around your brother seems at present a very wise move." Her secretary Millacent Yarrow wrote to her about a "Mrs. Thorpe [who had] called up. . . . She hadn't known you were not continuing. I told her you had stepped aside for your brother. 'O,' she said, 'he's doubtful of her reelection if she had run'; to which I heartily agreed." If Jeannette Rankin was emotionally down during the aftermath of her war vote, Wellington Rankin was more so because of his planned 1942 Senate race. Edna wrote to Jeannette that she had "talked with Wellington at Denver. . . . He was frightfully depressed. . . . I told him how badly you felt that he was forced to bear the brunt of all the criticism."

There appeared to be, however, a reason other than Wellington Rankin's primacy for Jeannette Rankin's stepping down—a deal with the Anaconda Company. At a Capitol lunch in summer 1941 with Winfield Page, one of her 1940 primary opponents, she explained why "the field was open" to him in 1942. She told Page that "she was not going to run for reelection" and that the "only reason she ran [before] was that President Roosevelt was pushing us into the war." "She ran" in 1940, Page said, "to register her vote against it." Having that sole goal for her second term, Jeannette had gone along with Wellington's election strategy for her in 1940 and himself in 1942. The Anaconda Company would stay out of Jeannette Rankin's 1940 western district race and, in exchange, the company—"strong for Mike Mansfield"—would get a free pass for Mansfield in 1942. The "Rankins fought the Company for many, many years," Page said. "But, then [in 1940] they got in with the Company. . . . [Jeannette Rankin] told both Alice [Page's wife] and me that she'd promised the Company that she wasn't going against Mike."

Jeannette Rankin's renunciation of congressional ambitions, however, was temporary. Her desire to be a politician and member of Congress never diminished. In 1943 she began to plan a race against U.S. representative Mike Mansfield, whom she had sarcastically started calling the "'pleasant young man' . . . in Congress from my district." She set out for Millacent Yarrow her options of fighting men directly or letting others do the job for her: "I'm either going to run for Congress or I'm going to live as peacefully as I can and let the world kill off the men." An ebullient Yarrow exhorted Rankin to run: "Two months more and only a year will be left you before filing day. . . . You must wake [the women] up. You can." Jeannette Rankin began to scout out her prospects in western Montana. To a supporter in Washington, she described her early tentativeness as "going out in the state and brows[ing] around a little." As in 1916 and 1940, she used a cover for testing the political waters. In 1943 it was talking about a "program with the women in Montana that will make it possible for us to express our determination to avoid war in the future." A year later she reported to Flora Belle Surles that planning had turned to action: "We started to campaign— doing Sanders County. . . . [It's] going to be a long hard struggle."

As always, Wellington Rankin was a major obstacle. Jeannette Rankin, with little money set aside and no income, was dependent on her brother. Not wanting to approach him directly, she wrote to her sister Grace about Wellington's assessment of her chances. Grace replied, "I asked him about your running [and] he said 'Oh not impossible' and I didn't press it." From a family perspective, Grace suggested that running for Congress might free Jeannette from the burden of caring for their eighty-nine-year-old mother.

"[I]f you run," Grace wrote, "you could have some peace." After Jeannette pushed her sister to get more information from Wellington, Grace sent back a discouraging reply: "I talked to Wellington yesterday [and] asked him . . . if he thought there would be a chance for you to run and he said 'Not a chance. Oh of course if Germany collapsed within thirty days there might be a chance.'" Four months later, Wellington told Jeannette unambiguously that he would not back her, even though he did not run for the U.S. Senate again until 1948. Jeannette Rankin reluctantly deferred to her brother even though she told herself that women's support would have outweighed pro-war sentiment. She wrote to her friend Flora Belle Surles: "Wellington feels I can't win—I think the women would put me over but I'm not willing to risk the campaign debt." To her old boss Frederick Libby, she confided: "I'm not willing to risk all I have and take a chance on having a debt and no office."

Twenty-four years later, Jeannette Rankin thought about running for Congress one more time. Wellington Rankin's death in 1966 freed her from his control, and his bequest of $75,000 gave her money to spend. In her new state of independence, the world in the form of women activists and Vietnam War protesters started "coming to [her] door." The glare of the public eye felt warm and welcoming; her old constituencies were calling out to be harvested and her old detractors had fallen to the wayside. Her sister Mary tried to dissuade her: "If you are unhappy about the way Congress acted toward the [Jeannette Rankin] Brigade, I wonder if you would enjoy being in Congress . . . daily associated with so many war-mongers. . . . You have had so much praise, but you are still unhappy because Congress was so horrid. . . . I should think so much attention would have given you a lift for some time." But her niece sent the report that an "election judge I know said you got ten [write-in] votes in the precinct we used to live in," and the national press depicted her as a vigorous woman "look[ing] a good quarter of a century younger" than her age. Some of her relatives had worried about "her problems of boredom," but now, with the prospect of another campaign, "she appear[ed] more happy or fulfilled" than ever. Late in 1967 she decided to test the political waters by hinting to the Montana press about a campaign. The intelligence from Wellington Rankin's widow was encouraging: "[Y]our news story [should] cause a lot of comment in Republican circles, and will no doubt scare Smiley to death." Ultimately Jeannette Rankin gave in to the realities of old age, and the unopposed Dick Smiley won the 1968 Republican nomination for Montana's western congressional district. But she "stump[ed] the country" with "cane in hand" for five more years, this last time not for her own election but for election reform.

First Term

A Brilliant Future Behind Her

FTER JEANNETTE RANKIN WAS ELECTED TO CONGRESS IN 1916, THE PRESS CLOSELY followed the unfolding story. Reporters continued to seek new angles despite feature articles running week after week. Businesses, too, tried to capitalize on Jeannette Rankin's fame by getting her to endorse their products. The toll on the family's privacy was enormous, and Wellington Rankin positioned himself at the front door of the Rankin home to screen callers going in and messages coming out. But the Rankin family had to face up to the fact that Jeannette Rankin had become the nation's "best known woman." She later recalled, "It's almost impossible for people . . . to understand what I was in 1917 . . . a symbol and a representative, not only of women in Montana or in the United States, but of women in all nations and ages." In her vast constituency, she raised great expectations. Some supporters predicted a Rankin presidency and world peace; most kept their eyes on the upcoming struggle for national woman suffrage. A history professor wrote to the congresswoman: "[I]n my capacity as a disenfranchised woman I feel very keenly that you are a sort of representative-at-large of the womanhood of the United States." Feeling women's eyes and hopes on her, Rankin told the *New York Times* that she would "put in as [her] first bill the Susan B. Anthony nationwide woman suffrage amendment." Suffrage's defeat and her association with radical labor, however, came to be the criteria used to assess her first term. Typical was the *Helena Independent*'s judgment when she was leaving Congress in 1918: "[S]he has a brilliant future behind her."

Wellington Rankin managed Jeannette Rankin's gradual emergence from the Rankin house following her election. Her first step was a speech from a flag-draped car in front of the University of Montana's main hall. "A great responsibility rests upon me," she told the assembly, "to my country . . . and to my alma mater." Cheerleaders shouted their approval: "Rankin, Rankin, bully for Rankin, Varsity, Varsity, Rah." Next she accepted an invitation to address university professors and, ironically, their wives at "an authors club, to which distinguished people say things once a month." Broadening her audience, she placed an article, written by Wellington Rankin, in the *Boston Traveler* that used the myth of the West to explain her election and aspirations: "Side by side the men and women have wrought their homes from the virgin country, struggling first with nature, and then with the man-made laws which control the results of their struggle with nature." Wellington Rankin's involvement was also seen in the *Boston Record-Herald*'s reporting the family's statement that "all alleged interviews [with Jeannette Rankin] previously published were unwarranted." Her next appearances were completely on her brother's terms. He negotiated a contract with a speaker's agency that gave her $500 (about $8,500 today) for each of twenty East Coast speeches ("a lot of money for a young girl from the country," Wellington Rankin said). He arranged through a client, as payment for legal services, to have a New York clothier make her four dresses—one a $200 "very elegant" design. He must have achieved the effect he desired, because a Western Union messenger on the Pennsylvania Railroad between Harrisburg and New York recalled Jeannette Rankin's "striking appearance in the Pullman car."

At Jeannette Rankin's inaugural speech at Carnegie Hall on March 2, 1917, she spoke on "Democracy in Government," another Wellington Rankin–crafted "eulogy of the West." Introduced by NAWSA president Carrie Chapman Catt and clothed in white satin and pink chiffon, she addressed 3,000 in a half-filled auditorium. Contemporary accounts of her remarks, delivered without notes, closely parallel Wellington Rankin's draft. She focused on the West and at times, to the bewilderment of her audience, provincially on Montana. She ran through a litany of progressive issues ranging from the evil of concentrated economic power, which for the Rankins meant the Anaconda Copper Mining Company, to the remedy of direct democracy, with which Montana had begun to experiment. There was only one reference to war, the issue that Wellington Rankin wanted most to control. To her audience she merely said, "[W]omen ought to have a right to say whether their men shall go to war."

While in New York, Jeannette Rankin stayed with Harriet and James Laidlaw and undoubtedly discussed with Harriet the topics of their recent correspondence: the split in the suffrage movement between the conservatives led by Carrie Chapman Catt, whom Rankin's New York friends called "old suf mossbacks" and the "old time 1880 ladies," and the radical Congressional Union led by Alice Paul; the personal tension between Catt and Rankin; and the tactics Rankin should use to push the national suffrage amendment through Congress. Newly elected congressman Fiorello LaGuardia took the two Rankins to lunch at the Waldorf Astoria, and former president Theodore Roosevelt invited them to his Oyster Bay home for dinner. Wellington Rankin had arranged the event hoping that Roosevelt would urge the congresswoman to support war should a vote occur, but the topic did not come up. Wellington Rankin did succeed, however, in getting the speaker's agency to threaten nonrenewal of his sister's contract if she voted against war.

Jeannette Rankin did not establish any distance between herself and her brother until her vote on World War I. In the meantime, she followed guidelines on which Wellington Rankin insisted. She "dressed well and sensibly" in public and described herself, in an interview with the *Washington Post,* as simply "very womanly." The *New York Herald* did not depart from her self-deprecating self-description when it observed how the first congresswoman's dress accented "her ankles and trim little feet." Jeannette accepted Wellington's tether in more important matters than fashion. From New York, he telegraphed her aide in Montana, Belle Fligelman, to send him "letters about Congressional Directory. Also letters from [NAWSA officials Molly] Hay and [Carrie Chapman] Catt." When Jeannette Rankin arrived in Washington for President Wilson's war address to Congress, she was still "accompanied by her brother" and his counsel of reticence.

Jeannette Rankin, the dauntless campaigner and expert lobbyist, spoke as a political novice to the press just a week before her vote against war: "I am a little afraid to say anything right now about anything. . . . You know, I am in a pretty predicament. I had no idea Congress was going to open so soon. I have so much to learn that I don't know what to say and what not to say. . . . I am going to put in all my time at present learning the ropes. No, I can't tell you what I'm going to stand for, as I haven't answered that question for anybody." She had been equally vague when answering reporters' questions in New York a month earlier. At that time the *Washington Post* described her as "a master politician" and "the eternal feminine" for her "evasion of issues and situations. . . . She talked with ten reporters for an hour, parried close to a thousand questions and did not commit herself definitely on anything excepting woman suffrage."

Jeannette Rankin soon began to establish herself in Washington. She rented a "vast rambling apartment" with "eleven beds" at the St. Nicholas on California Street. Living with her were her mother and two of her office workers from Montana, Belle Fligelman and Florence Leech. Jeannette's recently widowed sister Harriet Sedman and her two children later joined the household. As female staffers, Fligelman and Leech were as much oddities in the male-dominated Congress as their employer. Both were suffragists from Montana. Fligelman, a journalist, had graduated from the University of Wisconsin, and Leech had come east to work for the congresswoman or attend graduate school at Columbia. Besides Fligelman and Leech, Rankin hired a stenographer and a caseworker who "knew all the strings to pull when you wanted something done in one of the government departments." Fligelman said that "every other congressman had one" staffer, but Rankin managed to have four by paying them "considerably less" than the standard wage of $2,000 (her congressional salary in 1917 was $7,500) and using her income from "speaking engagements and the syndicated weekly stories that paid $100 a week." She also differed from her colleagues in her office space. She was assigned 332 Cannon but, because of her large volume of mail, was given the adjacent rooms.

Like the wages she paid, the working conditions in Jeannette Rankin's office were lower than might be expected of a labor reformer. Belle Fligelman remembered the congresswoman, wearing her sturdy and practical "Ground grippers," in control of the office. Asked if Rankin was "an affectionate woman" and whether she came to her wedding, Fligelman answered "no" to both questions. Asked if the atmosphere was "all business," Fligelman replied, "Yes. There was really nothing more. . . . [W]e never went out for lunch. We always had a sandwich in our desk drawers and we ate while we worked. We worked awfully hard there. Nobody had ever heard of an eight-hour day and she basically worked till around ten at night and was there at nine in the morning. The help, of which I was one, would come in at nine and we usually got off around six; quite often we would come back and work [until] eight at night, but not as much as she worked." Much of the staff's work stemmed from Rankin's heavy correspondence. Fligelman remembered that she got mail "from all over the world. We would get a couple of sacks like that every morning."

Belle Fligelman's principal task was answering the mail and doing other writing for Jeannette Rankin. Until she left to get married and was replaced by Harriet Sedman, Fligelman "was sort of the office manager and. . . . dictated all the letters." She said that Rankin "didn't write. It's an interesting thing, she never wrote a speech." A biographer makes the same point: "Jeannette all her life was a verbalizer . . . she had a great resistance to writing. . . . Everything that has appeared under her name in print represents . . . the composition . . . of others." Fligelman ghostwrote a fifty-article series in the *Chicago Herald* on labor reform that she "research[ed] in the Congressional Library." The collaboration between Rankin and Fligelman was described in a letter to Fligelman from an Illinois suffragist: "This scribbled article will give you additional ammunition for your promised (rather, Jeannette's promised) help for us through the *Herald*. Mrs. [Catharine Waugh] McCulloch sent Jeannette one on Methods of Enfranchising Illinois Women [and] a long typewritten argument for the amendment. I am enclosing a revised copy of my political statement. . . . You see Jeannette offered to do this and I am trying to help. We need your skilled pen and her big ideas." Wellington Rankin also had a hand in the publications that went out under Jeannette Rankin's name. In a telegram he reminded her that under the *Herald* contract "you must obtain consent to publish [other] articles," and added, "Glad you will let me see article before publication."

Wellington Rankin was referring to Katharine Anthony's ghosted article that was published in the *Ladies Home Journal* in August 1917. It contained the explanation, "through the courtesy of the *Chicago Herald*, by which she has been engaged to write exclusively a weekly letter." Jeannette Rankin's personal jottings suggest the extent of her participation in one of the *Chicago Herald* pieces that dealt with the "problem of child labor on our city streets." The article described the dangers of "street-roving habits," "using stimulants of various sorts," and "resorting to vice and crime" and suggested the remedy of paying "the little earners the meager amount they can earn in street trades and keep them off the streets." In her handwritten notes, Rankin had provided the following "big ideas" for Belle Fligelman to develop: "Begging—Bad influences—Red Light District—Saloons—Out all night—Business Spirit over developed—Public consciousness—picturesque, 'manly'—shouldn't be content to accept child's support of family—Boot Black—Push Carts—seven days a week, 7 A.M.–9 P.M."

In adapting to the House of Representatives, the first congresswoman— "disadvantaged in terms of seniority" and lacking a "critical mass" of allies—attempted at first to honor the House's expectations, even if they were biased, and blend into its life. She "invited two experienced members to lunch" to discuss securing support for the national woman suffrage amendment. With the assistance of her mother, she hosted Sunday evening suppers at their apartment for "prominent people to come in and talk things over." Characteristic of Jeannette Rankin, each gathering "wasn't so much a social affair as it was talking over what had to be done." On the House floor she downplayed her sex "to deflect the sexual innuendo that was certain to be used to explain the rise of a woman to such high rank." Not wanting to stand out prominently or appear flirtatious, she sat next to a first-term "man from Michigan who had white hair." Rankin recalled, "I never worked any female stuff. . . . I think men are tired of being flirted with, and they knew I never flirted with them."

For reasons other than dress and deportment, Jeannette Rankin and her office gradually earned the reputation of being different. She ignored the advice imparted by House veterans stopping by her office: "Do you know what is the first thing you do in Congress? . . . Begin your campaign for the next election." Despite her protestations of being a neophyte, she knew from lobbying that "the rules of Congress are made with [reelection] in mind" and that she would not play that game. She accented her status as "outsider" and risked further "marginalization" by taking on the role of a loner with a separate agenda. "I was working with myself," she explained. "I commanded myself. . . . I said what I wanted to say." With Wellington Rankin back in Montana, the congresswoman and her staff earned the reputation of being "so on the outside of what we should have been doing." Belle

Fligelman recalled walking one morning in front of the Capitol when Elizabeth Watson, Jeannette Rankin's Heterodoxy friend who had been hired to investigate abuses in the Bureau of Engraving and Printing, "called across. . . . 'Did you read the papers this morning? . . . Isn't it marvelous Russia has rebelled?' And we were so excited; it was the morning that Russia declared no more Tsar. . . . We weren't Communists but we knew there should be a change in government. . . . [I]t was that general attitude that made them call us 'Reds.'"

Jeannette Rankin's maverick nature, if carefully deployed, could have been an advantage in the Sixty-fifth Congress. Republicans in the 1916 House elections had gained ground on Democrats, and "[w]ith such a close division between the major parties, a handful of independents . . . would command special influence." Jeannette Rankin and Fiorello LaGuardia were among the "independents," and she especially, given her unique status and "energy and will to accomplish miracles," became immediately "one of the distinctly potential influences in the House." But disliking partisanship, parliamentary intrigue, and political nuance, she proved not adept at navigating the House's shoals. At the beginning of the session, House Democrats nearly persuaded her to vote for Champ Clark, their candidate for Speaker, but Wellington Rankin's intervention brought her back to political reality: "You have to vote for [James R. Mann, the Republican candidate]," Wellington told Jeannette. "That [is] the only thing to do." She speculated with Harriet Laidlaw that, because of her national reputation, she could be positioned at the center of congressional suffrage politics: "[I]t seems to me it would be a good idea to urge the creation of a Woman's Suffrage Committee in the House. . . . I believe it would be possible for me to be the chairman." The House did establish a special committee on woman suffrage, but a majority party Democrat emerged as its chair after the Republican caucus stopped Rankin's bid to become its leader.

On Jeannette Rankin's legislative agenda was not only suffrage but also the social reforms suffrage would make possible. But World War I soon derailed them. "I have always regretted," she said, "that there was no opportunity for really constructive legislation. There never is in wartime. So many things I was interested in, it was impossible to work on." Her legislative initiatives that fell by the wayside included government ownership and operation of hydroelectric plants; instruction of women in birth control, venereal disease, maternity, and infant care; a fair wage and an eight-hour day for women working in government offices; and U.S. citizenship for women regardless of the citizenship of their husbands. The bill on female and infant hygiene, drafted by Florence Kelley and the Children's Bureau of the Department of Labor, was enacted after Rankin left Congress. The citizenship bill was introduced at the request of Crystal Eastman—poet, Heterodoxy member, "self-proclaimed socialist-feminist," sister of socialist editor Max Eastman, and militant member of the New York City branch of the Congressional Union and Women's Peace Party—who wanted to marry a British citizen and retain her U.S. citizenship. It, too, later became law. Other unsuccessful measures she sponsored aimed at softening the hardships of World War I on soldiers, their families, and farmers. She wanted to relax homesteading requirements for settlers who had gone into the military, provide free use of the mail to military personnel, exempt them from taxes on admission tickets and transportation fares, and make payments to the dependents of soldiers and sailors. Explaining some of these efforts in a telegram to the editor of Wellington Rankin's Havre, Montana, *Promoter,* Jeannette Rankin said, "Am bending every effort toward relief of Montana farmers, appreciating that assistance is necessary if Montana is to make that contribution to the nation's food supply which is necessary to the successful conduct of the war."

Jeannette Rankin's first priority was gaining suffrage for all of the nation's women. Suffrage had "prompted her to run for Congress," and her "special duty" as a member of Congress, she told the *New York Times,* was "to express . . . the point of view of women." In her first East Coast interview, suffrage was the only issue to which she committed herself. Her first formal action, on the day after President Wilson's war speech, was to introduce with ten other members of Congress the national suffrage constitutional amendment. War pressures, however, caused the suffrage coalition to crack. The roots of the fissure ran back to 1912, when Alice Paul created the Women's Congressional Committee within NAWSA and began to champion a federal suffrage amendment instead of Carrie Chapman Catt's series of state suffrage amendments. Rankin was drawn more to Paul than to Catt. Both Rankin and Paul viewed suffrage "as a step forward in women's liberation from all political and social restrictions," and Rankin "liked Alice Paul; they were nearly the same age, both social workers, [and] both graduates of the New York School of Philanthropy." Jeannette Rankin's friend Mary O'Neill was an active member of the Congressional Union, and Rankin herself was "very much amused [at the] fear that the Nationals have of the Congressional Union."

On the morning of April 2, 1917, the day of the special session convened by President Wilson, the two competing suffrage organizations honored Jeannette Rankin at a Shoreham Hotel breakfast. Seated between Carrie Chapman Catt and Alice Paul, Rankin saw "her difficult position in visual and dramatic form." Her hosts differed not only on suffrage but also on war. Paul was a pacifist, and Catt had committed NAWSA to President Wilson's war policy in exchange for his endorsement of the state-by-state suffrage strategy. Later that day, when Rankin entered the floor of the House of Representatives and was introduced to the packed chamber, she appeared to signal her preference between the two organizations by carrying a bouquet of yellow and purple flowers, the colors of the Congressional Union, rather than yellow and white flowers, the colors of NAWSA. Suffragists throughout the nation, however, expected her to take a more definitive stand on the issues dividing the two organizations.

Bringing the controversy to a head were Congressional Union demonstrations near the White House. Jeannette Rankin's failure to denounce the picketers pleased some but infuriated others. Helen Gardener, NAWSA vice-president, wrote to Harriet Laidlaw that "Miss Rankin is losing out every day in public opinion and with the men in the House because she declines to take any stand whatever on the picketing. . . . [It] has gone to the length of being public disorder and is a disgrace to woman suffrage, for the simple reason that the newspapers speak of them all the time as 'the suffragists are doing this and the suffragists are doing that,' and we all get the result of it." Especially angering to Gardener was Rankin's ambivalence: "The newspapers tried to interview Jeannette on the question of whether she approved it or not. She laughed as usual and said, 'I am deaf, dumb and blind on that question!' Now, Mrs. Laidlaw, if she is going to continue to be deaf, dumb and blind on that question she is putting the women of the country in the worst possible light. . . . [The] effect that this lawlessness and stupidity of the Congressional Union is having upon the work here . . . is just as bad as it could possibly be. Can you and Mr. Laidlaw do anything with the Honorable Jeannette? If not, I am afraid that some of the rest of us will have to make a statement that will be decidedly to her detriment."

The Congressional Union's picketing aimed to pressure President Wilson to support the national suffrage amendment. Jeannette Rankin's aide Belle Fligelman recalled, "I used to go down to watch them. . . . They came out of the Congressional Union headquarters at four o'clock every afternoon, dressed in white, carrying banners with quotes from the U.S. Constitution on them, and they walked to the White House with crowds watching them. The police and the 'Paddy Wagons' were waiting for them." A Congressional Union demonstrator from North Dakota gave the press a vivid account of the picketing: "I have . . . seen a police officer laugh while a crowd of hoodlums snatched at me, and a sailor in the uniform of the United States navy doubled up his fist and deliberately struck me in the chest. I have seen a woman who weighed less than 100 pounds knocked down by another sailor in uniform and dragged twenty feet by the ribbon around her neck. . . . I have seen six policemen, a policewoman and a plain clothesman snatch a woman's property from her hands, cruelly twisting her arms as they did so. . . . This was the day Miss Alice Paul, national chairman of the Woman's party, was knocked down three times, though her only fault was to stand quietly on Pennsylvania avenue, with no banner in her hand, and with the only symbol of suffrage, a purple, white and gold ribbon, across her shoulder. . . . Thursday forty policemen appeared in Pennsylvania avenue and Madison place, and themselves did the banner snatching and mistreatment which they had permitted the men to do the day before; 147 banners were destroyed that day. Five women had their arms twisted and their hands scratched and bruised."

By not taking a public stand on the picketing, Jeannette Rankin was hoping to minimize political damage. Like her mail, she was running in two directions. She sympathized with a Milwaukee woman who wrote: "Common decency demands you act immediately in behalf of pickets." Like many members of Heterodoxy who had been "radicalized" by the picketing, she was "friendly to the action of the militants" and quietly visited those jailed at the Occoquan workhouse, some who were her "personal friends." But a Montana woman gave Rankin pause: "I am intensely anxious that . . . you prove yourself above everything else a true American. . . . That woman should push her individual claims and be to any degree a clog or irritant in this time of real peril fills me with shame and regret." Another woman said that she was "ashamed" of the demonstrators "who have been making a spectacle of themselves at the gates of the White House" and warned the congresswoman: "We are watching you Miss Rankin." Her dilemma boiled down to respecting her Montana constituents' conservatism or acting upon her sympathy for the radical suffragists. Caught between conflicting values, she described to her Montana suffrage and Good Government colleague Eleanor Coit her sense of a compromise: "We have been quite excited in the office this morning over the pickets—you know sixteen are in prison. . . . I wrote a note to the President this morning and urged him to work for the federal amendment. . . . I have kept very quiet about the picketing, thinking that it was the best thing to do under the circumstances."

The pressure she was under clearly upset Jeannette Rankin. To the attorney general of Montana she wrote, "I hope . . . you have not met with as many difficulties in your office as I have in mine." To a Missoula woman she confessed, "Things are much harder than I had dreamed they could be before I came to Washington." Near the top of her frustrations was the struggle between herself and NAWSA, the woman suffrage organization with which she had long labored in common cause. Eleanor Coit tried to draw out her feelings on the conflict. She acknowledged the "heartaches and difficulties" Rankin must have been experiencing and admitted that her own "feeling of resentment" toward NAWSA "grows and grows." Coit's letter, which also went to Mary O'Neill, continued: "I get letters by the dozen from both Mrs. Catt and now Mrs. Maud Wood Park about this, that and the other that Mrs. Catt, Mrs. Park, and the rest of the SELECT do, but never a word about you, the most prominent woman in the whole world today. . . . Can it be possible they are the arrogant, egotistical persons they appear, and are jealous of any power that does not come through their 'divine right of rule'?" In a separate letter that went just to Jeannette Rankin, Coit wrote more intimately: "I really am boiling over the way the Nationals treat you. . . . Perhaps it is all personal feeling on my part, because you are to a certain extent my very own. . . . I do not think they are half giving you a chance to do what you might. . . . I hope you will feel you can tell me what you think about it, and I shall treat what you say as confidential."

Responding to Eleanor Coit's "sweet letter," Jeannette Rankin first restrained herself regarding the NAWSA leaders: "[W]e all love to have those we have a grudge against called down. I have been very much amused at the actions of some of the people here . . . although my sister, Hattie, has been on her high horse a good many times." Then, unable to resist the urge to vent her anger, Rankin climbed up next to her sister: "I could tell you so many things but they seem so hard when I write them. . . . I would not mind their ignoring me, but it does make me furious when they act as though I didn't have sense enough to be out alone." What especially bothered Rankin was that "the Nationals" were ignoring the advice of the first congresswoman on how to move the suffrage amendment through Congress. She had been plotting strategy with Congressman James R. Mann, the minority leader in the House of Representatives. As Rankin told Coit, "Mr. Mann told me that he would do all he could to help me with the suffrage amendment and the people you refer to keep trying to make me think that he is simply putting me in a trap." Her first term had quickly become very tiring to Jeannette Rankin, who always pushed the limits of her endurance. She ended her letter to Coit with an admission of burdens and worries and said, "I am going to take a little time off this afternoon to see if I can be ready for work next week."

Jeannette Rankin's big moment in the congressional suffrage fight did not come until January 10, 1918, when she presented her only formal remarks on suffrage in the House of Representatives. It was not, however, her first speech in Congress. That came on May 28, 1917, when she offered an amendment to an agricultural bill that urged the government to employ women in the war work of food conservation. In the three-minute speech, "braced . . . upon the back of the preceding row of chairs," Rankin used her New York education and Jane Addams's housekeeping trope to argue that women were naturally suited to preventing waste: "And when these activities are so closely related to the home . . . women are especially well fitted by their training and experience. . . . Women as housekeepers must learn to think of food in carload lots, in transit, in storage, in the board of trade, and in the national markets as well as in the small portions on the family table. . . . Our higher educational institutions have been turning out a large body of women who are trained to deal with fundamentals from a scientific standpoint. . . . Food conservation on a national scale is but the natural outgrowth of woman's traditional work." The speech, coming seven weeks after her vote against war, was well received and successful. The United Press referred to the "stir on the floor as she rose" to speak and the "vociferous applause" and favorable vote she received. An Atlanta newspaper said that the House of Representatives gave "a significant parliamentary reception [to the] first woman's voice ever lifted in the Congress." Despite the reservations of her NAWSA detractors, there was no reason to believe that Jeannette Rankin's colleagues would be any less open to her suffrage speech eight months later.

Jeannette Rankin knew well the historic nature of her suffrage speech and prepared accordingly. Belle Fligelman had labored over the text "for months," and Rankin "had rehearsed it." For the special occasion, she ordered from New York a $75 brown silk dress (about $1,300 today). To Eleanor Coit she confided her sense of moment: "The New York election has had a great influence on some of the recalcitrant Members of Congress, and conditions generally have helped to turn the tide. . . . [H]owever, I don't think we shall have any votes to spare. The Suffrage Committee of the House, of which I am a member, has been holding hearings for the last several days, and I cannot tell you how impatient it makes me, and how absurd it seems after having voted myself, to hear women still pleading for the right to vote. . . . Thursday is the big day for me. . . . It thrills me to think it may be my only suffrage speech ever made in the House. And I feel a very solemn responsibility about it, too." In her earlier food conservation speech, she had argued women's suitability for war work. Wellington Rankin had responded enthusiastically: "Congratulations your success with amendment. It is work of that kind that will do more to prevent revolt in Montana than anything else, something to lead the women to some service [during the] present war. . . . [S]omething to show that you are going to assist not hinder in preparation for war." Encouraged by the response to her first speech, she returned to pragmatic and patriotic themes in her suffrage remarks.

The pragmatic part focused on women and social evolution. The New York School of Philanthropy had taught that society was in the process of improving itself. Edward T. Devine, who directed the New York School just before Jeannette Rankin's arrival, saw as a "not too distant goal" a society where "heredity and environment shall be joined in a holy wedlock of which high physical and moral character shall be the offspring." In her speech, she argued that "we are facing today a question of political evolution" and, with woman suffrage factored in, "universal justice" was a possibility. It was evident, she explained, that society was stalled without the participation of women. Despite the efforts of men, "something is still lacking. . . . Might it not be that the men who have spent their lives thinking in terms of commercial profit find it hard to adjust themselves to thinking in terms of human needs? Might it not be that a great force that has always been thinking in terms of human needs, and that always will think in terms of human needs, has not been mobilized? Is it not possible that the women of the country have something of value to give the Nation at this time? It would be strange indeed if the women of this country through all these years had not developed an intelligence, a feeling, a spiritual force peculiar to themselves, which they hold in readiness to give to the world." Next she sounded her patriotic theme. She openly used the war she had voted against as ammunition for suffrage. How ironic it is, she pointed out, that democracy is "our national religion," that the nation is fighting for democracy elsewhere, that women are making sacrifices for the war effort, and that they lack "a voice in their own government." In her conclusion she asked, "[H]ow shall we explain . . . the meaning of democracy" to Americans who are "giving their all for the cause of democracy" and to foreigners fighting for democracy "if the same Congress that voted for war to make the world safe for democracy refuses to give this small measure of democracy to the women of our country?"

Jeannette Rankin's suffrage speech in Congress, just like her speeches in the state suffrage campaigns, relied on racist and nativist arguments. Directing her attention to the South, the "section of the country [that] seemed unwilling to budge" on suffrage, she tried to convince southern congressmen that the white vote produced by woman suffrage would outweigh the expanded black vote: "Are you gentlemen representing the South, you who have struggled with your negro problem for half a century, going to retaliate after fifty years for the injustice you believe was done you so long ago? . . . The women of the South have stood by you through every trial. . . . Are you going to deny them the equipment with which to help you effectively simply because the enfranchisement of a child-race fifty years ago brought you a problem you were powerless to handle? There are more white women of voting age in the South today than there are negro men and women together."

Jeannette Rankin's suffrage speech did not carry the day in 1918. Needing a two-thirds majority, the proposed amendment passed the House by one vote but failed in the Senate by two votes. After she left Congress in 1919, both chambers passed the amendment and sent it to the states for ratification. But Rankin's politicking in 1918 might have closed the gap a bit, as it seemed to in several anecdotes she was fond of telling. One story had Representative James Mann, the Republican floor leader, asking her about Mrs. Catt and the suffrage amendment. After Rankin replied, Mann said, "You and I will put through this woman's suffrage." Mann was later hospitalized, but he came to the floor at the time of the suffrage vote, Rankin said, "looking just like death. . . . [W]hen the House saw him they rose in a body . . . and applauded, and the tears were running down so many of the cheeks and mine. . . . [H]e knew it would take his vote to put it through." Another of Jeannette Rankin's allies was Joe Walsh, a senior Republican representative "violently opposed to woman suffrage" but also her "best friend." "I always sat back of him," Rankin said, "so that he couldn't see me, and I wouldn't be a thorn in his flesh." For the Republicans, Joe Walsh was an effective floor fighter. Rankin recalled how "every time the Democrats did an irregular thing . . . he'd get up and stop them, by objecting." To turn him around on suffrage, she went to his district and told his constituents that, although an "able man . . . he isn't for woman's suffrage." Walsh thanked Rankin "for saying such nice things about him," and she replied, "I'm not asking you to vote for [suffrage]. But I am asking you not to make a speech against it." Walsh went beyond not speaking against suffrage. He told suffrage supporters, "If you change your vote, I'll change mine." Another story, not of Jeannette Rankin's telling, featured one of her antagonists. At a hearing on suffrage, she rebutted the argument that citizenship's privileges should be denied if a citizen can't perform every duty with the observation that men can serve in the Senate even if they can't serve in the army. One senator, however, insulted her with the "stereotype of women as weepy wimps who don't belong in the business of serious affairs." He told her that the "two most important personal duties of citizenship are military service and sheriff service, neither of which a woman is capable of performing. . . . If an outlaw must be arrested, are you going to order a woman to get a gun and come with you on such an errand? If you did, she would sit down and cry."

While one of these anecdotes depicted Jeannette Rankin and other members of Congress crying at the suffrage vote, she adamantly denied that she cried during the vote on World War I. But she did cry, as both male and female politicians have cried at critical moments since. Belle Fligelman said that she was "sure [that Jeannette Rankin] was weeping" on the House floor during the after-midnight roll call. Fligelman also remembered that she was weeping when she arrived home several hours later, having walked with Wellington Rankin from the Capitol to California Street in the April early morning: "I remember hearing them come in the door and Jeannette was definitely weeping at the time." Given Jeannette Rankin's wrenching decision, her tears were understandable. But as the years went by, the details of her 1917 war vote became reconfigured in her mind. In 1938, when Metro-Goldwyn-Mayer was filming a movie with a scene showing Jeannette Rankin voting against war, she required the studio to use two fictions. She insisted that she be shown "not in tears" and that her statement accompanying her vote be "I want to stand by my country but I cannot vote for war. I vote NO." In contrast, a contemporaneous account in the *Washington Times* had Rankin omitting an explicit negative on war: "Her appearance was of a woman on the verge of a nervous breakdown. She clutched at her throat repeatedly. Her hands were alternately wrapped around each other. She sat upright, then dropped forward in her seat. Occasionally she threw back her head and looked fixedly at the white lights shining through the stained glass ceiling of the house of representatives. She stroked her head tiredly. . . . Slowly Miss Rankin arose to her feet. . . . Every eye in the chamber was fixed upon her. There was no sound. As she came fully to a standing posture Miss Rankin threw back her head and looked straight ahead. Her hands groped for the back of the seat before her; they found it, and she gripped it hurriedly, nervously. 'I want to stand by my country, but I cannot vote for war,' she said. . . . A score of men called upon Miss Rankin to answer 'aye' or 'no,' not understanding that she intended to vote 'no' without actually using the word."

It is understandable why Jeannette Rankin voted obliquely against war. All of the important influences in her life were pressed upon her, not in unison but as opposing forces. She was put, said Harriet Laidlaw, under "the most terrible strain . . . one of the most terrible mental struggles any woman ever had." Belle Fligelman recalled that Jeannette Rankin "really didn't know when she got into the congressional hall which way she was going to vote." Wellington Rankin—her only brother, surrogate father, political adviser, financial angel, and expert trial attorney—came to Washington to secure a vote for war. His fear was that a negative vote would "destroy" her politically. Summing up his argument, he told her, "After the vote there'll be nothing." That his appeal weighed on Jeannette Rankin is evident from her admission: "I knew that being the first woman in Congress I would have a chance to fulfill almost any ambition." Wellington Rankin enlisted the assistance of Harriet and James Laidlaw, who "pleaded with her not to betray the cause of suffrage." This argument, too, reached Jeannette Rankin. The "hardest part of the vote," she said, "was the fact that the suffragists were divided, and many of my beloved friends said that you will ruin the suffrage movement if you vote against war." From Montana, her friend Eleanor Coit argued in a telegram that fundamental American values were at stake: "We cannot be a free nation if we submit longer to violation of the rights of our individual citizen. This German order challenges civilization." Such evils concerned Jeannette Rankin, but unresolved in her mind was the right response to the "horror of war" by women's first and only representative.

Jeannette Rankin resolved her dilemma by acting as a feminist and not as a pacifist. The "pressure might have pushed me in," she said, "if I hadn't realized that the first woman had to take the first stand" on war. A former associate director of the New York School of Philanthropy understood the symbolism. She wrote to Rankin: "[I]t would have been so much better and easier for you if two or more women had been the inaugurating element of our sex. . . . The responsibility would have been divided and you would not have stood for womanhood, but only for Miss Rankin." But Jeannette Rankin did not think she was standing completely alone. Her allies came from the quarter that most inspired and comforted her. From New York, Nina Swinnerton sent the encouragement of Rankin's Greenwich Village soul mates: "Jeannette Dear, don't sell us out as Mrs. Catt and all the rest of them have done. We count on you to vote for peace." Just before the vote in the House, Alice Paul "called her out from the floor to ask her to oppose the resolution." A Montana woman who supported the war also appreciated her struggle: "What I really want to convey to you is that while I earnestly believe in the righteousness of our cause in this war, I am indeed thankful that the first Congresswoman had the insight and stability to vote against war. This would sound paradoxical to some, but I think you understand." Jeannette Rankin did understand, as she wrote to a New York supporter: "I thought I must vote as I did in order to make a protest against war for the women of the future."

In the following months the symbolic nature of Jeannette Rankin's antiwar vote became clearer. She heeded the *Christian Science Monitor*'s advice to use "other opportunities perhaps equally golden" to prove that she was "clear and firm on the right side." Ill with ptomaine poisoning and against the advice of a doctor, she left her sick bed and went to the House floor to vote for war against Austria. Writing to California radical Charlotte Anita Whitney, she rationalized the army's disruption of a draft-protest meeting as "a logical result of war." She spoke for the Liberty Loan campaign and Red Cross fund drives. At a Fourth of July celebration, she argued that the United States was not only "fighting for our own freedom but for freedom and justice for others." With the argument that she was representing womanhood and not opposing war, she tried to patch over her differences with Wellington Rankin. She told him that her vote had come from her very being as a woman: "[It] was the only way I could go." He tried to make amends by repenting of his heavy-handed tactics: "[T]he only one that did her any harm was myself." But on subsequent issues, when she tried to steer by her ideals, he was no less forceful in trying to make her see the practical side. Conscription was such an issue.

Two weeks after the war vote, Jeannette Rankin sent a telegram to Wellington Rankin about her opposition to conscription. "The more study given the draft bill," she told him, "the more it appears to be undemocratic and unnecessary. I shall consider it very carefully and vote my conviction regardless of future of political life." Wellington immediately sent a biting reply: "Vote your conviction but let your conviction be right not sickly. A vote against president's conscription is morally wrong and a vote to slaughter the volunteer. More American lives will be lost without conscription and many of us expecting to be at front will need assistance. . . . Realize that war has been declared and how unstatesmanlike and anarchistic a vote against the country actually is and fifty years hence it will be so regarded. . . . We are in war. No need to hold back. A vote against [conscription] will and should be condemned hundred times more than vote against war." This time Jeannette Rankin found a way to follow her brother's advice. She voted for a committee conscription bill—not President Wilson's—which exempted nineteen- and twenty-year-olds from the draft and authorized draftees to join "territorial units" and take appeals to "civilian tribunals." To justify the measure, she relied on the scientific education she had received at the New York School of Philanthropy. A Washington newspaper reported, "Manifesting an active interest in legislation for the first time since she came to Congress, Miss Jeannette Rankin . . . is urging that the young unmarried men of the nation be withheld from the army in order that the mothers of the next few years will not have to pick their mates from the old men, the feeble and the worst of the race." While eugenics motivated Jeannette Rankin, Wellington Rankin's main concern in his congratulatory telegram was reelection: "Very happy you voted for conscription. . . . Feel thousand pounds lighter."

Other war problems that drew upon Jeannette Rankin's time and energy were civil liberties, taxes, food conservation, and troop conditions. She generally accepted the war as a given and worked to ameliorate its impact. She voted, however, against the Espionage Act, supported "the freest circulation possible" of the socialist publications *The American Socialist* and *The Masses*, warned that Columbia's dismissal of two pacifist trustees would lead to a nation of "dullards," and voted against the Postal Revenue Bill that would have taxed magazines according to the distance they were mailed. She was a consistent advocate of taxing the wealthy and war profits to pay for the war. To a constituent who argued that "all personal income over $100,000 should be taxed 100 percent, she replied: "You have expressed my sentiments exactly." To another who urged that "individuals with large incomes and corporations, both of which profit by the growth of war industries, be compelled to contribute a large part of their incomes to defray the cost of the war," she responded, "I am absolutely in sympathy with these views." In the same vein she wrote to a constituent, "I assure you that I am heartily in sympathy with the policy of placing the burden of the war on the country's unneeded increment in incomes rather than on industry and the necessities of life."

The issue of food conservation drew from Jeannette Rankin the same class sentiments. Her *Ladies Home Journal* article advocating community meals in public food kitchens and her congressional speech calling for food conservation by the carload instead of by small portions were responses to angry complaints she had been receiving from women throughout the country. Eleanor Coit had written, "The women of Montana are tired and sick of hearing and reading how 'women can and must save the country and world from starving' by conserving the food supply, and economizing, with never a word about the money wasted by men for booze, not to speak of the food used in its manufacture." An outraged Texas woman appreciated Rankin's radical approach to food conservation: "I cannot express to you the feeling of relief it gives me in these troubled times just to know that one woman in Washington can not only speak and write some other message to women than saving crusts. . . . [M]en are urging already overburdened women to do without wheat bread and eat meal to send the best to 'our allies.' And Mrs.

Millionaire wives are gravely telling us how they manage to exist on three-course meals instead of five!"

Jeannette Rankin's involvement in the debate over troop conditions stemmed from humanitarian if not utopian sentiments. Some letters told tragic stories about camp life. A Massachusetts woman informed her of shortages of tents, winter clothing, and hospital space and deaths from pneumonia and measles. A Pennsylvania woman conveyed a rumor of "three soldiers . . . killed attempting to keep 'bootleggers' out of the camp." A sociology student wrote to Rankin several times about troop conditions, addressing her as "a God-made social worker and more than any woman in America the inspiration of the women of America." One of the student's letters was occasioned by a newspaper report that Rankin had discussed with President Wilson "the necessity for establishing good moral surroundings at the cantonments for the new National Army and at the training camps for the Navy." A New York woman encouraged her to "introduce a bill in the House forbidding our soldiers to be on duty more than eight hours—and maybe, another appointing a commission to see to the proper ventilation of the trenches." In her responses to these messages, the congresswoman assured her correspondents that she had urged the president to make "protection of soldiers in the camps" a priority. She suggested to Eleanor Coit that "it might be a good plan for the Montana women to make a thorough study of the conditions surrounding the army camps and to make an intensive campaign for the improvement of those conditions." And with no hint of irony, she replied to the New York woman that "your suggestion in regard to the hours for soldiers in the trenches seems to me a good one. You may be interested to know that when I was in New Zealand last year I learned that the soldiers had protested because afternoon tea was not served in the trenches."

Early in her first term Jeannette Rankin became more concerned with conditions in the Bureau of Engraving and Printing than with those in military camps and trenches. She received a complaint from a Montana woman whose sister worked at the bureau. It prompted Rankin to invite female bureau employees to a Sunday morning meeting in her apartment. What she heard from these "dozens and dozens of girls" sitting on her living-room floor caused her to hire Elizabeth Watson of New York to conduct an investigation. Watson, a Heterodoxy member, had extensive experience in labor controversies. She had joined the Women's Trade Union League, worked as an investigator for the New York Commission on Prison Reform and the National Child Labor Commission, and "testified to the New York Factory Investigating Commission after the Triangle Shirtwaist Factory fire in 1911." Both Rankin and Watson believed that it was the duty of feminist reformers to investigate women's work conditions. Florence Kelley, Rankin's instructor at the New York School of Philanthropy, had been "chief inspector of factories for Illinois" and contributed to Louis Brandeis's brief in *Muller v. Oregon* (1908) that championed a ten-hour day for women. Kelley was committed to "educating college and university students, with the hope of recruiting them to her causes," and Rankin was a willing convert.

A Greenwich Village publication, *The Masses*—edited by Max Eastman, brother of Jeannette Rankin's friend and Heterodoxy member Crystal Eastman—published Elizabeth Watson's findings. The article, Rankin said, was "absolutely true. . . . The hours that the girls were obliged to work and the conditions described in this statement were quite as bad as you would infer from this description." *The Masses* reported that, "of about 3,000 women and girls, 81 percent were working twelve hours or more every day, seven days a week. . . . One girl, whose mother was dying, wanted to leave work at four o'clock on Saturday afternoon; she was denied permission, and only permitted as a great favor to get away at 9:00 P.M. The mother died at 4:00 A.M. Monday morning. Many girls work fourteen, fifteen, and sixteen hours. Workers not reporting for work Sundays were demoted and put on night shifts. Women with children at home requiring their care at night were told to take positions (at reduced wages) in departments not requiring so much overtime. Others were told to resign, and were handed resignation blanks to fill in. The hospital of the Bureau is fitted up with beds, and ambulance tables . . . are wheeled out into the workrooms to pick up workers who have fallen by their machines. . . . Girls helping printers on power presses (making bank notes, Liberty Bonds, etc.) lift their arms 6,000 times in a day of eight hours. Twelve hours of this is exhausting and the accumulative effect of thirteen, fourteen, and fifteen hours drives them to the point of insanity. . . . Overtime work is paid for at the same hourly rate as regular work." Rankin and Watson also discovered that the "head of the department was making improper suggestions and invitations to the girls" and that bureau employees were printing "private calling cards . . . wedding announcements and Christmas cards" for bureau and union officials.

Jeannette Rankin kept Wellington Rankin informed about her "exploit" that had kept Washington in a stir "for a week." In a telegram she told him about the "unspeakable" conditions in the bureau and her intended plan: "Public sentiment aroused. Indisputable official records sufficient to compel congressional investigation. Minority leader and many congressmen back of me. Will probably introduce resolution for investigation Wednesday." Then Jeannette Rankin confronted Treasury Secretary William G. McAdoo with her information and a threat to turn over employees' affidavits to a congressional committee. McAdoo immediately put all bureau employees on an eight-hour schedule and "appointed a committee to make immediately a full, frank and impartial investigation and report." For months after the Treasury's change of course, Rankin maintained an interest in the affairs of the bureau. She pressured McAdoo for a new director and was "gratified . . . upon the appointment of an officer in whose integrity and good faith [she had] full confidence." She "address[ed] a mass meeting of Bureau girls . . . held for the purpose of reorganizing [their] union" and allied herself with the "women employees of the Bureau" in their "protest against the action of the House Appropriations Committee [denying] increased pay to the women employees."

Jeannette Rankin's success at the Bureau of Engraving and Printing put her in great demand. Women were told: "Why don't you go to Miss Rankin . . . she wants to help all women in trouble." One writer implored, "you represent the people of Montana of course, but you are at the same time the sole representative of the women of the entire country." Letters poured in from women seeking her intervention at the U.S. Government Printing Office, Census Bureau, Washington Navy Yard, Post Office Department, and Bureau of Animal Industry. There were requests to improve the working conditions of a "widow charwoman," to help two "diseased" women working at "W. Wallis's Café" in Washington, and to secure higher wages for Butte "girls . . . in the Woolworths store, Casey Candy Company and several other places . . . [trying to keep] body and soul together on a mere pittance." An Indiana woman sought her help in finding "one or more little children to keep . . . or care for, say children of wealthy people who are perhaps dull or backwards and they want to put them away out of the home." Exhausted and exasperated, she wrote to Eleanor Coit that the "Bureau work has just about finished me," and to one supplicant, "Why do you not interest your own Representative to take up the matter."

Jeannette Rankin's success at the bureau did not please everyone. Male employees, numbering "nearly a thousand," adopted a resolution "asking that the eight-hour-day order be rescinded." To an eight-year-old girl who wrote to protest her father's loss of extra pay, Rankin replied: "I think I know just how you feel about your father working overtime and I do not doubt that he is able physically to stand the extra work now. But you must remember that there are other little girls whose fathers cannot stand the overtime and we must protect them." The *Nashville Banner* did not see the congresswoman's deed in that way and depicted her as a brash reformer. The newspaper editorialized that she should have taken time to "find out if the proposed beneficiaries desire help before unsheathing the sword in their behalf."

Jeannette Rankin's rush to do good got her into trouble during the 1917 Butte copper strike. Butte had become "the greatest mining center in the United States," and the Anaconda Copper Mining Company was attempting to corner the world copper market through unrestricted production. A rapid succession of events in Butte engulfed the crusading congresswoman and pitted her against the power of the copper-mining giant. On June 5, a new labor organization, the Metal Mine Workers' Union (MMWU), was formed in response to a "draft registration order that threatened young Irish migrants with having to fight against Ireland." Among its organizers were leaders of the "Pearse-Connolly Irish Independence Club," a local group formed the previous year "whose principles and policies . . . were much like . . . those of the IWW" and whose activities "practically begged . . . American patriots to league [the organization] with a German victory." Patrick Pearse and James Connolly were Irish nationalists, Pearse a poet and Connolly a labor leader. Both had become heroes in Ireland during the Easter Uprising of 1916. The like-minded organizers of the new Butte union included Dan Shovlin, Joe Shannon, and Tom Campbell. Shovlin and Shannon were "IWW and syndicalist inspired radicals." Campbell, a Canadian citizen who had been "in and out of Butte for fifteen or twenty years" and "denied citizenship papers," "admitted to being a member of [the IWW's] propaganda league" and advocated use of "strikes and sabotage."

Four days after the union's founding, Butte experienced the "most overwhelming disaster" in its history, a fire in the Speculator Mine. Of the 415 miners on shift, 164 died "of gas and smoke inhalation" and were found "in front of cement bulkheads that blocked escape to other tunnels." The

MMWU's issues included mine safety along with higher wages and elimination of the "rustling card" used by companies to screen out undesirable workers, but "the Speculator fire precipitated the strike" the new union called on June 11. The strike leaders were "Irish of settled habits . . . established miners" who resisted companies' turning "to new men [who] were cheaper" and "blacklisting the men who had built the city." But the "settled" workers soon threw in with the new men—called "transient hoodlums" and IWW fodder—and the strike spread from the miners to the craft workers.

As the strike events unfolded, Elizabeth Kennedy, writing "at the behest of the strike committee," sought to enlist Jeannette Rankin in the new union's cause. Kennedy, the wife of a mine foreman and president of the Butte Housewives League, sent Rankin newspaper clippings about the mine disaster and labor violence. One story described how Anaconda-backed "automobile loads of gunmen" were "flying about the city, assaulting strikers, who are defenseless and unprotected." Kennedy asked Rankin to secure a government investigation of the mine fire and of the company's refusal to recognize the union. The congresswoman turned to her brother, asking him to "get all facts . . . in regard to labor situation at Butte and send me night letter." Wellington Rankin's same-day response cautioned his sister against believing the union's interpretation of events: "Butte trouble I.W. work. Mining companies no possible way to blame. . . . Could you meet me in Chicago or St. Paul talk things over June 30th."

On the day of Jeannette Rankin's telegram to Wellington Rankin, the MMWU Press Committee sent her a copy of its strike bulletin. The union's "true statement . . . of the causes which led up to the present strike" was directly opposite Wellington Rankin's interpretation. The circular—edited by William Dunne, a radical who had "applauded the Bolshevik Revolution in Russia"—proclaimed: "In this the largest mining camp on earth are gathered as avaricious, subservient and insatiable a group of businessmen as could be assembled [bent on] ruthlessly and brutally crushing all opposition." The union asked Jeannette Rankin to "use your influence with Mr. Wilson the Secretary of Labor to send a representative . . . to investigate." During the following weeks the congresswoman stayed in contact with Elizabeth Kennedy and the MMWU. She sent Kennedy a telegram pledging her assistance, which Kennedy read to "a mass meeting of fully 6,000 men at the baseball park." She reported to the union that she had visited with Samuel Gompers, head of the American Federation of Labor, and W. B.

Wilson, the Secretary of Labor, about an investigation. But because the Department of Labor had already sent an investigator to Butte, Jeannette Rankin seemed ready to close her file on the crisis: "If there is anything else I can do for you, I assure you that any suggestion you make will receive my earnest consideration. . . . [A]ll kind wishes to you for the success of your union."

The MMWU, however, had raised the stakes in its battle with the mining companies. In a telegram responding to Jeannette Rankin's wishing-you-well-in-the-future letter, the union told her that the "[r]ustling card" had become "the main issue" and was a "[s]tumbling block in way of settlement." Hatred of the rustling card stemmed from its use by the Anaconda Company to exclude known or suspected labor radicals from its workforce. The MMWU told Rankin that "the principal object of the card is . . . crushing any attempt of the Miners in the Butte District to organize," and Elizabeth Kennedy explained how would-be workers had to undergo intimidation and investigation in order to get the company's approval to "rustle up" a job. As a strike settlement became more doubtful and tensions increased, Kennedy warned Rankin that the company might be "interfer[ing] with Uncle Sam's postal service" and encouraged her to take "precautions" in her communications.

Beginning in mid-July, the union's principal line to Jeannette Rankin became Mary O'Neill, whom Elizabeth Kennedy referred to as Rankin's "able assistant." O'Neill's goal was to bring Rankin to Butte. A July 14 telegram from O'Neill appealed to the congresswoman's reputation as a labor reformer: "[Y]our friends here believe that if personally present you can bring about a settlement of miners' troubles with companies." On July 16, Thomas Campbell, Dan Shovlin, and other strike leaders complained to Rankin that the Department of Labor investigator was showing "scant consideration to the striking miners" and should be recalled. In a next-day reply to Shovlin and Campbell, Rankin agreed that recall of the investigator was "the logical next step in the solution to this problem." The union's *Strike Bulletin* took the same position, saying that the investigator "laid down" when "the companies informed him that they would not recognize our union, nor abolish the Rustling Card." In a July 26 telegram to Jeannette Rankin, Mary O'Neill heightened her rhetoric: "Crisis in labor situation is here. . . . Practically all miners still out. Any drastic measure likely to bring an open war. . . . Big company grants some concessions but insists on maintaining many objectionable features of rustling card system and black-listing. Miners want you to appeal to President Wilson to invest you with authority to come here and meet with them and see for yourself conditions existing and endeavor to bring about peace between workers and operating companies." Rankin sent O'Neill's telegram to President Wilson and pleaded, "I hope that this will seem so important to you that you will let me talk to you about it at once." To O'Neill Rankin wrote, "Have the miners make their request direct to President Wilson as an added appeal to mine." O'Neill continued to pressure Rankin in a July 28 telegram: "Conditions need immediate action. Miners will agree to suspend strike conditions with you commissioned to make personal settlement. . . . All business dead."

Two days later Mary O'Neill further pressured Jeannette Rankin and advised her to use caution and the appearance of fairness in her communications to Butte: "Just got word operators intend to run leading miners out of town tonight. Gunmen, game wardens, soldiers all ready for the work. . . . If operators take drastic action tonight terrible conditions sure to follow. . . . Secure credentials as advised. If possible cannot be too careful in responding to wires and letters from those involved. Attitude impartial." Heeding Mary O'Neill's advice, Jeannette Rankin turned to Wellington Rankin in two coded telegrams with decoding instructions: "Read telegram first word. Postal second word." Wellington Rankin read the following message: "Mary O'Neill advised me regarding developments of situation in copper camp and requests my presence there to attempt settlement. Conferences with Department labor not satisfactory despite warning that situation demanded immediate procedure. Conciliation commissioner sent out but left without securing concessions for men making demands. Telegram today from one Joe Kennedy describes atrocities and urges protection from here. Am urging federal aid. Will welcome suggestions from you."

Before Wellington Rankin could formulate a response, the MMWU fueled the crisis by scheduling Frank Little to speak at the Butte union hall. Little, a national IWW leader, had declared in Arizona that he cared more about labor solidarity than the war effort. On August 1, vigilantes dragged Little from his boardinghouse and hanged him from a railroad trestle. Suspended around Little's neck was a message that put on notice Jeannette Rankin's union contacts: "L-D-C-S-S-W-T" warned "Bill Dunne, Tom Campbell, Daniel Shovlin, Joe Shannon, John Williams, and John Tomich—

all leaders of the strike"—that they were next. Just days before, Campbell and Shannon had shared the platform with Little when he exhorted an overflowing crowd: "[T]he working man in every trade . . . must rise up as a unit and in a great rebellion overthrow the yoke of the capitalist." Wellington Rankin later discovered that "the company," the object of Little's hatred, was behind the hanging, and agreed with Montana news-papers that the lynching was "a patriotic act." Jeannette Rankin, too, was told that "Little was lynched because the A.C.M. wanted to force the U.S. to intervene . . . to act as a strike breaker." "[S]hocked at [the] turn of events," Jeannette Rankin asked the War Department to use the army to guard the Butte mines. Soldiers were stationed in Butte after "more than 1,000 Pearse-Connollys, resplendent in their 'green sashes,' marched second in line to the red-sashed IWW at the funeral of the murdered IWW radical Frank Little."

After Frank Little's death, Mary O'Neill became more insistent. She told Jeannette Rankin that her "highest duty [was] to come instantly to investi-gate these conditions and methods first hand. . . . You can take the people here into your confidence at a great mass meeting and win cooperation in bringing peace here and power in Congress. . . . My plan demands big courage, big comprehension and close discrimination. . . . It is a tremendous opportunity for even the biggest man in the nation. . . . This is the hour to prove the quality of your courage and your justice. All is ready." Emboldened by her success at the Bureau of Engraving and Printing, Jeannette Rankin nonetheless sought her brother's advice. His reply cautioned about the "vi-sionary" O'Neill and struck a brotherly tone: "Use your own judgment. . . . Do not come if too tired." Before leaving for Butte, Jeannette Rankin intro-duced in the House of Representatives a resolution authorizing the federal government "to provide further for the national security and defense" by taking over and operating the nation's copper mines. Worried that his sister's House remarks would be slanted toward labor, Wellington Rankin dis-patched a telegram using language that eleven days later ran through Jeannette Rankin's speech to Butte residents: "Hope you will present Butte situation in non partisan manner if you address House. Present facts that will warrant investigation but do not prejudge. No doubt that the IWW are in some instances endeavoring to harass the government and should be stopped. The capitalist should also pay wages." At the end of her House speech, however, Jeannette Rankin paid her brother no heed: "For some years the Anaconda Copper Mining Company has been using what is called in Butte the 'rustling-card system.' . . . [It] has effectively discouraged the men from organizing . . . prevented them from demanding the enforcement of laws requiring safety devices in the mines. . . . John D. Ryan of New York, the president of the Anaconda Copper Mining Company, is the man responsible for this situation. . . . If Mr. Ryan says the rustling-card system must be abolished, it will be."

When interviewed by the *Washington Times* the next day, Jeannette Rankin continued to disregard Wellington Rankin's caution: "'I think I know perfectly well what the Amalgamated will try to do to me,' Miss Rankin declared, her eyes sparkling and her ready smile showed she rather enjoyed the prospect than otherwise. 'They'll try to do to me just what they have done to everyone who ever tried to oppose them in and out of Montana. They own the State, they own the government. They own the press. . . . [T]hey use political ruin, social ostracism, financial ruin. . . . Years ago they used to put people out of the way that tried to organize the miners. . . . I didn't want to fight the copper crowd. I wanted above and beyond everything else, to get some relief for those poor miners out there. I didn't put my resolution before the House until I had exhausted every other means. . . . I would have preferred John D. Ryan, the president of the company and the man responsible for the awful situation out there, to have answered my appeal to settle this strike as a patriotic duty.'" The Montana press immediately criticized Jeannette Rankin's remarks. The *Great Falls Tribune* accused her of representing "particularly the I.W.W. element in Montana" and derided her telling "Mr. Ryan how he could run his business to the entire satisfaction of the I.W.W." The *Lewistown Democrat-News* found her irresponsible "in seeking to play upon a prejudice which is always more or less strong in this state when she calmly places the blame for the murder of the man, Little, in Butte on John D. Ryan, president of the Anaconda Copper Mining Company." The *Helena Independent* asked her to reconcile her judgment about a bought-and-paid-for state government with the politics practiced by her friend, Sam C. Ford (the Montana Attorney General), and by her brother.

Mary O'Neill and Wellington Rankin reacted differently to Jeannette Rankin's House speech. O'Neill hoped that Rankin had put herself on the path to a showdown with the Anaconda Company. "Prompt action is needed," she telegraphed to the congresswoman. "Ryan coming. It is up to you now." But on the same day Wellington Rankin advised a more moderate approach: "If not too tired you might wire Cornelius Kelley Vice President Anaconda Company Butte telling him you have been invited by number workers to come to Butte to endeavor to adjust strike difficulties with company. Inquire whether company officials will meet with you for purpose adjusting difficulties. . . . If thought you could settle difficulties would want you to come but doubt whether company will abandon rustling. . . . Let me know company's answer in case you wire company." Jeannette responded that she was coming to Montana and wanted Wellington to "join her." He replied, "Will be glad to see you. Let me know when you expect to arrive and will try to meet you somewhere in eastern Montana." After Wellington boarded the Milwaukee before it reached Butte, he wrote the impartial remarks Jeannette gave four days later at the "great mass meeting" organized by O'Neill, sent O'Neill a go-slow message: "Do not under any circumstances have parade or demonstration," and urged his sister to repudiate her remarks to the *Washington Times*. Three days before the Butte speech, Jeannette Rankin told the *Anaconda Standard* that the report that the company was out to get her was "absurd on the face of it" and the rest of the story was "fiction, pure and simple."

Wellington Rankin also blunted Mary O'Neill's influence when the two Rankins arrived in Butte. O'Neill and Tom Campbell had brought Jeannette Rankin to Butte and arranged her schedule. Campbell "headed the reception committee of the Metal Workers' union at the Milwaukee Railroad depot," where "the I.W.W. turned out in full force . . . expecting to participate in a grand parade and a lively demonstration in [Jeannette Rankin's] honor." But the Butte mayor "explained that the parade had been cancelled." O'Neill had "hired and paid for an automobile" for the party, but given the presence of the mayor and police escort, she "had an awful time finding a seat in the car." To O'Neill's further disappointment, the message Jeannette Rankin shouted from the car was Wellington Rankin's and not O'Neill's: "Good Americans must obey the law. There will be no demonstration tonight."

Instead of a rally, a "lengthy conference" on the labor crisis was held the night of Jeannette Rankin's arrival in Butte. Attending besides the Rankins were Mary O'Neill and Burton K. Wheeler, the U.S. Attorney for Montana. Scheduled to join the group was J. Harry Covington, a federal judge "delegated by President Wilson to investigate the so-called I.W.W.

activities in Butte and the northwest." Jeannette Rankin said that she also wanted "to meet the men," meaning Tom Campbell and the other union leaders. Her statement to the press, reflecting Wellington Rankin's presence, was devoid of pro-union or populist language: "So far I have formed no definite opinion, and I am open to conviction until I have heard both sides of the question, and then I will endeavor to judge, fairly and impartially, to the best extent of my ability. I hope to meet officials of the Anaconda Copper Mining Company and leaders of the labor movement, and draw my own conclusions from the opinions of the two opposing factions." Following Wellington Rankin's advice, she had asked the company for a meeting, but Cornelius J. Kelley, an Anaconda Company vice-president, declined the invitation: "The unwarranted attack made by you without investigation upon the Anaconda Company and its officials preclude your being acceptable as mediator or my conferring with you relative to existing troubles."

On August 18, three days after her arrival in Butte, Jeannette Rankin addressed a "standing up" crowd of 6,000 at a ballpark under a threatening storm. On the platform "over the home plate . . . decorated with the national colors" were the "most radical union leaders in Butte" and Jeannette Rankin "dressed in something simple and white." The speakers preceding Rankin included Tom Campbell and William Dunne. Scheduled to speak was James Larkin, who was "prominently connected with the I.W.W.," but at noon on the day of the gathering it "was announced . . . that [Larkin would] not take part in the speaking." An advance text of Rankin's speech was distributed to the press, "from which she departed" to discuss the rustling card. She argued that copper was needed in the "great war" and that business and the union had to compromise in order to get a settlement. Her balanced rhetoric reinforced her theme: "The development of Montana has been accomplished by the combined efforts of capital and labor. . . . I have no patience with that spirit which seeks to destroy property to satisfy personal grievance. . . . Nor have I any patience with that spirit which seeks to destroy the truth by printing false and misleading statements. . . . It is unpatriotic for labor to strike without just cause, but it is equally unpatriotic for capital to take advantage of men when patriotism causes them to continue to work [and risk] their lives." Toward the end of her speech, Jeannette Rankin abandoned Wellington Rankin's text and asked a question dear to Tom Campbell and the other radicals on the platform: "I ask you again, will you be willing for the purpose of settling the troubled conditions, to accept the existing scale of wages and go back to work if the rustling card be abandoned?" The rank and file in the bleachers, however, objected. From them came cries of "No, wages is what we're after." The rift in the union never healed. After the ballpark meeting, "when one of the Metal Mine Workers' leaders advised the strikers to follow [Jeannette Rankin's] suggestion, he was censured."

Satisfied with the day's events, Jeannette Rankin telegraphed her mother in Washington: "Meeting a tremendous success. Biggest meeting ever held in Butte." Tom Campbell did not have the same reaction. He asked the other three members of the Montana congressional delegation by telegram if they would make their "best effort to have the rustling card abolished in Butte provided it means a settlement of controversy." As unsatisfying as Jeannette Rankin's speech was to Campbell, Senator Thomas Walsh's reply was more so: "[T]hough [the rustling card] might be indefensible in ordinary times, it may be indispensable now to keep I.W.W. destructionists and others with treasonable purposes out of the mines, where they might imperil the lives of those therein engaged in honest labor. My counsel to the Butte miners given in earnest and sympathetic concern for their welfare is to disassociate themselves utterly from the I.W.W., whose disloyalty is notorious and almost a matter of boast."

Montana newspapers continued to link the MMWU with the IWW. The union reported in its *Strike Bulletin:* "The companies have made use of every agency they control. . . . [T]heir newspapers . . . have howled 'I.W.W.' since the strike began." Mary O'Neill echoed the MMWU when updating Jeannette Rankin after she returned to Washington, but O'Neill admitted that the union's tie to the IWW had to become less obvious: "You know this I.W.W. howl is only a poisonous cloud. . . . But there is a new scheme on now. . . . The sixth floor [Anaconda Company's headquarters] is to take action as soon as the Canadian conscription goes into effect and get Campbell deported to Canada and put into the trenches in France! I got him into the office today and told him about it and we agreed that we must make arrangements to have the union taken into other hands." Two days later O'Neill told Rankin that the rustling card was still "the chief factor" and that "at a conference here in the office tonight . . . we shall get things lined up pretty well for the beginning of the big struggle. The men are coming so I'll quit."

The Butte strike continued until the end of 1917, but its final stage was marked by declining worker support and not "the big struggle" Mary O'Neill had forecast. Back in Washington, Jeannette Rankin turned her attention to gathering information on mine wages and safety and pressuring President Wilson to have Butte included in the federal investigation of western labor problems his administration was conducting. Her contacts with the MMWU became less frequent, and she was "somewhat embarrassed" when she was caught using inaccurate information in her "daily communication with the White House." She wrote to a union official, "I learned today that the MMWU strike was settled on December 18. I cannot imagine why you did not acquaint me with this fact immediately." She had become so out of the loop that she was forced to admit to Montana's U.S. Attorney, "I, too, cannot understand why the Labor Commission did not stop in Butte." Throughout the Butte labor crisis there was much that Jeannette Rankin did not get right. Well meaning but imprudent, she failed to fashion a solution to a complex problem. The hard fact was that "when the men returned to work, they carried their rustling cards with them." The strike ended, but Montana remembered Jeannette Rankin's association with the IWW. Although she steadfastly maintained, "I have never had dealings with the I.W.W.," the Montana press continued to accuse her of "championing the cause of the I.W.W." The average Montanan, too, bestowed on Jeannette Rankin not the political laurels that Mary O'Neill had promised but a maligned political reputation the Rankin family referred to as "the poison."

Despite the political fallout of her Butte efforts, Jeannette Rankin maintained a letter-writing relationship with Montana voters up to the 1918 election. The correspondence in and out of her office reveals everyday concerns of constituents and routine activities of the first congresswoman. A frequent correspondent was Eleanor Coit who felt free to capitalize on her friendship with the new member of Congress. In a telegram three days after the 1916 election, Coit celebrated Rankin's win as a "signal victory for the cause of women." But Coit was soon asking Rankin to help her in a personal matter. In one letter she sent the intelligence that Big Timber was against Rankin "to a man" after the war vote, but then moved on to her son's situation about which she was "all but frantic": "We have not heard from Robert for almost one month. . . . Can not you take up the matter with the American Ambassador, and find out for me that he is safe?" Two months later Coit continued to lean on Rankin: "Here I am again about Robert.... If we do not do something to get him work of some kind for the war and America, he will enlist; so I am asking you what you can do. . . . A message to the American Ambassador from the Secretary of War would undoubtedly place Robert in line for the position in which he would be of most use to the U.S." Subsequent exchanges showed Rankin as resourceful in serving her friend. She told Coit that she was "taking the matter . . . up at once" and "just had an interview with Secretary of War Baker in reference to a position for Robert. . . . Am now writing a letter to him, which he will refer to General Pershing in Paris, with a letter of his own." Several weeks later Coit told Rankin, "we had a cablegram from Robert yesterday saying 'am with [Pershing's staff].'. . . We feel you are to be thanked for it all." After Rankin's speech in the House of Representatives advocating the hiring of women for food conservation work, Coit asked her to be on the lookout for a good wartime job: "I want to tell you that I am ready to do anything I am fitted for during the war." Jeannette Rankin was as willing to help Eleanor Coit as she was her son: "I am looking for jobs with fat salaries and you may be assured that, as far as I am concerned, you are in line for the very fattest."

Another set of letters Jeannette Rankin received concerned independence for Ireland. She was interested because of the prominence of Irish immigrants in the Butte union and electorate. Her stated reason for addressing the issue was consistency in foreign policy: America's going to war should benefit the oppressed Irish no less than the victims of Germany. In summer 1917, the president of the Butte Pearse-Connolly Club sent her a resolution that called upon the United States to back Irish independence. In her reply Rankin was fully supportive: "I assure you that I am heartily in sympathy with the ideas which you have expressed and I shall take pleasure in doing everything possible to aid this cause. I agree with you that this Government is honor bound to help to preserve democracy in all cases of peoples held in subjection and I regret deeply that our Government has not taken a stand for the independence of Ireland." On January 4, 1918, she introduced a resolution backing "the rights of Irish independence": "Resolved . . . That this Government recognize the right of Ireland to political independence, and that we count Ireland among those countries for whose freedom and democracy we are fighting."

The *Helena Independent* saw the resolution as more disloyalty: "[T]he resolution must be regarded . . . as only a bid for votes and the woman knew very well when she introduced it that it would not be passed, but she wanted to do something more for the Sinn Feiners and the pro-German agents." The Adrian, Michigan, *Daily Telegram* stung the first congresswoman more sharply, accusing her not only of "lacking both in loyalty and in common sense" but also of "moral treason": "Fate tossed a magnificent opportunity into Miss Rankin's lap by placing her in congress at the greatest epoch in history. She was there avowedly as the advance guard of feminism. . . . She had a chance to rise to the stature . . . of a wisely patriotic woman. . . . [Her resolution is] discouraging because of the fact that men expect so much from women in the way of fundamental moral qualities." When Harriet Laidlaw sent Jeannette Rankin suffragists' criticism of her support for Ireland, she responded defensively: "I am writing to tell you that my Irish resolution is only one of six similar resolutions that have been introduced during this session. . . . [The criticism is] simply another instance of the vicious way in which public attention is concentrated on every move of mine. . . . It seems reasonable and consistent to me that we should make no distinction be- tween the rights of small nations which are now subservient to our enemies and those which are subservient to . . . our allies. . . . I am trying with every atom of my being to do the thing which seems to me to be right. . . . I hope that you women will not suffer greatly as a result of the principles I am trying to follow." Rankin was still unapologetic at the end of her term when she noti- fied a Catholic bishop that she had reintroduced her Irish-independence resolution.

Other letters to Jeannette Rankin's office exposed her to religious and racial intolerance. These correspondents gave her the opportunity to com- promise more than her pacifism, but, despite her willingness to use racist and nativist themes in suffrage politics, she resisted sympathizing with the letter writers' biases. Her typical response to the hate mail was "I assure you that this matter has my earnest consideration." The objects of hatred included blacks, Chinese, Catholics, Mormons, and Jews. A Bureau of En- graving and Printing employee asked Rankin to "stop the appointing of so many Negroes into this department. . . . [The director] made the threat that he would employ four colored to each white person [and] the Negroes have been swarming like bees ever since. . . . It is very hard for us girls, especially those of us of the South, to be compelled to work beside a Negro and to stand by and see each day places in the Bureau filled by the colored race that some worthy white girl on the eligible list at the Civil Service Commission would

be glad to have as it is rightfully hers. It is also a bitter dose for the Protes-
tants of the force to take a back seat and see the Roman Catholics handed the
fat jobs in I might safely say eight cases out of every ten." A Government
Printing Office worker sent similar observations: "There are many colored
women in the employ of these two Bureaus and they are husky enough to do
all kinds of work that would be a hardship to white women. . . . I have never
known a Roman Catholic in power who didn't drive his employees like
slaves." A state of Washington resident asked Rankin to confirm that eight
of ten cabinet officers were "Romanist." Several Montana unions decried
"coolie labor": "[T]here are things that should be talked of at home, though
not published, such as if we do not put a stop to this war, why the yellow
races would step in and take our country." Anti-Catholic bigots sought help
for women "subject to the rapings of priestly satyrs at all hours"; warned
that the "Roman Catholic situation [is] one of the greatest perils to our
public schools and our nation"; and revealed that "Jesuit power" controlled
Congress, the nation's newspapers, and women's clubs. Mormons were
equally despised: "no man or woman who goes through the Salt Lake temple
and takes that oath of treason against the government is fit to have a franchise. . . . [T]he Mormon 'church' should be wiped completely off the map."
Anti-Semitism was no less spiteful: "[I]t is high time some Gentile scribe
unloaded Something on the subtle, hypnotizing, 'Thus saith the lord' type
of Jewish scribe and the ubiquitous Jewish financier. They are the busy
breeders of . . . 'Black Internationalism.'" Although Jeannette Rankin did
not censure the bigotry and routinely ridiculed organized religion, she later
sympathized with the civil rights cause. In her old age she said that she had
always been concerned about the plight of American Indians and was proud
of sharing a room in Paris in 1919 with the head of the National Association
of Colored Women. She told an interviewer: "[W]e had a colored woman in
our party, Mary Church Terrell—a very able, beautiful woman—and when
we got to Paris [Jane Addams] put me in the room with . . . Terrell, and
[Addams] was quite disappointed at some of the women who didn't want
her."

Some of the correspondence Jeannette Rankin received was in response
to the June 6, 1917, "circular letter" she mailed to her constituents. Although
her stated goal was to share useful information about canning and baking
("I know you . . . will be interested in the bulletins I am sending you"), she
also wanted to detract attention from her war vote. Wellington Rankin had

urged her "to show that you are going to assist not hinder in preparation for war," and in the circular she called attention to her efforts to further the war effort ("we are anxiously doing what we can to help with the war"). She also planted doubt about the veracity of her newspaper critics: "No doubt you have read in the papers about my 'red hair' and 'sending the fathers to war' and other inventions of the eastern press. I wish you were here to . . . know the true facts." The circular was addressed "Dear Friend," but its text made it clear that her intended audience was the women of her district: "[W]e must not forget that the homes we are fighting to protect and the children . . . need the attention of every woman." The tone she tried to strike was personal. Several times she invited her audience to stay in touch with her: "[F]eel perfectly free to call upon me whenever I can be of the slightest service to you. . . . I wish you would find a moment to write to me."

Many women responded to the first circular. They "believed that [Jeannette Rankin] had written personally to them," and their messages demonstrated that her letter rekindled their support and uncovered a hidden reservoir "of opinion, concern, anger, and bitterness." One woman must have heartened Rankin by her tale that at "eight months pregnant . . . she rode fourteen miles on a cold windy day to vote for her and . . . would do it again gladly." But another woman's story of home life on the eastern Montana plains must have greatly frustrated the "special representative" of women. "Dear Friend," Jessie Nakken wrote, borrowing the salutation Jeannette Rankin had used in her circular. Nakken's tragic story could not have belied more Rankin's sense of a woman's proper role in the home. "Glad to here of you," Jessie Nakken began, "for I was wishing to know where to write to you and impose upon you with a number of questions. Yes the war is quite bad but I have so much to think of at home. . . . I was 26 years when I was married and my husband 25. . . . [H]e appeared to me such a kind hearted man and pleasant. . . . [H]e told me he did not drink or chew, which he did boath. But that is not our main trouble. . . . [F]irst night of our married life . . . he picked up my hand bag . . . and said you wont need that any more. [A] married woman has no business with a pocket book. . . . [H]e did not sware at me till five month after we were married. I told him I beleaved I was in family way. Oh how he cursed at me and said he supposed I would be sickly and he would have to spend on me. [H]e called me an old bitch hore and everything. . . . All I knew of married life was what he told me so he used me rough first six years of our married life. I had to let him—14 to 20 times a weak. Couldn't stand it. I got poor waighing around 100 lbs wher my weight was 137 lbs to 140 lbs before married. [W]hen I would feel worst he would be rougher. . . . We will be married 10 years. . . . [O]ur boy is 8 years old. . . . [O]ur little girl died. . . . I have had no miscarriages but I had operations 3 years ago female trouble and I was not allowed to take care of myselfe as I should and I am in worse condition then before. . . . [M]y glasses kneed changing. I have been chewing with out teath for several years and I kneed care in other ways and he puts me off from fall to fall. [H]e spends mainly the yeare round for beer and a lot but all ways tell me I can do without. . . . [W]e are on a claim 320 acres and good crops. We have the horses in good condition 8 be & 1 cow 4 pigs and 5 chickens. I am not alowed any chicken feed or I would sell and care for myself. . . . I left him once because he got to taking me every day or so and so rough. [H]e is a large man and can hit hard 220 lbs. [H]e promised to be good to me and for the sake of the child I came back. . . . [L]ast winter he commenced to kick me again. . . . What do you think if I do go to Plentywood to get a divorse he will buy them off and these batchelors of his neighbors will tell any thing he says them to. . . . I would loose my boy. . . . [Do] you think I could keep my boy and get enough money to support myself and boy. . . . I am going to sell soap and face cream for a little money and if things were quite here I could crochet but so much cursing. . . . I beleave I could make a living raising chickens and crocheting and tatting. . . . Please do not address your answer to me but to my brother. [O]ur claims join his."

Jeannette Rankin's reaction to Jessie Nakken's tragic story can easily be imagined. As a social worker and the first congresswoman who had publicly advocated women's rights, child protection, female hygiene, and woman's special role but had personally rejected a life with a man, she must have felt outraged and vindicated by her constituent's plight. A greater distance between two women's worlds is hard to imagine: one totally powerless and the other empowered to an unprecedented degree. But the resources provided by the narrow scope of early twentieth-century government limited Jeannette Rankin's response. Her socialist and utopian leanings toward an array of government agencies and programs availed her not at all. Her greatest resources were her campaigning, fame, and brother. She could afford an investigator to look into the problems of women in the Bureau of Engraving and Printing and find wartime employment for Eleanor

Coit and her son, but she could do little for Jessie Nakken. Her frustration is evident in the goodwill but ineffectualness of her reply: "I have read your long letter and wish you to know that I sympathize deeply with you in your troubles and hope that it will be possible for me to be of assistance to you. Were you thinking of filing on a homestead for yourself or of taking part of your husband's farm? If you had a part of the homestead that you and your husband are now living on could you make a living raising chickens? I shall appreciate it greatly if you will write to me about this and will tell me just what you want to do." Jessie Nakken's tale of abuse on a Montana homestead highlights Jeannette Rankin's actions as the first congresswoman. By concentrating on incremental gains rather than radical solutions, Jeannette Rankin possibly could have moved the nation toward her vision of a government that could help women like Jessie Nakken.

Another tale of prairie challenge and frontier spirit so impressed Jeannette Rankin that she couldn't resist identifying with her constituent. Mrs. C. D. Carlson, in response to the government's call for food conservation, wrote to Rankin: "Saving is easy, that comes natural, but raising more is difficult for us and most everyone else around here. We have only four horses, two of them are ponies and one of the others got in the wire last fall and won't be as strong as he used to be. We have only fifteen acres broke on our homestead yet. . . . The sod is so firm and hard that the horses can't stand it very long at a time on the breaking plow and this spring it will be harder because we have no grain to feed them. Our oats last year didn't even head out. Oats is $3.75 a hundred pounds. We haven't money to buy oats or anything else for that matter. Our total income from April 1917 to date was $303.22. Can't buy another horse for they want $175 for just a small gelding and we have our last years debts for next fall. . . . No use putting in a crop unless its fenced, ranch horses eat it all up. . . . All the planning in the world won't keep the rust away (1916) nor the drought (1917). We have been planning and saving to get a tractor but we are no nearer getting it now than when we first came, two years ago, and they're going up in price right along. If we don't get a crop this fall we'll have to sell our cows and go. . . . About all we have is time. . . . As soon as the snow goes, I'll take baby in the children's wagon and we'll go out to poison gophers, while husband ['doesn't use tobacco nor is he a boozer'] digs and hauls off rock until the frost is out of the ground. I want to raise a big garden but its so discouraging trying to have anything, the gophers are so thick. I have six turkey hens. Will tend them very carefully to raise as many as I can. Can't raise many chickens for we haven't much feed. The turkeys can live on grasshoppers, green oats and clabbered milk. This will be my part to help win the war." To this homestead wife and other farmers hurt by the drought of 1917, Jeannette Rankin wrote that she was working to provide them grain for feed and seed. But in her reply to Mrs. Carlson, she went further: "[H]ow much I appreciate . . . letters from women living on homesteads and I think I understand many of the hardships they have to overcome. I was born on a ranch near Missoula, Montana, and know some-thing about the problems of the farmer." The privileged nature of Jeannette Rankin's life, however, distanced her from both the struggle of Mrs. Carlson and the tragedy of Jessie Nakken.

The tensions between Jeannette Rankin's several worlds got in the way of her return to Congress. Her East Coast radicalism mixed poorly with the individualism of her home state. Montana's Mrs. Carlsons had little pa-tience with "the poison" produced by Jeannette Rankin's association with labor and farm radicals. Her constituents had sent her on a historic mission to Washington but now "hoped [she] wouldn't come back to Montana." She left Congress with more than a ruined political career. She took with her a notoriety for her antiwar vote. Her constituents were willing to overlook it, but Jeannette Rankin never allowed anyone to forget it. Joan Hoff Wilson has observed that Rankin's "vote against World War I . . . became part of her persona. . . . [Her] original opposition to World War I became a raison d'être for the rest of her career." After she was denied reelection, her feminism and pacifism blended and she became a single-minded crusader against war. Her deepening pacifism appeared in "congratulations" she sent to a col-league in 1918 who had been "chosen a member of the Peace Commission." "There is a large group of people in every country," Rankin wrote to Con-gressman Henry White, "many of them women, who are convinced that there will always be war as long as we have secret international rela-tions and governments are used to protect special economic privileges. . . . From what I can ascertain, it seems there is a possibility of this Peace Conference being made up on the assumption that the world is inhab-ited by men and men only, so may I plead with you, as one member, to keep in mind that there are women in the world and that they have an interest in the world's affairs." For the rest of her life, especially in Congress during her second term, Jeannette Rankin proclaimed that she was a woman who wanted to be heard on war. Her message was that men should be rejected for their centuries of war-making and women should be embraced for their inherent pacifism.

Second Term

Women and War

THE FIGHT AGAINST WAR JEANNETTE RANKIN HAD BEEN WAGING FOR TWENTY years reached its climax in 1941. Sent to Congress for the second time, she confronted for the second time—but quite differently—the war plans of a U.S. president. In 1916 she had presented herself to voters as a symbol of woman suffrage. In 1940 she campaigned for Congress as an absolute pacifist. In her first term, war had surprised her and thwarted her legislative plans. In her second term, stopping a war that had long obsessed her was her only goal. It is not that Jeannette Rankin lacked pacifist sentiments in 1917. Childhood tales of violence had stirred up antiwar feelings, and two strong women—Minnie Reynolds and Jane Addams—had nurtured a nascent opposition to war. But Jeannette Rankin's first-term pacifism was preliminary and easily set aside because of her desire for reelection. Her antiwar philosophy did not mature until the ruin of World War I battlefields shocked her, British sociologist Benjamin Kidd's woman-based theory of pacifism inspired her, and antiwar politics became her identity. By the time of Pearl Harbor, all doubt about opposing war had vanished. Her negative vote on World War II was unwavering and without regret: "[N]o one could bring any pressure on me because I knew what I was going to do. And so it was very simple, at last."

In a late-in-life reflection on her vote against World War I, Jeannette Rankin said that two childhood stories "shaped [her] thinking about the stupidity and cruelty of force and the power of non-violence." One depicted U.S. soldiers massacring Indians moving to a new hunting ground. The other featured a courageous woman's simple act of diplomacy—inviting an Indian warrior to hold her baby—to forestall violence against settlers. Rankin's early memories of warring men and a pacifying woman were reinforced by her father and Minnie Reynolds. John Rankin, she recalled, "always made fun of the army" because "they were too stupid for words." Wellington Rankin, however, remembered their father as Jeannette Rankin would later see other men: ready to fight "at the drop of a hat," and thought that his own pugilism—not his sister's pacifism—was his father's legacy. More clearly influencing Jeannette Rankin's opposition to war was her mentor during the Washington suffrage campaign, Minnie Reynolds. She taught Rankin the essential difference between men and women: "[W]omen produce the boys and the men take them off and kill them in war."

Jane Addams, because of her reasoned pacifism and personal attention, left an even deeper impression on Jeannette Rankin. From Addams's writings, the young woman borrowed several ideas about war that she freely used thereafter: war was "a wasteful and ineffective method of solving social problems," and war would eventually be overcome because "in the progress of society sentiments and opinions have come first, then habits of action, and lastly moral codes and institutions." Addams's attraction to Rankin was evident in 1919 when the international peace activist and former congresswoman attended the Women's International Conference for Permanent Peace in Zurich and toured battlefields in France, a sight Rankin "could hardly face." During her life, Addams was "passionately involved" with several women and showed a special interest in the younger Rankin. In Zurich, Rankin said, "Miss Addams was wonderful to me. . . . She used to have me sit next to her at her table. I think I didn't sit well with the thirty other women at the meeting. When she had callers she always had someone with her, and she always took me. . . . Those were wonderful times." So taken was Rankin that she said "she most admired [Addams] . . .

of all the people she had ever known." Addams had a similar effect on Florence Kelley at Hull House, where "Kelley sat beside Addams at the evening meal—an important daily ritual where Addams presided." Kelley's judgment was similar to that of Rankin: Addams "was a truly great woman" whose mind had "more floor space in it than any other I have known."

An even more significant influence on Jeannette Rankin's pacifism was British author Benjamin Kidd. Reflecting as an elderly woman on the intellectual underpinnings of her life, Rankin said that the Cambridge scholar's *The Science of Power* (1918) was the "most important book" she had ever read. Like other feminists exposing the fraudulence of men (Charlotte Perkins Gilman, for example, had "strongly criticized the 'man-made world' for its aggression, competition, and destruction of female values of peace, cooperation, and life giving"), Rankin said that *The Science of Power* was "the only thing in this man-made world that indicates that women have anything to contribute to our social organization." At the New York School of Philanthropy she had read Kidd's earlier book, *Social Evolution* (1898). It reinforced Jane Addams's and the New York School's message that a more advanced human race was in the process of evolving from "a holy wedlock of . . . heredity and environment." What she especially liked about *Social Evolution* was its argument that "things can change, and that the evolution of the human race was different. . . . [W]e had the power to do things." Kidd's other book, *The Science of Power,* published after Rankin's vote against World War I, built upon his evolutionary theory by arguing that women were the primary agents of social change.

The Science of Power substantiated what Jeannette Rankin had taken away from the childhood story of the brave settler woman protecting her family. She told a national television audience in 1972: "Benjamin Kidd says . . . men like force [and] women have more experience with human relations." Given her regard for Kidd, a supporter's judgment that she embodied the author's highly evolved woman must have pleased her: "[Y]ou seem really to epitomize . . . in one personality what Kidd is driving at for a coming generation of women who will allow the emotion of the peace ideal to totally possess them." After Rankin left Washington in 1943 and before Wellington Rankin quashed her plans to run for Congress in 1944, she commissioned an article-size condensation of *The Science of Power* and mailed it to her backers across the United States. Faced with criticism that the world had passed her by, Jeannette Rankin thought that the best campaign endorsement was Kidd's implicit judgment that she was a woman of the future.

Years before, when Americans were criticizing Jeannette Rankin's vote against entering World War I, *The Science of Power* had been an epiphany. Depressed by her fall from power, she discovered that Kidd's woman-based theory celebrated her antiwar vote. Rather than being at odds with feminist principles, as her suffrage critics charged, her vote had quintessentially "linked pacifism to feminism." War, Kidd argued, was "a passing phase of the world [because in Woman] we have the future centre of Power in civilization." Although "the fighting male, . . . the creature of those short-range animal emotions," has ruled the "existing world in every phase of its life, . . . [Woman] by the necessities of her being [is] the ruling principle of this new era of Power." What was uniquely feminine and expeditious for social evolution, Kidd continued, was women's "emotion of the ideal," their capability "of subordinating their minds, their lives, and all the interests within the span of their lives to an ideal which is beyond their lives." The ideal that animates women is the "social or other regarding self," stemming from the "Absolute or Universal Mind which we attribute to God." In contrast, "the male [is] intimately connected with . . . the emotions of the fight." Because the female ideal expresses itself through care of the next generation, only in women can be found the promise of destroying the "military utilitarianism in which self is glorified." For fifty-four years of her life, from 1919 to 1973, Jeannette Rankin strived to be living proof of Kidd's theory.

For Benjamin Kidd—as for Jesus Christ, Henry David Thoreau, and Mohandas Gandhi—peace would arrive only after individuals perfected themselves one by one. Jeannette Rankin, however, never placed a high value on spiritual development and inner peace. To her young sisters she had been an "irritable and domineering" surrogate mother, and in her peace work she always ended up crosswise with her usually male superiors. The habits that she developed had more to do with stubbornness and self-reliance than patience and cooperation. For five decades, her peace work was characterized by an unbending will, not a gentle spirit. Inconsistency creeps into each person's life, but in Jeannette Rankin's case—given the discrepancy between her peace ideal and feisty demeanor—it became more pronounced and—given her unreflective nature—less perceived. At age ninety-one, still lacking the inner peace on which a peaceful world depends, she admitted that her peace crusade had failed: "It's hard to push and push and push and never get anywhere." In contrast to Rankin, reformers like Florence Kelley and Julia Lathrop learned to persevere and work through "the obstacles of male political authority."

Two recurring motifs ran through Jeannette Rankin's twenty years of professional peace work: her inability to synthesize her antiwar arguments and her unwillingness to get along with others. With the Women's International League for Peace and Freedom, she advanced a variety of proposals. One was based on her lifelong, all-purpose notion of democracy: the peace sentiment of ordinary people would prevail in the League of Nations if that body's international council were popularly elected. She pushed John Dewey's and Senator William E. Borah's outlawry of war plan: "Instead of laws about war, we should have laws against war." She espoused her insight about women's unique role in attaining peace: "Disarmament will not be won without their aid. . . . Half of the human race does not fight and has never fought. . . . [W]hy should men not learn something . . . from the non-fighting female." But in the 1920s, Rankin began to fault women for not seeing that the "peace problem is a woman's problem" and for their inability to sacrifice their comfort for radical change: "[Peace] cannot be gotten by avoiding every danger including what is to so many women the most painful consequence of all, the loss of social approval."

Another of Jeannette Rankin's peeves was the Women's International League's scheduling and tactics. Her travel as field secretary was extensive and exhaustive, taking her in one two-week period to Boston, Philadelphia, Wilmington, Niagara Falls, Toronto, Dayton, Detroit, and Cleveland. In one month she visited Winona, Red Wing, St. Paul, Duluth, Minneapolis twice, and St. Cloud in Minnesota; Ames, Iowa; Lincoln and Omaha in Nebraska; Boulder and Denver in Colorado; Kansas City and St. Louis in Missouri; and Champaign, Illinois. Knowing Jeannette Rankin's growing resistance to her schedule ("I wrote you some time ago that there could be no plans for May"), her supervisor expressed concern about her health ("I know how busy you are and how tiring your job must be [and] hope you are keeping up your strength") but chastised Rankin for criticizing and taking liberties with her itinerary ("I do not quite understand about what you meant that 'time is wasted unless better arrangements are made.' . . . St. Louis is greatly disturbed by your telegram. I insist you be there for large luncheon Tuesday as per agreement"). Rankin became further upset when her employer rejected her plan to concentrate Women's International

League resources in the sparsely populated western states to make it easier to win over U.S. senators. She left the league's employment saying, "I wouldn't go on because they just wanted me to go and speak, and then go and speak . . . and [there was] no organization, no purpose, no definite thing."

Georgia was Jeannette Rankin's next peace venue. With the Georgia Peace Society, which she had founded with some university faculty, Rankin plied Jane Addams's evolutionary theme in her lectures, "Civilization Outgrows War" and "War Can Be Outgrown," and tried to avoid tension with her colleagues by running things herself. Her associates, however, called her dictatorial and "accus[ed] her of using the name and letterhead of the organization to her own end." Peace work in Georgia unsettled Rankin for another reason. Prior to a lecture at Brenau College, she was introduced with the wish that Brenau "might have a 'Chair of Peace' . . . and if so [the college] would nominate Miss Rankin as 'Professor of Peace.'" When a newspaper wrongly reported that Brenau had established a "Chair of Peace" and Rankin would be its first occupant, the American Legion exploded with outrage: "It is the aim of the department to try to prevent any such communistic ideas being taught in the state, and the department will utilize every effort possible to combat the policies being encouraged by Brenau College." In a subsequent newspaper article the American Legion linked Rankin with the *Daily Worker, The Masses,* the Garland Fund, and Emma Goldman. Both the American Civil Liberties Union and Wellington Rankin advised against litigation, but the National Council for the Prevention of War gave Jeannette Rankin $500 to bring a libel suit against the newspaper. She settled the matter short of trial for a payment of $1,000 and the newspaper's publication of the statement that "Miss Rankin . . . is not a Communist [and] has never been so branded." She later said that the episode was "the worst experience of her life."

From her rural retreat Jeannette Rankin returned to national peace work with the Women's Peace Union. She received $300 a month for six months to lobby for a constitutional amendment, introduced by U.S. senator Lynn Frazier, to put teeth into the Kellogg-Briand Pact's no-war policy. Her arguments sounded the themes of Jane Addams ("War is doomed because it is a stupid waste. It always fails to settle a dispute or adjust a conflict"; "Only when a world-mindedness is created and that world-mindedness is expressed in our laws and institutions and is backed by a collective and informed public opinion will there be the same feeling of security in our international relations that exists in our internal and personal relations") and of Benjamin Kidd ("Women do not want war. . . . The dominant impulses of woman in her woman's nature are those of creation"). Aware of Rankin's independent streak, the Women's Peace Union required her to limit her activities to the Frazier amendment. Soon, however, she began to advocate disarming unilaterally, building roads to eat up military funds, and establishing replicas of her Georgia Peace Society throughout the country instead of lobbying in Washington. The Women's Peace Union wanted to work "from the top down," she said, but she wanted to work "from the bottom up." Feeling "muzzled," she left the organization.

With the National Council for the Prevention of War, her next employer, Jeannette Rankin was again unable to get along with her colleagues and superior. Unhappy as a lobbyist and lecturer regarding the Kellogg-Briand Pact, the League of Nations, the World Court, disarmament, neutrality legislation, and a war referendum, she asked her boss, Frederick Libby, to assign her to grassroots organizing. She was "preaching to the already converted," she believed, and wanted to make the NCPW "get down to real things" by setting up a Peace Action Service like her Georgia Peace Society. She also called for an "armaments for defense only" campaign—in Libby's mind, her "panacea of 'we can't be attacked'"—to derail President Roosevelt's war. (Ironically, Eleanor Roosevelt used a Kidd-like argument to try to persuade Jeannette Rankin to see things from her husband's perspective: "If the will for peace can grow in the hearts of women everywhere we may be able to bridge over the present tense situation in Europe.") The religious Libby, however, preferred his "mandate from God" to the advice of his employee, and the continued prospect of one-night speaking engagements dispirited Rankin: "I don't see how I could possibly spend three months traveling and survive. . . . It is quite necessary for me to be at home to relax and secure courage to go out and face the cold, stupid world again."

Despite her frustrations, Jeannette Rankin's decade with the NCPW was not without success. People who heard her speak praised her ideas ("practical, workable and inspiring") and her manner ("heart-to-heart talks with their amusing angles"), and Frederick Libby admitted that her campaigning in a Tennessee congressional district turned around public opinion and a critical congressman on 1936 arms-embargo legislation. On her own initiative, she had gone to the district of Representative Sam McReynolds, chairman of the House Foreign Affairs Committee. Working out of Abbie Crawford Milton's Chattanooga home, Rankin used all of her political skill to build ten counties of antiwar pressure on McReynolds. For ten days she visited newspapers, colleges, and schools and spoke on the radio and at church services, luncheons, and afternoon teas. In the morning Milton brought her breakfast in bed, "a beautiful little steak and a huge grape-fruit," knowing that she "wouldn't have anything more to eat" that day. At the end of the campaign, she returned to Washington so worn out that she "didn't send one card . . . didn't do one thing for Christmas." From Rankin's perspective, Congressman McReynolds's introduction of neutrality legis-lation made her effort "her greatest single achievement in the thirties" and "the greatest political victory for pacifism of the interwar years." But her triumph was not complete. When Libby heard that she was working in Tennessee, he sent a male staff member to assist in the campaign without consulting Rankin. She was deeply hurt by Libby's lack of confidence: "[I]t was just exactly what we wanted. . . . [I]t was a wonderful demonstration of what could be done. . . . But they all knew so much better than I did. . . . [T]hat's why I was so unhappy. . . . [T]hey'd get me to do such trivial things."

One of these "trivial" assignments, lobbying unsuccessfully against the $800-million Navy Appropriation Act of 1938, ultimately left Jeannette Rankin "flatter than a pancake." Then the NCPW's donations began to dry up "because people were getting war minded," and Frederick Libby asked her to work without pay or take a salary reduction. She wrote to him, "I've no doubt money is slow in coming in but if you can send me some or put me on a weekly payroll it will help a lot. It hurts my spirits so to be broke." A source of irritation for Libby was Rankin's "increasingly critical" attacks on the Roosevelt administration and her uncompromising pacifism when the nation was becoming aware of Hitler's evil. Rankin said that Libby "never would have hired" her if he had known what she really believed, and her old disagreement with Libby about political tactics continued: she wanted to use "county-by-county methods of organization" while Libby "wanted to work right in Congress . . . to beat out the brains of the men who were voting." Libby rejected her "advice on how to campaign and what to do," and she left the NCPW, her last peace employer, saying it was too "ladylike." In old age Rankin continued to believe that she would have been more successful in peace work if she had been "nastier."

Having run through peace groups and been frustrated by their bureaucracy, Jeannette Rankin decided to wage her battle for peace directly as a member of Congress. By then an absolute pacifist, she hoped her candidacy would be seen as a vote on war. Help came from several U.S. representatives who put two of her antiwar speeches into the *Congressional Record*. In the first address she emphasized her tenets of isolationism (war "creates more conflicts than it solves," America's "geographical position makes us safe from attack," and Americans should do "everything that money, science, and ingenuity can devise to protect our shores from invasion") but reserved her rhetorical force for women's role in bringing about a war-free world ("Mothers alone can prevent our entering the war if they will express their opinions now"). In the second speech—"Prepare to the Limit for Defense; Keep Our Men Out of Europe," which became her 1940 campaign slogan—she criticized President Roosevelt's interventionism (if America builds "a highly modernized, mechanized military defense . . . to make our entire coast as impregnable as Corregidor, every man, woman, and child can go to sleep knowing that no enemy can reach us") and concluded with her coda: "governments make war, women can prevent war." Having made her name synonymous with antiwar sentiment, Rankin was returned to Congress by a war-fearing electorate.

Insular Affairs, Jeannette Rankin's principal committee assignment in the House of Representatives, did nothing to assist her fight against World War II. On her own, she implemented a grassroots campaign using "[l]etters from mothers." Writing to her New York friend Jane Thompson Bausman, she explained: "I still feel sure that [President Roosevelt] can be bluffed out of going to war if the women will do their part." Next Rankin coordinated her antiwar effort with the America First Committee, an isolationist organization notorious for its fascism and anti-Semitism. To new America First chapters, Rankin conveyed her pleasure that they had joined the antiwar struggle: "Congratulations on your patriotic services in keeping this country out of war." Her staffers sent America Firsters suggestions for antiwar activities that "might be helpful." Rankin especially recommended the tactic of "[t]elephoning the White House," which, she told the America First groups, "should not be underrated." Her aides cooperated with America First in a postcard mailing that supported antiwar politicians and opposed "the draft extension." She accepted a series of invitations from America First's national office to speak around the country. After Congress declared war against Japan, the chairman of America First's speakers bureau thanked Rankin for her willing service to the organization: "I used to call you on the telephone and try to persuade you to speak when you should have been home resting. You did such a grand job for America First and we are all so proud of you." A woman who had been in one of Rankin's audiences made it clear that her sacrifices for America First were worthwhile: "I heard you speak in Jersey City recently at an America First Meeting and it gave me much courage and hope." One local chapter sent Rankin an America First lapel button and congratulations for her vote against World War II: "Our sincere appreciation of your outstanding courage and faithfulness and loyalty. It was a bright flame in a dark hour. We love you for it."

Jeannette Rankin's support of America First included the organization's most publicized action: Charles Lindbergh's October 1941 speech in Des Moines. Lindbergh argued that the "three most important groups who have been pressing this country toward war are the British, the Jewish and the Roosevelt administration" and that "the Jewish groups in this country should be opposing it in every possible way for they will be among the first to feel its consequences." Rankin approved of Lindbergh's "calling for new leadership [that] can control the notions of the President," mailed to her supporters Lindbergh's position on the war, and adopted Lindbergh's argument that America's going to war would be worse for Jews and other minorities than the Nazi persecutions. To civil rights advocate and old friend Mary Church Terrell, she wrote: "I feel that the colored people are in a tight spot right now. . . . [If President Roosevelt] takes us into war, the reaction that will come later against those groups who have supported him—the women, the colored people and the Jews—will be like the reaction in Germany, if not worse. For the protection of themselves, it seems to me that the colored people should take an open stand against war now. I know of nothing that is going to be so tragic as the race riots that will result from the hate generated if we go to war. This, to me, will be the most tragic part of the war." The remarks of one America First sympathizer demonstrated the downside of Rankin's courting radical bedfellows: "You are the only member of Congress with any common sense. . . . This gang of Jew thugs headed by Baruch, Frankfurter and Roosevelt have bankrupted our country."

Jeannette Rankin's flirting with extremism stemmed from her frustration. After years of striving, she had failed to advance the cause of pacifism. Her anger intensified as she heard repeated the same arguments she had heard during World War I. She complained, in opposition to President Roosevelt's lend-lease program, that the "1917 propaganda was exactly the same as the propaganda today." For twenty years, however, Rankin had been using her same antiwar arguments, especially her Benjamin Kidd–inspired, woman-based philosophy. In a 1941 Mother's Day speech on the floor of the House of Representatives, she proclaimed that the "mothers of this country . . . want to protect our shores from invasion, . . . do not believe the war method can be used to settle disputes, . . . [and] refuse to have [their] work sacrificed for the profits of a few. . . . [The] mothers of America . . . are not going to have their sons sent to war if they can prevent it—and they can." But despite her two decades in the antiwar trenches, Rankin could feel another war bearing down on the country. "I knew it was coming," she said. "Roosevelt was deliberately trying to get us in the war."

Jeannette Rankin could not escape the war but she could escape prowar pressures. To shield herself from arguments she despised, she cut herself off from the public. "I didn't let anybody approach me," she recalled. "I got in my car and disappeared. Nobody could reach me. . . . I just drove around Washington and got madder and madder because there were soldiers everywhere I went. . . . I don't remember whether I thumbed my nose at them or not, but I resented them." She even shut herself off from those closest to her. Wellington Rankin could not reach her to make his argument: "She can't be for peace again—after Pearl Harbor." Maury Maverick, a reform mayor from San Antonio who had backed her World War I vote, failed with his argument: "This time Germany has a chance to conquer the world. . . . [D]on't stick to your ideas because you've had them since the last war. This situation IS different, I tell you." Her brother-in-law Grant McGregor in London got nowhere by describing his and Harriet's dilemma of remaining in their "flat at the top of the building" or going to a bomb shelter. Emerging from her self-imposed isolation and taking her seat on the floor of the House, Rankin "clamored for recognition" so she could oppose immediate consideration of the war resolution. But House Speaker Sam Rayburn "steadfastly looked the other way." After her one-word vote of "No," Rankin was "hissed by some of her colleagues," confronted by a "mob in the cloak room," and forced to take "refuge in a telephone booth." She was escorted by Capitol police, a newspaper reported, to her office where she "barricaded herself . . . and wept."

Condemned and derided in the press, Jeannette Rankin took solace from the words of friends. Katharine Anthony sent praise and an invitation: "I always knew you were like the Rock of Gibraltar. And so you are. I feel proud to know you and prouder that I can say that we are friends. What you have done today will go down in history. Darling, you have made an impression on the whole world. . . . We are all hoping to see you next week-end." Elisabeth Irwin included a comforting note: "Bully for you darling." Old suffrage colleague Katherine Devereux Blake simply honored Rankin's solitary stand, "Congratulations for courage," as did civil libertarian Roger Baldwin: "[Y]our act is heartening to all who cherish fidelity to principle and ideals." A long-time admirer wrote: "Once in Athens, you kissed me on the forehead and said, 'Come to see me in Washington sometime.' I'm proud to have had my thinking influenced by the 'pacifist lady from the West.'" Other supporters paid tribute with the rhetoric of mythic accomplishment: "fearless," "brave," "courageous," "Christian," "righteous," "common-sense," "principled," "moral," "wise," "firm," "inspiring," "marvelous," "glorious," "great," "heroic," "noble."

But the American public was as black and white in its judgment as Jeannette Rankin had been in hers. Newspaper editorials overran with horror and rage, and hostile letter writers struggled for words that could adequately express their anger and disgust: "sentimental," "move to Japan," "made an ass out of yourself," "feeble minded," "consult a psychiatrist," "Judas," "dastardly, unpatriotic conduct," "contempt for a traitor such as you," "stubborn and stupid," "a sign of weakness, of stubbornness, of willful blindness," "yellow-livered publicity-seeking disgrace to woman-kind," "a final fling of publicity," "unpardonable feminine exhibitionism," "when concentration camps open you should be occupant number one." A female professor from the University of Chicago, the kind of intelligent and sophisticated woman Rankin thought she represented most, wrote: "You have turned the clock back for women! . . . Thank God our country does not have to depend on such unrealistic persons as you! You doubtless flatter yourself on standing by your 'principles,' but inflexible principles like yours would put us under the Nazi heel. You will not hold an enviable position in the history of our times." More moderate letters asked her to resign or explain her vote. The Republican National Committeeman from Montana wrote, "I urge and beseech you to redeem Montana's honor and loyalty and change your vote as early as possible." Rankin was not about to resign or change her vote, but on the day Congress declared war against Japan she did send a press release to Montana newspapers.

Some explanation by Jeannette Rankin was clearly needed. Before her vote she had strengthened her resolve by grounding her position in both conscience and constituency: "Everyone knew that I was opposed to war, and they elected me." But after her vote she stood out as the only member of Congress opposing war after an aggressor's attack. Even Belle Fligelman Winestine, her first-term secretary, disagreed with Rankin: "I'm afraid I would have voted for war. . . . I think by that time we just had to get into the war." Rankin's press release of December 8, 1941, ignored what Winestine meant when she said, "by that time": systematic persecution of Jews and the bombing of Pearl Harbor. In her statement Rankin returned to her well-worn arguments: "taking our army and navy across thousands of miles of ocean to fight and die certainly cannot come under the head of protecting our shores"; "in casting my vote today, I voted my convictions and redeemed my campaign pledges"; "I voted as the mothers would have had me vote." Rolled up together were Jane Addams's idea that war was wasteful and ineffective, the conclusion of Senator Gerald P. Nye's Munitions Investigating Committee that America had entered World War I out of corporate greed, and Benjamin Kidd's theory that war was a male invention. To these arguments Rankin added several rationalizations. One relied on parliamentary procedure: "I tried repeatedly to get the floor to ask some questions. I felt there were not enough facts before us." Another was an odd use of democratic principle: "Had the vote to go to war been unanimous, it would have been a totalitarian vote." What was absent from her statement was, despite her supporters' praise of her "Christian" principles, any discussion of the morality of ignoring the Nazi persecution of Jews.

A moral justification for war was anathema to Jeannette Rankin. As a realist, she viewed politics from the perspectives of public opinion and money. In her suffrage days she said that prohibition was "not a moral issue." Rather, it was "economic" and would "be decided not by woman suffrage but by the corporations of the country." Similarly, she thought running war through a moral filter a mistake. The NCPW, the last peace organization to employ her, had softened its pacifism because "Hitler was so bad," but Rankin's absolute pacifism would not tolerate the compromise. Toward the end of her career as a peace lobbyist, she wrote in the church publication *World Outlook* that she was especially troubled by "holy wars."

Citizens are rightfully skeptical, she explained, about the argument that war is good for the nation's economy, but "ask them to fight for a lofty ideal . . . and that is quite a different story." Throughout her life she was interested in religion only instrumentally. Churches were good places for rallies and speeches, and missionaries—especially Quakers—provided lodging when she was traveling on a tight budget. The Bible, too, could be useful when making peace arguments to the God-fearing. Just before she died, Rankin turned to the Bible for rhetoric but not comfort. She asked an aide to scour the Old Testament and the New Testament for useful passages, and he reported back: "I have read Genesis, Exodus, Leviticus, Numbers, Deuteronomy, and Joshua in the Old Testament, and have, following your suggestion, . . . been looking for references to Peace. There are very few. . . . Perhaps the references to Peace will have to await the Gospels."

Jeannette Rankin's pacifism, however, bore no relationship to Christian pacifism. Augustine of Hippo had begun the just-war tradition by teaching, "True religion looks upon as peaceful those wars that are waged not for motives of aggrandizement, or cruelty, but with the object of securing peace, of punishing evil doers, and of uplifting the good." Thomas Aquinas, citing Augustine, posited three requirements for a morally defensible war: legitimate authority, just cause, and right intention. Martin Luther asked, "What else is war but the punishment of wrong and evil?" John Calvin found support in Scripture for arming states "to defend the subjects committed to their guardianship whenever they are hostilely assailed." Reinhold Niebuhr, Rankin's contemporary, believed that the "Christian realist must recognize that power is necessary for the exercise of justice." And Michael Walzer concluded that Nazism was "evil objectified in the world . . . in a form so potent and apparent that there could never have been anything to do but fight against it." Christian just-war theory, because it does not glorify passivity and is inspired by peace, should have interested Jeannette Rankin. She did sign her Christmas cards with "Pax," but more telling was the holiday greeting from one of her nieces who referred to herself and her aunt as "infidels and anti-Christians." Rankin said that Mohandas Gandhi, not Jesus Christ, appealed to her because "Gandhi said, 'Resist evil. Resist it with your life if necessary, but resist with nonviolence.' But Jesus said, 'Resist not evil.' And he let himself be crucified." Jeannette Rankin was not going to submit to her enemies without a fight. Her description of her state of mind at the time of her World War II vote—that she couldn't "bear to be a worm"—expressed her hatred of passivity. So for Jeannette Rankin in late September 1939, war itself was absolute evil, and she was bent on ensuring that the United States was "not going to use violence" to stop the "Hitler methods of violence."

Jeannette Rankin's total, uncompromising pacifism promoted bizarre behavior. An anomalous use of force occurred during her final days with the NCPW. Tensions between her and her colleagues increased as the extent of Nazi Germany's anti-Semitism became known. When her boss, Frederick Libby, saw that his organization's pacifism was hindering fundraising, he muted his own message and tried to tone down his most outspoken employee. Rankin's description of the resulting relationship between her and Libby—"he got so that he wouldn't let me talk if he could help it"—indicates that she defied his orders. But her antiwar convictions pushed her beyond clashing with Libby to the point of confronting Jewish employees of the NCPW ("'we had lots of Jews in our organization,'" she said). She recounted a dinner at which she discussed "the problem" of European Jews with "this Jewish woman." When their disagreement about using war to stop the widening persecution of Jews became obvious, the two women, Rankin said, nearly came to blows: "I wasn't mad: I was just earnest. And she wasn't mad, but she was so emotional about it that . . . somebody came and pulled us apart; they thought we were going to have a fight. I didn't feel emotional, but she did, maybe to protect her people." Rankin did not hide her belief that pacifism should outbalance the plight of the Jews. "Anyway," she emphasized, "I didn't feel it," referring to the pressure some NCPW employees were trying to bring on behalf of European Jews. Even the gentle Francis of Assisi saw no "inconsistency between loving men and fighting them," but the feisty Jeannette Rankin said that she could find "no way of making force and violence right."

Most Americans, unlike Jeannette Rankin, believed that it was right to use force and violence against Japan and Germany in 1941. When she voted against war in December, "70 percent of Americans thought it was more important to aid England than to continue to keep out of the European theater. Likewise, 70 percent were willing to risk war with the Japanese rather than permit their unabashed aggression in the Far East." Rankin knew that her vote placed her "completely out of step with the times" and, having "been discredited," there would be "little to do" for the rest of her term. She said that "her second term ended for all practical purposes the day the Japanese bombed Pearl Harbor." Her war vote impaired not only her effectiveness in Congress but also her emotional life. Even before Pearl Harbor her sister Edna wrote to her that she "hope[d] things are not too discouraging for you," and two months after the World War II vote her sister Grace, struggling with the ordeal of caring for their mother, wrote: "I hope you aren't having as fearsome a time as you sound. I am hoping it is for Mother's sake you are making it sound so."

About the time she received Grace's letter, the ostracized Jeannette Rankin confided to her mother her depression and the everyday concerns that had become a diversion: "I am inviting a couple of Congressmen and their wives to dinner tonight. . . . I did not go to sleep until 4 A.M. so am feeling very dull and stupid and now have to have a party tonight. I set the table last night when I could not sleep—literally not figuratively. . . . As usual when I have nothing else to do I spend money on clothes. I bought an evening dress. I do not know why since I have not had one on this winter, but it was for sale and is what I have been thinking about for a very long time. . . . I have been attending towel sales and am going to send you my promiscuous collection of seconds. . . . I am still worried about the apartment curtains. I think I will have to starch and iron the ones I had last summer." In other letters to her mother, Rankin continued to convey her solitariness and static official life. She told her mother that she had stayed home from Congress "and covered a chair with tan-and-rose striped material, and then went up to the roof garden and sat alone for a long time." Another time she told her mother of her habit of using the apartment building's roof garden "just before going to bed." It provided her an escape from the wartime activity of Washington, making her "feel as though" she were back in Montana, "out in the open."

Prior to Jeannette Rankin's becoming Congress's persona non grata, her congressional office—often in her absence—contended with huge volumes of correspondence. Her office manager informed Rankin, who was in Montana "enjoy[ing] the soul refreshing weather," that the staff, suffering through Washington's "heat and humidity," were preparing address cards on incoming mail, sending out "peace material," and mailing her "quantities of letters to sign." "We worked last night [sending out anti-draft information]," the staff assistant wrote to Rankin, "and Sigrid is going to work tonight too. I have to do my washing or I won't be able to come to work. . . . Sigrid worked on filing yesterday too. The amount of work to be done on that alone is staggering." After the war vote there was less official activity. Rankin spent enough time in Washington to introduce her antiwar schemes and measures "to mitigate the effects of World War II," none of which was enacted into law. They included congressional approval of any offensive military activity, voter approval of conscription, an advisory national referendum before Congress could vote on war, no money for foreign wars, no arming of civilian ships, limits on the president's lend-lease authority, free use of the mail for military personnel, no statute of limitations for prosecuting war-contract fraud, liberalized draft deferments, and no death penalty for wartime sabotage.

One of Jeannette Rankin's bills stemmed from an unpleasant incident when she was returning from a visit to Katharine Anthony and Elisabeth Irwin's summer home in Connecticut. The railroad claimed that she hadn't purchased a ticket for her trip to Washington, and she asked her friends to come to her defense. Anthony replied: "Of course I saw you buy the ticket at New Haven and pay for it. I was standing right by you when you did it. Elisabeth was there too and saw it. She is at school now and will write you a letter this evening. I can't imagine how there could have been any mix-up about it. Would you like me to send you an affidavit?" For a remedy, Rankin decided to introduce HR 6153, which called for "receipts for fares paid on common carriers." Another problem with a purchase bothered Rankin during her second term, possibly because big problems had been put out of her reach or because of her "cheapness," one of her defining traits according to a family member. After leaving Congress in 1943, she asked a staffer to look into a Washington department store's claim that she had not paid for a pair of stockings. The secretary wrote back: "I took the bill you sent down to Woodward & Lothrope to the adjustment department. I know you didn't order but the one set of stockings and I remember returning them to the stocking counter [and] got a credit slip for them, which I gave to you. Of course you don't have it now. . . . [A]ll I know to do is just not pay it." Paying for the stockings was not an option Rankin entertained. She wrote to the store four months later: "I hope you will not feel it is necessary to continue to send the bill which is very irritating."

Jeannette Rankin's detachment from the official life of Washington was evident in other ways. She spent considerable time caring for her mother. Immediately after the 1940 election, the eighty-seven-year-old Olive Rankin lived with the congresswoman in a small apartment in Washington's northwest section. When Olive became ill the next summer, Jeannette "had to get a series of nurses [but ultimately] do much of the nursing herself . . . for Mrs. Rankin couldn't get along with the nurses." The strain on Jeannette in Washington compared with her brother's freedom in Montana became an issue. In a letter to an acquaintance she complained, "I cannot get out very much. . . . [I] spend the evenings at home." In a note to Wellington she seemed to be irritated at his expression of brotherly concern: "Don't worry about me, I'm all right." When their mother's illness became unmanageable for Jeannette, Wellington recruited Edna to accompany Olive by train back to his Montana ranch. Jeannette's nursing responsibilities did not come to an end, however, as she spent parts of July, August, and September in 1941 and April, May, September, and October in 1942 in Montana to relieve Edna and Grace. For each of the sisters the responsibility was imprisoning, and Grace—who then bore the brunt of caring for their mother—frequently expressed her need to escape. Grace wrote to Jeannette in September 1941: "I've only been out of the house twice since you left. . . . You will be just rolling around in your apartment alone." When Jeannette returned to Washington after a nursing stint at the ranch, Grace's envy was obvious: "I'll bet you hardly know what to do with all your freedom. It's like being turned out of jail." In another letter Grace could not check her bitterness about being trapped with Olive: "She fell off the pot in the night last Wednesday. . . . It was all the nurse and I could do to put her on the bed. She didn't have any bruises much to her disappointment." Toward the end of Rankin's second term, Grace tried to be understanding of Jeannette and Edna's holiday in New York: "Going to plays sounds just grand and knowing someone in one must have been fun. . . . I had to laugh when you spoke of your quiet week in New York. If you spread that over two and a half months for me it would seem like a wild orgy."

Traveling provided Jeannette Rankin a more pleasant distraction from the ruin of her second term. To fulfill his part of the bargain with his sisters, Wellington paid for Jeannette's trips along with his mother's expenses and an occasional vehicle for his sisters. (Edna once begged for hers: "I am very sure Jeannette thinks she is willing to share her car—but past experience has shown repeatedly that one goes and comes when and if she is ready and willing.") Throughout Jeannette Rankin's life, traveling relieved her boredom and consumed her energy. Her stamina during a 1952 trip through Africa was described by Edna in a letter to Grace and Mary: "There were no airplanes to the places we wanted to go and the nights on the train were just plain rugged, but how Jeannette can take them! She beds down on those long hard bench seats—without even a pillow—and sleeps!" In 1941 and 1942 she was constantly on the go—journeying repeatedly from Washington to Montana, Georgia, and New York by train, plane, bus, car, and truck. When a constituent inquired about her being in Montana and missing a vote on a "highway measure," she explained: "I made a reservation on the plane which would have arrived in Washington in time for the vote, but I missed the plane because my car arbitrarily refused to run." Another time a secretary telegraphed that Senator Burton K. Wheeler was urging her to return to Washington for a draft-extension vote. After the vote to enter World War II, Millacent Yarrow fretted about the congresswoman when she drove cross-country to Montana: "Glad of your word that you were safely out so far as near Fargo but sorry snow was holding you up." After Rankin's brief visit to Georgia to see her burned-down house in the country and her house in town that had become infested by "[r]ats, mice and moths," a friend sadly recalled their parting when "your bus left today." To Abbie Crawford Milton she wrote that she would "fly out to take Mother to the ranch" after Wellington had telephoned that the early spring roads between Grace's home in Idaho and his Montana ranch would be "dry enough." When Wellington wanted Jeannette home again five months later to help with his U.S. Senate race, she told Flora Belle Surles: "[W]e all must work" and "it looks as if I would leave this week." After driving to Montana to campaign for her brother and returning east in a new truck, she closed down her office and was soon heading back to Idaho to help with her mother's care, driving alone through severe winter weather and with the uncertainties of gas rationing.

Once during her second term, Jeannette Rankin remained in Washington long enough to complete a task of her own making. After brooding for months over President Roosevelt's responsibility for Pearl Harbor, she set out to give the nation her interpretation of why America went to war. She had always been dismissive of others' attempts to identify the causes of war. "What they call 'causes of war,'" she said, "are always lies. The real cause is that we have a military system that has to exist, and that military system creates disputes." Backing up her condemnation of the military was Benjamin Kidd's theory that warring men run the world. Exactly one year after Congress declared war against Japan, Rankin entered into the *Congressional Record* her explanation of how the two men she detested most— Franklin Roosevelt and Winston Churchill—duped the United States into entering World War II. In "Some Questions About Pearl Harbor," she revealed their treachery: "Three years before Pearl Harbor, Britain's imperialists had figured out just how to bring the United States once more to their aid, . . . [by establishing] an economic blockade [of Japan]—in other words, sanctions—an admitted provocation to war. . . . [I]n less than a week after the Atlantic Conference [between Churchill and Roosevelt] the machinery of economic sanctions was getting under way. . . . Six weeks later the economic stringency in Japan had become acute. . . . [A] prominent non-Japanese oriental [told Rankin that] 'Japan has no choice but to go to war or to submit to economic slavery for the rest of her existence.' . . . [N]ot only did President Roosevelt accede to Churchill's pressure to send an ultimatum to, and impose sanctions upon Japan but he made a blanket commitment to bring America to the war even if Japan did not attack."

Jeannette Rankin was proud of the research she had conducted for her analysis—she told a constituent that she had "a pile of material ten inches high" on her desk concerning President Roosevelt's machinations to bring the United States into war—but one of Rankin's biographers concluded that Ralph Baerman of the Institute for Christian Economic Action had written her remarks. Regardless of who wrote "Some Questions About Pearl Harbor," the statement reflected Benjamin Kidd's male-conspiracy theory. Rankin wrote in a similar vein to a Montana soldier a month after Pearl Harbor: "There are always more than two choices. . . . This 'either/or' is the method of the Fuehrer. I can speak to you frankly and it is a great comfort. . . . I felt the President would not push the Japanese too far if he really wanted to avoid an attack until we were prepared. I do not know and have not yet been given the facts regarding the negotiations with Japan. I have hardly recovered from the shock that we are actually at war and now have a Fuehrer that we must obey blindly and enthusiastically."

Throughout her life Jeannette Rankin fumed at anyone—especially men—who got in her way, but her deep dislike of Franklin Roosevelt spanned sixty-one years. It began during the 1912 New York state suffrage campaign when he "ridiculed western states that had adopted suffrage," and it persisted until her death. In her California retirement apartment, a visitor found the failing Rankin "almost mute" but outraged at newly discovered "incriminating evidence" that her archenemy had purposely misled the American people. At their first meeting she had found Roosevelt to be "manipulative" and "condescending," and by World War II she was describing Roosevelt even more pejoratively. By then he and Winston Churchill had become "the two dictators." In a 1943 letter, she expressed how angry and bitter she was because they had succeeded and she had failed: "I have been pretty quiet since the eighth of December, 1942, but evidently enough people are reading my speech to worry some of the 'super' patriots. Perhaps some day the people will learn that every country loses every war, and then they will hang all the dictators, including Roosevelt and Churchill." But the people never seemed to learn, and Rankin remained angry because men continued to lead the nation into war and women were incapable of understanding their maternal nature and the lesson of men and war.

Jeannette Rankin might have been the first but she was not the only political woman to be "disappointed to learn that women voters do not automatically rally around [women's] candidacies" and causes. Soon after suffrage "the women's vote had been revealed to be a paper tiger" because "when women did vote, they did not vote differently from men." Rankin expressed her disappointment with women in 1943 when she was "much discouraged over the women and their work when they let this war come with so little protest." In 1944 she was even more disillusioned because women failed to turn Franklin Roosevelt out of office. As a result of women's careless use of their vote, the election meant "a continuation of war and deaths." During the Vietnam War, women upset her by being politically lazy and devoting themselves to lesser causes than peace. To the Associated Press she said: "The draft could be abolished if women spoke loudly enough to be heard. But they don't. Women remind me of the cows on our ranch in Montana. A cow has a calf and after a while some man comes along and takes the calf away. She bawls for a while, then goes on and has another calf." Five years later *Life* magazine reported the elderly reformer criticizing young women activists for lacking her determination and drive: "I tell these young women that they must get to the people who don't come to the meetings. It never did any good for all the suffragettes to come together and talk to each other. There will be no revolution unless we go out into the precincts. You have to be stubborn. Stubborn and ornery." The year before she died she criticized women even more sharply in an interview with a Washington newspaper: "They don't know who they are voting for or why. . . . It is time they woke up. . . . They're dumb because men have told them a beautiful face is all that's important." That same year she told another interviewer that women's typical concerns were: "What [will it] do to my husband's job. . . . Will I have to wear the same dress two or three times?" What seemed to bother Rankin most about modern women activists was that their goals were "trivial," by which she meant they were not about peace. She expressed her own singular dedication to peace "[i]n an encounter with Margaret Sanger at the international meeting on birth control in New Delhi": "All you talk about is vaginas, vaginas, vaginas. I'm getting out of here."

Fundamentally, however, Jeannette Rankin had no problem with vaginas. Years before, she had shared with her suffrage sisters her ideas "about sex": birth control, abortion, prostitution, and "all these underground things." She once told an audience of feminists: "Certainly I believe in the right to abortion and in women's rights and an end to discrimination on the basis of sex." She spoke approvingly of a suffragist who "got up one time and said she had seventeen abortions." Even though Rankin reserved her energy and reputation for the cause of peace, she backed—albeit reluctantly—the cause of women's reproductive rights. When the Women's National Abortion Action Committee requested her to "send a greeting to our rally," she scribbled on the invitation an instruction to her aide: "Give support to march? No!! Statement but not name!" Rankin's problem was that the abortion-rights organization did not understand that peace-making was women's naturally ordained role.

Jeannette Rankin's fundamental problem was with penises. Her belief in social evolution sustained her optimism in women, but history sustained her pessimism about men: "They start too many wars." She harbored only a perverse hope for maleness—that the era of women and peace would arrive after the men were dead. With a friend she shared her essentialist belief that "after four or five more devastating wars, . . . women will be willing to assert their primitive instincts for the protection of the young and do something about war. . . . [T]here will be so few men to protest because they're out killing themselves." Out of office in 1943, having set aside her desire to return to Congress because of Wellington's own campaign plans, Jeannette thought that her only course of action was to let evolution take its course: "I'm going to live as peacefully as I can and let the world kill off the men." Another time when her frustration with men had boiled over, her cure was again violence; speaking of men in general and the military in particular, she exploded, "Why we don't shoot those men, I don't know." But in her notes for her remarks when the National Organization of Women inducted her into the Susan B. Anthony Hall of Fame in 1972, she delivered her more characteristic message when she told feminists that they would "have to subdue the killer man by nonviolence."

Throughout her sixty-plus years of political activism, Jeannette Rankin continuously exhorted and relied on "the women." Philosophically, politically, and personally, men were unimportant to her. Although some other feminists discarded the "idea of a unitary female identity" (Estelle Freedman notes Simone de Beauvoir's judgment that "it's quite obvious that once they are in power, women are exactly like men"), Jeannette Rankin persisted in her belief in the unique goodness of women and in her "low view" of men. Like her soul mates a century earlier, she continued to insist—in the words of Carroll Smith-Rosenberg—that "male not female desires fostered political corruption and civic vice." She continued to believe, in the words of Estelle Freedman, that the promise of social progress "rested in large part on ideals of female difference from and moral superiority to men, as well as on a social authority based on the common experience of motherhood." Some twentieth-century women reformers "claimed equality with men" and "were less likely to invoke their own womanhood as a justification for their efforts," but Jeannette Rankin continued to assert a feminism whose goal was the "gendering of the political and the public."

Jeannette Rankin vigorously rejected the argument that her gender-role ideology was passé. She was dismayed to discover that young feminists were just coming to the positions she had pioneered long before they were born. At age eighty-nine, as an angry "foremother," she "more or less told [a university dean] that she was a hundred years out of date with her 'continuing education for women plans.'" At age ninety, she called contrary women at a peace conference "a lot of old ladies." In defense of her position, she would have triumphantly cited Ralph Nader who, after visiting her in 1972, described her as "a future-directed person." Her female-identity philosophy from which her pacifism stemmed bears a striking similarity to three interconnected premises in the writing of contemporary feminist Catherine MacKinnon: male dominance in sex, male dominance in law, and male dominance in society. MacKinnon's argument "treats sexuality as a social construct of male power: defined by men, forced on women, and constitutive of the meaning of gender." Similar to Rankin's criticism of male politicians, MacKinnon condemns the acting out of male sexual dominance in lawmaking: "Those with power in political systems that women did not design and from which women have been excluded write legislation, which sets ruling values." MacKinnon concludes her argument by describing a state that "protects male power through embodying and ensuring existing male control over women at every level"—evidenced by a world of sexual abuse, sexual harassment, rape, domestic battery, prostitution, pornographic depiction, unequal pay, disrespected work, and economic destitution.

Catherine MacKinnon's logic moves from sexuality to legislation to society. Her belief that sexuality is socially constructed binds together the three parts of her argument. "Sexuality," she believes, "is not a discrete sphere of interaction or feeling or sensation or behavior in which preexisting social divisions may or may not be played out. It is a pervasive dimension of social life, one that permeates the whole, a dimension along which gender occurs and through which gender is socially constituted. . . . Sexuality becomes, in this view, social and relational, constructing and constructed of power." Because MacKinnon's continuum of sexual intimacy admits as equally meaningful such diverse sexual arrangements as man and man, woman and woman, man alone, and woman alone, a different kind of society arguably could come into being. Rankin's evolutionary argument used similar logic: a world without war would be possible only when there existed a world without men. An unanswered question is whether Jeannette Rankin's orientation toward women was total; that is, did the political become personal just as the personal became political?

Another scholar of feminist jurisprudence in her description of two feminist camps provides reason to believe that Jeannette Rankin's orientation toward women was complete. According to Robin West, contemporary "radical feminists" assert that "women's connection with the 'other' [i.e., with a man and/or a child] is above all else invasive and intrusive: women's potential for material 'connection' invites invasion into the physical integrity of [women's] bodies and intrusion into the existential integrity of [women's] lives. . . . [W]omen's connection to others is the source of women's . . . debasement, powerlessness, subjugation, and misery." In contrast, "modern cultural feminists" argue that "women value intimacy." Women inherently "are more nurturant, caring, loving and responsible to others than are men. This capacity for nurturance and care dictates the moral terms in which women, distinctively, construct social relations." Jeannette Rankin's values and activities tell us that she had her feet in both feminist

camps. Completely woman-oriented, she tended to be a cultural feminist in her political life and, with respect to men, a radical feminist in her personal life.

Assessment

A Paradoxical Reformer

J EANNETTE RANKIN WAS ALWAYS QUICK TO JUDGE PUBLIC FIGURES. SHE CALLED Franklin Roosevelt "the Dictator," had "no kind words for Ike," and "could not stand [Lyndon] Johnson." When U.S. Secretary of State William F. Rogers panned her disarmament plan, she replied: "Your hollow comments . . . are more insane than inept." When California congressman Pete McCloskey, an opponent of the Vietnam War, stole her limelight, she lashed out: "Perhaps [redistricting] is a better way of defeating him for reelection than shooting him." Others received kinder treatment. She felt that Jane Addams "could have made a great President" and that only Norman Thomas, of all the presidential candidates she had voted for since 1920, deserved her support. She told Wellington Rankin that she was "grieved and depressed" when Huey Long was murdered and that the country had "lost a great man" when Senator William Borah died. Just as Jeannette Rankin did not hesitate to judge other politicians, she deserves more than automatic praise.

A close look at Jeannette Rankin's life reveals tension between her political

positions and her private life. As a radical reformer, she campaigned for woman suffrage, safe workplaces, high wages, world peace, and reconfigured election systems. But as a private person she derided women, benefited from shameful work conditions, reveled in her nastiness, and sought to impose her will on others. Some public figures—for example, John F. Kennedy and Martin Luther King, Jr.—have been criticized because of inconsistencies between their public image and private lives, while others—such as Thomas More and Mohandas Gandhi—are hailed for their ability to integrate the two spheres. In Jeannette Rankin's case, an outsized and radical public life seems to have contributed to a surprisingly limited private life. While a deficient public life suggests a lack of altruism or an excessively full private life, an exaggerated public life suggests an unsatisfying private life or an inordinate need for acceptance. The paradoxes in Jeannette Rankin's story help to explain her initial promise, short-term stardom, and years of isolation and frustration.

Publicly, Jeannette Rankin was a radical reformer. Like Henry David Thoreau, whom she admired and tried to imitate, she went to live by herself in the country. Her Walden Pond was "sixty-four acres of scrub land" near Bogart, Georgia. And, like Thoreau, she designed a one-room hut and "hired neighborhood men to construct it under her direction." In time she added rooms to accommodate extended stays by her mother and Edna Rankin's two children, Dorothy and John McKinnon. Years later Dorothy recalled Jeannette's eccentric residence. The main part was connected to a cooking shack by a "gangway," and the downstairs had access to upstairs sleeping rooms by way of a recycled narrow spiral staircase that Olive Rankin had trouble negotiating. The structure was nothing like Jeannette Rankin's childhood home. The Rankin family mansion had been grand and state-of-the-art, but the rural Bogart house was Spartan and idiosyncratic. It lacked electricity and plumbing, its interior was "practically lined with books," and its outhouse "had *Nation* and the *New Republic* for toilet paper." Jeannette Rankin's skimping extended to food and her guests. Dorothy McKinnon remembered being sent to school by her aunt "with a piece of hardtack and fat for lunch."

When Jeannette Rankin's Bogart house burned in the mid-1930s, she moved to a 45-acre plot near Watkinsville where she lived in another little house almost to the time of her death. Raising money by selling off acreage and timber, Rankin turned her shack into a Frank Lloyd Wright–inspired

"rammed earth" structure. One visitor called the result the "damndest house I ever saw," but Jeannette's sister Grace was more flattering: "I had no idea it was so pretentious [and] wasn't prepared for anything as nice outside." Dorothy McKinnon described it as a "sharecropper shanty with one room added"; it sat on stilts "a foot and a half above the ground" and was connected by concrete-block steps to an outbuilding with a dirt floor. Like Henry David Thoreau, Jeannette Rankin went without common conveniences. Heat came from "second-hand oil stoves [in] the kitchen and the bedroom"; a "homemade tin bathtub [sat] in a tiny cubbyhole off the kitchen"; and in another "little cubbyhole off her bedroom [was located] a railroad toilet, with a pit underneath." Thoreau had gone to the woods to live simply in order to recover the meaning in his life he felt he had lost. Living by herself, Rankin plotted how she could recover the political influence that she had lost. In rural Georgia, as at Wellington Rankin's ranch in Montana, she spent much of her time "thinking and working peace ideas."

Jeannette Rankin's "non-consuming life style" was dictated more by political than personal reasons. She needed to send a message to her radical supporters that she was keeping the faith. Carroll Smith-Rosenberg's essay on "The New Woman" suggests that the contemporaries Rankin identified with were characterized by their college education, freedom from traditional family ties, and economic independence from fathers, husbands, and lovers. Most of the Greenwich Village–based Heterodoxy women became "through their own efforts economically independent." Katharine Anthony, for example, "argued that 'the emancipation of woman'. . . was the fundamental aim of feminism" and achieved economic independence by writing books and through personal sacrifice. Once, when waiting for a manuscript to be published, she wrote to Rankin: "I haven't any clothes, worse still, no money to buy any. . . . [H]aving to pay over $300 to the type-writer for copying my book . . . is the only luxury I can afford." Rankin achieved economic independence only a few times in her life—during her two congressional terms and brief periods of employment with peace organizations. Otherwise she met her needs and wants partially by frugality but principally through Wellington Rankin's wealth and beneficence. She maintained the appearance of poverty because of her radical ideology and her reputation among her admirers as a self-sufficient woman. Living on the edge in Georgia, therefore, was both a personal choice and a political necessity.

While living simply in rural isolation, both Jeannette Rankin and Henry David Thoreau filled their small spaces with radical ideas. Both philosophized about protesting war by withholding tax payments. They differed, however, in that Thoreau thought that a protester's mark depended on moral integrity and Rankin emphasized that the demonstrators' influence depended on their gender, number, and vigor. In "Civil Disobedience," Thoreau wrote: "I know this well, that if one thousand, if one hundred, if ten men whom I could name—if ten honest men only—ay, if one HONEST man, in this State of Massachusetts, ceasing to hold slaves, were actually to withdraw from this copartnership, and be locked up in the county jail therefor, it would be the abolition of slavery in America." The moralistic Thoreau had no interest in achieving reform by political means—exhorting followers and building majority coalitions: "As for adopting the ways which the State has provided for remedying the evil, I know not of such ways. They take too much time, and a man's life will be gone." In contrast, Rankin conceived of politics more practically. She tried her entire life to motivate women to experiment with "the ways which the State has provided for remedying evil."

Mass politics for Jeannette Rankin began conventionally enough with her assumption that a politician's top priority is gaining public support. She said that "members of Congress are more concerned with their reelection than any issue that could come up, . . . so anyone who can influence voters is of great importance to a Congressman." Her underlying, radical meaning was that women could become a political force. Throughout her life she beat the drum for protests by women. A stock response to letters opposing World War II was "if mothers wish to save their sons, they must have the courage immediately to protest, and protest vigorously." Like Thoreau during the Mexican War, Rankin thought that jail was the proper place for the just during the Vietnam War. "If we had 10,000 women willing to go to prison if necessary," she said, "that would end it."

With only rhetorical exceptions, the woman-based protests she advocated and led were nonviolent. During the Montana suffrage campaign she said, "I do not want to be understood as advocating violence." Fifty-four years later, she was at the head of the Jeannette Rankin Brigade—5,000 black-clad women marching from Washington's Union Station to Capitol Hill. The FBI reported that the brigade was "composed predominantly of white, middle-aged women . . . well behaved and orderly," even though "two hundred self-styled 'radical' young women . . . in miniskirts and high boots" said the demonstration was too peaceful and "wanted to stir up 'some illegal action.'" House Speaker John McCormack, when he met Rankin in his office, "did a polite put-down number," and Senate Majority Leader Mike Mansfield, whose idea of protest was even quieter diplomacy, turned his meeting with his fellow Montanan into "a social occasion." Some feminists, however, came to view the Jeannette Rankin Brigade as "a focal point in the development of the women's liberation movement."

Jeannette Rankin's radical thinking in secluded retreat turned to other methods of bringing about political change. One reform, first formulated when she visited New Zealand, would have changed how newspapers shape public opinion. Her suggestion, which she said caused newspapers to turn against her in 1918, was that newspapers should be owned by the government and "run the same as the public schools. We should select our press board who should select the managing editor and the papers should be delivered free at our doors." The crux of her proposal was that newspapers would become "purely educational," by which she meant devoid of a male-dominated perspective. They would "only print the news and the expressions of the people in the community, public letters and opinions, but not have editorial opinions by some man." Rankin's ideas to increase the political influence of women also included proportional-representation elections. In 1922 she opposed a progressive Illinois constitution because it would have junked the system by which a minority, most importantly women, could gain a share of power by winning a fraction of the vote. The head of the constitutional reform effort asked suffragist Catharine Waugh McCulloch to "explain [to Rankin] the much broader proposition of adopting a new Constitution [because] she would doubtless recognize the necessity of considering the whole question rather than just one feature." But Rankin's passionate commitment to her own reform agenda prevented her from seeing the larger picture.

Much of Jeannette Rankin's reform passion in her later years was devoted to congressional and presidential election schemes. Frustrated but not losing faith in women voters after Franklin Roosevelt's repeated victories, she criticized single-member, winner-take-all congressional districts because they favored the better-known and better-credentialed male candidates and also the Electoral College because it restricted the voter's choice to the two men nominated by the Democratic and Republican Parties. Her initial education in the possibilities of multiple-member districts had come in 1916 when she won election to Congress by telling voters in Montana's statewide, two-member district to vote for the local man and for her. Her presidential-election reform was formulated during her 1952 sojourn in India when, "bored" in the Himalayas, she began to critique the Electoral College process that had produced such "horrible" results. To her sister Grace she wrote: "I play with the idea of working for a new method of selecting a president. . . . I have an idea. I want to be prepared to 'dig in' when the [opportunity] comes." That chance came in 1968 when Vietnam War protesters and feminist activists gave her the hero's status she had desired but been denied since 1917. From her new platform to the time of her death, she linked her perennial cause of women and peace to her electoral reforms. Once again she was inspired by Jane Addams and Benjamin Kidd. Addams's feminism, "far from breaking down the myth that temperament is a function of sex, tended to perpetuate it." What women had to contribute, Addams believed, was "a set of distinctive interests of their own, which could no more be served by men than the interests of the proletariat could be served by the bourgeoisie." And Rankin was still striving to realize Kidd's hope that women would "take the lead in the future of civilization" because the "other-regarding self" resides in the "mind of women" and "short-range animal emotions" in the "fighting male."

Jeannette Rankin's electoral reforms were based on, besides Addams's and Kidd's theories, her own belief in democracy. In her 1917 Carnegie Hall speech she had argued that "only through the extension of the democratic process could effective reforms be brought about in the body politic." This grassroots philosophy repeatedly put her at odds with her peace employers in the 1920s and 1930s. She left the Women's International League for Peace and Freedom because "they just wanted me to go and speak," the Women's Peace Union because they "thought they could bring about changes by working from the top down," and the National Council for the Prevention of War because it insisted upon lecturing and lobbying. Nothing had changed when she was in her eighties and nineties. In 1967 she told the Associated Press that the "draft could be abolished if women spoke loudly enough to be heard." In 1969 she told a New York gathering of women, "It is of the utmost importance to the goal of peace that we perfect the machinery through which the people express their wishes." And in Nashville the year before she died she exhorted women from twelve states to commit themselves to "grassroots political organizing."

The electoral reform Jeannette Rankin supported the longest was multiple-member congressional districts, having discarded proportional representation as her favored election system by 1930. Her other electoral reform, "Direct Preferential Vote for President," was a popular-election alternative to the Electoral College. But Congress—where she had hoped to make a difference—was her most pressing concern, as she explained to a resident of her California retirement home: "I still believe Congress is the really important problem. We need larger districts and more from the districts to get real representation." Propelled by the fiftieth anniversary of her entering Congress, the notoriety of the Jeannette Rankin Brigade, and her ninetieth birthday celebration in Washington, she took to the campaign trail to convert her newfound popularity into political clout for women. She urged her two plans on Walter Lippman, Henry Steele Commager, Mike Mansfield, Birch Bayh, James Abourezk, David Frost, Dick Cavett, Edwin Newman, Mike Wallace, Eric Sevareid, Merv Griffin, and Gore Vidal. She presented her presidential-election proposal to the U.S. Senate subcommittee on constitutional amendments and told the Jeannette Rankin Rank and File, women from the Jeannette Rankin Brigade who remained close, that she had "been invited to appear in Washington before the House Committee." She spoke to the Georgia legislature and addressed the Montana constitutional convention. She "accepted all invitations for newspaper, magazine, and television interviews and speaking engagements." A law student, who had left school to be of "devotional service" to Jeannette Rankin, became her scheduler, chauffeur, coauthor, and cook. At every appearance that she, her aide, or someone else could finagle and she could get to, she "made a plea for the preferential vote [and] urged multiple-member districting."

Jeannette Rankin had long hoped that Georgia would be her guinea pig for multiple-member congressional districts. After the 1930 census when Georgia's number of U.S. representatives dropped from twelve to ten, she unsuccessfully encouraged legislators to consider an apportionment plan with two districts, each containing five representatives. After a 1971 lobbying visit to the Georgia legislature, she made a follow-up written plea that drew on her 1916 election experience: "Under the current arrangement . . . only a single man and a single set of ideas represent each district. With multiple member districts, each voter could elect at least two representatives and differing points of view could find a vote in Congress. . . . [W]omen are reluctant to participate in the balloting if they feel their ideas and perspective are not represented. . . . [I]f they feel their needs will find effective voice through the ballot, they will seek expression through our democratic processes."

In an interview just before her death, Jeannette Rankin showed her continued disgust for middle-of-the-road politics and her passion for multiple-member districts. The gist of her argument was that every single-member congressional district has "about 40 percent who are reactionary, and about 40 percent who think they're liberal. Then there's 20 percent in between. . . . [T]he politicians that want to keep their job . . . swing to one side or the other. So that those who are against him never have a representative and those who are for him don't have a representative; they're representing the 20 percent in between [they need] in order to win. . . . [T]hey [don't] dare offend anyone in the 20 percent because they'd lose the election. . . . [T]he great good of the multiple-member district is that you can be a minority and get elected." The standard objections to her plan, which she ignored, were that single-member districts were required by federal law and multiple-member districts would "dilute urban votes," "substantially increase campaign costs," and "further increase buck-passing."

At the Carmel Valley Manor nine months before her death, Jeannette Rankin put in pamphlet form her "Case for the Direct Preferential Vote for President." Her arguments came from the speech she had been delivering for several years. When the National Organization of Women recognized her as the "world's outstanding living feminist," she told the assembly: "[E]verybody knows the Electoral College is a sham. What we need is a participatory democracy through a preferential election." Two of her reform's benefits, she told her audience, were that "anybody who wants to can run" and the "differences between men and women" would be manifested in public policy. The next month at the Montana constitutional convention she again pushed her presidential-election reform and supported it with Jane Addams's argument that "men have progressed as much as they could without the help of women." Her subtext was Benjamin Kidd's theory that the difference between men in power and women in power is the difference between war and peace.

In her pamphlet Jeannette Rankin argued that the "sham" of the Electoral College was its "distort[ing] the meaning of the popular vote and tak[ing] the final choice out of the hands of the voters." In contrast, her reform would allow each presidential candidate to get on the popular ballot through petitions and each voter to list "the candidates in order of individual choice, from first to last." With some precision she described the next steps: "[T]he computer counts all the 1st choice votes; any candidate with a majority of votes is President. If there is no 1st choice majority, the 2nd choice votes are counted as equal to the 1st, and the candidate with the highest number of votes and a majority is President. If there is still no majority, the 3rd choice votes are counted as equal to the 1st and 2nd and, etc." In 1972, when she was demonstrating her plan to various audiences, she included Shirley Chisholm among the thirteen candidates on the sample ballot. Her system, she argued, would provide a varied field and, therefore, would return "to the people the sovereign power of choice," make "the President directly responsible to the voters rather than to pressure groups," and provide "an invaluable index of public opinion."

Jeannette Rankin's reform campaign brought her personal acclaim. Ralph Nader, commenting in his newspaper column on her proposals but mostly on her energy, said that her "stamina behind these ideas and ideals is absolutely staggering." The National Organization of Women honored her, and a New York friend urged past recipients of the Nobel Peace Prize to nominate her for the 1973 award. A typical compliment came from a New York supporter: "You are a constant beacon of truth and good judgment." But support for Rankin's radical reforms was not as strong. Common Cause chairman John W. Gardner was politely but clearly critical: "It appears to produce very lively controversy among any group that begins to talk about it." Since Rankin's death, similar plans have been debated by several states and adopted by a few localities. The radicalness and continued unpopularity of her ideas are reflected in the fate of Lani Guinier, who was derided as a "quota queen" when President Clinton nominated her to be Assistant Attorney General for Civil Rights. She had become known for advocating at-large elections, multiple-member districts, proportional representation, and cumulative voting to correct flaws in the U.S. system of legislative representation.

Even more radical than Jeannette Rankin's election reforms were the social policies she espoused. By 1908, she was aware of the positions of feminist reformers, and a few years later she made their acquaintance in New York. Heterodoxy members who were her friends and supporters campaigned for woman suffrage, but they were also interested in birth control, sexual experimentation, anarchism, communism, socialism, prohibition, pure food and drug regulations, child labor laws, release of political prisoners, and the revolutionary goals of the Industrial Workers of the World. Many of these women "had been radicalized by their experiences" on the Congressional Union picket lines and, as denizens of a new social frontier, anguished in the "void midway between two spheres—the man's sphere and the woman's sphere." Greenwich Village, a mecca for woman reformers, sustained Rankin intellectually and emotionally throughout her life. Just a few months away from her death the pull was still there. "I'd love to call and say I am on my way to New York," she wrote to an acquaintance.

While under Wellington Rankin's influence, Jeannette Rankin was kept within the bounds of rural orthodoxy. But in the company of Katharine Anthony, Elisabeth Irwin, and other New York friends, her unorthodoxy knew only the boundaries of her radical imagination. She was as comfortable with educational innovations, monetary reform, communal living, eugenics, and old age benefits as with quota democracy. Many of her ideas matched up closely with the feminist-utopian prescriptions of the period. The imagined societies of Lillie Devereux Blake, Winnifred Harper Cooley, Mary H. Ford, and Charlotte Perkins Gilman seem no more far-fetched than Jeannette Rankin's support of "hours for soldiers in the trenches," mammoth highway appropriations "to drain away military funds," or "gunpowder–versus–face powder" and "don't-shop-on-Tuesdays" antiwar campaigns.

Feminist utopians found a "refuge or shelter" in their stories from whose safety they could advocate "a changed society." The protagonist was typically "a critical outsider wondering at the folly of the crowd." The folly—victimization of women—was always attributed to the male world of individualism, militarism, sexual dominance, and unsafe work conditions. In the place of a male-run society the utopians offered a splendid new order arising out of "cooperative or communitarian solutions." In Lillie Devereux Blake's "feminine Republic," the woman-inspired changes ranged from "[c]ommon-sense shoes" to arbitration replacing war. In Winnifred Harper Cooley's imagined twenty-first century, "corrupt marriages" and "restrictive sexual relationships" gave way to women free "to select their sexual partners" and "mates . . . 'striv[ing] to please each other.'" Oppressive work conditions and their accompanying evils disappeared, and the incredulous visitor found, instead, "equal wages regardless of sex" and short workdays affording women free time "for inventions, art, and letters."

These feminist utopian proposals resemble the ideas that populated Jeannette Rankin's speeches and the causes that defined her life. Like the feminist utopians, Rankin presented herself as a "critical outsider" who was calling society's attention to its secular sins. Her safe harbor was not utopian storytelling but her unique public status, an economic independence bargained from her brother and purchased by self-denial, and her late-life status of endearing crank whose critics had been silenced by death. Like the utopian figures, Rankin presented herself as a "self-sufficient" woman fleeing the curses of domestic subordination and rural shallowness. Her journal entry at age twenty-two—"'Go! Go! Go! It makes no difference where just so you go! go! go!'"—was as heartfelt as the Edward Bellamy–smitten heroine in Mary H. Ford's utopia who declared: "I want freedom and fresh air in such large, unlimited doses!" Rankin's complaint that Florida suffragists were "sex women" obsessing about her "single blessedness" restated the contempt that the gender-essentialist Charlotte Perkins Gilman expressed for the "sex mania" that made a single woman "unnatural," an "old maid," and a "social reject." Her decision to forego a "beau" and go "the other way" rid her of contending with Winnifred Harper Cooley's "nineteenth-century horror—the city bachelor." The "Ground grippers" she wore in Congress qualified as the "common-sense shoes" in the feminine republic of Lillie Devereux Blake, mother of Rankin's friend and suffrage colleague, Katherine Devereux Blake. Her calls to "abolish the profit system" and socialize copper mines and hydroelectric plants were echoed in Cooley's twenty-first-century utopia where women "abolished oil trusts, private ownership of mines, railways, electric-light plants, and express and telegraph companies." Her argument that eight hours of work would leave a woman "wholesomely tired at the end of the day, and [fit] to devote a few hours in the evening to sane enjoyment and further education," repeated the feminist utopian prescription that women receive "three hours daily of mental or manual labor, whichever was not a person's means of livelihood." Her warning that "child labor" led to "street-roving habits" reflected Cooley's tale of "ragged little newsboys" and children "swarm[ing] the back streets like rats."

A recurring concept in feminist utopias was the "wild zone," a place apart from the world of men where radical feminists were free to experiment and bring forth a "women's reality . . . whose practices may be crucial to the survival of humankind." In Lillie Devereux Blake's writings, Volumnia, "a matron of notable appearance" and "the great leader among women," guided her followers to a feminine republic. Abandoned by women, men consumed enormous amounts of liquor, brawled incessantly, and threatened "to declare war against all the world." Meanwhile in their "wild zone," Volumnia's subjects "had grown self-reliant" and physically developed through their "outdoor lives." They had taken to wearing "blouse waists, short skirts and long boots" for their "out-door labors" and "graceful and flowing robes of Grecian design" for their "home life." Under Volumnia, "[p]eace and tranquility prevailed through all the borders of the feminine Republic."

Jeannette Rankin became a Volumnia-like figure in Katharine Anthony's poetic rendition of Rankin's country life in Georgia. In her *Woman's Home Companion* trilogy, Anthony calls Rankin "Aspasia" after Pericles's mistress and transforms Rankin's sixty-four acres and quaint Bogart house into a "wild zone." In the summer the pioneering Aspasia cultivates virgin land with her hands and boys and girls with her "stories for young citizens." Like her namesake, Aspasia "stir[s] up" and commands the women. She guides the compliant Katharine Anthony, Elisabeth Irwin, and Flora Belle Surles on an outing "to Atlanta for haircuts and manicures." In her "Girls' Club," she permits the adventurous Sparta to stay in the swimming hole, a decision Sparta's older sister, Pearl, reluctantly accepts. In all of the events of the summer, Aspasia is portrayed as consummate and compelling: presiding at breakfast, putting up fruit, and, with her guests in the heat of the summer, "abandon[ing] all clothing except [their] thin cotton dresses." From this "wild zone" Aspasia, through her chronicler Anthony, teaches the external realm lessons about life properly lived. Her story is an allegory of simplicity, commitment, community, organization, leadership, hard work, education, and leisure.

In the feminist utopias, the "wild zone" or "woman's culture" was characterized by experimentalism and communitarianism. Charlotte Perkins Gilman's reformed New York featured a woman happily surrendering her baby to a community playground for the first "two or three years" instead of subjecting the infant to the "bungling experiments of an unaided mother." The mothers benefited from advances in nature as well as nurture. An official in Gilman's utopia explained: "We are constantly improving the quality of the stock as a whole. . . . [T]he female . . . selects among males. That's another idea of the new motherhood. We will not marry the inferior men. . . .

[T]hey enjoy life as human beings and become—extinct." Abandoned along with maternal child-care and "low grade" men was individualistic and inefficient housekeeping. In the place of the cooking-together and eating-together family, Gilman's utopia featured communal "blocks" of 750 residents and "twenty-five cooks, dishwashers and servers to a kitchen." A proud inhabitant of the new New York announced to a visitor: "Come and see the dining rooms. . . . In no part of that foolish, wasteful, wicked way of living did we squander more than in what was called 'housekeeping.' We wasted . . . over a third of our labor and two-thirds of our living expenses." In "Applepieville," another utopian creation, Gilman depicted a "self-sufficient experimental" community "laid out with farms radiating like pie-wedges from its center, where cultural activities and domestic services may be concentrated."

In most of these feminist utopias, ethics replaced religion. In Winnifred Harper Cooley's dream of the "first day of the twenty-first century," the death of traditional religion launched massive social change: the advent of "rational religion . . . destroy[ed] the spite and fight over hair-splitting theological problems," enabled residents "to turn their zeal and energy into practical ethics and philanthropy," and brought about "Universal Peace." In Lillie Devereux Blake's "feminine Republic," schools were placed "under the care of feminine Boards of Education" and "each child was trained to develop a special gift" through daily doses of ethical instruction. In Charlotte Perkins Gilman's reformed New York, schools took the place of churches, social service replaced Christian duty, practical ethics dethroned theology, and results—not principles—became the measure of success. One crusade in Gilman's utopian community was a "special campaign against falsehood" that fined a "proven liar . . . like a spitter." The guide providing a tour of twenty-first-century New York explained that "the average of behavior rises faster every year." In the old order, women were "pre-social individuals" and "kept the world selfish [by spending] their lives in the closest personal relations and car[ing] little for anything outside them." But in the new order women "worship God all the time—by doing things [for] the Bureau of Agriculture and the Health Commission and . . . transportation."

Throughout her life, not just in Katharine Anthony's stories, Jeannette Rankin's ideas and causes resembled the radical inventions of the feminist utopians. Like these visionaries, she emphasized ethics over religion and results over doctrine. To the Christian Science beliefs of her mother and siblings she had a "bitterly negative reaction." She placed religion, drugs, alcohol, and mysticism in the category of "mind-clouding" experiences—all rendering a person out of touch with the here and now. But even though Rankin "had no spiritual base" ("Christianity made people into sheep," she said), "ethical principles—like telling the truth—were extremely important to her." Late in life she summed up women's innate virtue and unique challenge. Women could change the world, she said, if their "compassion, honesty, integrity, and love . . . were incarnated through . . . daily actions and . . . sustained in adversity." Although Rankin's peace habits bring to mind the Sermon on the Mount, she, like the feminist utopians, wanted to produce results not preach beatitudes.

Also bordering on the utopian were Jeannette Rankin's ideas about education. Bright and inquisitive as a child, she had found her own schooling "a dreadful bore." When challenged by her graduate-school instructors, she feared that the inadequacy of her Montana education would prevent her from measuring up to her peers. Later she was drawn to the progressive ideas of her friend Elisabeth Irwin who was experimenting with intelligence testing and ability grouping. When traveling in foreign countries, Rankin inquired into other educational innovations. In Denmark she was impressed by "folk schools." She wrote to an acquaintance that they had accomplished what she had always wanted to do—accelerate the evolutionary process. Their feat, Rankin said, was to "chang[e] Denmark from a dull, sodden peasantry to an enlightened, cooperative, fearless people." Their method, called "the living word," must have reminded Rankin of how she had learned at her father's sawmill and on the campaign trail. Boys "when their work was slack" and girls "when they had less work to do at home" came to the folk schools where "they sang and they read and they . . . did their own cooking and everything, and there was no formality." By doing things—"work[ing] at their economic problems" and taking care of themselves—they learned "to express themselves through language and sayings and history and knowledge of their country."

Jeannette Rankin was even more fascinated by Gandhi's educational methods at the Sevagram ashram, which she called "the most thrilling thing I saw in India." Compared with conventional schooling, Gandhi's pupils "went from the other end." Rankin explained that he "would take the children in a certain community and start them on a project. . . . [I]f they were in the cotton district, they worked with cotton. . . . [T]hey had . . . 'ministers' of housework . . . of streets . . . of toilets and everything. . . . [T]he children did all the work. . . . [What] the teachers did was to perform all the processes very crudely so that the children saw them from the beginning. . . . They got all their arithmetic . . . from the kitchen and the cooking. . . . After dinner at night, the older children or anyone who wanted to listen to the head woman could hear an account of current events. . . . All the [writing] they did was in their diaries. Every word they knew was a word they used." Gandhi's reforms excited Rankin because as an instrumentalist she believed that participatory learning would improve "democratic processes."

No less utopian were Jeannette Rankin's ideas about childcare, eugenics, and collective living. As a suffrage campaigner she had argued that the Montana state orphanage should become a model of child-rearing. She explained to a convention of club women that "the effect of work and play and idleness on character building could be studied, watching the children twenty-four hours a day. In time a store house of information on child life and care [could be used in] a scientific course . . . that would prepare women for scientific motherhood." The result she anticipated was both evolutionary and revolutionary. She challenged her audience, "Is it too much to hope that in time we have no 'Topsies.'" Rankin's interest in eugenics was apparent when World War I placed conscription on the nation's agenda. She fought President Wilson's induction plan with a preservation-of-the-fittest argument: "[B]y drawing exclusively upon the young men between nineteen and twenty-five years of age for the first army the country will strip itself of the future fathers of the race. . . . [T]o take away the marriageable men would force women in selecting husbands to draw upon less desirable classes and types and produce a generation far inferior to the standard set in this country." As an old woman she was still enamored with eugenics, telling an interviewer that "the whole trouble with England today is, every generation she kills off the good bulls [and] they just have the scrubs." Rankin was equally in tune with the utopians' praise of communal living. In 1917 she and Katharine Anthony instructed American women in the *Ladies Home Journal* to conserve for the war effort not by "return[ing] to primitive housekeeping customs [such as] soap making, candle making and home grinding" but by imitating the "public food kitchens, free school lunches and other forms of community feeding" being used in France and Germany.

Even closer to the "wild zone" was Jeannette Rankin's decision to build a "roundhouse" on her Watkinsville property. Her idea for a commune was hatched earlier—possibly in young womanhood when she read Charlotte Perkins Gilman and discovered in "Applepieville" a model for her round-house. In 1966, anticipating her inheritance from Wellington Rankin, Jeannette Rankin told Flora Belle Surles that her plan had taken definite shape: "I suggested that [a retired neighbor] help me build my co-op home-stead for old ladies. I'm all excited about it." In letters to prospective residents, Rankin described the layout and location of her roundhouse: "[T]en small bedrooms . . . on the perimeter of the circular house [provide] each woman a measure of privacy, while the large central living area offers op-portunity for companionship and communal activities. There is one shower and one full bathroom . . . and there is a community kitchen. . . . Each woman has a half bath that is a toilet and hand basin. . . . Exterior landscaping and beautifying would be left to the occupants. There is also ample space for vegetable gardening. . . . The house has electricity and can have a phone . . . [and is] within walking distance from the country store. . . . I hadn't planned to furnish the bedrooms unless someone wanted it furnished. I'm expecting some furniture from Montana [Avalanche Ranch discards after Wellington Rankin's death] and I have more than I need in my house." To a Montana newspaper she explained that she was going to charge a "fifteen dollar monthly rental" and was hoping that the selected ten elderly women would "live like a family."

Designed by Jeannette Rankin and built under her supervision, the cement-block roundhouse went begging for tenants. Aspasia's zeal, in this instance, failed to inflame any disciples. One drawback was that the round-house was unfinished and, far from being a care facility, anticipated able and industrious inhabitants. To an elderly "unemployed homemaker" from Georgia, Rankin explained: "It is not a nursing home, but for women . . . in the habit of doing [their] own work. It can't really be finished until each one puts on some finishing touches." Another obstacle was its communal and spare regimen. A widow from Florida told Rankin that she had read about "The Cooperative Home" but that the single refrigerator was a problem: "I simply cannot picture ten women using one refrigerator." Another woman was initially excited ("Please put my application in right now . . . for your Heart 'n Brain Child-Home for Retirees") but later withdrew her application because her daughters were skeptical and wanted to make an inspection.

With her dream of elder communal life dashed, Jeannette Rankin, undeterred, turned to another generation for the idealism she was seeking in her tenants. She rented the roundhouse to members of the local Students for a Democratic Society whose peace sentiments she shared. The roundhouse, however, soon became the setting for more than peace radicalism. Police arrested the occupants for marijuana possession and being "part of a main supply line for marijuana in northeast Georgia." Rankin saw the incident differently: "They just wanted the house so I let them have it. I don't know the circumstances of the charges but they are welcome to return. Hippies are doing a very interesting thing, and I think we ought to help. Hippies are very much like Gandhi in not conforming." In a letter to her mother, Rankin's niece Dorothy surmised that rural Georgia was no more open to her aunt's radicalism in 1969 than it had been in 1934: "Poor Jeannette—It ain't safe to be different."

Being different, however, was what defined the public Jeannette Rankin. In 1917 she and her office staff were called "Reds" by their colleagues in Congress because "[we were] so on the outside of what we should have been doing." At the 1919 Women's International Conference for Permanent Peace in Zurich, she continued to support the Russian revolution. There she "asked for an explanation of the 'warfare being waged without open declaration . . . upon people who are experimenting in a new social and economic order which had not yet had a fair trial, but which may prove to have a great contribution to make to the future of the world.'" In 1925 Katharine Anthony and Elisabeth Irwin presumed it to be "very disappointing" to Rankin that her planned trip to Russia "was off." She did travel to Moscow in 1962 to attend a "world conference on peace that Khrushchev organized." There she revealed the basis of her infatuation with the Soviet Union. "I was [so] disgusted with the peace attitude of the American group," she said, "that I told them that since the Russians controlled their military organization they could do what we couldn't do . . . disarm immediately and totally and unilaterally. And I said, 'But we can't do it because we're controlled by the army! But you control your army; therefore, you could do it.'"

The state socialism of the Soviet Union had something in common with Jeannette Rankin's economic beliefs. During the Great Depression she indicated several times that she had grown disillusioned with nationalism and capitalism. To a sympathizer she wrote: "[W]ith increasing unemployment and a definite tendency toward Fascism in the Government, it seems to me that there is no possible way of establishing a world organization as long as the profit system controls. Our present efforts must be directed toward facing the facts and preparing for a peaceful elimination of the profit system." This view never changed. As an elderly woman she was still calling capitalism a "stupid money system." Another tenet of communism Rankin appeared to favor was radical equality. During the economic distress of the 1930s she enthusiastically supported the ideas of Huey Long, Upton Sinclair, Dr. Francis Townsend, and the Reverend Charles Coughlin—all political enemies of the too conservative Franklin Roosevelt. Jeannette Rankin especially liked Huey Long's anti–big business sentiments and minimum-income schemes, telling him "how much she appreciated his efforts to redistribute wealth" and, "When you bring out the point that interest is usury, . . . it gives me great pleasure." After Long's murder, she confided to Wellington Rankin her sense of the conspiracy that was responsible for the death of her radical hero: "It has been known for some time that the plan was to draw straws to select the one to shoot him. Of course, we all knew that the easiest way for the opposition to dispose of his ideas would be to shoot him. . . . [I]t will be a long time before we find anyone else to have the ability to live through the attack of the newspapers and the scandal mongers and the political organizations to arrive at the point where the only way they can reach him is by killing him. . . . I can see nothing but chaos ahead." There were other radicals on the scene, however, who gave Rankin some comfort. She supported Upton Sinclair's plan of agricultural socialism, "End Poverty in California," and Dr. Townsend's "Old Age Revolving Pension Plan," which would have provided every person sixty and older $200 a month. She was in sympathy with Father Coughlin's radio diatribes against Franklin Roosevelt and his argument that passé capitalism should be replaced by a new system of social justice. Rankin also had her own ideas for social equality and her expression of them was typically blunt: "I feel," she testified before a congressional committee, "that you should pay . . . whatever the soldier's wage is . . . to every one, and let every one have a tin cup and bread card and subsist on the same food that the soldier does beginning with the President."

To the day she died Jeannette Rankin did battle with the established order. But, in comparison with her radical political causes and methods, her personal affairs were far more conventional and comfortable than she lct on. Taking up space in her psyche were not only a feminist, a socialist, and a pacifist but also a woman dependent on her brother, a capitalist and a fighter. By reputation she was a Gandhi-like reformer, but in reality she resembled her power-hungry brother. She wanted influence and fame as much as Wellington Rankin did and competed with him for the spectral approval of their father. She repeatedly submitted to Wellington Rankin's directives about what she should do and how she should look and became, as a result, a well-dressed and wealthy woman. Although she benefited greatly from her family's material success, her comfort came not without emotional distress. Undoubtedly her radical reform bent resulted, in part, from her feelings of guilt.

Jeannette Rankin's manner of dress symbolized her conflicted person. On her Georgia plot or Wellington Rankin's ranch she "expressed disdain for people who dressed well" and angered her mother by her sloppy dress, donning her relatives' discarded "ski pants" and "ragged sweater[s]." But in the public eye she followed the Rankin family's standard of elegant dress. In 1914 in her "gold colored velvet suit," she leapt upon the Montana suffrage stage looking "like a young panther." In 1917, opening her post-election speaking tour at Carnegie Hall, she charmed the audience with her "becoming pink chiffon dress, cut rather short to show her ankles and trim little feet encased in white silk stockings and white satin slippers." A month later, making her inaugural appearance in Congress, she appropriately wore a "dark blue silk and chiffon suit, with open neck and wide crepe collar and cuffs." In 1961, when accepting an honorary Doctor of Laws degree from Montana State University, she "looked perfectly lovely in a new sort of raw silk fawn colored dress with her hair done in that grey-ginger color." In 1968 she showed up for an interview with a graduate student "dressed in a tailored blue plaid suit and silk printed blouse complete with a patterned scarf and pin, black calf-high boots, and a Shirley Temple ash blond-copper blended wig." The internal struggle manifested in the clothing she wore continued to her death. In 1972, after her television interview with David Frost, she told her aide to "return the [Shanghai Silk] dress" she had bought and worn for the occasion.

Jeannette Rankin's two modes of dress symbolized the distance between her political beliefs and her Rankin roots, but more telling were her public-private inconsistencies involving war protest, labor justice, and property ownership. Despite her affinity with the jailed Congressional Union demonstrators, her pronouncement that she would lead militant Vietnam War protesters all the way to prison, and her regret that she had not been "nastier" in her politics, Rankin was always more genteel than radical in her protest. In 1913 she told a newspaper, "I do not want to be understood as advocating violence," and she led suffragists in a pageant that was "simultaneously feminine and feminist." In 1917 she admonished striking miners, "Good Americans must obey the law. There will be no demonstration tonight." During the Vietnam War, her personal protest consisted of not paying the federal excise tax on her telephone calls. She had been inspired by Henry David Thoreau who had written, "one HONEST man" willing to "be locked up in the county jail" could bring an end to slavery. But after withholding her telephone tax, Jeannette Rankin went not to jail but to Wellington Rankin's partners for legal assistance. Wellington Rankin's widow replied: "I have the following information for you. . . . I hope it is what you want. You have two accounts—an ordinary savings account, and an account for C/D's. . . . I will be interested to know how you come out with the Internal Revenue. We will be glad to defend you if it comes to that. . . . The bank . . . said [the IRS] could serve them with an attachment on $21.00 of it."

In the matter of labor justice, too, there was incongruity between Jeannette Rankin's public stands and private affairs. At the start of her congressional career, she did battle for workers in the Bureau of Engraving and Printing and Butte's underground mines. Articles were published under her name that championed an eight-hour workday for women and an end to child labor. But Jeannette Rankin was not above benefiting personally from wretched working conditions. In the mid-1950s, before Wellington Rankin bought her the Weiglow Ranch, she twice asked him to finalize the transaction before she left for South America: "I would like to sign that deed we talked about before I sail." Her eagerness about the ranch carried over in a letter to Flora Belle Surles: "Did I tell you that I'm buying a ranch ten miles toward Helena from 71? Of course Wellington is going to run it and make the payments but I have 100 cows and a brand . . . 'Lazy one O one.'" Wellington Rankin's widow confirmed Jeannette Rankin's description of the arrangement: "In 1954, Wellington bought the 71 Ranch. Soon after he bought for Jeannette the nearby Weiglow Ranch to supplement her income. Wellington provided 125 head of cattle for the ranch and managed it with his employees from the 71." Persistent rumors about the work conditions Wellington Rankin forced upon his ranch employees should have given the labor reformer pause. But Jeannette Rankin, whose public position on labor conditions was enlightened, did not hesitate to accept the proceeds from her ranch run by her brother.

Jeannette Rankin's credentials as a capitalist involved more than absentee ownership of a ranch. Even though she said on more than one occasion that she opposed business profits, she entered into a series of moneymaking ventures. With her mother in the mid-1930s, she bought a house in Athens, Georgia, and asked Wellington for a loan so that she could increase their profits: "I am trying to have the house Mother and I bought in Athens made over into four apartments. . . . The house cost $4,200 and has ten good rooms. . . . [We can] get $100 a month rent for the four apartments. It now looks as if I'll have to pay $1,400 or $1,500 to get it in good shape. I have only $500 that I can put in. I have the $500 of mother's you sent but I think she likes to feel she has that much on hand. If you think it all right for mother to put in $700 and lend me $200 it will help me out a lot. . . . Mother and I have made 5 percent on the building for each year. I think I could sell it for what we've put in it and could make something on it." Jeannette was still getting income from the building in 1944, as was evident from Grace's telling Wellington, "Jeannette is debating about selling her apartment house." Wellington's reply to Grace was that of the family's premier capitalist: "Sure, if she can get her money out."

Jeannette Rankin was involved in another apartment-house venture, which she ran to maximize her profits. As the owner of the Benton Avenue Flats and Broadway Flats in Helena, she allowed the two buildings to deteriorate in the same way Wellington Rankin had run his ranches. When sending Jeannette the monthly rent receipts, Wellington's widow informed Jeannette that a notice had been received from the City of Helena "to either fix up the two places or tear them down." The City's order read: "An inspection was made January 18, 1968, of the Jeannette Rankin property at 604-6-8-10 Broadway. . . . The building, through inadequate maintenance, has become dilapidated, unsafe and a public nuisance. . . . [It] must be abated by repair and rehabilitation or by demolition and removal." Wellington's widow advised Jeannette that "it would cost too much money to do either," thereby creating the certainty that "the City will tear them down and charge it against the property."

Over the years Jeannette Rankin also contradicted her belittling of capitalism by becoming a shareholder in U.S. corporations. During the Vietnam

War she even "continued to hold stock in . . . companies that produced modern weapons of war." Her stock transactions, as many of her other practical affairs such as driver's licenses, income taxes, and passports, were managed by the Rankin law office before and after his death. In 1969 Wellington's widow told Jeannette that she and her law partner "wouldn't think of charging you for anything" because their services to her were "still part of [their] office work." A constant stream of information and instructions from the Rankin law office in Montana to Jeannette Rankin in Georgia between 1965 and 1971 reveals her extensive investments and comfortable financial condition: "enclosing your Montana Flour Dividend check"; "enclosing a paper from the Equitable Assurance Company. . . . [Y]our annuity [is] here at the office"; "are you watching Boeing and United go up—Are quite a bit higher than when you left"; "will keep you informed as to the balance in your account . . . and of all deposits which should include the Broadway Flat check, Social Security, and any and all dividend checks"; "deposited . . . dividends [from] Montana Flour Mills—$354, United Aircraft—$108, Boeing Co.—$55"; "enclosing a dividend check from Fairchild Hiller"; "found some men willing to buy the Rim Rock oil wells. . . . [T]hey want to buy yours too [and you would] be paid off out of production"; "ninety shares of United Aircraft and 1,569 shares of Helena Hotel Co. stock have also been placed in your safety deposit box. . . . Further enclosed a copy of a Promissory note . . . for $30,000, the balance due on the cattle"; "deposited three checks [for] Social Security—$123.10, United Aircraft—$121.50, Boeing Co.—$66.00"; "Big West Oil people had deposited to your account $1,058.14, as your share of the production from the Kalispell-Kevin lease property"; "You have 1,180 shares [of Montana Flour Mills stock] . . . give the matter of selling serious consideration"; "check for the 1,180 shares which came to $43,424 came."

Year after year the dividends and deposits accumulated. In 1972, Jeannette Rankin added to her wealth by selling the Weiglow Ranch and using some of the proceeds for gifts of $3,000 each to thirteen members of the Rankin family. After Jeannette Rankin's death in 1973, her lawyer placed the value of her estate at $162,000 (approximately $720,000 today). Her death and the immediate appearance of a celebratory biography occasioned a vigorous protest by Edna Rankin to the author that she had fallen for the public Jeannette Rankin and missed entirely the private person. "[Y]ou have made it sound as though Jeannette was desperately poor," Edna complained.

"Jeannette knew that [Wellington] had meant for her to have whatever she needed. Actually, she had greater access to any funds that my father left than any of us—and I never knew of a time when Jeannette did not have money to travel. She had a peculiar sort of neurosis of WANTING to APPEAR poor—and she seemed to *enjoy* living in privation as though it was sort of *indecent* to have any money. I feel that it is rather pathetic that she should appear to the world as one who was in desperate 'want of money' when that actually was not the case. [Both Jeannette and Wellington] had a most peculiar attitude toward money, but Jeannette felt she must advertise that she was desperately poor—when she was NOT."

Jeannette Rankin was like Wellington Rankin in another way. In her will she left her money to Rankin family members and a few associates but not to further the good work of others. Among Jeannette Rankin's beneficiaries was Wonder Robinson whose family lived for years on her Watkinsville land and helped her with chores. He received his house and its plot of land, five more acres, and the fishpond near the roundhouse. Each of Robinson's three children received $2,000. The man who built the roundhouse and another helper each received five acres of her Georgia property. A "charitable foundation" to be set up by the will's administrator, Edna's daughter Dorothy, received the roundhouse, Jeannette's house, and ten acres with the stipulation that it continue her experiment to "serve the needs of unemployed mature women workers." Four nieces and nephews—Grace's three children and Dorothy—received $10,000 each, and another niece and a great-niece received $5,000 each. The balance of the estate was divided among the remaining great-nieces and great-nephews. Lawyer Edna believed that Jeannette's disposition of her wealth amounted to "the dumbest will I could imagine. . . . I really don't know what was in her mind and I sometimes wonder if she did!" Dorothy, frustrated in implementing her aunt's plan for the roundhouse, agreed with her mother: "I have fit, fought, bled, and died over Jeannette's estate lately. . . . Five years and I still haven't settled the round house business." Another peculiarity, in Edna's judgment, was that two nieces, Harriet's daughters, received nothing. Edna believed that they had angered Jeannette by ignoring her example and getting married. Jeannette's silence about peace in her will—the cause that had been her identity for fifty-six years—also bothered Edna. Jeannette Rankin had frequently said that "she wanted to leave everything to a peace organization," but she left nothing because "she didn't feel any of them were doing a proper job!"

Epilogue

A Rankin First

J EANNETTE RANKIN WAS A POLITICAL PHOENIX, REAPPEARING FROM TIME TO time as her nature dictated. Her seasons in the sun were notorious as well as glorious, but undeterred, she kept coming back to accomplish what she felt she was ordained to do. Women, especially, were drawn to her because she represented so strikingly their aspirations and dreams. Given her electric presence, she was "eminently suited" to symbolize the emergence of women in national politics. But given her drive to keep going, she ended her life as a faint image of the victor she was in 1916.

Jeannette Rankin was a political woman to her core. She was fascinated by government, yearned to exercise authority, and believed herself as capable as the men who possessed political power and prestige. Like her successors, she defined politics "to include both public and private realms." She introduced what came to be known as the Sheppard-Towner Maternity Act, just as Representative Patricia Schroeder years later sponsored the Family and Medical Leave Act. But to become the successful politician she wanted to be, the first woman of American politics did what politicians

223

of both genders and all stripes commonly do. She starved her private realm in order to fuel her public career.

In one significant way, however, Jeannette Rankin distinguished herself from ordinary politicians. Political commentators from Plato to the *Washington Post* have criticized politicians for being slavish to the public in defining their stands. In the metaphor of "a large and powerful animal," Plato criticized the politician's habit of "going out of his way to make the public his master and to subject himself to the fatal necessity of producing only what it approves." In 2001, when Rankin's successors numbered fifty-six in the U.S. House and nine in the U.S. Senate, the *Washington Post* criticized both political men and political women for relying on "poll-driven politics" and promising slices of the public pie to critical groups of voters. In contrast, Jeannette Rankin—like one of Plato's Guardians—refused to pander to the public when she presented solutions to society's problems. She never ceased using power-to-the-people rhetoric, but she had little confidence that correct answers would come from the common man and, at times, even despaired that they would come from the common woman. She deferred to the people at election time, but once in power she pushed her own ideas, apparently believing in a "Government of the people by an elite sprung from the people."

Jeannette Rankin's life was filled with other anomalies. Her electoral success came from both her extraordinary campaign talent and her brother's savvy and money. Her stellar campaigning contrasted with her modest success as a member of Congress. Despite commitment to labor reform, maternal health, and woman suffrage, her two votes against war are her legislative legacy. Possibly to explain her largely symbolic congressional record, her admirers have created another anomaly by depicting her not as a politician but as a person of conscience—unwilling to compromise principle to get reelected. Jeannette Rankin, however, was eminently political. She understood that political success depends on both power and flexibility. Despite finding compromise impossible after pacifism became her identity, she backtracked from her vote against World War I during her first term and tried to build bridges to congressional opponents.

The story of another unique congresswoman further teaches us about political pioneering and personality. In 1972 Barbara Jordan became the first African American woman elected to Congress from a southern state. From an early age Jordan felt different from others and worked hard to convert her personal traits into political assets. She cultivated a commanding presence by perfecting her distinctive voice and judiciously dressing her ample figure. She converted her special status into the de facto office of women's representative. She welcomed her deluge of mail, made frequent appearances, and gave many interviews. To cope with the burdens of public life, she demanded privacy in her personal life, shunned marriage, maintained a sustaining relationship with a woman, and put up with whisperings about her sexual orientation. More completely than Jeannette Rankin, Barbara Jordan earned fame for herself and acceptance for her causes by accommodating personal principle to political realities.

Jeannette Rankin's political success, in comparison, is less apparent and her place in history less secure. What emerges from her story is a struggle between the flawed and the noble: cheapness as well as the common good, arrogance as well as democratic spirit, meanness as well as lofty ideas, and self-preoccupation as well as public service. Her Spartan lifestyle stemmed not only from fear of poverty, guilt because of her family's wealth, and a need to appear self-sufficient, but also from a "stingy soul." Her crusades were propelled in part by noblesse oblige and rarely placed a claim on her money and vanity. She lacked a genuine common touch, could rarely rise above the concrete, and failed to fire the imagination of her followers with clear and beautifully expressed ideas. Preoccupied with herself and her causes, she was unable to touch listeners with self-deprecating humor. The complex and conflicted Jeannette Rankin was charismatic and inspiring but not personally endearing. A relative said that he "felt close to her" only in her last days "when her fear of death made her seem humanly vulnerable."

Jeannette Rankin, in sum, was both a Rankin and a radical. She grew up in a mansion with modern plumbing, but she lived as an adult in a shack without a toilet. She enjoyed the benefits of wealth, but she attacked people of privilege. She dressed splendidly, but she ridiculed others who wore fancy clothes. She was a stock-trading capitalist, but she espoused socialist solutions to society's problems. She ignored peonage on her Montana ranch, but she advocated labor reforms. She followed her brother's worldly advice, but she condemned the world's injustice. She submitted to her brother's rule, but she was a New Woman. During her first term in Congress, Jeannette Rankin briefly reconciled her two selves by subordinating her radical principles to political success. Later, she willed her radicalness to the fore, but she could never completely deny that she was a Rankin first.

Essay on Sources

J EANNETTE RANKIN HAS BEEN THE SUBJECT OF BIOGRAPHIES, DOCTORAL DISSER-
tations, master's theses, journal articles, speeches, oral histories, and
children's books. These interpretations of her life have been generally
favorable; she is described as "the country's most dedicated pacifist,"
"the greatest woman in American political history," "hav[ing] done more
for women in this country than any other political figure," "the greatest
feminist this century has seen," and "one of the great humanitarians of this
age." Rankin was not happy, however, with some other assessments—especially by Ronald Schaffer in his doctoral dissertation, "Jeannette Rankin:
Progressive Isolationist" (Princeton, 1959). After its appearance she likely
resolved to do a better job of controlling the telling of her story.

Throughout her life, Jeannette Rankin tried to control the judgment of
others about her. She stored her first-term papers at the family residence in
Missoula, Montana, and her second-term papers at her brother's ranch.
When the house was razed and dampness crept into the ranch buildings,
some of these documents were ruined. It has even been rumored that she

deliberately destroyed some of her papers. Whether she went to such an extreme to protect her reputation is not known, but it is clear that she became selective about which scholars were allowed to use the surviving documents. Scholar John C. Board was entrusted with many of her papers and responded with a positive master's thesis, "The Lady from Montana: Jeannette Rankin" (Wyoming, 1964). What remained of Jeannette Rankin's and Wellington Rankin's papers were donated by their niece Dorothy McKinnon Brown and Wellington's widow Louise Rankin Galt to the Montana Historical Society and the Schlesinger Library at Radcliffe College. The University of Montana library lost whatever Rankin papers it once possessed and received no further gifts because, as Dorothy Brown said, the family was "furious at the University . . . for never giving [Jeannette Rankin] an honorary degree."

Jeannette Rankin also learned to be selective with information during interviews with scholars. Although she freely granted these sessions—seemingly to anyone who asked—she repeated over and over again the same anecdotes with a self-serving spin. Some interviewers, however, were able to provoke her into revealing deeper feelings. The interview record includes verbatim interviews conducted by Hannah Josephson for *Jeannette Rankin: First Lady in Congress* (1974); Malca Chall for the Suffragists Oral History Project at the University of California, Berkeley; and Katrina Cheek for "The Rhetoric and Revolt of Jeannette Rankin" (University of Georgia, 1969). The Josephson and Chall interviews are available through the University of California's Bancroft Library, and the Cheek interviews are appended to her thesis. Another scholar, Helen Bonner, made available through the University of Montana transcripts of her interviews with some of Rankin's acquaintances and political contemporaries that she conducted for her doctoral research. These interviews contain some revealing recollections, but the dissertation itself—"The Jeannette Rankin Story" (Ohio University, 1982)—is a fictionalized screenplay ("the story of Jeannette's life the way I think it was, and as it might have been") complete with a love affair with a red-bearded mountain man.

Focusing on their scholarly perspective, the writings on Jeannette Rankin can be labeled as friendly or critical. The "friendly" authors readily admit that they became "captivated" by their subject. Norma Smith's *Jeannette Rankin: America's Conscience* (2002) grew out of her friendship with Rankin, beginning in 1962, which included regular summer visits with

Rankin in Georgia. A Montanan, Smith placed Rankin solidly and approvingly within a western tradition and adamantly refused to "sex up" her account. Ted Harris's dissertation, "Jeannette Rankin: Suffragist, First Woman Elected to Congress, and Pacifist" (University of Georgia, 1972), had its roots in rural Georgia. As a local minister, he was associated with Rankin's Oconee County Neighborhood Committee for a Participatory Democracy. Like Smith, he does not try to hide his admiration for his friend's courage and vision. Most hagiographic are John Kirkley's "An Afternoon with Jeannette Rankin," published by the University of Georgia in 1971, and "A Chapter in a Life," written in 1973 and unpublished, both of which make clear that the "devotional service" Kirkley rendered Rankin included his biographical essays. Hannah Josephson's celebration of Rankin's life was influenced by the two women's relationship, which stemmed from their ties to a mutual friend, Katharine Anthony. About the biography the *New York Times Review of Books* commented that if Jeannette Rankin "did have a below-the-surface life filled with the usual run of personal agonies, thwarted hopes, and ambitions, her biographer, Hannah Josephson, a friend of twenty years' standing, prefers not to tell. . . . In an age of intimate biography, it is singularly unencumbered by psychological, political, or anecdotal revelations."

The critical works partially fill the void noted by the *New York Times Review of Books* because they begin the process of humanizing "Saint Jeannette." Belle Fligelman Winestine—a journalist, first-term aide to Jeannette Rankin, and a longtime acquaintance—was able to move beyond her fascination with Rankin in her interviews, speeches, published article, and unfinished manuscript. Winestine's soft criticism, however, seems for the purpose of establishing that she, too, was at the center of activity in Rankin's first-term congressional office. Kevin S. Giles's *Flight of the Dove: The Story of Jeannette Rankin* (1980) speculates, amidst fulsome praise, about Rankin's sexual ambiguity ("a man in a woman's body") and notes her anxiety and bitterness in old age. Its usefulness, however, is undercut by an unclear focus and dearth of documentation. Ronald Schaffer's 1959 Princeton dissertation, written under the direction of historian Eric Goldman, earned him Jeannette Rankin's scathing criticism. She was incensed that he suggested that Wellington Rankin had his own political agenda, her peace ideas were jumbled, and her life was marred by inconsistencies. When Wellington Rankin said suing the graduate student was out of the question,

Jeannette dismissed Schaffer's judgments as the ravings of a love-struck young man. (Schaffer was newly engaged.) Of special interest among the critical works are two 1980 articles in *Montana: The Magazine of Western History* and several speeches by historian Joan Hoff Wilson. Using, among other sources, the National Council for the Prevention of War Papers at Swarthmore College and Norma Smith's research materials, Wilson provides a fuller understanding of Jeannette Rankin's personality, pacifism, and impact on U.S. foreign policy. Most significant are her conclusions that Rankin was wracked by self-doubt and insecurity, her ideas were simplistic, her World War I vote was the pinnacle of her career, and her legacy was largely symbolic.

Although some of the secondary works on Jeannette Rankin are perceptive and bold, the primary-source materials—especially personal correspondence—provide the most valuable insights into Rankin's life. At the Montana Historical Society are the Jeannette Rankin Papers and the Wellington Rankin Papers. The Jeannette Rankin collection focuses on her 1916 congressional campaign and her first term in Congress and consists primarily of correspondence from New York friends and allies, constituents, and strangers from across the country. Included are several hundred letters from Montana women who responded to the form letter Rankin sent out from Washington shortly after her vote against World War I. This correspondence has been analyzed by historian Mary Murphy in a speech, "Women in the West Telling Their Stories." Wellington Rankin's papers, donated by his widow in 1985 and recently catalogued, contain a constant flow of letters from family members to Wellington, the acknowledged head of the Rankin family. Two studies of Wellington Rankin—Richard K. Hines's "Wellington Duncan Rankin: The Man Behind the Myth" (Washington State University, 1996) and Volney Steele's *Wellington Rankin: His Family, Life and Times* (2002)—relied on the unsorted Wellington Rankin Papers to document his law, ranching, and political activities.

The Schlesinger Library at Radcliffe College was chosen by Dorothy McKinnon Brown to house the remaining Jeannette Rankin papers that were in the Rankin family's possession. Found in the microfilm collection "Women in National Politics, Part B: Republicans," these papers (not all are yet open to the public) shed light on Rankin's second term in Congress, family and personal relationships, peace work, and, to a limited degree, suffrage and first-term activities. Brown also placed in the Schlesinger Library the papers of her mother, Edna Rankin McKinnon. This collection covers Edna's long experience in the birth-control movement and includes a large body of family correspondence whose frequent subject is Jeannette. Also at the Schlesinger Library are the papers of some of Jeannette Rankin's friends and political colleagues. The collections of Flora Belle Surles, Harriet Laidlaw, Mary Ware Dennett, Margaret Foley, Catharine McCulloch, Belle Fligelman Winestine, Harriet Yarrow, and Hannah Josephson provide even more perspective on the political woman Jeannette Rankin.

Notes

RANKIN FAMILY

DMB	Dorothy McKinnon Brown
ERM	Edna Rankin McKinnon
GRK	Grace Rankin Kinney
HRM	Harriet Rankin McGregor
HRS	Harriet Rankin Sedman
JR	Jeannette Rankin
MRB	Mary Rankin Bragg
WR	Wellington Rankin

MANUSCRIPT COLLECTIONS

ERMP	Edna Rankin McKinnon Papers
JRP	Jeannette Rankin Papers
WRP	Wellington Rankin Papers

LIBRARIES AND ARCHIVES

LOC	Library of Congress
MHS	Montana Historical Society
SL	Schlesinger Library, Radcliffe College
SOHP	Suffragists Oral History Project, Bancroft Library
UML	University of Montana Library

1. PROLOGUE : POSSESSED BY POLITICS

1   "driven by a demon": *Augusta Chronicle,* 11 November 1971, JRP, SL.

she lived everywhere: Norma Smith, "Fighting Pacifist: Jeannette Rankin and Her Times" (unpublished manuscript, 1999), 241.

Like many political women who came after her: Linda Witt, Karen M. Paget, and Glenna Matthews, *Running as a Woman: Gender and Power in American Politics* (New York: The Free Press, 1994), 76–77.

2   loved each of his seven children: Hannah Josephson, *Jeannette Rankin: First Lady in Congress* (New York: Bobbs-Merrill, 1974), 10.

"unresponsive 'problem' child": Kevin J. Giles, *Flight of the Dove: The Story of Jeannette Rankin* (Beaverton, OR: Touchstone, 1980), 24.

"didn't like it": Smith, "Fighting Pacifist," 30

"probably of a sexual nature": Norma Smith, interview with authors, 3 July 1999.

other possibilities: Volney Steele, *Wellington Rankin: His Family, Life, and Times* (Bozeman, MT: Bridger Creek Historical Press, 2002), 29.

3   "Go! Go! Go!": quoted in Ronald Schaffer, "Jeannette Rankin: Progressive Isolationist" (Ph.D. dissertation, Princeton University, 1959), 6.

left the New York School: Katrina Rebecca Cheek, "The Rhetoric and Revolt of Jeannette Rankin" (M.A. thesis, University of Georgia, 1969), 62; Alfred J. Kahn, "Themes for a History: The First Hundred Years of the Columbia University School of Social Work," June 1998, www.columbia.edu/cu/ssw/events/ajkahn, accessed 21 August 2000.

with her sophisticated education: Josephson, *First Lady,* 25.

While Wellington was settling: Smith, "Fighting Pacifist," 44.

"suffocating": quoted in Josephson, *First Lady,* 25.

"I couldn't take it": quoted in Smith, "Fighting Pacifist," 46.

Oral Expression: ibid.

"self-denying, domestic, subservient" voice: Martha J. Cutter, *Unruly Tongue: Identity and Voice in American Women's Writing, 1850–1930* (Jackson: University Press of Mississippi, 1999), 8.

4   peculiarly a woman's issue: Smith, "Fighting Pacifist," 52, 64.

"erotic experimentation": John D'Emilio and Estelle B. Freedman, *Intimate Matters: A History of Sexuality in America* (New York: Harper & Row, 1988), 229.

5   "[T]hey all did as I said": quoted in Cheek, "Rhetoric and Revolt," 160.

her contribution to the campaign's success: Doris Buck Ward, "Winning of Woman Suffrage in Montana" (M.A. thesis, University of Montana, 1974), 108, 122, 131.

"tumultuous welcome": Josephson, *First Lady,* 44, 47.

weighing a campaign for Congress: Kathryn Anderson, "Steps to Political Equality: Woman Suffrage and Electoral Politics in the Lives of Emily Newall Blair, Anne Hennrietta Martin, and Jeannette Rankin," *Frontiers* 18 (January–April 1997), 106; Smith, "Fighting Pacifist," 98.

"a man's world": Witt, Paget, and Matthews, *Running as a Woman,* 50.

"altruism" and "toughness": ibid., 30, 249.

"perfect little lad[y]": ibid., 56.

"hot dirty trains": Mackey Brown, "Montana's First Woman Politician: A Recollection of Jeannette Rankin Campaigning," *Montana Business Quarterly* 9 (autumn 1971), 23.

"ran as a woman": Witt, Paget, and Matthews, *Running as a Woman*, 31.

"[T]he first time it was suffrage": JR, interview with Malca Chall, SOHP, 53.

"multiple winners": Nancy E. McGlen et al., *Women, Politics, and American Society*, 3rd edition (New York: Longman, 2002), 102.

6   "She will win for us the fight": Margaret Van Slate to JR, 16 March 1917, JRP, MHS.

Rankin's campaign rash: Anna Howard Shaw to JR, 20 March 1917, JRP, MHS.

not sufficiently "intellectual": quoted in Smith, "Fighting Pacifist," 107.

"The day of our deliverance": quoted in *Daily Missoulian*, 7 April 1917, JRP, MHS.

"I am going to Washington": quoted in *New York Times*, 12 November 1916, MHS.

"'transcendent power to remake humanity'": Estelle B. Freedman, *No Turning Back: The History of Feminism and the Future of Women* (New York: Ballantine Books, 2002), 70.

"You are the instrument": Mary O'Neill to JR, 23 November 1916, JRP, MHS.

7   mission began with a railroad journey: WRP, MHS.

"sexual innuendo": Witt, Paget, and Matthews, *Running as a Woman*, 10.

"doubtful if I shall go to Washington": JR to Jean Bishop, 24 February 1917, JRP, MHS.

"came and destroyed everything": JR, interview with Josephson, SOHP, 178.

sister worked at the Bureau: Belle Fligelman Winestine, "The First Woman in Congress," 8 July 1981, UML.

On June 9, 1917, a mining disaster: *Butte Miner*, 10 June 1917, JRP, MHS; Jerry Calvert, *The Gibraltar: Socialism and Labor in Butte, Montana, 1895–1920* (Helena: Montana Historical Society Press, 1988), 104.

Industrial Workers of the World–inspired miners: David M. Emmons, *The Butte Irish: Class and Ethnicity in an American Mining Town* (Urbana: University of Illinois Press, 1989), 364–366.

8   "in the best tradition of American journalism": Michael P. Malone, Richard B. Roeder, and William L. Lang, *Montana: A History of Two Centuries*, revised edition (Seattle: University of Washington Press, 1991), 369.

"We heartily wish that some of the excellent things": *Lewistown Democrat-News*, 11 August 1917, MHS.

"a ploy that has been used": Witt, Paget, and Matthews, *Running as a Woman*, 249.

Her congressional colleague: *Missoulian*, 13 August 1917, MHS; E. W. Brickert to JR, 9 May 1918, JRP, MHS; *Great Falls Daily Tribune*, 27 April 1918, JRP, MHS.

Catt endorsed Senator Walsh and asked Harriet Laidlaw: Carrie Chapman Catt to Harriet Laidlaw, 11 September 1918, JRP, SL; Schaffer, "Progressive," 147.

"most awful person": quoted in Cheek, "Rhetoric and Revolt," 182.

"to fall back on": Witt, Paget, and Matthews, *Running as a Woman*, 257.

9   "social worker-politician": ibid.

"no social worker would have anything to do with me": quoted in Cheek, "Rhetoric and Revolt," 182.

"no place to go but home": Witt, Paget, and Matthews, *Running as a Woman*, 257.

"essentialists": Freedman, *No Turning Back*, 329; Witt, Paget, and Matthews, *Running as a Woman*, 33; Susan Ware, *Partner and I: Molly Dewson, Feminism, and New Deal Politics* (New Haven: Yale University Press, 1987), xvii.

Moskowitz "served as the right-hand woman": ibid., 32.

"to play the game by the men's rules": Ware, *Partner and I*, xviii.

attended the Women's International Conference for Permanent Peace: Josephson, *First Lady*, 108.

U.S. branch of the Women's International League: Schaffer, "Progressive," 160–161; Josephson, *First Lady*, 110.

"Wobblies": Smith, "Fighting Pacifist," 172.

goals that "fitted nicely": Schaffer, "Progressive," 164.

"wanted to do grassroots organizing": JR, interview with Chall, 102–103.

10   Kelley, with her "deep capacity for affection": Kathryn Kish Sklar, *Florence Kelley and the Nation's Work: The Rise of Women's Political Culture, 1830–1900* (New Haven: Yale University Press, 1995), 182.

impressed Rankin as a lecturer: Smith, "Fighting Pacifist," 41.

The two women shared a capacity for hard work: see Josephine Goldmark, *Impatient Crusader* (Urbana: University of Illinois Press, 1953).

the most important work of her own career: ibid., 93.

"a colony of efficient and intelligent women": Sklar, *Florence Kelley*, 194.

"applied social science techniques": ibid., 295.

"back in college again, . . . transforming spinsterhood": quoted in ibid., 191, 187.

one of Hull House's "core" residents: ibid., 186.

"take a 'drummers' room'": Smith, "Fighting Pacifist," 174.

Rankin left the National Consumers' League: Josephson, *First Lady*, 118.

she had "piddled around": Cheek, "Rhetoric and Revolt," 182.

living in Georgia made sense: Smith, "Fighting Pacifist," 178.

11   "I am enclosing two checks": WR to JR, 8 October 1925, JRP, SL.

"single-handedly," the Georgia Peace Society : Smith, "Fighting Pacifist," 201.

"'center of infection'": Josephson, *First Lady*, 126.

Her plan was to spread her message first locally: Schaffer, "Progressive," 171.

referring to her as a "renegade": JR, interview with Josephson, 275.

"I have been in the country long enough": JR to Elinore Byrns, 6 April 1929, quoted in Josephson, *First Lady*, 12.

Women's Peace Union censored a press release: Schaffer, "Progressive," 176.

Rankin contacted Frederick Libby: ibid., 177.

the initial conditions of her employment: ibid.

"Nobody wants me": JR quoted in Frederick J. Libby diary, 21 December 1929, quoted in Schaffer, "Progressive," 177.

12   during several summers in the 1930s: JR to WR, 25 July 1937, WRP.

"a rested point of view": JR to WR, 30 June 1937, WRP.

cooperatives in Sweden: Belle Fligelman Winestine to Hannah Josephson, 16 April 1974, Hannah Josephson Papers.

rise of Nazism: Smith, "Fighting Pacifist," 192.

"There is a possibility of my going to Geneva": Mary Huntington Williams to JR, nd, WRP.

"gave the speech and left out the sentence": Smith, "Fighting Pacifist," 198.

"I wasn't going to be under his direction": quoted in Cheek, "Rhetoric and Revolt," 183.

"learned the lessons of networking and cooperation": Ware, *Partner and I*, xix.

"The most important thing about a candidate": JR to Benny, 4 August 1938, JRP, SL.

With her brother's assistance: Tom Haines, interview with Helen Bonner, 8 July 1980, transcript, UML, 1–2.

13   "every night . . . a fresh snowstorm": JR to Gladys Heinrich Knowles, 17 December 1940, JRP, SL.

"shipped the car from Minneapolis to Pittsburgh": JR to Mary O'Neill, 14 December 1940, JRP, SL.

"a cold in [her] eyes and nose": JR to Elizabeth Kennedy, 14 December 1940, JRP, SL.

"not be thrilling like the last time": JR to Jane Bausman, 28 December 1940, JRP, SL.

"I learned from the first [vote]": JR, interview with Chall, 9–10.

She isolated herself from all pressure: confidential interview.

"second term ended for all practical purposes": *New York Times*, 30 May 1973, JRP, SL.

"We are in the war": JRP, SL.

But the war activity depressed her: JR to Abbie Crawford Milton, 11 April 1942 and 14 September 1942, JRP, SL.

"Where are you": Cornelia Swinnerton to JR, Christmas 1942, JRP, SL.

"Where in the world are you?": Mary O'Neill to JR, 31 December 1942, JRP, SL.

She stayed in New York: ERM to JR, 3 January 1943, JRP, SL.

Rankin had made a "bargain": DMB to ERM, 6 September 1946, ERMP.

for her "travel and needs": confidential interview.

14   "One of the women in his family": Witt, Paget, and Matthews, *Running as a Woman*, 95.

"money of my own": JR, interview with Josephson, 232.

"how to get out of it": DMB to ERM, 17 April 1946, ERMP.

died in a "gruesome apartment": DMB to Hannah Josephson, 31 August 1973, and ERM to Hannah Josephson, 27 August 1973, Hannah Josephson Papers; confidential interview.

He bought her a ranch: Louise Rankin Galt, interview with authors, 25 April 2000.

To the time of his death in 1966: WRP; Cheek, "Rhetoric and Revolt," 189.

"chipper as a lark . . . just the sort of life she loves": ERM to MRB and HRM, 18 April 1961, JRP, MHS.

"as long as she is happy": ERM to MRB, 5 April 1963, ERMP.

"about the finest hotel service": ibid.

"in idle splendor on a houseboat": Josephson, *First Lady*, 180.

"Jeannette seemed to have a good time": ERM to WR, 11 April 1948, WRP.

"I'm getting too bored": JR to ERM, October 1952, JRP, SL.

15   "I am not going to allow you to say that you are a futile person": Katharine Anthony to JR, 7 February, 1954, JRP, SL.

"I hope you are getting along": Katharine Anthony to JR, 17 March 1955, JRP, SL.

Mary Weible, a North Dakota friend: JR to Flora Belle Surles, 3 May 1965, Flora Belle Surles Papers.

"intimate relationship": Nancy C. Unger, "Jeannette Pickering Rankin," in John A. Garraty and Mark C. Carnes, eds., *American National Biography* (Oxford University Press, 1999), 142.

"He had a tacit understanding with age": JRP, SL.

after her facial pain became unbearable: JR to Flora Belle Surles, nd, Flora Belle Surles Papers.

operation to sever a nerve: Smith, "Fighting Pacifist," 270.

"like an old woman": Vivian Hallinan, interview with Helen Bonner, 16 July 1980, UML, 4.

Occasionally her spirits were raised: Cheek, "Rhetoric and Revolt," 189.

She thanked Kennedy for the "cheering effect": JR to John F. Kennedy, April 1958, JRP, SL.

Then she appeared on national television: JR to WR, 3 December 1958, WRP.

"dimly remembered figure": Warren Hinckle and Marianne Hinckle, "A History of the Rise of the Unusual Movement for Women Power in the United States, 1961–1968," *Ramparts* (February 1968), 26, MHS.

At the ceremony she challenged her new entourage: *Denver Post*, 19 May 1967, JRP, MHS.

flirted with fully emerging from political exile: MRB to JR, 29 January 1968, JRP, SL; Flora Belle Surles to JR, 5 January 1968, Flora Belle Surles Papers.

not paying her telephone tax: Louise Rankin Galt to JR, 23 September 1968, JRP, SL.

not shopping on Tuesdays: JR, interview with Chall, 31.

16   direct preferential election of the president: JR to GRK, 3 September 1952, JRP, SL.

she could push herself no further: Smith, "Fighting Pacifist," 276.

"dizzy spells": JR to New Jersey ACLU, 8 November 1972, JRP, SL.

She inquired of little children: quoted in Giles, *Flight of the Dove*, 234.

"index pages": ibid.

A stroke weakened her: DMB to JR, 16 January 1973, JRP, SL.

"further cold nights on the floor": DMB to JR, nd, JRP, SL.

begging her doctor to end her life: confidential interview.

Her final days were passed: ERM to Hannah Josephson, 12 June 1973, Hannah Josephson Papers.

"I want to get back to my apartment": DMB to Hannah Josephson, 31 August 1973, Hannah Josephson Papers.

2. FAMILY: IN HER BROTHER'S SHADOW

17 "many of the hardships": JR to Mrs. C. D. Carlson, 12 March 1918, JRP, MHS.

"lived an aristocratic lifestyle": Richard K. Hines, "Wellington Duncan Rankin: The Man Behind the Myth" (M.A. thesis, Washington State University, 1996), 19.

"thought themselves superior to others": confidential interview.

red-bearded, and bullheaded: John C. Board, "The Lady from Montana: Jeannette Rankin" (M.A. thesis, University of Wyoming, 1964), 5.

18 He was a "rounder, getting drunk with the boys": confidential interview.

he served a term as a Republican: Smith, "Fighting Pacifist," 15.

flooded roads and washed-out bridges: John Rankin to Jessie [Rankin Wilson], 14 May 1893, ERMP.

"I have too many irons in the fire": John Rankin to Jessie, 14 May 1893, ERMP.

"Rankin nose": confidential interview.

Patricia Limerick's observation: Patricia Nelson Limerick, *The Legacy of Conquest: The Unbroken Past of the American West* (New York: W. W. Norton, 1987), 26.

Olive challenged her children: Wilma Dykeman, *Too Many People, Too Little Love* (New York: Holt, Rinehart, and Winston, 1974), 20.

filling the house with books: Cheek, "Rhetoric and Revolt," 186.

large map of the United States: GRK to JR, 1 December 1943, JRP, SL.

surrendered household management: Smith, "Fighting Pacifist," 7.

business affairs to Wellington: Dykeman, *Too Many People,* 21.

"self-isolated": Board, "Lady from Montana," 6.

Increasingly inert but domineering: confidential interview.

19 Grace spoke for the others: GRK to ERM, 9 January 1946, ERMP.

Their first concern was their reputation: confidential interview.

"he insulted your sister": ibid.

"it looked an enormous gang": DMB to ERM, nd, ERMP.

"And they are formidable": Winfield Page, interview with Helen Bonner, 9 July 1980, transcript, UML, 1.

"the most energetic ones": Belle Fligelman Winestine, interview with Helen Bonner, 14 July 1980, UML, 10.

toss glasses and silverware: Dykeman, *Too Many People,* 21.

the topic was usually politics: Galt interview.

"one knifing the other": confidential interview.

"were incapable of self deprecation." Both were "publicity hounds": ibid.

"I hope you warned Jeannette": DMB to ERM, 23 May 1951, ERMP.

"was not a strict or harsh disciplinarian": Cheek, "Rhetoric and Revolt," 160.

"'the family claim'": Ware, *Partner and I,* 51.

strict and harsh as a surrogate mother: Josephson, *First Lady,* 16.

20   "no choice": Smith, "Fighting Pacifist," 7.

"dictatorial": ibid., 7–8.

"irritable and domineering": ibid., 8.

"restless and unhappy": Giles, *Flight of the Dove,* 31.

"I disliked my experience in Montana": ERM to Wilma Dykeman, 20 March 1973, ERMP.

Olive became a Christian Scientist: confidential interview.

Wellington became a convert at Harvard: Steele, *Wellington Rankin,* 47.

religion was not a priority for John Rankin: Smith, "Fighting Pacifist," 16.

Rankin did not believe in God: Smith interview.

"bitchy about Christians": ERM to DMB, 2 October 1972, ERMP.

called Christians "Christers": confidential interview.

"infidels and anti-Christians": DMB to JR, 17 December 1968, JRP, SL.

"goddamn Christian words": confidential interview.

deep dislike of Christianity: Smith, "Fighting Pacifist," 67.

"into sheep": confidential interview.

"I never go unless I can preach": quoted in Cheek, "Rhetoric and Revolt," 82.

"a visceral, bitterly negative reaction": confidential interview.

"There is little one can do for her": ERM to MRB, 3 September 1963, ERMP.

21   "mother superior of the family": confidential interview.

satisfaction her instruction and reading brought her: MRB to WR, 18 July 1952, WRP.

"When I returned from Bali": ERM to WR, 22 November 1963, WRP.

"I usually read my lesson in the bathroom": ERM to MRB, 26 February 1963, ERMP.

"prayerful work": ERM to WR, 16 June 1959, WRP.

"My Religion": ERM to Wilma Dykeman, 20 March 1973, ERMP.

he was more like Jeannette and Grace: Hines, "Wellington Duncan Rankin," 115.

"I went to church this morning": ERM to WR, 26 June 1934, WRP.

"to cover his butt": confidential interview.

his habit of wagering: WRP.

22   "the perfect law of God": John Ellis Sedman to WR, nd, WRP.

"put to rout all false symptoms": ibid., 4 September 1954.

as a "Child of God": Maria Soubier to WR, 25 January 1955, 20 November 1958, 25 June 1962, WRP.

"well and free of the claim": ibid., 29 June 1963.

"God knows nothing about any of this": Paul Stark Seeley to WR, 14 June 1957, WRP.

"Still need help on old condition": WR to Paul Stark Seeley, 27 August 1957, WRP.

"enormous bag of fluid": DMB to ERM, 8 July 1961, ERMP.

"extra-wide left legs": WRP.

his stallion, White Man: confidential interview.

"arguing with a Child of God!": ibid.

23   she had not enjoyed school: Smith, "Fighting Pacifist," 26.

"an extremely timid girl": quoted in *Montana Kaimen*, 16 November 1916, JRP, SL.

"[I]t's hard for me to realize": Samuel J. Wright to JR, 26 November 1916, JRP, MHS.

"to come out immediately": JR to Abbie Crawford Milton, 11 April 1942, JRP, SL.

"going to be a very hard week in Congress": JR to Olive Rankin, 11 April 1942, JRP, SL.

"Wellington phoned me": JR to Mr. and Mrs. Duncan Barnet, 11 April 1942, JRP, SL.

24   "treated her like a turd": confidential interview.

criticizing "her morals": Giles, *Flight of the Dove*, 25.

"the best brother in the world": JR to WR, 3 January 1937, WRP.

"You are just too wonderful": JR to WR, 26 December 1953, WRP.

"claims of any beauty": quoted in Steele, *Wellington Rankin*, 33.

"the saint of the Rankin family": Helena Stellway to JR, 1 June 1954, JRP, SL.

"The money will help": MRB to WR, 17 November 1933, WRP.

followed her brother's directives: Dykeman, *Too Many People*, 23–24.

worked for a time in Wellington's office: Galt interview.

"a more 'social' creature": Dykeman, *Too Many People*, 24.

"a pretty woman": Vivian Halinan, interview with Helen Bonner, 16 July 1980, transcript, UML, 14.

"married for money": confidential interview.

25   "one who has 'cracked up'": ERM to WR, 11 September 1935, WRP.

she began her birth-control career: ERM to Wilma Dykeman, interview notes, June 1972, 122–123, ERMP.

"far more controversial than suffrage": McGlen et al., *Women, Politics, and American Society*, 255.

birth-control reform was "too sordid": quoted in ibid.

prospect "very distasteful": ibid.

"wreck his prestige": Dykeman, *Too Many People*, 49.

"she couldn't stay in Montana": Winestine interview, 14.

"The Boy": quoted in Dykeman, *Too Many People,* 21.

"The Little Boy from Oxford": *Park County News,* 7 April 1955, MHS.

"huge in everything but height": William F. Crowley, interview with authors, 28 November 2001.

"damn big man": Haines interview, 2.

"would roll over you": Crowley interview.

"boxer and s.o.b. of formidable reputation": ibid.

"strong, compact and heavy set": Radio address manuscript attributed to George Niewoehner, White Sulphur Springs, Montana, 1948, WRP.

"the best 'Indian wrestler' in Montana": K. Ross Toole to WR, 19 November 1965, WRP.

"ready at any time to accept a physical challenge": *Great Falls Tribune,* 6 July 1966, MHS.

"proud of being on the Harvard boxing club": confidential interview.

boxing lessons in his law office: Gary Cooper to WR, 1946, WRP.

26   "Several men need pasting": JR to WR, July 1917, JRP, MHS.

Wellington Rankin's first job: Winestine interview, 12.

"very handsome": Haines interview, 6.

"to analyze my feelings for you": Elizabeth Wallace to WR, 16 August 1913, WRP.

"My sentimental idea of love": ibid.

"very vain" man: ERM to JR, 19 December 1941, JRP, SL.

"admired himself in the mirror": Page interview, 2, 18.

27   "Deary Wellington": Nina Swinnerton to JR, 23 April 1917, JRP, MHS.

"Sally is disappointed": ERM to WR, 5 March 1929, WRP.

she had been "charmed": Peggy Heinrich to WR, 10 September 1935, WRP.

"letting me come and visit you": Rita Shields to WR, 17 September 1941, WRP.

"I hope that business or pleasure will bring you back": Rita Shields to WR, 2 February 1950, WRP.

"You better get rid of that stuff": Marjorie Graves to WR, 6 October 1946, WRP.

"exhibiting your physical prowess": ibid., 18 February 1947.

28   "You have too many interests": ibid., 24 August 1948.

"I'm driving over next week": ibid., 6 May 1954.

Louise Replogle's many achievements: *Great Falls Tribune,* 5 July 1966 and 7 July 1966, MHS.

"[S]he has a pretty face": DMB to ERM, 6 June 1949, ERMP.

"has a stunning ring": DMB to ERM, 15 July 1953, ERMP.

"what she thought about Wellington's wife": Halinan interview, 12.

29   "I do want you to have the money": ERM to JR, 11 December 1966, JRP, SL.

sending Jeannette a $10,000 advance: Louise Rankin to JR, 19 December 1966, JRP, SL.

"was totally taken by him": Crowley interview.

"just loved Wellington": Halinan interview, 4.

"a sharper intellect, a higher native intelligence": Galt interview.

"urged in his college years to become a dramatic actor": *Great Falls Tribune,* 6 July 1966, MHS.

speaking ability was "whiz like": Page interview, 21.

"Wellington got right up and made a speech": Haines interview, 2.

"He is so wonderful in court": DMB to ERM, 4 April 1951, ERMP.

"the most successful and widely known": Belle Fligelman Winestine to Hannah Josephson, 16 April 1974, Hannah Josephson Papers.

"in court he was one of those lawyers": Crowley interview.

"Two days and he would be fed up": Helena Stellway to JR, 18 January 1945, JRP, SL.

he opened his own practice: *Great Falls Tribune,* 6 July 1966, MHS.

"one of the top criminal lawyers": Hines, "Wellington Duncan Rankin," 17; *Hardin Tribune,* 15 October 1920, MHS.

"better prepared than anybody else": Haines interview, 2.

30   "I appreciate your loyalty": Hazel to WR, 13 January 1956, WRP.

Other beneficiaries were more prominent: *Great Falls Tribune,* 3 July 1966, MHS.

"tentacles that reached everywhere": Crowley interview.

"amoral": Smith interview.

"ruthless"; "Any means": Crowley interview.

"glories in the trial of a case": Niewoehner radio address, WRP.

"claim on two Supreme Court justices": Crowley interview.

"fear[ed] him for physical reasons": Niewoehner radio address.

"the most selfish, inconsiderate and unreliable attorney": Anonymous to WR, 20 November 1952, WRP.

"never to be relied upon": ibid.

"calls from Rankin at 1:00 A.M.": *Great Falls Tribune,* 5 July 1966, MHS.

31   "he'd tamper with witnesses": Crowley interview.

"big cases with big fees": ibid.

"he charged 40 to 45 percent": Hines, "Wellington Duncan Rankin," 110.

"exacted a fee of $7,500": *Great Falls Tribune,* 8 July 1966, MHS.

"Rankin told you, you didn't tell Rankin": quoted in ibid.

"standard fee of $5,000": Haines interview, 2.

Another rumor: MHS.

defendant drove up in a Cadillac: Crowley interview.

lawyers right out of law school: ibid.

"a good office lawyer": ibid.

"gone off on some junket": Louise Rankin to JR, 1 March 1967, JRP, SL.

"fiery temper": Page interview, 8.

"walked on eggshells": Crowley interview.

"It is a shame he does not care": Helena Stellway to JR, 18 January 1945, JRP, SL.

32   "creaky stairs": *Great Falls Tribune*, 14 July 1991, MHS.

After a fire: confidential interview.

"flat didn't spend money": Page interview, 17.

"not a bit bashful": ibid., 9.

"avoided paying his debts": Hines, "Wellington Duncan Rankin," 111.

His files were filled with overdue notices: WRP.

"[Y]ou never contribute a dime to charity": Anonymous to WR, 20 November 1952, WRP.

"Please do not give any publicity to it": 1947, WRP.

"He didn't have friends": Crowley interview

"probably the only person this side of the divide": DMB to ERM, 19 September 1961, ERMP.

"Some day, on the streets": Harry L. Burns to WR, 11 August 1948, WRP.

"Put the Anaconda Company out of Montana Politics": quoted in Board, "Lady from Montana," 75.

33   "like a cemetery": Hines, "Wellington Duncan Rankin," 69.

decided against running for governor: Frank Hayes to WR, 1932, WRP.

"did not want to be one of 435 members": Galt interview.

The more prestigious U.S. Senate: Belle Fligelman Winestine to Hannah Josephson, 16 April 1974, Hannah Josephson Papers.

"Hang on tight, Wellington": quoted in Hines, "Wellington Duncan Rankin," 73.

chairman of the party's state executive committee: Board, "Lady from Montana," 74.

"At a little conference this afternoon": Mary O'Neill to WR, 18 November 1917, JRP, MHS.

34   Rankin spoke to the strikers: *Butte Miner*, 19 August 1917, JRP, MHS.

"newspaper is now an assured fact": Mary O'Neill to JR, 19 September 1917, JRP, MHS.

Anaconda Copper Mining Company's "complete control": *Joint Strike Bulletin*, 27 September 1917, JRP, MHS.

Dunne's *Strike Bulletin*: Calvert, *Gibraltar*, 111.

"unabashedly revolutionary": ibid.

"probably the widest acquaintance among lawyers": *Hardin Tribune*, 15 October 1920, MHS.

"progressive and anti-company": Hines, "Wellington Duncan Rankin," 53.

"in league with the anti-progressive wing": ibid., 54–55.

He opposed the plans: ibid., 53.

"to use convicts as strike breakers": ibid., 56.

As attorney general he opposed charging the Anaconda Company: ibid., 62.

earning him the label "lackey": ibid., 63.

"women's vote but also the miners": Josephson, *First Lady*, 118.

35   "They own the state, they own the government": quoted in *Washington Times*, 8 August 1917, quoted in *Helena Independent*, 16 August 1917, JRP, MHS.

"anti–Anaconda Company forces": Hines, "Wellington Duncan Rankin," 70.

"all the dignity of a baboon": *Anaconda Standard*, nd, quoted in Hines, "Wellington Duncan Rankin," 71.

"says you'll carry the county": ERM to WR, 2 July 1934, WRP.

"Have they become reconciled?": Katharine Anthony to JR, 7 February 1954, JRP, SL.

"old and dear friends": Roy to WR, 7 June 1955, WRP.

"Rankins always blamed the Company": Belle Fligelman Winestine to Hannah Josephson, 16 April 1974, Hannah Josephson Papers.

"cunning tricks upon the electorate": Niewoehner radio address, WRP.

"You had definitely made up your mind": Harry L. Burns to WR, 1948, WRP.

"a good many men who will do as he says": ERM to WR, 13 June 1934, WRP.

"handle Red Lodge in his own way": ERM to WR, 18 June 1934, WRP.

36   "pretty bad dope on Swords": ERM to WR, 20 June 1934 and 22 June 1934, WRP.

"Russell White Bear": ERM to WR, 24 June 1934 and 26 June 1934, WRP.

"to buy it": quoted in Steele, *Wellington Rankin*, 144.

"circumvent the election thieves": Mary O'Neill to JR, 15 June 1942, JRP, SL.

"the Murrays will stop at nothing": Elizabeth Kennedy to JR, 18 August 1942, JRP, SL.

"precincts have been 'jokied'": Mary O'Neill to JR, 5 November 1942, JRP, SL.

"a crooked politician": quoted in Steele, *Wellington Rankin*, 145.

"too big a bully": ERM to WR, 15 June 1934 and 8 July 1934, WRP.

"frustrated but relentless ambition": anonymous, 1948, WRP.

37   "a race between two sons-of-bitches": anonymous, 20 November 1952, WRP.

"I am thoroughly convinced you cannot win": quoted in Smith, "Fighting Pacifist," 239, 240.

"Above all Judge get out": W. R. Hopkins to WR, 18 August 1952, WRP.

"you might say arrogant": Page interview, 10–11.

"If I'd called Jeannette to come back": quoted in Steele, *Wellington Rankin*, 181.

her birth-control work would embarrass him: ERM to WR, 11 April 1948, WRP.

"Wellington offered to pay my way home": JR to GRK, 1 June 1952, JRP, SL.

"covering more than one million acres": *Helena Independent Record*, 30 April 1964, MHS.

His widow set the value of his estate: Louise Rankin to Montana Department of Revenue, 30 August 1967, ERMP.

Montana ranches with "historic names": *Great Falls Tribune*, 1 July 1966, MHS.

Savage Brothers Ranch: *Great Falls Tribune*, 19 February 1964, MHS.

Miller Brothers Ranch: *Helena Independent Record*, 30 April 1964, MHS.

38   "He bled them white": Crowley interview.

"every property he acquired": quoted in Hines, "Wellington Duncan Rankin," 99.

Unsubstantiated stories: Michael MacDonald manuscript, MHS.

disdained keeping up property: Crowley interview.

Cattle buyers came from afar: ibid.

"Rankin poured in cattle by the thousands": Ivan Doig, *This House of Sky: Landscapes of a Western Mind* (New York: Harcourt Brace, 1978), 47.

"His cowboys were shabby stick figures": ibid.

"the men": confidential interview.

personally hired his "men": Hines, "Wellington Duncan Rankin," 114.

Their peonage included the requirement: Crowley interview.

They hitchhiked to Helena: Page interview, 8.

"pay me or I'll kill you": Crowley interview.

storehouses of candy and cigarettes: confidential interview.

39   "a bare bedspring to sleep on": Jerry G. Ross to WR, 8 December 1962, WRP.

"put us out of the ranching business": Louise Rankin to JR, 12 March 1965, JRP, SL.

"the lord of the manor": confidential interview.

haystacks, a horse barn, and an icehouse: ibid.

"white snow on the mountains": JR to Flora Belle Surles, 18 May 1944, Flora Belle Surles Papers.

"From our front window": ibid., 12 August 1943.

"several hundred cows and their calves": ibid., 21 May 1944.

"still sleep with blankets": JR to Genevieve Hastide, 11 June 1943, JRP, SL.

"The country is beautiful": JR to Mrs. Herbert Brown, 12 October 1943, JRP, SL.

"apple crop is short this year": JR to Frederick J. Libby, 11 October 1943, JRP, SL.

40   "luscious, big tomatoes": JR to Mrs. Mary M. Wright, 11 October 1943, JRP, SL.

Avalanche summers were family affairs: confidential interview.

could appear "slovenly": Galt interview.

"looking like a bag of potatoes"; "shit kicking": confidential interview.

"putting the fish in her mouth": ibid.

She placed the household on a strict budget: DMB to ERM, 7 July 1951, ERMP.

"poor old fool probably feels so frustrated": ERM to Family, 4 March 1964, ERMP.

41   "I feel that we must 'loose her'": ERM to MRB, 3 September 1963, ERMP.

"grappling with the false sense of *self*": ERM to Family, 14 September 1963, ERMP.

"takers not givers": Page interview, 17.

"I'm not big enough in spirit": JR to WR, 26 December 1958, WRP.

3. FRIENDSHIPS: A WOMAN-CENTERED LIFE

43 Molly Dewson, Rankin's contemporary: Ware, *Partner and I*, xvi.

44 escape from rural isolation: D'Emilio and Freedman, *Intimate Matters*, 226–227.

"the family became less central as an economic unit": Leila J. Rupp, *A Desired Past: A Short History of Same-Sex Love in America* (Chicago: University of Chicago Press, 1999), 40.

Frustrated in Montana, . . . daydreamer: Giles, *Flight of the Dove*, 24.

"restless and unhappy": ibid., 31.

"The kid crowd went sleighing": JR, 29 December 1902 journal entry, quoted in Schaffer, "Progressive," 6.

"quickened [Jeannette Rankin's] social sympathies": ibid., 61.

"long struggle, as a young woman": Christopher Lasch, ed., *The Social Thought of Jane Addams* (Indianapolis: Bobbs-Merrill, 1965), 84.

"advantages of women studying social work": JR, interview with University of Washington students, 4 December 1968, quoted in Cheek, "Rhetoric and Revolt," 60.

"social arrangements in which young people were expected to grow up": ibid.

traumatized by her sexual "slip": Lillian Faderman, *Odd Girls and Twilight Lovers: A History of Lesbian Life in Twentieth-Century America* (New York: Columbia University Press, 1991), 32.

The New York School opened its doors: Kahn, "Themes for a History."

"hadn't taught her to think": Smith, "Fighting Pacifist," 26.

"such well-trained college girls": Schaffer, "Progressive," 8.

values of "the first generation of New Women": Smith-Rosenberg, *Disorderly Conduct: Visions of Gender in Victorian America* (New York: Alfred A. Knopf, 1985), 245, 254.

"granted social license to arrange their lives": Faderman, *Odd Girls*, 17.

"adequate wives": ibid., 12.

"love unimpaired by repressive male dominance": Sklar, *Florence Kelley*, 192.

45 "our Greenwich Village days": ERM to JR, 1 January 1945, JRP, SL; see Judith Schwarz, *Radical Feminists of Heterodoxy: Greenwich Village, 1912–1940*, revised edition (Norwich, VT: New Victoria Press, 1986).

"in the old Italian quarter of the Village": Katharine Anthony to JR, 2 May 1957, JRP, SL.

Cornelia Swinnerton, Jeannette Rankin's suffrage colleague: JR, interview with Josephson, 184.

"luncheon club for 'unorthodox women'": Schwarz, *Radical Feminists of Heterodoxy*, 1.

"It was the time of social change": ibid., 31.

"liberal/radical small town": ibid., 34.

"translation from personal experimentation to social activism": D'Emilio and Freedman, *Intimate Matters*, 231.

The 110 members of Heterodoxy: ibid., 85.

"new Bohemia" . . . "social pressures": ibid., 36.

"she never once mentions a male": ibid., 90.

"friendship between a lesbian and a straight woman": ibid., 91.

46 "a horrible alternative" to a single, unencumbered state: ibid., 191.

she was "tough as nails": confidential interview.

"intimate adult relationships": ibid.

"did love to have company": Galt interview.

"be a charmer when she likes people": ERM to Martha Ragland, 4 May 1971, ERMP.

"hi-ing here and hi-ing there": Page interview, 2.

"to sit in the middle of the plane": confidential interview.

"whole days waiting by the phone": *Washington Evening Star and Daily News,* 2 September 1972, JRP, MHS.

"the most feminine woman in the world": Halinan interview, 13.

While on a Mediterranean cruise: ERM to GRK, nd, JRP, SL.

47 "[M]y Denver 'Experience'": ERM to JR, 23 November 1944, JRP, SL.

"'doing' for a man rather than a 'cause'": JR to ERM, 25 November 1945, ERMP.

"the Rankin nose": confidential interview.

detracted from her prettiness: *The Nation,* 31 May 1917, quoted in Cheek, "Rhetoric and Revolt," 84.

Journalists in 1916 focused "on what she looked like and wore": Witt, Paget, and Matthews, *Running as a Woman,* 186.

"an object for the readers' gaze": Sara Hayden, "'The House Beautiful': Media Responses to Jeannette Rankin's Election to Congress and Vote Against U.S. Entry into the First World War," unpublished paper, University of Montana, 15.

"feminine charm": *Boston Traveler,* 10 November 1916, JRP, SL.

"striking personal appearance": *Woman's Journal and Suffrage News,* nd, JRP, SL.

"a slender creature with a wealth of soft, curly hair": *San Francisco Sunday Chronicle,* nd, JRP, SL.

"such beautiful clothes": *The Woman Citizen,* nd, JRP, SL.

"tall and slender, with hazel eyes": *New York Times,* 19 November 1916 and 3 March 1917, JRP, SL.

"in her first thirties": *Chicago Tribune,* 14 March 1917, JRP, SL.

"so disgusted . . . go to hell": Witt, Paget, and Matthews, *Running as a Woman,* 186.

offers of marriage: Smith, "Fighting Pacifist," 28.

"To think you would have to fight it out for second place": Max to JR, 12 November 1916, JRP, MHS.

"Since having heard your little, impromptu speech": Leslie Wandby to JR, 27 May 1917, JRP, MHS.

48 "Your kind letter has been received": JR to Leslie Wandby, 2 June 1917, JRP, MHS.

"Your much-prized favor reached me": Leslie Wandby to JR, 5 June 1917, JRP, MHS.

"saving for the day": Smith, "Fighting Pacifist," 258.

"what remains of life and love": ibid., 259.

"not very satisfactory": JR to WR, 1952, WRP.

"I asked Chester Van Allen out here": JR to ERM, 18 August 1952, ERMP.

"I have felt a growing sense of loneliness": W. Vernon Edenfield to JR, 16 January 1972, JRP, SL.

49   one special male companion: Giles, *Flight of the Dove*, 173; Smith, "Fighting Pacifist," 183–184.

"You don't know how hard [I] tried": Smith, "Fighting Pacifist," 183–184.

"With all your faults, I love you still": Fiorello LaGuardia to JR, 26 December 1942, JRP, SL.

"close personal friend": Smith, "Fighting Pacifist," 185.

"He was my best friend from then on": JR, interview with Josephson, 255.

"She had a number of men friends": Belle Fligelman Winestine, "Belle Fligelman Winestine: Feminist and Suffragette," 1976 audio recording, UML.

"She liked the company of men": Galt interview.

"I don't think there was ever any man in her life": Haines interview, 2–3.

50   "male-dominated . . . family that restricted women's full development": Smith-Rosenberg, *Disorderly Conduct*, 254.

"parasitic life": JR to Katherine Black, 14 August 1943, quoted in Wilson, "'Peace Is a Woman's Job . . .'—Jeannette Rankin and American Foreign Policy: Her Lifework as a Pacifist," *Montana: The Magazine of Western History* 30 (spring 1980), 49.

"You know I don't believe in marriage": JR to Peter Besag, nd, JRP, SL.

"women are too dependent on men": *The New Mexican*, 11 June 1970, JRP, SL.

"scared off men because she . . . had to dominate everybody": Galt interview.

"did not want to be tied down again": ibid.

"sweet little handkerchief": Fernie Macready to JR, 3 January 1916, JRP, SL.

"When your package came Sunday": Helena Stellway to JR, 25 December 1917, JRP, MHS.

"I only live for the day": Helena Stellway, 18 January 1945, JRP, SL.

"I am delighted I never married": ibid., 4 October 1961.

her incomparable charm: Belle Fligelman Winestine interview, 1, 7, Norman and Belle Fligelman Winestine Papers, MHS.

"Your continued refusal to come to Jersey": Minnie J. Reynolds to JR, 16 July 1911, JRP, SL.

51   "with the sweetest love in my heart for you": Mary O'Neill to JR, nd, JRP, SL.

"You don't know how jealous I am": Mrs. J. B. Ellis to JR, 9 June 1917, JRP, MHS.

first woman physician in Helena: *Helena Independent Record*, 4 November 1999.

"I do hope she succeeds": Maria M. Dean to Mary Stewart, 22 July 1918, JRP, MHS.

in code: Lillian Faderman, *Surpassing the Love of Men: Romantic Friendship and Love Between Women from the Renaissance to the Present* (William Morrow, 1981), 189.

"new possibilities of love between women": ibid., 188.

"not recovered from the good news yet": Rosalie G. Jones to JR, 12 November 1916 and 31 January 1917, JRP, SL.

"For a long time I've been wanting to see you": Mary Stewart to JR, 9 December 1917, JRP, MHS.

"Chicago Woman's Club cleared expenses": Minna C. Smith to JR, 22 March 1917, JRP, MHS.

won the heart of her friend's companion: ibid., 27 March 1917.

52   "I feel an interest in you": Bertha A. Yoder to JR, 2 March 1917, JRP, MHS.

"[C]ome to see me soon": JR to Bertha A. Yoder, 18 June 1917, JRP, MHS.

woman from New York hinted at a special affinity: Elizabeth Waldron to JR, nd, JRP, MHS.

"I have longed to write you a hundred times": Ada Willard to JR, 1 October 1917, JRP, MHS.

"do not hesitate to call upon me": JR to Ada Willard, 9 October 1917, JRP, MHS.

"I am so pleased with the thought": JR to Irma Hockstein, 27 March 1925, JRP, SL.

"I am going to be in Chicago": JR to Wilma Ball, 18 April 1925, JRP, SL.

"I felt very near you": JR to Mary Weible, 18 April 1925, JRP, SL.

"You know you captured our hearts": Jean Bishop to JR, 24 January 1917, JRP, MHS.

"such a lovely person": Helena Stellway to JR, 4 October 1961, JRP, SL.

"very good work you did in the campaign": JR to Jean Bishop, 26 December 1940, JRP, SL.

53   "classy double room on the *S.S. Argentina*": Jean Bishop to JR, 27 August 1955, JRP, SL.

Katharine Anthony . . . closest lifelong friend: Katharine Anthony to JR, 12 September 1955, 3 October 1955, and 8 January 1956, JRP, SL.

Another of Jeannette Rankin's longtime friends: Schaffer, "Progressive," 55.

Her New Woman argument: ibid.

"[I]t's nearly nine o'clock and I am getting sleepy": Massey to ERM, 11 December 1917, JRP, MHS.

"a small dinner with certain selected people": Jane Thompson to HRS, 25 July 1918, JRP, MHS.

"[It was] a joy to have your gift": JR to Mrs. R. Fenby Bausman, 28 December 1940, JRP, SL.

54   "She asked for you of course": ERM to JR, 7 March 1944, JRP, SL.

"Jane asks all about you": ibid., 15 March 1944.

"she was horribly disappointed": ibid., 6 November 1944.

"she fairly shouted with joy": ibid., 4 December 1944.

"I wish she might find a thoroughly congenial person": MRB to ERM, 19 November 1945, ERMP.

she had been enticed to Mexico: GRK to JR, 13 February 1945, JRP, SL.

Milton visited Rankin in Washington: Smith, "Fighting Pacifist," 232.

"[L]et's go adventuring into Florida this winter": Abbie Crawford Milton to JR, 24 October 1944, JRP, SL.

"Enclosures make the trip seem realistic": ibid., January 1945.

"like a bat out of Hell": ERM to JR, January 1945, JRP, SL.

"After you get through dashing around": GRK to JR, 13 February 1945, JRP, SL.

"[A]rrived home last night": JR to Abbie Crawford Milton, 11 April 1942, JRP, SL.

55   "I don't know how long I shall stay": ibid., April 1942, JRP, SL.

"And was your letter a welcome one to me!!": Abbie Crawford Milton, December 1942, JRP, SL.

"sobbing fiction": Cornelia Swinnerton to JR, 23 April 1917, JRP, MHS.

Rankin responded with a "Dear Nina" letter: JR to Cornelia Swinnerton, 22 May 1917, JRP, MHS.

56   "It is perfectly grand that you are coming Sunday": Cornelia Swinnerton to JR, nd, JRP, MHS.

Carroll Smith-Rosenberg's analysis of correspondence: Smith-Rosenberg, *Disorderly Conduct*, 56–57.

"My but it was a wonderful—a marvelous experience": Cornelia Swinnerton to JR, 24 July 1917, JRP, MHS.

"Where are you going to speak Labor Day[?]": ibid., 28 August 1917.

57   "I was frightfully disappointed not to see you Labor Day": ibid., September 1917.

"I am enclosing some postals": ibid., 2 August 1918.

"does seem good to have a family circle again": ibid., Christmas 1942.

"let her do the calling up": Katharine Anthony to JR, 18 January 1943, JRP, SL.

58   "Swinnie has been a little ailing": ibid., 12 March 1943.

"Swinnie is all right": ibid., 18 March 1943.

"Darling your postal is better than a letter": Cornelia Swinnerton to JR, 12 May 1943, JRP, SL.

taking lessons from a "lady pilot": ibid., 10 October 1945.

"[G]lad we had our little visit with her": Katharine Anthony to JR, 2 September 1947, JRP, SL.

Millacent had been a teacher: Millacent Yarrow to JR, 22 November 1940, JRP, SL.

a secretary in the congresswoman's office: Spriggs and Yarrow Secretaries to JR, 31 December 1942, JRP, SL.

"I hope [you have] read some of these fine letters": Millacent Yarrow to JR, 4 January 1942, JRP, SL.

"[I] wish I could look into your eyes": ibid.

"You just can't have powers": ibid., 30 March 1943.

"You don't know how this old Millacent loves you": ibid., 14 April 1943.

59   she conveyed a "daydream" of herself: JR to Millacent Yarrow, 24 April 1943, JRP, SL.

"I almost think I want to go to Georgia with you": Millacent Yarrow to JR, 14 May 1943, JRP, SL.

"I am interested in your daydreams": Katharine Anthony to JR, 29 March 1943, JRP, SL.

"[H]ow I love and honor you": Millacent Yarrow to JR, 7 March 1944, JRP, SL.

"dear little friend": Helena Stellway to JR, 4 October 1961, JRP, SL.

"in a little apartment by ourselves and so happy": Millacent Yarrow to JR, 22 November 1940, JRP, SL.

Harriet taught at a school in Turkey: Harriet Yarrow to JR, 24 February 1942, JRP, SL.

"I've been having tea ready for the three": Millacent Yarrow to JR, 14 May 1943, JRP, SL.

Later that year Harriet visited Rankin in Montana: ibid., 11 July 1943; Harriet Yarrow to JR, 1 August 1943, JRP, SL.

In 1944 Harriet worked in the laundry of a Chicago school: JR to Harriet Yarrow, 30 November 1944, Harriet Yarrow Papers.

attached to a Quaker house in Massachusetts: Harriet Yarrow to JR, October 1970 and 27 December 1971, JRP, SL.

"the delightful Miss Yarrow": Hannah Josephson to JR, 18 June 1970, JRP, SL.

60   "on a boat in the Merain harbor": Harriet Yarrow to JR, nd, JRP, SL.

"Your pink blouse will be the best": ibid. (three-fourths of page cut out following "I love you!").

"The army came out here to register all 'colonists'": ibid., 24 February 1942.

"I had a very difficult time getting things straightened [out]": Smith, "Fighting Pacifist," 232.

A year later Harriet Yarrow was in California: Millacent Yarrow to JR, 30 March 1943 and 14 May 1943, JRP, SL.

"This is all that goes this year": Harriet Yarrow to JR, January 1943, JRP, SL.

61   "The beast lacks nothing": ibid., 1 August 1943.

"You are such a joy in this world": JR to Harriet Yarrow, 25 September 1943, Harriet Yarrow Papers.

"I had breakfast by the little stove": ibid., 11 November 1944.

"If all the thoughts I've had of you since your sweet letter": ibid., 30 November 1944.

Rankin escaped from caring for her mother: JR, interview with Josephson, 270–271; American Export Lines to JR, 27 May 1946, JRP, SL.

She stayed with Yarrow at a "school for girls": JR, interview with Josephson, 269.

"[S]o sorry not to be home when you came to Montana": JR to Harriet Yarrow, 20 January 1953, Harriet Yarrow Papers.

"Come to the ranch if you can": ibid., 21 May 1953.

62   "Shady Grove cottage will be most anxious to have you": ibid., 14 December 1956.

"It was such a joy to see your handwriting": ibid., 5 September 1961.

"I'm thinking about a trip to Russia": ibid., 16 December 1961.

she sent Rankin a "blessing . . . for your dear one": Harriet Yarrow to JR, 23 January 1965, JRP, SL.

"If I could have an hour with you": ibid., October 1970.

"Christmas . . . in Cambridge": ibid., 27 December 1971.

"I haven't taken the poverty oath for you": JR to Harriet Yarrow, 30 November 1944, Harriet Yarrow Papers.

"jolly little presents": ibid., 21 May 1953.

63   "I appreciate your taking time": Harriet Yarrow to JR, 24 February 1942, JRP, SL.

"I'm coming home to settle down in Georgia": JR to Harriet Yarrow, 20 January 1953, Harriet Yarrow Papers.

Yarrow sought Rankin's assistance: Harriet Yarrow to JR, 8 July 1948, JRP, SL.

"I'm so happy you made it possible": JR to Harriet Yarrow, 14 December 1956, Harriet Yarrow Papers.

Rankin recommended books to Yarrow: ibid., 30 November 1944 and 20 January 1953.

"When the Big Three take their hands off of Asia": ibid., 30 November 1944.

"fed up with all this bla about internationalism": ibid., 20 January 1953.

"The Dictator's majority": ibid., 30 November 1944.

"Ike seems to be really in earnest": ibid., 14 December 1956.

"How do you explain Taft?": Harriet Yarrow to JR, 8 July 1948, JRP, SL.

"How did you like the way Dewey won his nomination?": ibid., 17 August 1948.

64   "I am just sick about your and Wellington's personal disappointment": ibid.

"Wellington did not get in": JR to Harriet Yarrow, 20 January 1953, Harriet Yarrow Papers.

"I know you are sad to have Flora Belle go": JR to Esther Gregorie, 11 March 1971, Flora Belle Surles Papers.

"[W]hen I first saw you, in Birmingham": Flora Belle Surles to JR, 12 February 1966, JRP, SL.

"There [was] something in the look of [your] . . . face": ibid.

"the loveliest vacation I ever had": Flora Belle Surles to JR, 12 May 1969, JRP, SL.

describes "Florabel" as alien and lacking in beauty: Katharine Anthony, "A Basket of Summer Fruit," *Woman's Home Companion* 53 (August 1926), 12.

65   Surles's "old man": JR to Flora Belle Surles, 17 March 1948, Flora Belle Surles Papers.

Surles occupied herself with helping Gregorie's brother: Flora Belle Surles to JR, 19 March 1945, JRP, SL.

to Mexico or Canada in a new "Ford 60": ERM to WR, 3 August 1936; JR to WR, 2 July 1938, WRP.

Rankin invited Surles to visit her: JR to Flora Belle Surles, 22 July 1935, Flora Belle Surles Papers.

"[I]f you and Anne want to come up [to Washington]": ibid., 15 January 1938.

"why he distrusts the people": ibid.

"How do the people feel about saving the Red menace?": ibid., 28 June 1941.

"Next winter I expect to spend in the South with mother": ibid., 4 September 1942.

66   "[J]ust whenever it suits you hop a bus": Flora Belle Surles to JR, 19 March 1945, JRP, SL.

"[C]ome at any moment that the impulse strikes": Anne Gregorie to JR, 8 December 1945, JRP, SL.

"I'm ready for you any time": JR to Flora Belle Surles, 10 January 1948, Flora Belle Surles Papers.

"I went out to the ranch with a woman to help clean": ibid., 7 June 1949.

"It was very hard to leave you": ibid., 7 February 1944.

"missed you so much that the heavens wept with us": ibid., 28 March 1944.

"[I]t was very hard to give you up and come home alone": ibid., 29 November 1944.

"How I miss you!! . . . It seems almost like a dream": ibid., 8 April 1946.

"I don't know when I'll ever see you": ibid., 22 July 1947.

sending "your girls . . . a batch of fudge": GRK to JR, 7 November 1944, JRP, SL.

67   "taking such good care of the little red button": JR to Flora Belle Surles, 6 March 1962, Flora Belle Surles Papers.

"wish I could drop in for a visit with my precious friend": ibid., nd.

"I'm wearing the fancy pretty nighty": ibid., 1961.

"I think of you every day in cool or cold weather": Flora Belle Surles to JR, 2 October 1966, JRP, SL.

"If you want to stay dressed all day": JR to Flora Belle Surles, 20 October 1970, Flora Belle Surles Papers.

"Haven't been feeling any too pert": ibid., 3 March 1944.

"[Y]our papers have given me a lot of information": ibid., 21 May 1944 and 22 June 1944.

"Mother is still in town with Mary and three nurses": ibid., 22 July 1947.

"Did I tell you that I'm buying a ranch": ibid., 29 July 1955.

In 1938 she reported: ibid., 15 January 1938, 5 July 1950, 4 October 1955, 3 May 1965.

68   "Can't make my head work": ibid., 22 July 1947.

"I had an attack of pain but it's over now": ibid., 4 October 1955.

"I've had such a time with pain": ibid., March 1962.

"I have been in such pain I couldn't write": ibid., nd.

In her letters, Flora Belle Surles recounts her own daily activities: Flora Belle Surles to JR, 19 March 1945 and 7 September 1955, JRP, SL.

her opinion on urban riots: ibid., 12 May 1969.

"I thought you were more or less joking": ibid., 20 October 1965.

"I know you will miss Katharine": ibid., 26 November 1965.

"I keep wishing you had Katharine Anthony": ibid., 5 January 1968.

"beloved Wellington had to go before you": ibid., 25 August 1966.

"[I]t was given to you to love all mankind": ibid., 5 January 1968.

69   "armor against a hostile environment": Faderman, *Odd Girls*, 21.

She taught English at Wellesley: Maureen Flanagan, "Katharine Susan Anthony," in John A. Garraty and Mark C. Carnes, eds., *American National Biography* (New York: Oxford University Press, 1999), 546–547.

In New York she worked in a settlement house: Floyd M. Hammack, "Elizabeth Antoinette Irwin," in John A. Garraty and Mark C. Carnes, eds., *American National Biography* (New York: Oxford University Press, 1999), 692–693.

"economic dependency on husbands": Flanagan, "Katharine Susan Anthony," in John A. Garraty and Mark C. Carnes, eds., *American National Biography* (New York: Oxford University Press, 1999), 547.

"emphasized memorization rather than experience": Hammack, "Elizabeth Antoinette Irwin," in John A. Garraty and Mark C. Carnes, eds., *American National Biography* (New York: Oxford University Press, 1999), 692.

70   She stayed for several weeks: Josephson, *First Lady*, 84.

"What We Women Should Do": Jeannette Rankin, "What We Women Should Do," *Ladies Home Journal* (August 1917), 17, MHS.

Her three *Woman's Home Companion* articles: Katharine Anthony, "Our Gypsy Journey to Georgia" 53 (July 1926), "A Basket of Summer Fruit" 53 (August 1926), "Living on the Front Porch" 53 (September 1926), *Woman's Home Companion.*

71   emotional convalescence at Anthony's Greenwich Village apartment: Smith, "Fighting Pacifist," 232.

Rankin and Anthony also visited in New York: Frances Elge to JR, 24 June, 25 June, 27 June, and 23 July 1942, JRP, SL.

Elisabeth Irwin was in a hospital: JR to Ernestine Evans, 1 August 1942, JRP, SL.

"Was at Katharine's when the real cool spell came": JR to Flora Belle Surles, 21 July 1946, Flora Belle Surles Papers.

72   "I've just written to Katharine to come down": ibid., 10 January 1948.

"Did you know that Elisabeth Irwin is ill": ibid., 4 September and 14 September 1942.

Irwin's death in late 1942: ibid., 1 October 1942.

Gloomy weather: Katharine Anthony to JR, 18 January 1943, JRP, SL.

Also weighing on Anthony: ibid.

"It gave me a thrill to get a letter from you": ibid., 21 January 1943.

73   "We must write to each other often": ibid., 21 February 1943.

"I'll be glad when you are there": ibid., 18 April 1943.

"Somehow I feel better about you": ibid., 9 June 1943.

"I think of you every day and every night": ibid., 18 April 1943.

"I think of you so often, and so lovingly": ibid., 7 June 1946.

"Washington or Georgia would do": ibid., 21 January 1943.

"spend some time in the Rockies": ibid., 28 January 1943.

74   "stay in the city and suck it dry": ibid., 8 January 1951.

"Hope you had a good visit in Butte": ibid., 18 May 1943.

"your day dream about going to India is swell": ibid., 9 June 1943.

"Your mother must have been so delighted to see you": ibid., 9 February 1947.

"restlessness seems to be satisfied": ibid., 9 September 1956.

"She is alone now and foot-loose": ibid., 5 February 1943.

"feel rather lonely to have you in India": ibid., 18 December 1949.

After Rankin's return from India: ibid., 17 June 1950.

"Go on with your travel plans": ibid., 12 September 1955.

75   "Mrs. Miller has a bad cold": JR to ERM, April 1961, JRP, MHS.

"few and far between and of short duration": Flora Belle Surles to JR, 26 November 1965, JRP, SL.

"[Y]ou will stay with me of course": Katharine Anthony to JR, 5 November 1955, JRP, SL.

"You know you have a home in New York": ibid., 6 October 1956.

She asked Rankin to join her on a research trip: ibid., 8 January 1951.

In July 1953, Anthony was "still hoping": ibid., 26 July 1953.

visit Rankin in her Georgia "hide-out": ibid., 7 February 1954.

"snatched that visit with you": ibid., February 1955.

"you should come here next summer": ibid., 21 July 1954.

"make me very happy if you would say yes. YES": ibid., 25 April 1955.

"on tenter hooks till I hear from the publisher": ibid., 10 February 1958.

"I can refer to your card": ibid., 2 March 1958.

"My social life is not so active as yours": ibid., 10 March 1958.

76   "your sweet Georgia kitchen": ibid., 9 December 1954.

"your elegant pink boudoir": ibid., February 1955.

"all those Indian things [that] give it so much character": ibid., 2 May 1957.

"so sweet and attractive": ibid., 17 March 1955.

"I am thinking of you and wish with all my heart": ibid., 25 April 1955.

"wish I could come down and play around with you": ibid., 27 October 1957.

"Come noon and lunch time I say to myself": ibid., 28 April 1959.

"How lovely to hear your voice": ibid., 24 January 1959.

"I have had the kitchen painted for you": ibid., 5 February 1959.

"I don't believe any of those expenses kept you from coming up": ibid., 1 March 1959.

"I miss you a lot": ibid., 28 April 1959.

"I got homesick for you": ibid., 4 May 1959.

"Viola is going to her Maine resort": ibid., 19 May 1965.

77   "Mary Elizabeth . . . will pick you up at Katharine Anthony's": HRM to JR, 18 October 1965, JRP, SL.

"I am so anxious to see you": Katharine Anthony to JR, 3 November 1965, JRP, SL.

"Jeannette was so undone at Katharine Anthony's death": DMB to ERM, 16 December 1965, ERMP.

"[D]on't be rash": Katharine Anthony to JR, 20 January 1955, JRP, SL.

"I often think of you and your brisk way": ibid., 27 October 1957.

4. SUFFRAGE: A GLIMPSE OF SELF

79   "the most male of roles": Witt, Paget, and Matthews, *Running as a Woman*, 100.

introduced her to a female candidate: Cheek, "Rhetoric and Revolt," 172.

"remarkable voice": Goldmark, *Impatient Crusader,* 71; Smith, "Fighting Pacifist," 41.

80   she volunteered to put up posters: Smith, "Fighting Pacifist," 47.

"I paid my way": Cheek, "Rhetoric and Revolt," 158.

Her father's estate provided $75 a month: ibid., 31, 47.

"nearly every county west of the Cascade mountains": Smith, "Fighting Pacifist," 58.

"No service was too commonplace": ibid., 59.

"singularly sweet personality": ibid.

"slim and slightly above medium height": ibid., 24.

"straight posture . . . abundant hair": ibid.

her brother's sartorial strategy: ibid., 31, 47.

floor and gallery "were helpless": *Helena Independent,* 2 February 1911, JRP, MHS; Cheek, "Rhetoric and Revolt," 85.

"a gold colored velvet suit": Winestine, "The First Woman in Congress."

"looked just marvelous": Winestine, "Feminist and Suffragette."

81   "looked like a young panther ready to spring": quoted in Winestine, "The First Woman in Congress."

"thin and lacking in the curvaceous form": Sara J. Moore, "Making a Spectacle of Suffrage: The National Woman Suffrage Pageant," *Journal of American Culture* 20 (spring 1997), 92, 94, 96.

"dashing and glowing": Belle Fligelman Winestine, "Equal Suffrage and Jeannette Rankin's First Year in Congress," unpublished paper, Belle Fligelman Winestine Papers, SL.

"simultaneously feminine and feminist": ibid., 94.

"women would become an important bloc": McGlen et al., *Women, Politics, and American Society,* 36.

"attended meetings . . . on wage and hour legislation": Smith, "Fighting Pacifist," 35.

Her course of study at the New York School: Kahn, "Themes for a History"; Schaffer, "Progressive," 18.

Her reading of Jane Addams: Lasch, *Social Thought,* 143–144.

"pacifism should be a part of woman suffrage": Smith, "Fighting Pacifist," 110.

"men are doing their own work": *Butte Miner,* 10 July 1913, JRP, MHS.

"straight from the shoulder": ibid.

"timid and retiring girl": *Montana Kaimen,* 16 November 1916, JRP, SL.

"worked over her speeches": quoted in Lita Barnett, "Who is Jeannette Rankin and What Will She Do?" *The Woman's Journal* (18 November 1916), 370, cited in Cheek, "Rhetoric and Revolt," 63.

82   "I didn't write it clear through": quoted in ibid., 165.

what "worked and what didn't work": quoted in ibid.

"the highest standards of grammar, diction, and enunciation": Galt interview.

"You can't get an audience reading": quoted in Cheek, "Rhetoric and Revolt," 165.

"We often speak of you": Mrs. D'Arcy Hamilton to JR, 7 August 1916, JRP, MHS.

"she never wrote a speech": Winestine interview, 23.

"Well, you write something": ibid.

"when Jeannette got up to speak": ibid.

"an exquisite voice": *The Independent,* Kansas City, Missouri, nd, JRP, MHS.

"rare combination of femininity and force": unidentified newspaper, nd, JRP, SL.

"Everyone speaks of you": ERM to JR, 1 April 1972, JRP, SL.

83   "almost mute": Elinor Richey, *Eminent Women of the West* (Berkeley: Howell-North Books, 1975), 205.

"firstborn daughter to mother the lastborn children": Smith-Rosenberg, *Disorderly Conduct,* 33, 65.

followed the Tammany Hall model: Schaffer, "Progressive," 28.

"old Tammany Hall organization": quoted in Cheek, "Rhetoric and Revolt," 65.

"We are busily at work in this state": quoted in *Anaconda Standard,* 10 July 1913, JRP, MHS.

"money is a great essential": JR to Miss Clara Park Oliver, 6 June 1936, JRP, SL.

84   Seeing an opportunity to apply at home: Smith, "Fighting Pacifist," 78.

Her speech that February to the Montana legislature: Ward, "Winning of Woman Suffrage," 110.

"[E]scorted to the reading desk": Ida Husted Harper, ed., *The History of Woman Suffrage,* vol. 6 (New York: National American Woman Suffrage Association, 1922), 362.

challenged the two chambers: Cheek, "Rhetoric and Revolt," 172.

Addams saw suffrage as women "pursuing their traditional activities": quoted in Lasch, *Social Thought,* 144.

"Men want women in the home": *Helena Independent,* 2 February 1911, JRP, MHS.

Despite Rankin's success: ibid.

"has worked day and night, heart and soul": New York organizers to James L. Laidlaw, 21 March 1912, JRP, MHS.

State senator Franklin Delano Roosevelt: JR, interview with Josephson, 185.

85   Rankin never forgave Roosevelt: Galt interview.

"how quickly she could get signatures": Smith, "Fighting Pacifist," 65.

"go into a saloon or anyplace": JR, interview with Josephson, 209.

"came home with pages of signatures": ibid.

"All progressive movements were started by the few": quoted in *Helena Independent*, 10 October 1914, quoted in Schaffer, "Progressive," 52.

"sent into the country districts": JR, "Why the Country Folk Did It," *The Woman Voter* (19 December 1911), 13, JRP, MHS.

"We had entered—most of us who were sent out to help": ibid.

86 Upton wrote to Laidlaw: Harriet Upton to Harriet Laidlaw, July 1912, JRP, SL.

87 "so untrained and held down by the church": quoted in Schaffer, "Progressive," 35.

"fearing I might have pushed her from town to town": Harriet Upton to Harriet Laidlaw, July 1912, JRP, SL.

"I'm sorry that my work was unsatisfactory": JR to Harriet Upton, 28 July 1912, quoted in Schaffer, "Progressive," 36.

Upton sent Laidlaw an explanation: Harriet Upton to Harriet Laidlaw, July 1912, JRP, SL.

In her response to Harriet Upton: Harriet Laidlaw to Harriet Upton, 24 July 1912, JRP, SL.

88 "find a whacking good position": Harriet Laidlaw to JR, 1912, JRP, SL.

president of Montana's chapter of the National Men's Suffrage League: Harper, *History of Woman Suffrage*, 364.

Once back in Montana: Ward, "Winning of Woman Suffrage," 115.

"We got every party . . . strik[ing] out the word 'male'": quoted in Cheek, "Rhetoric and Revolt," 160.

"[Then we] wrote to every candidate": quoted in ibid.

"county to county appointing chairmen": Smith, "Fighting Pacifist," 84.

talking to legislators at the state capitol: Josephson, *First Lady*, 41.

"the power of organization": quoted in Cheek, "Rhetoric and Revolt," 16.

89 "traveling wherever she was needed": Smith, "Fighting Pacifist," 68.

"woman suffrage would not create race suicide": Schaffer, "Progressive," 40.

NAWSA, which was "often racist in nature": McGlen et al., *Women, Politics, and American Society*, 36.

"suitable accommodation" on trains for blacks: ibid.

the objection of southern women: quoted in ibid.

"Mrs. C. P. Gilman's sex women": JR to Mary Ware Dennett, 15 May 1913, Mary Ware Dennett Papers, SL.

"who had worked with the more militant British suffragettes": McGlen et al., *Women, Politics, and American Society*, 38.

90 organizing "more than five thousand women": Moore, "Making a Spectacle," 91–92.

"Daring to make a spectacle of themselves": ibid., 89.

"Women were spat upon": *The Woman's Journal*, quoted in Schaffer, "Progressive," 39.

"a powerful tool in the political process": Moore, "Making a Spectacle," 90.

"[S]uffrage is all right for the women of the North": quoted in Smith, "Fighting Pacifist," 71.

"use the same laws against them that you do against the Negro": quoted in Cheek, "Rhetoric and Revolt," 171.

"You can't hit your baby's nurse": quoted in ibid.

"exploit[ed] popular racist and nativist sentiments": Estelle B. Freedman, "Separatism as Strategy: Female Institution Building and American Feminism, 1870–1930," in Moses and Hartmann, eds., *U.S. Women in Struggle: A Feminist Studies Anthology* (Urbana: University of Illinois Press, 1995), 80.

"a white, middle-class, native movement": Hinckle and Hinckle, "History of the Rise," 26.

91   "libelous statements circulated about her": Smith, "Fighting Pacifist," 72.

"condemn[ed] female friendships as lesbian": Smith-Rosenberg, *Disorderly Conduct*, 34–35.

"morbid and pathological": D'Emilio and Freedman, *Intimate Matters*, 228.

politically active women . . . were labeled homosexuals: Smith-Rosenberg, *Disorderly Conduct*, 35.

"Jane Addams, for instance, shrugged it off": Smith, "Fighting Pacifist," 72.

"a very important spoke in the wheel": Antoinette Funk to JR, 2 April 1915 and 17 April 1915, JRP, SL.

"This sort of thing is not as serious as it seems": ibid., 17 March 1915.

"too contemptible to be worthy of notice": WR to JR, 16 April 1915, JRP, SL.

"be very careful": JR, interview with Chall, 47.

"punishment and social ostracism": D'Emilio and Freedman, *Intimate Matters*, 228.

"bossy ways" of its president: Smith, "Fighting Pacifist," 99.

92   sharp division within NAWSA: ibid.

"hoity-toity grand ladies": JR, interview with Josephson, 248.

"a jealous 'brimstone heart'": Harriet Laidlaw to JR, nd, JRP, SL.

NAWSA removed the dissident Paul: McGlen et al., *Women, Politics, and American Society*, 39.

"[a]fter decisive state referenda defeats": ibid.

She was personally closer to Paul: Smith, "Fighting Pacifist," 99.

"were generally among the better educated and propertied": ibid., 63, 68.

Dr. Maria M. Dean had been fighting for suffrage: Harper, *History of Woman Suffrage*, 360.

Mary O'Neill had been running suffrage's press campaign: ibid., 361.

Woman's Christian Temperance Union (WCTU) had been such an effective voice: Ward, "Winning of Woman Suffrage," 123.

"legitimate targets" of the liquor industry: McGlen et al., *Women, Politics, and American Society*, 33.

"gave the WCTU suffragists plucky leadership": ibid., 34.

93   Another political woman was Ella Knowles: ibid., 36, 40.

"by far the most prominent woman": ibid., 35.

"mounted a campaign that was energetic and efficient": ibid., 44.

Montana House of Representatives invited Knowles: ibid., 58.

"suffragists gave testimony in both chambers": ibid., 110.

"honor of floor privileges was not new": ibid.

Catt spoke and organized in Helena and Butte: Harper, *History of Woman Suffrage*, 360; Ward, "Winning of Woman Suffrage," 81.

"every town of importance, organizing more than thirty clubs": Harper, *History of Woman Suffrage*, 360.

"largest copper producing mine in the world": Hines, "Wellington Duncan Rankin," 22.

supporters of "revolutionary industrial unionism": Calvert, *Gibraltar*, 50.

"included equal franchise in a large package of reforms": Ward, "Winning of Woman Suffrage," 102.

"broaden the base for reforms": ibid.

In 1900 the northern High Line: ibid., 103–105.

94   "earned the generous credit traditionally awarded her": ibid., 108.

sending out "each week a letter of suffrage news": Harper, *History of Woman Suffrage*, 363.

"violent public temper tantrum": Smith, "Fighting Pacifist," 100.

"afraid of my speaking ability": quoted in Ward, "Winning of Woman Suffrage," 131.

"I would go to the Union Hall night after night": JR, interview with Josephson, 284.

She co-opted campaign appearances: Cheek, "Rhetoric and Revolt," 162.

She debated anti-suffragists: Harper, *History of Woman Suffrage*, 366.

"went to mines and talk[ed] to the men": JR, interview with Josephson, 284.

"spoke at a three-county picnic": Winestine, "The First Woman in Congress."

organized a "Woman's Day and a Suffrage Pageant": JR to Catharine Waugh McCulloch, 7 September 1914, Catharine Waugh McCulloch Papers, SL.

95   staged a "picturesque," "mile-long" parade: Harper, *History of Woman Suffrage*, 366; Schaffer, "Progressive," 57–58.

the "great" Katherine Devereux Blake: Cheek, "Rhetoric and Revolt," 175; Harper, *History of Woman Suffrage*, 364.

"charmed [the local women] with her beauty and style": Harper, *History of Woman Suffrage*, 364.

James Laidlaw, who "surprised" Montanans: ibid.

"successor as field secretary": Schaffer, "Progressive," 55.

Ida Craft, East Coast labor organizer: Harper, *History of Woman Suffrage*, 364.

"at least one school in every county": Winestine, "The First Woman in Congress."

"I want my mother to vote": Cheek, "Rhetoric and Revolt," 162.

She personally "organized every county": ibid.

she could campaign in "kitchen[s]": ibid.

"reason we found her": Cheek, "Rhetoric and Revolt," 175.

"the money was totally lost": *Seattle Times,* 31 August 1916, JRP, SL.

suffrage was "being counted out in Anaconda": Cheek, "Rhetoric and Revolt," 163.

"the company that controlled the state": Cheek, "Rhetoric and Revolt," 163.

executive secretary of the National Anti-Suffrage Association: Harper, *History of Woman Suffrage,* 366.

96   "jumping around throughout the state": JR to Margaret Foley, 29 July 1914, Margaret Foley Papers.

"became confident of the 'dry' vote": Ward, "Winning of Woman Suffrage," 130.

"not to dare to bring prohibition into the campaign": quoted in ibid., 133.

"sweepingly declared that they were not interested in social reforms": ibid., 130.

"persuade the foreign-born that equal suffrage was in their interest": ibid., 134.

"effective participation by minority elements": ibid.

"take the old men and leave the young men": quoted in Board, "The Lady from Montana," 115.

"we could see that these children were given intensive study": JR, speech to State Federation of Women's Clubs, Lewistown, Montana, 4 June 1914, JRP, MHS.

"natural rights and equal justice": Ward, "Winning of Woman Suffrage," 157.

willing to muzzle the cry: Freedman, "Separatism as Strategy," 80.

"women needed the vote to perform their traditional tasks": ibid.

"All over the country": quoted in *Daily Missoulian,* 2 May 1914, quoted in Cheek, "Rhetoric and Revolt," 150.

97   "all the dope you can": Mary O'Neill to JR, nd, JRP, SL.

98   more than two million: McGlen et al., *Women, Politics, and American Society,* 32–34.

"modified Victorian concept of women": Ward, "Winning of Woman Suffrage," 124.

"the best single-handed campaigner": quoted in Josephson, *First Lady,* 52.

"I could be elected where other women couldn't": JR, interview with Josephson, 180.

"[A]ll during the suffrage campaign": quoted in Cheek, "Rhetoric and Revolt," 64.

"I didn't run for Congress": quoted in ibid.

"I was sitting on your porch in Lewistown": JR to Josephine Reynolds, 10 January 1941, JRP, SL.

"I thought I was the only one": JR, interview with Chall, 80.

"mentioned this war a good many times": ibid.

"speeches . . . on the streets of Butte": JR, interview with John C. Board, 1965, UML.

99   "[I]t was entirely on suffrage": ibid.

"I would never describe her as a politician": Winestine, "Feminist and Suffragette."

"woman's place is in the house, baking bread": Mabel M. Peck to JR, 8 February 1941, JRP, SL.

"Can you make a blueberry muffin?": Witt, Paget, and Matthews, *Running as a Woman,* 216.

"staggering" campaign difficulties: Brown, "Montana's First Woman Politician," 24.

organized "[m]any of the suffrage work-horses": Ward, "Winning of Woman Suffrage," 150.

"you will be the central figure": Mary O'Neill to JR, 6 April 1915, JRP, SL.

"citizen lectures"; "course of civic study": Schaffer, "Progressive," 62.

100 "The cause would surely profit by such a move": Lynn Haines to JR, 8 April 1915, JRP, SL.

5. CAMPAIGNING: WHAT SHE LOVED MOST AND DID BEST

101 barriers that have frustrated political women: McGlen et al., *Women, Politics, and American Society*, 92–102; Witt, Paget, and Matthews, *Running as a Woman*, generally.

"perceptual screen of general female stereotypes": Witt, Paget, and Matthews, *Running as a Woman*, 116.

Not having a predecessor to learn from: ibid., 100.

"decidedly negative" attitudes: quoted in McGlen et al., *Women, Politics, and American Society*, 67.

"freakish thing": Board, "The Lady from Montana," 67.

"Tonight a hen will attempt to crow": Mrs. M. J. Baker to JR, 6 July 1917, JRP, SL.

"tradition of principled, altruistic" service: Witt, Paget, and Matthews, *Running as a Woman*, 30.

career and credible credentials: Witt, Paget, and Matthews, *Running as a Woman*, 9, 100; McGlen et al., *Women, Politics, and American Society*, 95.

saddled with "family demands": ibid., 96.

"double duty as caregivers": Freedman, *No Turning Back*, 338.

"male party structure": Witt, Paget, and Matthews, *Running as a Woman*, 217.

102 "outmanned" in the Republican Party: Ware, *Partner and I*, 149.

"run by men": ibid.

lacked personal financial resources: Witt, Paget, and Matthews, *Running as a Woman*, 128.

run for office "anomalous": ibid., 31.

urinated on the paper: Daphne Bugbee Jones, interview with authors, 13 September 2002.

"[Y]ou are always on the jump": Mary O'Neill to JR, 6 April 1915; Mary O'Neill to JR, nd, JRP, SL.

"I did everything in the suffrage campaigns first": JR, interview with Josephson, 285.

"I had tried out everything": ibid., 246.

"abounding enthusiasm throughout the state": *Three Forks Herald*, 17 August 1916, MHS.

"Brass bands and street parades": ibid.; *Kalispell Times,* 17 August 1916, MHS.

"Jeannette Rankin clubs are being organized": Anderson, "Steps to Political Equality," 108.

103   "the best known person": JR, interview with Board.

postcard mailings: Winestine, "The First Woman in Congress."

telephone calling: Cheek, "Rhetoric and Revolt," 117.

"walls were hung with the maps": Winestine, "The First Woman in Congress."

"to every woman on the polling lists": ibid.

Each volunteer signed the postcards: ibid.

"[e]veryone who had a telephone was greeted": Cheek, "Rhetoric and Revolt," 117.

going house to house: ibid.

giving street-corner talks: JR, interview with Board.

"Let the People Know": JR, interview with Chall, 43–44, 57.

"[A]ll the rules of Congress": ibid., 38–39.

"controlled" by the Anaconda Copper Mining Company: JR, interview with Josephson, 179.

"Greater publicity in Congressional committees": JRP, MHS.

"I was born on a Montana farm": ibid.

"war was not then a campaign issue": Smith, "Fighting Pacifist," 110.

"I was running on issues": JR, interview with Chall, 53.

"[Being anti-war] wasn't a thing we talked about": ibid., 58.

"seven mediocre men": quoted in Schaffer, "Progressive," 62.

"too much dignity [to] stand on the street corner": JR, interview with Board.

104   "less male, somehow unsexed": Witt, Paget, and Matthews, *Running as a Woman,* 50.

"beaten by a woman": *San Francisco Bulletin,* 5 May 1917, JRP, MHS.

"Do you want to keep a woman in Congress?": Senate Bill No. 7, 15th Legislative Assembly, 1917, *Montana Session Law;* JR, interview with Board.

"'I could be the first [woman to go to Congress]'": JR, interview with Chall, 37.

"[V]ote for your local candidate": JR, interview with Board.

she usually "had the second vote": ibid.

"they all got out and voted": ibid.

"intoxicating liquors of any kind": Ellis Waldron and Paul B. Wilson, *Atlas of Montana Elections, 1889–1976* (Missoula: University of Montana Publications in History, 1978), 62.

Allied on the dry side: ibid.

"big-gun war": *Great Falls Daily Tribune,* 8 November 1916, JRP, MHS.

"bankers, cattlemen, labor leaders": Waldron and Wilson, *Atlas of Montana Elections,* 62.

"one of the bitterest political fights ever waged": *Great Falls Daily Tribune,* 8 November 1916.

"total number [of] legal voters": ibid.

105   Across the state the successful measure passed: Waldron and Wilson, *Atlas of Montana Elections*, 62.

The turnout for the prohibition measure: ibid.

"he would elect her if she ran": Anderson, "Steps to Political Equality," 106.

"I'll pay for your campaign": quoted in Richey, *Eminent Women*, 191.

"half of the first salary": Winestine, "The First Woman in Congress."

She reported spending even less: *Portsmouth Times*, 24 November 1916, JRP, MHS.

"spent $20,000 on buying the 1916 election": confidential interview.

He was sufficiently confident at election time: Hines, "Wellington Duncan Rankin," 32.

"a trap that was set for you": J. A. Williams to JR, 13 November 1916, JRP, MHS.

"rumor current in Butte": Mrs. H. N. Kennedy to JR, 15 November 1916, JRP, MHS.

"outlined a plan for the campaign": Schaffer, "Progressive," 64.

placed himself at the center of its execution: Galt interview.

"never traveled" during campaigns: Board, "The Lady from Montana," 74.

concentrate on the more populated eastern part: Schaffer, "Progressive," 64.

106   "My brother was in touch": JR, interview with Board.

"Twice you were posted here as lost": Julia Skillman to JR, 12 November 1916, JRP, MHS.

"no conflict between his and Jeannette's political ambitions": Galt interview.

Despite the opposition of "Old line Republicans": Smith, "Fighting Pacifist," 108.

"Our father was a Republican": WR, interview with Board, quoted in Hines, "Wellington Duncan Rankin," 24.

"In the South, the aristocrats were Democrats": JR, interview with Chall, 58.

"who helped put [Jeannette] on the map": *Montana News*, 20 November 1916, MHS.

"brother was a powerful Republican": Belle Fligelman Winestine, interview with Helen Huppe, nd, 7, Norman and Belle Fligelman Winestine Papers, MHS.

"going to send me out with a young lawyer": JR, interview with Josephson, 243.

"stand on the platform and praise me": ibid.

107   "more people than the Missoula theater could hold": *Daily Missoulian*, 7 November 1916, JRP, MHS.

"interrupted with tremendous applause": ibid.

"50 percent of the vote and one more": JR, interview with Josephson, 244.

"fit of female hysteria": *Bozeman Chronicle*, 19 April 1917, JRP, MHS.

"[W]e hold Miss Rankin wholly sincere": *Lewistown Democrat-News*, 11 August 1917, JRP, MHS.

"is putting the women of the country in the worst possible light": Helen H. Gardener to Harriet Laidlaw, 27 June 1917, Harriet Laidlaw Papers, SL.

"the Joan of Arc of the I.W.W.": *Montana American*, 19 August 1917, JRP, MHS.

"It would be a tremendous stretch": *New York World,* nd, quoted in *Livingston Enterprise,* nd, JRP, MHS.

108 "[O]pponents of your sister Gerrymandered the State": Bill Keeley to WR, 1952, WRP.

"geographical limitations now set": *Missoulian,* 13 August 1917, JRP, MHS.

Evans "warned her": ibid.

"Little Mother Jones": Mrs. Thomas Burns to JR, 29 August 1917, JRP, MHS.

Its partisan split favored her: for example, see Reverend E. W. Brickert to JR, 9 May 1918, JRP, MHS.

"Of course you know the homesteaders had no crop": Margaret N. Bright to JR, 3 March 1918, JRP, MHS.

"Yes, I will run in the eastern Montana district": quoted in *Great Falls Daily Tribune,* 27 April 1918, JRP, MHS.

109 "quickly corrected herself": ibid.

Reports of Jeannette Rankin running for the Senate: *Helena Independent,* 9 August 1917, JRP, MHS.

"[W]hy did Miss Rankin adopt a partial attitude": *Butte Tribune-Review,* nd, quoted in *Missoulian,* August 1917, JRP, MHS.

"I cannot tell you how much I regret": *Helena Independent,* 19 August 1917, JRP, MHS.

"Everything arranged and in my hands": WR to JR, 17 September 1917, JRP, MHS.

Wellington's moderating influence: Calvert, *Gibraltar,* 124.

He sent her a copy: WR to JR, 24 August 1917, JRP, MHS.

110 "Carried along on the waves": *Butte Miner,* 19 August 1917, JRP, MHS.

president of the *New York Evening Post*: Oswald G. Villard to JR, 5 October 1917, JRP, MHS.

"It is being alleged here": ibid.

"to take up the matter fairly and squarely": ibid., 14 November 1917.

"I appreciate more than I can tell you": JR to Oswald G. Villard, 10 December 1917, JRP, MHS.

"cancelled" by her secretary: Belle Fligelman handwritten note on JR to Oswald G. Villard, 17 November 1917, JRP, MHS.

"the only violence that has occurred": JR to Oswald G. Villard, 17 November 1917.

"The more radical of the [union membership]": JR to Oswald G. Villard, 10 December 1917.

"The men do not want a sliding scale": JR to Oswald G. Villard, 17 November 1917.

"As to the wage question": JR to Oswald G. Villard, 10 December 1917.

111 "I ask you again, will you be willing": quoted in *Butte Miner,* 19 August 1917, JRP, MHS.

"[D]ynamic" and full of "new ideas": *Montana Standard,* nd, Butte–Silver Bow County Archives.

"one of the so-called radicals": Mary Murphy, *Mining Cultures: Men, Women, and Leisure in Butte, 1914–1941* (Urbana: University of Illinois Press, 1997), 154.

"simply progressive women": quoted in ibid.

dismissed her as a "visionary": WR to JR, 10 August 1917, JRP, MHS.

"[Y]our friends here believe": Mary O'Neill to JR, 14 July 1917, JRP, MHS.

"Miners and unions depend on your personal presence": ibid., 10 August 1917.

"It all depends on you": ibid., 12 August 1917.

"could see that he had you in mind": ibid., 19 September 1917.

To settle the Butte strike: JR, "Government Control of Metalliferous Mines," *Congressional Record* (7 August 1917), JRP, MHS.

112 "Walsh just told me": Mary O'Neill to JR, 19 September 1917, JRP, MHS.

"be a candidate for the U.S. Senate": *Helena Independent,* 9 August 1917, JRP, MHS.

"The lineup will then be": ibid.

"represents Montana, and more particularly the I.W.W. element": *Great Falls Daily Tribune,* 9 August 1917, JRP, MHS.

"association with the disloyal elements": unidentified newspaper, nd, JRP, MHS.

"German books and histories": *Boulder Monitor,* 27 April 1918, JRP, MHS.

113 "The attitude of the citizens who attended": ibid.

"Miss Rankin is on the right track": *Sanders County Signal,* 10 August 1917, JRP, MHS.

"As for your labor speech about the I.W.W.": Nina Swinnerton to JR, 28 August 1917, JRP, MHS.

"she is in touch with a group of malcontents": *Montana American,* 10 August 1917, JRP, MHS.

"champion the cause of the most lawless and dangerous set of men": *Lewistown Democrat-News,* 11 August 1917, JRP, MHS.

"the destructive and lawless activities": ibid., 13 August 1917.

"seeking to play upon a prejudice": ibid., 11 August 1917.

"peculiar school of politics": *Helena Independent,* 15 August 1917, JRP, MHS.

114 "emphatic need of a daily labor press in Butte": *Butte Miner,* 19 August 1917, JRP, MHS.

"Press reports about Butte and Anaconda": Mary O'Neill to JR, 13 September 1917, JRP, MHS.

Another Butte politico, Elizabeth Kennedy: Murphy, *Mining Cultures,* 24, 152.

"sending out 'doctored' reports": Mrs. H. N. Kennedy to JR, 18 June 1917, JRP, MHS.

"our press investigated for suppression of news": ibid., 23 June 1917.

she had contacted a press service: Mary O'Neill to WR, 18 November 1917, WRP.

contributed $500: *Butte Miner,* nd, JRP, MHS.

"called for state ownership of grain elevators": Calvert, *Gibraltar,* 124.

Nonpartisan League added planks: Schaffer, "Progressive," 142.

"*Butte Bulletin* made contact with the League": Calvert, *Gibraltar,* 125.

115   "an active player in the Nonpartisan Club's political drive": ibid., 127.

"nest" of the Nonpartisan League: *Butte Miner,* nd, JRP, MHS.

"the farmers and their wives": E. A. Meyer to JR, 7 September 1917, JRP, MHS.

"[T]he farmers of Flathead County": ibid.

"Dear Comrade": Don McLeod to JR, 14 February 1918, JRP, MHS.

"I hope you will try for the Senate next year": James L. Wallace to JR, 7 September 1917, JRP, MHS.

legal counsel to the Society of Equity: *Hardin Tribune,* 15 October 1920, JRP, MHS.

"close working relationship with organized labor": Jules A. Karlin, *Joseph M. Dixon of Montana, Part 1: Senator and Bull Moose Manager, 1867–1917* (Missoula: University of Montana Publications in History, 1974), 228.

at a Montana labor convention: Don McLeod to JR, 14 February 1918, JRP, MHS.

"Jeannette Rankin announced today": *Great Falls Daily Tribune,* 6 July 1918, JRP, MHS.

116   Montana effort run by Wellington Rankin: HRS to Harriet Laidlaw, 27 July 1918, JRP, MHS.

"I have been in New York only a few weeks": Mary Stewart to JR, 9 December 1917, JRP, MHS.

family emergency called her away: HRS to Marie Virginia Smith, 26 July 1918, JRP, MHS.

organize a "campaign stunt": Marie Virginia Smith to HRS, 19 July 1918, JRP, MHS.

"I am earnestly hoping": Margaret Dreier Robins to Mary Stewart, 19 July 1918, JRP, MHS.

"enormous amount of cordial support": Marie Virginia Smith to HRS, 6 August 1918, JRP, MHS.

117   "I have talked with a few of Miss Rankin's friends": ibid., 19 July 1918, JRP, MHS.

"I will go on Jeannette's committee": Harriet Laidlaw to HRS, 23 July 1918, JRP, MHS.

"She doesn't love me": Jane Thompson to HRS, 25 July 1918, JRP, MHS.

"Mrs. Vanderlip declines": ibid., nd.

"I am fond of your sister": Helena Louise Johnson to HRS, 25 July 1918, JRP, MHS.

"put the passage of the Federal Amendment": Minnie Fisher Cunningham to Mrs. Jane Deeter Reeppin, 25 July 1918, JRP, MHS.

118   address the 75,000 postcards: HRS to Harriet Laidlaw, 27 July 1918, JRP, MHS.

"The Bureau girls are working in the office": HRS to Ida Craft, 26 July 1918, JRP, MHS.

"in a state the size of Montana": HRS to Mrs. Amos Pinchot, 15 August 1918, JRP, MHS.

Contributions were slow to arrive: JRP, MHS.

"jumps in line with prejudice and fear": Maria M. Dean to Mary Stewart, 22 July 1918, JRP, MHS.

"The primaries will be August 27th": HRS to Jane Thompson, 25 July 1918, JRP, MHS.

"a dinner here would be a good thing": Jane Thompson to HRS, 25 July 1918, JRP, MHS.

"long to have a luncheon for you": Nina Swinnerton to JR, 2 August 1918, JRP, MHS.

"a huge working women's . . . reception": ibid., September 1918, JRP, MHS.

119   "Such a really painful time of year": Marie Virginia Smith to HRS, 6 August 1918, JRP, MHS.

"The women are all so busy": Ida A. Craft to HRS, 10 August 1918, JRP, MHS.

"counteract much of the [IWW] poison": HRS to Harriet Laidlaw, 27 July 1918, JRP, MHS.

"I have been traveling 150 miles a day": quoted in *Daily Missoulian,* 23 August 1918, JRP, MHS.

In "daily letters": HRS to Harriet Laidlaw, 27 July 1918, JRP, MHS.

"five or six times as many people": HRS to Rosalia L. Whitney, 26 July 1918, JRP, MHS.

Republican primary vote would be split: HRS to Jane Thompson, 25 July 1918, JRP, MHS.

"strong labor vote," and the "farmer vote": HRS to Rosalia L. Whitney, 26 July 1918, JRP, MHS.

"politicians are admitting that she will win": HRS to Ida Craft, 26 July 1918, JRP, MHS.

"Wellington writes that the women": HRS to Belle Fligelman Winestine, 27 July 1918, JRP, MHS.

"signal victory": Eleanor Coit to JR, 10 November 1916, JRP, MHS.

"You will now be in a position": Florence W. Stephens to JR, 9 November 1916, JRP, MHS.

"stand for everything noble": Mrs. J. E. Geyer to JR, 14 November 1916, JRP, MHS.

"some over-zealous [suffragists]": Eva Ammen to JR, 22 June 1917, JRP, MHS.

120   "some women think you have ruined suffrage": Mildred Isabel Hunt to JR, 12 September 1917, JRP, MHS.

"more influence with Jeannette Rankin": Carrie Chapman Catt to James and Harriet Laidlaw, 11 September 1918, HLP.

"a great epidemic of flu": JR, interview with Board.

121   recruited Lanstrum: Carrie Chapman Catt to James and Harriet Laidlaw, 11 September 1918, Harriet Laidlaw Papers.

"stopped campaigning": ibid.

"contrary to the principles of the Republican party": quoted in Hines, "Wellington Duncan Rankin," 39.

"threatened" the national party committeeman: ibid.

"to buy [his] Havre newspaper": ibid.

"composed largely of outspoken admirers": *Daily Missoulian,* 23 August 1918, JRP, MHS.

122   "a vehicle for her candidacy": Schaffer, "Progressive," 141.

"make the world safe for humanity": ibid., 144.

"would support President Wilson": Smith, "Fighting Pacifist," 158.

sought the vote of the Montana Nonpartisan League: Schaffer, "Progressive," 144.

"candidate of the 'toilers'": *Butte Weekly Bulletin,* 24 October 1918, quoted in Calvert, *Gibraltar,* 129.

"suspected of disloyalty": Schaffer, "Progressive," 143.

"would attract left-wing votes": ibid., 140.

"every influence possible be brought to bear": quoted in C. B. Nolan to Thomas J. Walsh, 30 August 1918, quoted in Schaffer, "Progressive," 141.

Wellington's complicity: Archibald Spriggs to Thomas J. Walsh, 2 September 1918 and 23 September 1918, quoted in Schaffer, "Progressive," 141.

"get a position with the government": Schaffer, "Progressive," 141.

viewed the arrangement as "politics": WR, interview with John Board, quoted in Hines, "Wellington Duncan Rankin," 38.

"I was offered bribes not to run": JR, interview with Board.

"make it possible for me to do what I intended to do": JR, interview with Chall, 76.

123   prevent its publication: JR, interview with Josephson, 209.

"No one will read his book": JR, interview with Josephson, 209 (refers to Schaffer, "Progressive").

"correct any mistakes": Reita Rivers to JR, 6 October 1972, JRP, SL.

"buckled, . . . bent with the wind": Michael P. Malone and Richard B. Roeder, *Montana: A History of Two Centuries* (Seattle: University of Washington Press, 1978), 215.

"ample financial and newspaper support": Hines, "Wellington Duncan Rankin," 40.

She lost Butte to Walsh: Waldron and Wilson, *Atlas of Montana Elections,* 70.

Catt told a Montana newspaper: *Helena Independent,* 18 April 1918, JRP, MHS.

"separate [female] institutions did support women": Estelle B. Freedman, "Separatism Revisited: Women's Institutions, Social Reform, and the Career of Miriam Van Waters," in *U.S. History as Women's History,* ed. Linda K. Kerber et al. (Chapel Hill: University of North Carolina Press, 1995), 186.

"a real desire for peace": JR to Benny, 4 June 1938, JRP, SL.

accompanied by her mother: JR to WR, 24 January 1940, WRP.

"I don't know whether I told Wellington": JR, interview with Josephson, 238.

driving force of her campaign: Halinan interview, 5.

124   "she could never have done it without him": ibid., 4.

"one of the ablest campaigners": Haines interview, 8.

"feel out the situation": JR to WR, 7 January 1940, WRP.

She visited precinct committeemen and high schools: quoted in Cheek, "Rhetoric and Revolt," 183, 189.

district had recently favored Democrats: JR, interview with Board.

"an American first, a Progressive second": JR to Fred R. Uhde, January 1941, JRP, MHS.

chairman of the Montana Republican Party: Page interview, 2.

"What do you think about my running?": quoted in Cheek, "Rhetoric and Revolt," 189.

"how stupid war was": quoted in ibid., 183.

avoided mentioning Roosevelt: ibid.

"some day we'll have a woman president": quoted in ibid., 239.

finally took the difficult step: JR, interview with Board.

"I would not run without the consent": ibid.

"Wellington decided that it was all right to run": JR, interview with Josephson, 245.

"tremendous influence with Jeannette": Page interview, 6.

"I always thought he guided her": Haines interview, 2.

125   "to the best dress makers": Page interview, 10.

"I believe we should use every means": campaign literature, nd, WRP.

"an appeal to women": JR to WR, 24 January 1940, WRP.

"We all want to do whatever you think is best": MRB to WR, 25 May 1940, WRP.

"Rankin girls had been there": Page interview, 5.

"Go see Harold K. Near": campaign itineraries, 1940, WRP.

Campaigners on the road reported: Elge and McCall to WR, 21 October 1940, WRP.

126   "very glamorous picture": Belle Fligelman Winestine to Hannah Josephson, 28 December 1973, Hannah Josephson Papers.

"She never really looked like that picture": ibid.

"on the telephone incessantly": Page interview, 5.

"was a tough person": Haines interview, 1, 2, 8, 9.

"vivacious with a quick, nervous speech": *Kansas City Star,* 1940, MHS.

"slogan my opponents planned to use": JR, interview with Josephson, 245.

"hadn't been in the state for a long time": Page interview, 4.

"to know I was in their district": JR, interview with Chall, 67, 68.

"the women [who] don't want war": JR, interview with Board.

127   "I have 5,000 copies": JR to WR, 24 January 1940, WRP.

"America was morally committed": JR, "Democracy and Women," 16 January 1940, *Congressional Record,* 29 September 1939 radio address, WRP.

"By voting for me": JR, "Prepare to the Limit for Defense—Keep Our Men Out of Europe," 7 August 1940, *Congressional Record,* 8 July 1940 radio address, WRP.

"symbol against war": JR, interview with Board.

Jacob Thorkelson, "an isolationist": Schaffer, "Progressive," 233.

referred to him as "a good man": JR, interview with Josephson, 245.

128   "I want the power trust to know": quoted in *The Western Progressive,* 4 January 1935, MHS.

"records of the two were roughly similar": Schaffer, "Progressive," 234.

"red baiting": Joan Hoff Wilson, ". . . Her Lifework as a Pacifist," 42.

"she endorsed a widely distributed radio script": ibid.

"in the interests of Americanism": American Legion Post No. 20, Athens, Georgia, 15 October 1940, JRP, MHS.

129   "a very good enemy": JR, interview with Board.

"not . . . much interest" in the race: Schaffer, "Progressive," 235.

"the women in all of these communities": JR, interview with Board.

"drove around the district": ibid.

"[Y]ou ought to be in Congress yourself": the Hills to JR, 9 April 1942, JRP, SL.

"stepped aside for your brother": Millacent Yarrow to JR, 4 January 1942, JRP, SL.

"talked with Wellington at Denver": ERM to JR, 28 December 1941, JRP, SL.

130   "the field was open": Winfield Page, quoted in *Missoulian*, 1 December 1991.

"strong for Mike Mansfield": Page interview, 6.

"Rankins fought the Company": ibid.

"'pleasant young man'": JR to Frederick Libby, 11 October 1943, JRP, SL.

"let the world kill off the men": Millacent Yarrow to JR, 30 March 1943, JRP, SL.

"You must wake [the women] up": ibid.

"brows[ing] around a little": JR to Gladys MacKenzie, 11 June 1943, JRP, SL.

"program with the women in Montana": JR to Mrs. Berkeley Hayes, 12 June 1943, JRP, SL.

"We started to campaign": JR to Flora Belle Surles, 18 May 1944, JRP, MHS.

"I asked him about your running": GRK to JR and ERM, 28 December 1943, JRP, SL.

131   "you could have some peace": GRK to JR, 19 January 1944, JRP, SL.

"I talked to Wellington yesterday": ibid., 31 January 1944.

"Wellington feels I can't win": JR to Flora Belle Surles, 21 May 1944, Flora Belle Surles Papers.

"I'm not willing to risk all I have": JR to Frederick Libby, 2 June 1944, quoted in Schaffer, "Progressive," 255.

protesters started "coming to [her] door": MRB to JR, 29 January 1968, JRP, SL.

"the way Congress acted": ibid.

"ten [write-in] votes": DMB to JR, 1 December 1966, JRP, SL.

"good quarter of a century younger": Hinckle and Hinckle, "History of the Rise," 24.

"her problems of boredom": DMB to ERM, 30 May 1966, ERMP.

"cause a lot of comment": Louise Rankin Galt to JR, 15 December 1967, JRP, SL.

132   "stump[ed] the country": *Washington Evening Star and Daily News*, August 1972, MHS.

6. FIRST TERM: A BRILLIANT FUTURE BEHIND HER

133   getting her to endorse their products: unidentified newspaper article, nd, JRP, MHS.

positioned himself at the front door: ibid.

"best known woman": JR, interview with Chall, 72.

"It's almost impossible for people": ibid.

"a symbol and a representative": JR and John Kirkley, "Jeannette Rankin: Why I Voted Against War," unpublished paper, nd, JRP, MHS.

"[I]n my capacity as a disenfranchised woman": Mary W. Williams to JR, 30 March 1917, JRP, MHS.

134 Feeling women's eyes and hopes on her: JR to Fred Schottelkorb, 7 April 1917, JRP, MHS.

"put in as [her] first bill": quoted in *New York Times*, 7 April 1917, JRP, MHS.

"[S]he has a brilliant future behind her": *Helena Independent*, 17 November 1918, MHS.

"A great responsibility rests upon me": quoted in *Montana Kaimen*, 15 December 1916, SL.

Next she accepted an invitation: J. Harding Underwood to JR, 1916, JRP, SL.

"Side by side the men and women": *Boston Traveler*, December 1916, MHS.

"all alleged interviews": *Boston Record-Herald*, nd, MHS.

"a lot of money for a young girl": quoted in Smith, "Fighting Pacifist," 114.

"very elegant" design: ibid., 118; JR interview with Josephson, 195.

"striking appearance in the Pullman car": Guy P. DeLong to JR, 1 March 1972, JRP, SL.

"eulogy of the West": "Miss Rankin Addresses 3000," *The Woman's Journal*, 10 March 1917, quoted in Cheek, "Rhetoric and Revolt," 110.

Introduced by NAWSA president: *New York Herald*, 3 March 1917, JRP, MHS.

135 She focused on the West: *The Woman's Journal*, 10 March 1917, as quoted in Cheek, "Rhetoric and Revolt," 110–111; Smith, "Fighting Pacifist," 120–121.

"[W]omen ought to have a right to say": Josephson, *First Lady*, 65.

topics of their recent correspondence: JR to Harriet Laidlaw, 2 January 1917, JRP, SL.

"old suf mossbacks": Rosalie Jones to JR, 12 November 1916, JRP, SL.

"old time 1880 ladies": Cornelia Swinnerton to JR, 23 April 1917, JRP, MHS.

Newly elected congressman Fiorello LaGuardia: JR, interview with Josephson, 250.

Theodore Roosevelt invited them: Smith, "Fighting Pacifist," 119; Board, "The Lady from Montana," 103.

hoping that Roosevelt: Winestine interview, 19; Winestine, "The First Woman in Congress."

"dressed well and sensibly": John Kirkley, "A Chapter in a Life," unpublished paper, MHS.

"very womanly": *Washington Post*, 26 February 1917, MHS.

"her ankles and trim little feet": *New York Herald*, 3 March 1917, MHS.

"accompanied by her brother": *Washington Times*, 1 April 1917, MHS.

136 "I am a little afraid to say anything": quoted in ibid.

"a master politician": *Washington Post*, 26 February 1917, MHS.

"vast rambling apartment": Richey, *Eminent Women*, 193.

"eleven beds": JR to Mary Ware Dennett, 13 June 1917, Mary Ware Dennett Papers, SL.

As female staffers, Fligelman and Leech: *The Montana Weekly Record*, 1917, MHS.

Fligelman, a journalist: Florence Leech to JR, 1917, JRP, SL.

"knew all the strings to pull": Winestine interview, 9.

"every other congressman": ibid.

"considerably less" than the standard wage: Belle Fligelman Winestine to Hannah Josephson, 16 April 1974, Hannah Josephson Papers.

assigned 332 Cannon: Winestine interview, 9.

"Ground grippers": Belle Fligelman Winestine to Hannah Josephson, 16 April 1974, Hannah Josephson Papers.

"an affectionate woman": Winestine interview, 24.

137 "There was really nothing more": ibid., 18.

Much of the staff's work: ibid., 9.

"sort of the office manager"; "never wrote a speech": ibid., 23.

"Jeannette all her life was a verbalizer": Josephson, *First Lady*, 84.

Fligelman ghostwrote: Winestine, interview with Huppe, 4, Norman and Belle Fligelman Winestine Papers, MHS.

"This scribbled article": Gretta Shipman Erickson to Belle Fligelman Winestine, 2 January 1917, JRP, SL.

"you must obtain consent to publish": WR to JR, 20 June 1917, JRP, MHS.

138 "child labor on our city streets": *Chicago Herald*, 1 April 1917, JRP, SL.

In her handwritten notes: nd, JRP, MHS.

"disadvantaged in terms of seniority": McGlen et al., *Women, Politics, and American Society*, 104.

"critical mass" of allies: Witt, Paget, and Matthews, *Running as a Woman*, 271.

"invited two experienced members to lunch": Josephson, *First Lady*, 81.

"prominent people to come in": Winestine interview, 18.

"to deflect the sexual innuendo": Witt, Paget, and Matthews, *Running as a Woman*, 56.

"I never worked any female stuff": JR, interview with Chall, 20.

"first thing you do in Congress?": ibid., 36.

"the rules of Congress are made": ibid., 39.

"outsider"; "marginalization": Witt, Paget, and Matthews, *Running as a Woman*, 278.

"I was working with myself": JR, interview with Chall, 16.

"So on the outside": Winestine interview, 21.

139 "'Did you read the papers this morning?'": ibid.

"close division between the major parties": Howard Zinn, *LaGuardia in Congress* (Ithaca: Cornell University Press, 1959), 11.

"one of the distinctly potential influences": John Temple Graves, quoted in *Daily Missoulian*, 30 May 1917, MHS.

"That [is] the only thing to do": JR, interview with Josephson, 252.

"seems to me it would be a good idea": JR to Harriet Laidlaw, 2 January 1917, Harriet Laidlaw Papers, SL.

House did establish a special committee: Schaffer, "Progressive," 101.

"I have always regretted": quoted in Board, "The Lady from Montana," 139.

140   "self-proclaimed socialist-feminist": Harriet Hyman Alonso, *Peace as a Woman's Issue: A History of the U.S. Movement for World Peace and Women's Rights* (Syracuse: Syracuse University Press, 1993), 65–66.

"bending every effort toward relief of Montana farmers": JR to editor, *Promoter*, 24 January 1918, MHS.

"prompted her to run for Congress": Joan Hoff Wilson, "'Peace Is a Woman's Job . . .'—Jeannette Rankin and American Foreign Policy: The Origins of Her Pacifism," *Montana: The Magazine of Western History* (winter 1980), 36.

"the point of view of women": *New York Times*, 19 November 1916, MHS.

In her first East Coast interview: *Washington Post*, 26 February 1917, MHS.

"a step forward in women's liberation": Josephson, *First Lady*, 68.

"liked Alice Paul": Smith, "Fighting Pacifist," 68.

active member of the Congressional Union: *Montana Standard*, 8 February 1986, Butte–Silver Bow County Archives.

141   "very much amused": JR to Harriet Laidlaw, 2 January 1917, Harriet Laidlaw Papers, SL.

"her difficult position in visual and dramatic form": Smith, "Fighting Pacifist," 121.

Paul was a pacifist: ibid., 122.

when Rankin entered the floor of the House: ibid., 123.

carrying a bouquet of yellow and purple flowers: ibid.

"Miss Rankin is losing out every day": Helen H. Gardener to Harriet Laidlaw, 27 June 1917, Harriet Laidlaw Papers, SL.

142   "I used to go down to watch them": Belle Fligelman Winestine to Hannah Josephson, 16 April 1974, Hannah Josephson Papers, SL.

"seen a police officer laugh": Beulah Amidon, "What the Washington Mob Did to Women," unidentified newspaper, nd, MHS.

"Common decency demands": Mabel Search to JR, 20 November 1917, JRP, MHS.

"radicalized" by the picketing: Schwarz, *Radical Feminists of Heterodoxy*, 44.

"friendly to the action of the militants": Helen Gardener to Harriet Laidlaw, 27 June 1917, Harriet Laidlaw Papers, SL.

some who were her "personal friends": Smith, "Fighting Pacifist," 140.

"above everything else a true American": Sara Crawford to JR, 12 July 1917, JRP, MHS.

"spectacle of themselves at the gates of the White House": Frances Smith to JR, 9 August 1917, JRP, MHS.

143 "quite excited in the office this morning": JR to Eleanor Coit, 19 July 1917, JRP, MHS.

"difficulties in your office": JR to Sam C. Ford, 1 May 1917, JRP, MHS.

"Things are much harder": JR to Martha Edgerton Plassman, 19 May 1917, JRP, MHS.

"heartaches and difficulties": Eleanor Coit to JR, 1st letter, 11 July 1917, JRP, MHS.

"I really am boiling over": Eleanor Coit to JR, 11 July 1917, JRP, MHS.

"those we have a grudge against": JR to Eleanor Coit, 19 July 1917, JRP, MHS.

144 big moment in the congressional suffrage fight: Cheek, "Rhetoric and Revolt," 113.

"upon the back of the preceding row of chairs": United Press, Washington, D.C., 28 April 1917, JRP, MHS.

"activities are so closely related to the home": JR's remarks, "Extending the Right of Suffrage to Women," Hearings before the Committee on Woman Suffrage, HR 4186, 65th Congress, 3, 4, 5, 7 January 1918, JRP, MHS.

"stir on the floor as she rose": United Press, Washington, D.C., 28 May 1917, JRP, MHS.

"a significant parliamentary reception": John Temple Graves, quoted in *Daily Missoulian*, 30 May 1917, MHS.

145 "had rehearsed it": Smith, "Fighting Pacifist," 142.

she ordered from New York a $75 brown silk dress: ibid.

"New York election has had a great influence": JR to Eleanor Coit, 7 January 1918, JRP, MHS.

"Congratulations your success with amendment": WR to JR, nd, JRP, MHS.

"heredity and environment shall be joined": Kahn, "Themes for a History."

"question of political evolution": JR, "Woman Suffrage," *Congressional Record*, 65th Congress, 10 January 1918, JRP, MHS.

146 "our national religion": ibid.

"seemed unwilling to budge": Schaffer, "Progressive," 90.

"Are you gentlemen representing the South": JR, "Woman Suffrage," JRP, MHS.

"put through this woman's suffrage": JR, interview with Board.

147 "looking just like death": ibid.

"violently opposed to woman suffrage": JR, interview with Josephson, 253–255.

"women as weepy wimps": Witt, Paget, and Matthews, *Running as a Woman*, 205.

"two most important personal duties": JR, "Extending the Right of Suffrage," JRP, MHS.

"weeping" on the House floor: quoted in Winestine, "The First Woman in Congress."

weeping when she arrived home: Board, "The Lady from Montana," 133.

"hearing them come in the door": Winestine interview, 16.

148 "I want to stand by my country": Metro-Goldwyn-Mayer to JR, 17 March 1938, JRP, SL.

"on the verge of a nervous breakdown": *Washington Times*, 8 March 1917, MHS.

"one of the most terrible mental struggles": quoted in *New York Times*, 10 April 1917, MHS.

"really didn't know": Winestine, "The First Woman in Congress."

"destroy" her politically: Board, "The Lady from Montana," 12.

"After the vote there'll be nothing": JR, interview with Josephson, 213.

"being the first woman in Congress": quoted in *Washington Daily News*, 6 April 1937, MHS.

"pleaded with her not to betray the cause of suffrage": Belle Fligelman Winestine, "Mother Was Shocked," *Montana: The Magazine of Western History* 24 (July 1974), 75.

"hardest part of the vote": JR, interview with Board.

149   "We cannot be a free nation if we submit": Eleanor Coit to JR, 3 February 1917, JRP, MHS.

"horror of war": *New York Times*, 10 April 1917, MHS.

"pressure might have pushed me in": quoted in Board, "The Lady from Montana," 111.

"would have been so much better": Anna Garlin Spencer to JR, 12 May 1917, JRP, MHS.

"don't sell us out": Nina Swinnerton to JR, 5 April 1917, JRP, MHS.

"called her out from the floor": Smith, "Fighting Pacifist," 124.

"What I really want to convey to you": Mrs. E. A. Steere to JR, 25 May 1917, JRP, MHS.

"other opportunities perhaps equally golden": *Christian Science Monitor*, 11 April 1917, JRP, MHS.

Ill with ptomaine poisoning: *Washington Herald*, 8 December 1917, JRP, MHS.

150   "a logical result of war": Charlotte Anita Whitney to JR, 16 April 1917; JR to Charlotte Anita Whitney, 9 May 1917, JRP, MHS.

Liberty Loan campaign: *Daily Missoulian*, 20 April 1918, JRP, MHS.

Red Cross fund drives: *Great Falls Daily Tribune*, 20 May 1918, JRP, MHS.

"fighting for our own freedom": quoted in news clipping, nd, JRP, SL.

"only way I could go": quoted in Wilson, "The Origins of Her Pacifism," 37.

"only one that did her any harm": quoted in Board, "The Lady from Montana," 123.

"The more study given the draft bill": JR to WR, 22 April 1917, JRP, MHS.

"Vote your conviction": WR to JR, 22 April 1917, JRP, MHS.

She voted for a committee conscription bill: JR to Charles Elliott, 9 May 1917, JRP, MHS.

"territorial units": JR to Charles Edward Elliott, 9 May 1917, JRP, MHS.

"Manifesting an active interest in legislation": unidentified Washington, D.C., newspaper, 26 April 1917, MHS.

151   "Very happy you voted for conscription": WR to JR, 28 April 1917, JRP, MHS.

against the Espionage Act, Josephson, *First Lady*, 83.

"the freest circulation possible": JR to Blanche Watson, 20 July 1917, JRP, MHS.

nation of "dullards": *Chicago Sunday Herald*, 11 November 1917, quoted in Schaffer, "Progressive," 74.

against the Postal Revenue Bill: JR to LeRoy Scott, 8 December 1917, JRP, MHS.

"all personal income over $100,000": Veltere and Eva Logan to JR, 10 May 1917; JR to Veltere and Eva Logan, 17 May 1917, JRP, MHS.

"individuals with large incomes": Ed Boyd to JR, 5 July 1917; JR to Ed Boyd, 12 July 1917, JRP, MHS.

"I am heartily in sympathy": JR to James Kirkpatrick, 21 August 1917, JRP, MHS.

Her *Ladies Home Journal* article: JR, "What We Women Should Do," *Ladies Home Journal*, August 1917, MHS.

"women of Montana are tired and sick": Eleanor Coit to JR, 6 July 1917, JRP, MHS.

"I cannot express to you the feeling of relief": Mrs. E. A. Wallace to JR, 26 July 1917, JRP, MHS.

152 Massachusetts woman informed her: Amy G. Stephens to JR, 4 January 1918, JRP, MHS.

Pennsylvania woman conveyed a rumor: Laura E. Messerly to JR, 7 December 1917, JRP, MHS.

"a God-made social worker": Hattie Stein to JR, 23 October 1917, JRP, MHS.

"good moral surroundings": ibid., 7 July 1917.

"proper ventilation of the trenches": Julia Fownes Smith to JR, 10 July 1917, JRP, MHS.

"protection of soldiers in the camps": JR to Hattie Stein, 3 August 1917, JRP, MHS.

"good plan for the Montana women": JR to Eleanor Coit, 17 July 1917, JRP, MHS.

"hours for soldiers in the trenches": JR to Julia Fownes Smith, 28 July 1917, JRP, MHS.

invite female bureau employees: Belle Fligelman Winestine to Hannah Josephson, 16 April 1974, Hannah Josephson Papers, SL.

"dozens and dozens of girls": Winestine, "The First Woman in Congress."

hire Elizabeth Watson of New York: Winestine, "Mother Was Shocked," 77; Schwarz, *Radical Feminists of Heterodoxy*, 127.

153 "testified to the New York Factory Investigating Commission": Schwarz, *Radical Feminists of Heterodoxy*, 127.

Florence Kelley, Rankin's instructor: Smith, "Fighting Pacifist," 41.

contributed to Louis Brandeis's brief: Goldmark, *Impatient Crusader*, vii.

"educating college and university students": ibid., 60.

"hours that the girls were obliged to work": JR to Maude Jay Wilson, 27 November 1917, JRP, MHS.

The Masses reported: *The Masses*, September 1917, JRP, MHS.

"improper suggestions": Winestine, "The First Woman in Congress."

"private calling cards": JR to J. Ellis Sedman, 22 October 1917, JRP, MHS.

154 Washington in a stir "for a week": United Press, Washington, D.C., 6 July 1917, JRP, MHS.

"unspeakable" conditions: JR to WR, July 1917, JRP, MHS.

confronted Treasury Secretary William G. McAdoo: Winestine, "The First Woman in Congress."

bureau employees on an eight-hour schedule: ibid.

"frank and impartial investigation": William G. McAdoo to JR, 6 July 1917, JRP, MHS.

"an officer in whose integrity and good faith": JR to director, Bureau of Engraving and Printing, 8 December 1917, JRP, MHS.

"mass meeting of Bureau girls": Belle Fligelman Winestine to JR, 20 September 1917, JRP, MHS.

"increased pay to the women employees": Women's Union of the Bureau of Engraving and Printing, *Organization Work Week*, 17–22 June 1918, JRP, MHS.

"Why don't you go to Miss Rankin": Hattie Stein to Belle Fligelman Winestine, 4 January 1918, JRP, MHS.

"you represent the people of Montana": Stewart E. Blassingham to JR, 13 July 1917, JRP, MHS.

"widow charwoman": anonymous to JR, nd; Alice Ward to JR, February 1918, JRP, MHS.

"girls . . . in the Woolworths store": Anna L. Rogers to JR, 3 August 1917, JRP, MHS.

"one or more little children to keep": Mrs. J. V. White to JR, 8 August 1917, JRP, MHS.

"Bureau work has just about finished me": JR to Eleanor Coit, 19 July 1917, JRP, MHS.

"interest your own Representative": JR to G. H. Wetzel, 29 September 1917, JRP, MHS.

155 "asking that the eight-hour-day order be rescinded": *Nashville Banner*, 13 July 1917, MHS.

"I think I know just how you feel": JR to Dorothy Compton, 12 July 1917, JRP, MHS.

"find out if the proposed beneficiaries desire help": *Nashville Banner*, 13 July 1917, MHS.

"the greatest mining center in the United States": Malone and Roeder, *Montana*, 157–158.

"draft registration order that threatened young Irish migrants": Emmons, *Butte Irish*, 366.

"Pearse-Connolly Irish Independence Club": ibid., 366, 359.

"practically begged . . . American patriots": ibid., 362.

"IWW and syndicalist inspired radicals": ibid., 265.

"in and out of Butte for fifteen or twenty years": ibid., 365; *Helena Independent*, 18 August 1917, JRP, MHS.

"admitted to being a member"; "strikes and sabotage": Emmons, *Butte Irish*, 271, 270.

"most overwhelming disaster": ibid., 373.

"gas and smoke inhalation": Calvert, *Gibraltar,* 104.

156   "rustling card": John Doran to JR, 3 July 1917, JRP, MHS.

"the Speculator fire"; "Irish of settled habits"; "established miners"; "new men"; "blacklisting"; transient hoodlums": Emmons, *Butte Irish,* 365, 267, 380, 267, 383, 270.

"at the behest of the strike committee": Murphy, *Mining Cultures,* 24.

Kennedy, the wife of a mine foreman: Mrs. H. N. Kennedy to JR, 18 June 1917, JRP, MHS.

"automobile loads of gunmen": William F. Dunne Collection, Butte–Silver Bow County Archives.

"get all facts . . . in regard to labor situation": JR to Helena Stellway, 20 June 1917, JRP, MHS.

"Butte trouble I.W. work": WR to JR, 20 June 1917, JRP, MHS.

MMWU Press Committee sent her a copy: William F. Dunne Collection.

"true statement . . . of the causes": Metal Mine Workers' Union Press Committee to JR, 20 June 1917, JRP, MHS.

edited by William Dunne: Calvert, *Gibraltar,* 111.

"the largest mining camp on earth": *Strike Bulletin,* 12 June 1917, JRP, MHS.

"use your influence with Mr. Wilson": Metal Mine Workers' Union Press Committee to JR, 20 June 1917, JRP, MHS.

"a mass meeting of fully 6,000 men": Elizabeth Kennedy to JR, 23 June 1917, JRP, MHS.

visited with Samuel Gompers: JR to John Doran, 26 June 1917, JRP, MHS.

157   "If there is anything else I can do for you": ibid.

"[r]ustling card" . . . "the main issue": John Doran to JR, 2 June 1917, JRP, MHS.

"the principal object of the card": John Doran to JR, 3 July 1917, JRP, MHS.

"Uncle Sam's postal service": Elizabeth Kennedy to JR, 30 June 1917, JRP, MHS.

"able assistant": ibid., 15 August 1917.

"[Y]our friends here believe": Mary O'Neill to JR, 14 July 1917, JRP, MHS.

"scant consideration to the striking miners": Metal Mine Workers' Union Press Committee to JR, 16 July 1917, JRP, MHS.

"the logical next step": JR to Dan Shovlin, 17 July 1917, JRP, MHS.

"companies informed him": *Joint Strike Bulletin,* No. 17, 18 July 1917, JRP, MHS.

"Crisis in labor situation is here": Mary O'Neill to JR, 26 July 1917, JRP, MHS.

158   "I hope that this will seem so important to you": JR to President Woodrow Wilson, 27 July 1917, JRP, MHS.

"Have the miners make their request": JR to Mary O'Neill, 27 July 1917, JRP, MHS.

"Conditions need immediate action": ibid., 28 July 1917.

"Just got word operators intend to run": ibid., 30 July 1917.

"Read telegram first word": JR to Helena Stellway, 1 August 1917, JRP, MHS.

"Mary O'Neill advised me regarding developments": JR to WR, 1 August 1917, JRP, MHS.

Little, a national IWW leader: Calvert, *Gibraltar,* 108.

cared more about labor solidarity: *Butte Miner,* nd, JRP, MHS.

vigilantes dragged Little: Calvert, *Gibraltar,* 109.

Suspended around Little's neck: ibid.

159   "[T]he working man in every trade": *Butte Miner,* nd, JRP, MHS.

behind the hanging: WR, interview with John Board, quoted in Hines, "Wellington Duncan Rankin," 38.

lynching was "a patriotic act": WR to Mrs. Oscar Sedman, 2 August 1917, quoted in Schaffer, "Progressive," 134.

"Little was lynched": Frank Rogers to JR, nd, JRP, MHS.

"[S]hocked at [the] turn of events": JR to Joe Kennedy, 1 August 1917, JRP, MHS.

Soldiers were stationed in Butte: Calvert, *Gibraltar,* 113.

"more than 1,000 Pearse-Connollys": Emmons, *Butte Irish,* 376–377.

"highest duty [was] to come": Mary O'Neill to JR, 6 August 1917, JRP, MHS.

"visionary" O'Neill: WR to JR, 10 August 1917, JRP, MHS.

"Use your own judgment": WR to JR, 10 August 1917, JRP, MHS.

"to provide further for the national security and defense": JR, "Government Control of Metalliferous Mines," *Congressional Record,* 65th Congress, 7 August 1917, JRP, MHS.

"Butte situation in non partisan manner": WR to JR, 7 August 1917, JRP, MHS.

160   "For some years the Anaconda Copper Mining Company has been using": JR, "Government Control of Metalliferous Mines."

"'I think I know perfectly well'": *Washington Times,* 8 August 1917, MHS.

"particularly the I.W.W. element in Montana": *Great Falls Daily Tribune,* 9 August 1917, MHS.

"in seeking to play upon a prejudice": *Lewistown Democrat-News,* 11 August 1917, MHS.

Helena Independent asked her to reconcile: *Helena Independent,* 15 August 1917, MHS.

"Prompt action is needed": Mary O'Neill to JR, 10 August 1917, JRP, MHS.

161   "If not too tired you might wire": WR to JR, 10 August 1917, JRP, MHS.

wanted Wellington to "join her": Hines, "Wellington Duncan Rankin," 37.

"Will be glad to see you": WR to JR, 11 August 1917, JRP, MHS.

"Do not under any circumstances": JR to Mary O'Neill, 14 August 1917, JRP, MHS.

"absurd on the face of it": quoted in *Anaconda Standard,* 15 August 1917, MHS.

Campbell "headed the reception committee": *Butte Daily Post,* 18 August 1917, quoted in *Helena Independent,* MHS.

"the I.W.W. turned out in full force": *Boulder Monitor,* 18 August 1917, MHS.

"explained that the parade had been cancelled": Schaffer, "Progressive," 136.

"hired and paid for an automobile": ibid.

"had an awful time finding a seat": *Boulder Monitor,* 18 August 1917, MHS.

"Good Americans must obey the law": Schaffer, "Progressive," 136.

"lengthy conference"; "delegated by President Wilson"; "to meet the men"; "no definite opinion": *Butte Daily Post,* 16 August 1917, Butte–Silver Bow County Archives.

162 "unwarranted attack made by you": C. F. Kelley to JR, 12 August 1917, JRP, MHS.

addressed a "standing up" crowd: Belle Fligelman Winestine to Hannah Josephson, 16 April 1974, Hannah Josephson Papers.

under a threatening storm: *Butte Daily Post,* 19 August 1917; *Butte Miner,* 19 August 1917, JRP, MHS.

"over the home plate": *Butte Daily Post,* 18 August 1917, MHS.

"most radical union leaders in Butte": Schaffer, "Progressive," 138.

"dressed in something simple and white": Cheek, "Rhetoric and Revolt," 85.

"prominently connected with the I.W.W.": *Butte Daily Post,* 18 August 1917, MHS.

"not take part in the speaking": ibid.

"from which she departed": *Butte Miner,* 19 August 1917, MHS.

copper was needed in the "great war": quoted in ibid.

"development of Montana": quoted in ibid.

163 "when one of the Metal Mine Workers' leaders": Schaffer, "Progressive," 139.

"Meeting a tremendous success": JR to Olive Rankin, 18 August 1917, JRP, MHS.

"best effort to have the rustling card abolished": Washington, D.C., bureau story, quoted in *Butte Miner,* 19 August 1917, JRP, MHS.

"[T]hough [the rustling card] might be indefensible": quoted in *Butte Daily Post,* 20 August 1917, Butte–Silver Bow County Archives.

"The companies have made use": *Joint Strike Bulletin,* 1 September 1917, MHS.

"You know this I.W.W. howl": Mary O'Neill to JR, 6 September 1917, JRP, MHS.

rustling card was still "the chief factor": ibid., 8 September 1917.

164 "somewhat embarrassed": JR to W. G. Sullivan, 27 December 1917, JRP, MHS.

"MMWU strike was settled": ibid.

"Labor Commission did not stop in Butte": JR to Burton K. Wheeler, 19 January 1918, JRP, MHS.

"when the men returned to work": Schaffer, "Progressive," 139.

"I have never had dealings": JR to Oswald Garrison Villard, 10 December 1917, JRP, MHS.

"championing the cause": *Yellowstone Monitor,* 16 August 1917, MHS.

"the poison": ERM to WR, 28 June 1934, WRP.

"signal victory for the cause of women": Eleanor Coit to JR, 10 November 1916, JRP, MHS.

"We have not heard from Robert": ibid., 18 April 1917.

165 "Here I am again about Robert": ibid., 20 June 1917.

"taking the matter . . . up at once": JR to Eleanor Coit, 26 June 1917, JRP, MHS.

"interview with Secretary of War Baker": ibid., 28 June 1917.

"cablegram from Robert": Eleanor Coit to JR, 10 July 1917, JRP, MHS.

"I am ready to do anything": ibid., 29 May 1917.

"jobs with fat salaries": JR to Eleanor Coit, 17 June 1917, JRP, MHS.

"I am heartily in sympathy": JR to M. Ferriter, 25 July 1917, JRP, SL.

"rights of Irish independence": JR, "Proposing Recognition by the Congress of the United States of the Rights of Irish Independence," House Joint Resolution 2570, 65th Congress, JRP, SL.

"resolution must be regarded": *Helena Independent*, 17 January 1918, MHS.

166 "lacking both in loyalty and in common sense": *Daily Telegram*, quoted in *Butte Miner*, 20 January 1918, JRP, MHS.

"I am writing to tell you that my Irish resolution": JR to Harriet Laidlaw, 31 January 1918, JRP, MHS.

notified a Catholic bishop: JR's secretary to Bishop Nathan C. Lenihan, 14 December 1918, JRP, SL.

"stop the appointing of so many Negroes": anonymous to JR, nd, JRP, MHS.

167 "many colored women in the employ": anonymous to JR, nd, JRP, MHS.

cabinet officers were "Romanist": S. A. Wilkins to JR, 18 May 1917, JRP, MHS.

unions decried "coolie labor": Edith Ferguson to JR, 21 June 1917, JRP, MHS.

"rapings of priestly satyrs": Fredrik Stuart to JR, 16 August 1917, JRP, MHS.

"Roman Catholic situation": Emeline Chesley to JR, 2 September 1917, JRP, MHS.

"Jesuit power": M. M. Yates to JR, 31 October 1917, JRP, MHS.

"Salt Lake temple": George M. Veile to JR, 29 May 1918, JRP, MHS.

"some Gentile scribe": Mary Ines Todd to JR, July 1918, JRP, MHS.

"colored woman in our party": JR, interview with Chall, 81.

Some of the correspondence: Mary Murphy, "Women in the West Telling Their Stories," 5 March 1994, audio recording, UML.

"interested in the bulletins": JR, Circular, 6 June 1917, JRP, MHS.

168 "assist not hinder": WR to JR, nd, JRP, MHS.

in the circular: JR, Circular, 6 June 1917, JRP, MHS.

Many women responded: Murphy, "Women in the West."

"had written personally to them": ibid.

"she rode fourteen miles": ibid.

"special representative" of women: JR, Circular, 6 June 1917.

Jessie Nakken wrote: Jessie Nakken to JR, 19 July 1917, JRP, MHS.

170 "I have read your long letter": JR to Jessie Nakken, 24 July 1917, JRP, MHS.

"Saving is easy": Mrs. C. D. Carlson to JR, 26 February 1918, JRP, MHS.

171 "[H]ow much I appreciate": JR to Mrs. C. D. Carlson, 12 March 1918, JRP, MHS.

"wouldn't come back to Montana'": ibid.

"became part of her persona": Wilson, "The Origins of Her Pacifism," 37.

"became a raison d'être": ibid., 38.

"congratulations": JR to Representative Henry White, 30 November 1918, JRP, MHS.

7. SECOND TERM: WOMEN AND WAR

173 Childhood tales of violence: JR, "Why I Voted Against War."

174 "[N]o one could bring any pressure on me": JR, interview with Chall, 10.

"stupidity and cruelty of force": JR, "Why I Voted Against War."

"always made fun of the army": JR, interview with Josephson, 192.

"too stupid for words": ibid., 195.

"at the drop of a hat'": WR, interview with John Board, quoted in Steele, *Wellington Rankin*, 20.

"[W]omen produce the boys": quoted in Smith, "Fighting Pacifist," 110.

"a wasteful and ineffective method": Lasch, *Social Thought*, 218.

"in the progress of society": Jane Addams, "Newer Ideals of Peace," quoted in Lasch, *Social Thought*, 221.

"could hardly face": Smith, "Fighting Pacifist," 170.

"passionately involved" with several women: Faderman, *Odd Girls*, 26.

"Miss Addams was wonderful to me": JR, interview with Josephson, 199.

"she most admired": Smith, "Fighting Pacifist," 175.

175 "Kelley sat beside Addams": Sklar, *Florence Kelley*, 186.

"was a truly great woman": quoted in ibid., 304.

"most important book": Cheek, "Rhetoric and Revolt," 166.

"strongly criticized the 'man-made world'": Freedman, *No Turning Back*, 69.

"the only thing in this man-made world": JR to Rosalie Gardiner Jones, 17 August 1943, JRP, SL.

"a holy wedlock": Edward T. Devine, quoted in Kahn, "Themes for a History."

"[W]e had the power to do things": JR, Ninetieth Birthday Celebration Remarks, 11 June 1970, JRP, SL.

"men like force": JR, Transcript of *The Dick Cavett Show*, 17 April 1972, JRP, SL.

"[Y]ou seem really to epitomize": Robert O. Grady to JR, 25 September 1935, JRP, SL.

mailed it to her backers: JR to Porter Sargent, 11 June 1943, JRP, SL.

176 "linked pacifism to feminism": Freedman, *No Turning Back*, 329.

"a passing phase of the world": Benjamin Kidd, *The Science of Power* (New York: G.

P. Putnam Sons, 1918), 200.

"future centre of Power": ibid., 203.

"short-range animal emotions": ibid., 209.

ruled the "existing world": ibid., 203.

"ruling principle of this new era of Power": ibid., 209.

"emotion of the ideal": ibid., 234.

"subordinating their minds, their lives": ibid., 233–234.

"social or other regarding self": ibid., 235.

"Absolute or Universal Mind": ibid., 235–236.

"emotions of the fight": ibid., 211.

"military utilitarianism": ibid., 237.

"irritable and domineering": Smith, "Fighting Pacifist," 8.

"push and push and push": quoted in ibid., 276.

177 "obstacles of male political authority": Freedman, "Separatism Revisited," 184.

all-purpose notion of democracy: Schaffer, "Progressive," 167.

outlawry of war plan: ibid., 165.

"Instead of laws about war": quoted in Smith, "Fighting Pacifist," 188.

"Disarmament will not be won": quoted in Joan Hoff Wilson, "Jeannette Rankin," Speech to the Montana History Conference, Helena, 4 April 1977, audio recording, UML.

"peace problem is a woman's problem": quoted in ibid.

"[Peace] cannot be gotten": quoted in ibid.

"I wrote you some time ago": Dorothy Detzer to JR, 27 March 1925, JRP, SL.

"I know how busy you are": ibid., 11 March 1925.

"I do not quite understand": ibid., 2 April 1925.

"St. Louis is greatly disturbed": ibid.

plan to concentrate Women's International League resources: Schaffer, "Progressive," 169.

178 "they just wanted me to go and speak": JR, interview with Chall, 102.

"accus[ed] her of using the name and letterhead": Giles, *Flight of the Dove,* 167.

"might have a 'Chair of Peace'": *Brenau Bulletin,* February 1935, JRP, SL.

"prevent any such communistic ideas": ibid.

In a subsequent newspaper article: *Atlanta Constitution,* 18 December 1934, JRP, MHS.

American Civil Liberties Union: Schaffer, "Progressive," 188.

settled the matter short of trial: JR to W. G. Cornett, November 1936, JRP, SL.

"the worst experience of her life": Smith, "Fighting Pacifist," 204.

She received $300 a month: Josephson, *First Lady,* 121.

Her arguments sounded the themes: JR, "Everyone Wants Peace," 2 September 1929 radio address, JRP, MHS.

179 Women's Peace Union required her to limit her activities: Smith, "Fighting Pacifist," 190.

she began to advocate: JR, "Everyone Wants Peace."

"from the top down . . . from the bottom up": Josephson, *First Lady,* 123.

"muzzled": ibid., 124.

"preaching to the already converted": Smith, "Fighting Pacifist," 192.

"get down to real things": quoted in Cheek, "Rhetoric and Revolt," 182.

Peace Action Service: Schaffer, "Progressive," 182.

"'we can't be attacked'": Frederick Libby, quoted in Schaffer, "Progressive," 226.

"If the will for peace can grow": Eleanor Roosevelt to JR, 13 November 1933, JRP, SL.

"mandate from God": Smith, "Fighting Pacifist," 191.

"cold, stupid world": JR to Frederick J. Libby, 1933, quoted in Schaffer, "Progressive," 228.

"practical, workable and inspiring": Gaylord W. Douglass to Frederick J. Libby, 26 June 1936, JRP, SL.

"heart-to-heart talks": Clara Fuhr to JR, 14 November 1937, JRP, SL.

180 "a beautiful little steak": JR, interview with Chall, 89.

"didn't do one thing for Christmas": ibid.

"her greatest single achievement": Josephson, *First Lady,* 140.

"the greatest political victory": Joan Hoff Wilson, "Her Lifework as a Pacifist," 44.

"exactly what we wanted": JR, interview with Chall, 90.

"flatter than a pancake": JR to Mrs. J. J. Owens, 25 March 1938, quoted in Schaffer, "Progressive," 228.

"people were getting war minded": Cheek, "Rhetoric and Revolt," 182.

"money is slow": JR to Libby, 12 September 1938, quoted in Schaffer, "Progressive," 228.

"increasingly critical": Wilson, "Her Lifework as a Pacifist," 40.

aware of Hitler's evil: Cheek, "Rhetoric and Revolt," 182–183.

"never would have hired" her: JR, interview with Chall, 85.

"county-by-county methods of organization": ibid., 14.

too "ladylike": JR, interview with Chall, 85.

if she had been "nastier": *New York Times,* February 1972, SOHP, BL.

181 hoped her candidacy would be seen: JR, interview with Board.

In the first address she emphasized: JR, "Democracy and Women."

In the second speech: JR, "Prepare to the Limit for Defense."

she implemented a grassroots campaign: JR to Mrs. R. Fenby Bausman, 28 December 1940, JRP, SL.

"[President Roosevelt] can be bluffed": ibid.

"Congratulations on your patriotic services": JR to Helena Kelley, 16 August 1941, JRP, SL.

"might be helpful": Frances C. Elge to Willard E. Fraser, 19 July 1941, JRP, SL.

"[t]elephoning the White House": JR to W. E. Fraser, 16 August 1941, JRP, SL.

"the draft extension": Frances C. Elge to JR, 24 July 1941, JRP, SL.

America First's national office: Mrs. Bennett Champ Clark to JR, 28 October 1941, JRP, SL.

182   "I used to call you": Mrs. Hereford Dugan to JR, December 1941, JRP, SL.

"I heard you speak in Jersey City": Ida Walter to JR, 17 December 1941, JRP, SL.

America First lapel button: JR to W. Merle Savage, 22 May 1941, JRP, SL.

"your outstanding courage": Long Beach America First Committee to JR, 11 December 1941, JRP, SL.

"three most important groups": Lindbergh, "Des Moines Speech."

"calling for new leadership": standard JR response to antiwar letters, JRP, SL.

Lindbergh's position on the war: Elizabeth Kennedy to JR, 18 August 1942, JRP, SL.

"I feel that the colored people": JR to Mary Church Terrell, 16 June 1941, Mary Church Terrell Papers, LOC.

"gang of Jew thugs": anonymous to JR, 29 August 1944, JRP, SL.

183   "1917 propaganda was exactly the same": JR, "Remarks on Introducing Amendment to Lend-Lease Bill," 77th Congress, *Congressional Record*, 8 February 1941.

"mothers of this country": quoted in *The People's Voice*, 14 May 1941, MHS.

"I knew it was coming": JR, interview with Chall, 9.

"I didn't let anybody approach me": ibid.

"I got in my car and disappeared": JR, interview with Josephson, 214–216.

"She can't be for peace again": quoted in Dykeman, *Too Many People*, 84.

"Germany has a chance to conquer the world": Maury Maverick to JR, 12 November 1940, JRP, SL.

"flat at the top of the building": Grant McGregor to JR, 10 January 1941, JRP, SL.

"clamored for recognition": *Missoulian*, 9 December 1941, MHS.

"steadfastly looked the other way": ibid.

After her one-word vote of "No": Smith, "Fighting Pacifist," 226.

"hissed by some of her colleagues": *Missoulian*, 9 December 1941, MHS.

"mob in the cloak room": JR, interview with John C. Board, 1965, UML, 6.

"refuge in a telephone booth": *Tacoma News Tribune*, 9 December 1941, JRP, SL.

"barricaded herself . . . and wept": INS news account, nd, JRP, SL.

184   "I always knew you were like the Rock of Gibraltar": Katharine Anthony to JR, 8 December 1941, JRP, SL.

"Bully for you darling": Elisabeth Irwin to JR, 8 December 1941, JRP, SL.

"Congratulations for courage": Katherine Devereux Blake to JR, nd, JRP, SL.

"[Y]our act is heartening to all": Roger Baldwin to JR, 9 December 1941, JRP, SL.

"Once in Athens": Helen Strickland to JR, 8 December 1941, JRP, SL.

"fearless," "brave," "courageous": see correspondence to JR, JRP, SL.

"sentimental," "move to Japan": ibid.

"turned the clock back for women!": Mary B. Gilson to JR, 8 December 1941, JRP, SL.

"redeem Montana's honor": Dan Whetstone to JR, nd, JRP, SL.

185 "Everyone knew that I was opposed to war": JR, interview with Board.

"I would have voted for war": Winestine, "Feminist and Suffragette."

"taking our army and navy": JR's statement to Montana newspapers, 8 December 1941, JRP, SL.

"I tried repeatedly to get the floor": ibid.

"not a moral issue": quoted in *Western News,* 19 May 1916, MHS.

"Hitler was so bad": quoted in Cheek, "Rhetoric and Revolt," 182–183.

troubled by "holy wars": *World Outlook,* November 1938, quoted in Schaffer, "Progressive," 216–217.

186 "I have read Genesis": John Kirkley to JR, 20 February 1973, JRP, SL.

Augustine of Hippo had begun: Thomas Aquinas, "Of War," in *The Summa Theologica.* Accessed 23 December 2003. Available at www.Pewforum.org.

Thomas Aquinas, citing: ibid.

Martin Luther asked: Martin Luther, "Whether Soldiers, Too, Can Be Saved," *Luther's Works,* vol. 46: *The Christian in Society III.* Accessed 23 December 2003. Available at www.Pewforum.org.

John Calvin found: John Calvin, "Of Civil Government," *Institutes of the Christian Religion, Book IX.* Accessed 23 December 2003. Available at www.Pewforum.org.

Reinhold Niebuhr . . . believed: Jonathan Wilson-Hartgrove, "Faith and the Kingdoms: The Politics of Niebuhr and Yoder." Accessed 23 December 2003. Available at www.globalengagement.org.

Michael Walzer concluded: Michael Walzer, *Just and Unjust Wars* (New York: Basic Books, 1977), 253.

"infidels and anti-Christians": DMB to JR, 17 December 1968, JRP, SL.

"Resist evil": Cheek, "Rhetoric and Revolt," 180.

"bear to be a worm": JR, interview with Josephson, 217.

187 "not going to use violence": JR, "Democracy and Women."

"he wouldn't let me talk": quoted in Cheek, "Rhetoric and Revolt," 182.

"'we had lots of Jews in our organization'": JR, interview with Josephson, 276.

"the problem" of European Jews: ibid.

"inconsistency between loving men and fighting them": G. K. Chesterton, *St. Francis of Assisi* (New York: Image Books, 1957), 48.

"no way of making force and violence right": JR, interview with Josephson, 277.

"70 percent of Americans": Wilson, "Her Lifework as a Pacifist," 47–48.

"completely out of step": Josephson, 168.

"been discredited"; "little to do": Smith, "Fighting Pacifist," 229.

"her second term ended for all practical purposes": *New York Times,* May 1973, MHS.

188   "hope[d] things are not too discouraging for you": ERM to JR, 19 August 1941, JRP, SL.

"I hope you aren't having as fearsome a time": GRK to JR, 11 February 1941, JRP, SL.

"I am inviting a couple of Congressmen": JR to Olive Rankin, 10 February and 1 July 1942, JRP, SL.

"covered a chair with tan-and-rose striped material": Smith, "Fighting Pacifist," 231.

"just before going to bed": JR to Olive Rankin, 1 July 1942, JRP, SL.

"enjoy[ing] the soul refreshing weather": Frances Elge to JR, 2 August 1941, JRP, SL.

189   "mitigate the effects of World War II": Josephson, *First Lady,* 164–165.

"Of course I saw you buy the ticket": Katharine Anthony to JR, 13 October 1941, JRP, SL.

"down to Woodward & Lothrope": Rosa Nell Spriggs to JR, 7 June 1943, JRP, SL.

"you will not feel it is necessary": JR to Woodward and Lothrope, 11 October 1943, JRP, SL.

small apartment: JR to Harry M. Rawn, 25 January 1941, JRP, SL.

190   "had to get a series of nurses": Smith, "Fighting Pacifist," 237.

"I cannot get out very much": JR to Harry M. Rawn, 25 January 1941, JRP, SL.

"Don't worry about me": JR to family, May 1941, JRP, SL.

mother's illness became unmanageable: ERM to JR, 6 July 1941, JRP, SL.

"I've only been out of the house": GRK to JR, 19 September 1941, JRP, SL.

"It's like being turned out of jail": ibid., 7 November 1944.

"She fell off the pot": ibid., 13 March 1945.

"going to plays sounds just grand": GRK to JR, 4 January 1944, JRP, SL.

"it would seem like a wild orgy": GRK to JR, 9 January 1944, JRP, SL.

To fulfill his part of the bargain: WR's secretary to GRK, 6 March 1945; ERM to JR, 4 September 1941; MRB to JR, 1 December 1942; ERM to WR, 3 August 1936, WRP.

"Jeannette thinks she is willing to share": ERM to WR, 8 June 1959, WRP.

"There were no airplanes": ERM to Kinneys and Braggs, 18 December 1952, ERMP.

191   "highway measure": JR to W. P. Roscoe, 27 September 1941, JRP, SL.

"I made a reservation on the plane": JR to W. P. Roscoe, 27 September 1941, JRP, SL.

Wheeler was urging her: Frances Elge to JR, 8 August 1941, JRP, SL.

"Glad of your word": Millacent Yarrow to JR, 4 January 1942, JRP, SL.

"your bus left today": the Hills to JR, 9 April 1942, JRP, SL.

"fly out to take Mother": JR to Abbie Crawford Milton, 11 April 1942, JRP, SL.

ranch would be "dry enough": JR to Olive Rankin, 11 April 1942, JRP, SL.

"[W]e all must work": JR to Flora Belle Surles, 14 September 1942, Flora Belle Surles Papers.

driving alone through severe winter: Sigrid Scannell to JR, 20 December 1942, JRP, SL.

uncertainties of gas rationing: Nina Swinnerton to JR, Christmas 1942, JRP, SL.

"What they call 'causes of war'": JR, interview with Josephson, 278.

192 "Three years before Pearl Harbor": JR, "Some Questions About Pearl Harbor," 77th Congress, *Congressional Record,* 8 December 1942.

"a pile of material ten inches high": JR to George T. Spaulding, 10 March 1942, JRP, SL.

biographers concluded that Ralph Baerman: Smith, "Fighting Pacifist," 236.

"always more than two choices": JR to Garth Howser, 8 January 1942, JRP, SL.

"ridiculed western states": Galt interview.

"incriminating evidence": Richey, *Eminent Women,* 207.

"manipulative" and "condescending": Galt interview.

193 "the two dictators": JR to Gerald F.M. O'Grady, 16 August 1943, JRP, SL.

"I have been pretty quiet": ibid.

"women voters do not automatically rally": Witt, Paget, and Matthews, *Running as a Woman,* 169.

"women's vote had been revealed to be a paper tiger": ibid., 34.

"did not vote differently from men": ibid., 155.

"much discouraged over the women": JR to Ernestine Evans, 11 October 1943, JRP, SL.

"a continuation of war and deaths": JR to Harriet Yarrow, 30 November 1944, Harriet Yarrow Papers.

"draft could be abolished if women spoke": quoted in Associated Press, unidentified newspaper, April 1967, MHS.

"I tell these young women": quoted in *Life,* 3 March 1972.

"They don't know who they are voting for": quoted in *The Evening Star and Daily News,* 2 September 1972.

194 "do to my husband's job": JR, interview with Chall, 33.

their goals were "trivial": Galt interview.

they were not about peace: Smith, "Fighting Pacifist," 274.

"encounter with Margaret Sanger": quoted in Susan Brownmiller, *New York Times Review of Books,* 3 November 1974, JRP, SL.

shared with her suffrage sisters: Cheek, "Rhetoric and Revolt," 176–177.

"I believe in the right to abortion": quoted in *Newsweek,* 28 May 1973, JRP, SL.

"Give support to march?": Sherry Smith to JR, 8 November 1971, JRP, SL.

"They start too many wars": quoted in *Life,* 3 March 1972.

"after four or five more devastating wars": JR to Ernestine Evans, 11 October 1943, JRP, SL.

"I'm going to live as peacefully as I can": Millacent Yarrow to JR, 30 March 1943, JRP, SL.

"Why we don't shoot those men": JR, interview with Chall, 34.

195 But in her notes for her remarks: JR, handwritten notes, JRP, SL.

"idea of a unitary female identity": Freedman, "Separatism Revisited," 186.

"it's quite obvious that once they are in power": quoted in Freedman, *No Turning Back*, 331.

unique goodness of women: *Life*, 3 March 1972.

"male not female desires": Carroll Smith-Rosenberg, "Discourses of Sexuality and Subjectivity: The New Woman, 1870–1936," in Martin Duberman et al., *Hidden from History: Reclaiming the Gay and Lesbian Past* (New York: New American Library, 1989), 274.

"ideals of female difference": Freedman, "Separatism Revisited," 186.

"claimed equality with men": ibid.

"gendering of the political": Smith-Rosenberg, "Discourses of Sexuality," 274.

angry "foremother": Witt, Paget, and Matthews, *Running as a Woman*, 280.

"more or less told [a university dean]": DMB to ERM, 15 April 1969, ERMP.

"a lot of old ladies": quoted in Smith, "Fighting Pacifist," 257.

"a future-directed person": Ralph Nader, "In the Public Interest," *Sunday Star and The News*, 10 September 1972, MHS.

"treats sexuality as a social construct": Catherine A. MacKinnon, *Toward a Feminist Theory of the State* (Cambridge: Harvard University Press, 1989), 128.

196 "Those with power in political systems": ibid., 238.

"protects male power": ibid., 167.

"not a discrete sphere": ibid., 130.

"social and relational": ibid., 151.

"radical feminists" assert: Robin West, "Jurisprudence and Gender," *University of Chicago Law Review* 55 (winter 1988): 15.

"women's connection with the 'other'": ibid., 29.

"modern cultural feminists" argue: ibid., 15.

"more nurturant, caring, loving": ibid., 17–18.

8. ASSESSMENT: A PARADOXICAL REFORMER

199 "the Dictator": JR to Harriet Yarrow, 30 November 1944, Harriet Yarrow Papers, SL.

"no kind words for Ike": JR to WR, 18 July 1952, WRP.

"could not stand [Lyndon] Johnson": Smith, "Fighting Pacifist," 269.

"Your hollow comments": JR to William F. Rogers, 7 April 1969, JRP, SL.

"[redistricting] is a better way": JR to Reita Rivers, nd, JRP, SL.

"could have made a great President": JR, interview with Chall, 81.

only Norman Thomas: Wilson, "Her Lifework as a Pacifist," 51.

"grieved and depressed": JR to WR, 10 September 1935, WRP.

"lost a great man": ibid., 24 January 1940.

200 "sixty-four acres of scrub land": Smith, "Fighting Pacifist," 178.

"hired neighborhood men": DMB to Hannah Josephson, 31 August 1973, Hannah Josephson Papers.

connected to a cooking shack: ibid.

"practically lined with books": ibid.

"Nation and the *New Republic"*: ibid.

"hardtack and fat for lunch": confidential interview.

"rammed earth" structure: JR to Rosalie Gardiner Jones, 17 August 1943, JRP, SL.

"damndest house I ever saw": Halinan interview, 6.

201 "I had no idea it was so pretentious": GRK to JR, 25 March 1944, JRP, SL.

"sharecropper shanty": DMB to Hannah Josephson, 31 August 1973, Hannah Josephson Papers.

"a foot and a half above the ground": ibid.

"second-hand oil stoves": Smith, "Fighting Pacifist," 243–244.

"homemade tin bathtub": ibid., 244.

"railroad toilet": ibid.

"thinking and working peace ideas": JR to WR, 29 July 1932, WRP.

"non-consuming life style": Wilson, "Jeannette Rankin."

Smith-Rosenberg's essay: Smith-Rosenberg, "Discourses of Sexuality," 264, 266.

"through their own efforts economically independent": Schwarz, *Radical Feminists of Heterodoxy,* 53.

"argued that 'the emancipation of woman'": Flanagan, 547.

"I haven't any clothes": Katharine Anthony to JR, 7 February 1954, JRP, SL.

202 "I know this well": Henry David Thoreau, "Civil Disobedience," in *The Portable Thoreau,* ed. Carl Bode (New York: Viking Press, 1964), 120–121.

"As for adopting the ways which the State has provided": ibid., 120.

"members of Congress are more concerned": JR, "How to Write to Your Congressman," unpublished paper, 1972, MHS.

"if mothers wish to save their sons": standard JR response to antiwar letters, JRP, SL.

"If we had 10,000 women": *The Denver Post,* 19 May 1967, MHS.

"I do not want to be understood as advocating violence": quoted in *Anaconda Standard,* 10 July 1913, MHS.

"composed predominantly of white, middle-aged women": Federal Bureau of Investigation, field report, "Demonstration Protesting United States Policy on Vietnam, Washington, D.C., January 16, 1968."

"self-styled 'radical' young women": *Washington Post,* January 1968, MHS.

203   "did a polite put-down number": DMB to Hannah Josephson, 31 August 1973, Hannah Josephson Papers.

"a social occasion": Josephson, *First Lady*, 188.

"women's liberation movement": *Washington Post*, January 1968, MHS.

"run the same as the public schools": quoted in *Buffalo Express*, 24 September 1917, JRP, SL.

"purely educational": quoted in ibid.

"only print the news": JR, interview with Board.

"explain [to Rankin] the much broader proposition": Joseph C. Mason to Catharine Waugh McCulloch, 21 October 1922, Catharine Waugh McCulloch Papers.

204   "bored" in the Himalayas: JR to ERM, October 1952, JR, SL.

produced such "horrible" results: JR to WR, 18 July 1952, WRP.

"I play with the idea": JR to GRK, 3 September 1952, JRP, SL.

"far from breaking down the myth": Lasch, *Social Thought*, 152.

"a set of distinctive interests of their own": ibid., 152, 153.

"take the lead in the future of civilization": Kidd, *Science of Power*, 239.

"other-regarding self"; "mind of women": ibid., 235.

"short-range animal emotions"; "fighting male": ibid., 209.

"only through the extension of the democratic process": Josephson, *First Lady*, 65.

"they just wanted me to go and speak": JR, interview with Chall, 102–103.

"working from the top down": Josephson, *First Lady*, 261.

"draft could be abolished": JR, Associated Press, 19 May 1967, MHS.

"utmost importance to the goal of peace": JR, speech to the Jeannette Rankin Rank and File, New York City, 30 January 1969, JRP, SL.

"grassroots political organizing": *Life*, 3 March 1972.

205   proportional representation: *Chicago Sunday Herald*, 11 November 1917, quoted in Schaffer, "Progressive," 77; Wilson, "Her Lifework as a Pacifist," 42.

"Congress is the really important problem": JR to Antoinette Hamilton, nd, JRP, SL.

"invited to appear in Washington": JR, speech to the Jeannette Rankin Rank and File.

"accepted all invitations": Smith, "Fighting Pacifist," 273.

"made a plea for the preferential vote": Josephson, *First Lady*, 200–201.

unsuccessfully encouraged legislators: JR to Georgia Senate and House of Representatives, October 1971, MHS.

"Under the current arrangement": ibid.

206   The gist of her argument: see JR, interview with Chall, 25–26, 37–38, 42–44.

"dilute urban votes": Paul D. Coverdell to JR, 30 November 1971, JRP, SL.

put in pamphlet form: JR and John Kirkley, "Case for Direct Preferential Vote for President," MHS.

"world's outstanding living feminist": *New York Times*, February 1972, SOHP.

"Electoral College is a sham": quoted in *San Francisco Chronicle*, 9 May 1972, SOHP.

"anybody who wants to can run": ibid.

"men have progressed as much as they could": quoted in *Helena Independent Record,* 13 March 1972, MHS.

"distort[ing] the meaning of the popular vote": JR and Kirkley, "Case for the Direct Preferential Vote," 264.

207   "stamina behind these ideas": *Capital Times,* 11 September 1972.

New York friend urged: Clara de Miha to JR, 8 February 1972, JRP, SL.

"You are a constant beacon of truth": Dave Johnson to JR, 18 April 1972, JRP, SL.

"produce very lively controversy": John W. Gardner to JR, 7 April 1971, JRP, SL.

known for advocating at-large elections: Lani Guinier, *The Tyranny of the Majority: Fundamental Fairness in Representative Democracy* (New York: The Free Press, 1994).

Heterodoxy members who were her friends: Schwarz, *Radical Feminists of Heterodoxy,* 30.

208   "had been radicalized by their experiences": ibid.

"void midway between two spheres": quoted in Inez Hanes Gillmore, "Confessions of an Alien," *Harper's Bazaar,* April 1912, 170, quoted in Schwarz, *Radical Feminists of Heterodoxy,* 56.

"I'd love to call and say": JR to Hannah Josephson, 24 January 1973, Hannah Josephson Papers.

"hours for soldiers in the trenches": JR to Julia Fownes Smith, 28 July 1917, JRP, MHS.

"to drain away military funds": Josephson, *First Lady,* 122.

"gunpowder–versus–face powder": JR to Rosalie Gardiner Jones, 17 August 1943, JRP, SL.

"don't-shop-on-Tuesdays": *The Evening Star and Daily News,* 2 September 1972.

"refuge or shelter": Carol Farley Kessler, ed., *Daring to Dream: Utopian Fiction by United States Women Before 1950,* second edition (Syracuse: Syracuse University Press, 1995), xv.

"a critical outsider": ibid., xvii.

"cooperative or communitarian solutions": ibid., xxiv.

Blake's "feminine Republic": Lillie Devereux Blake, "A Divided Republic: An Allegory of the Future," in Kessler, *Daring to Dream,* 103.

"corrupt marriages": Kessler, *Daring to Dream,* xxii.

"restrictive sexual relationships": ibid., xix.

"to select their sexual partners"; "striv[ing] to please each other": ibid., xxii.

"equal wages regardless of sex": ibid., xxiii.

"for inventions, art, and letters": quoted in Winnifred Harper Cooley, "A Dream of the Twenty-first Century," in Kessler, *Daring to Dream,* 127.

209   "I want freedom": quoted in Mary H. Ford, "A Feminine Iconoclast," in Kessler, *Daring to Dream,* 110.

"sex mania"; "unnatural"; "old maid"; "social reject": Kessler, *Daring to Dream,* xxvii.

"nineteenth-century horror": Cooley, in Kessler, *Daring to Dream,* 128.

"common-sense shoes": Blake, in Kessler, *Daring to Dream*, 103.

"abolish the profit system": Smith, "Fighting Pacifist," 213.

"abolished oil trusts": Cooley, in Kessler, *Daring to Dream*, 127.

"wholesomely tired": *Chicago Sunday Herald*, 25 March 1917, MHS.

"three hours daily": Kessler, *Daring to Dream*, xxiii.

"ragged little newsboys": Cooley, in Kessler, *Daring to Dream*, 130.

"swarm[ing] the back streets": ibid., 128.

"wild zone": quoted in Kessler, *Daring to Dream*, xxvii.

"women's reality": ibid.

210   "a matron of notable appearance": Blake, in Kessler, *Daring to Dream*, 96.

"to declare war against all the world": ibid., 100.

"had grown self-reliant": ibid., 102.

"blouse waists, short skirts and long boots": ibid.

"[p]eace and tranquility prevailed": ibid., 99.

In her *Woman's Home Companion* trilogy: Katharine Anthony, "Our Gypsy Journey to Georgia," "A Basket of Summer Fruit," "Living on the Front Porch."

community playground: Charlotte Perkins Gilman, "A Woman's Utopia," in Kessler, *Daring to Dream*, 167.

"bungling experiments of an unaided mother": ibid., 171.

"constantly improving the quality of the stock": quoted in ibid., 172.

211   "low grade" men: ibid., 170.

"twenty-five cooks, dishwashers and servers": ibid., 169.

"Come and see the dining rooms": ibid., 169–170.

"farms radiating like pie-wedges": Kessler, *Daring to Dream*, xxvi.

"first day of the twenty-first century": Cooley, in Kessler, *Daring to Dream*, 126.

"rational religion": quoted in ibid., 129–130.

"feminine Boards of Education": Blake, in Kessler, *Daring to Dream*, 102.

"special campaign against falsehood": quoted in Gilman, in Kessler, *Daring to Dream*, 148.

"the average of behavior rises": quoted in ibid., 146.

"pre-social individuals"; "kept the world selfish": quoted in ibid., 149–150.

"worship God all the time": quoted in ibid., 152.

212   "bitterly negative reaction": confidential interview.

"mind-clouding" experiences: Smith, "Fighting Pacifist," 267.

"had no spiritual base": confidential interview.

"Christianity made people into sheep": confidential interview.

"ethical principles—like telling the truth": Galt interview.

"compassion, honesty, integrity, and love": JR and Kirkley, "Why I Voted Against War."

"a dreadful bore": Josephson, *First Lady,* 15.

challenged by her graduate-school instructors: Schaffer, "Progressive," 18.

"folk schools": JR, interview with Josephson, 201.

accelerate the evolutionary process: JR to Mrs. Berkeley Hayes, 12 June 1943, JRP, SL.

"dull, sodden peasantry": ibid.

"the living word": ibid.

"when their work was slack": JR, interview with Josephson, 202.

"work[ing] at their economic problems": JR to Mrs. Berkeley Hayes, 12 June 1943.

"the most thrilling thing I saw in India": JR, interview with Josephson, 220.

"went from the other end": ibid., 223.

"would take the children in a certain community": ibid., 220–222.

213 "democratic processes": JR to Mrs. Berkeley Hayes, 12 June 1943.

convention of club women: JR, 1914 speech to Federation of Women's Clubs, MHS.

"drawing exclusively upon the young men": unidentified Washington, D.C., newspaper, nd, MHS.

"the whole trouble with England today": quoted in Cheek, "Rhetoric and Revolt," 187.

instructed American women: JR, "What We Women Should Do," 17.

214 "I suggested that [a retired neighbor] help me": JR to Flora Belle Surles, 3 February 1966, Flora Belle Surles Papers.

In letters to prospective residents: JR to Mrs. M. A. Evans, 7 March 1967, and JR to Mrs. W. L. Davis, 30 April 1969, JRP, SL.

"fifteen dollar monthly rental": *Great Falls Tribune,* 6 March 1969, JRP, SL.

built under her supervision: Smith, "Fighting Pacifist," 248.

"It is not a nursing home": JR to Mrs. M. A. Evans, 7 March 1967, JRP, SL.

"ten women using one refrigerator": Clara Thomas to JR, March 1967, JRP, SL.

"put my application in right now": Elizabeth Sinclair to JR, 7 May 1967, JRP, SL.

daughters were skeptical: ibid., 10 May 1967.

215 rented the roundhouse: MRB to JR, 4 October 1968, JRP, SL; Smith, "Fighting Pacifist," 266.

"main supply line for marijuana": *Washington News,* 30 May 1969, JRP, SL.

"Hippies are doing": quoted in unidentified newspaper, 27 May 1969, JRP, SL.

"It ain't safe to be different": DMB to ERM, 1969, ERMP.

"so on the outside": Winestine interview, 21.

"'warfare being waged'": Schaffer, "Progressive," 164.

trip to Russia "was off": Katharine Anthony and Elisabeth Irwin to JR, 28 April 1925, JRP, SL.

"world conference on peace": JR, interview with Josephson, 263.

"disgusted with the peace attitude of the American group": ibid., 262.

"definite tendency toward Fascism": JR to H. C. Eklund, 19 April 1935, quoted in Schaffer, "Progressive," 190.

216   "stupid money system": Smith, "Fighting Pacifist," 274.

"efforts to redistribute wealth": Schaffer, "Progressive," 191.

"interest is usury": JR to Huey Long, 31 May 1933, quoted in Schaffer, "Progressive," 191.

"plan was to draw straws": JR to WR, 10 September 1935, WRP.

Upton Sinclair's plan: Schaffer, "Progressive," 191.

Father Coughlin's radio diatribes: ibid., 192.

"whatever the soldier's wage is": JR, House Military Affairs Committee Hearing, January 1935, quoted in Schaffer, "Progressive," 210.

217   "disdain for people who dressed well": confidential interview.

angered her mother by her sloppy dress: Smith, "Fighting Pacifist," 245.

"gold colored velvet suit": Winestine, "The First Woman in Congress."

"like a young panther": ibid.

"becoming pink chiffon dress": *New York Herald,* 3 March 1917, MHS.

"dark blue silk and chiffon suit": Ellen Maury Slayden, quoted in Smith, "Fighting Pacifist," 132.

"looked perfectly lovely": DMB to ERM, 26 August 1961, ERMP.

"dressed in a tailored blue plaid suit": Cheek, "Rhetoric and Revolt," 2.

"return the [Shanghai Silk] dress": John Kirkley to ERM, 24 January 1972, ERMP.

218   "I do not want to be understood": quoted in *Anaconda Standard,* 10 July 1913, MHS.

"simultaneously feminine and feminist": Moore, "Making a Spectacle," 94.

"Good Americans must obey the law": quoted in Schaffer, "Progressive," 136.

"one HONEST man": Thoreau, "Civil Disobedience," 121, 119.

"I have the following information for you": Louise Rankin Galt to JR, 23 September 1968, JRP, SL.

"I would like to sign that deed": JR to WR, 30 November 1955, WRP.

"Did I tell you that I'm buying a ranch": JR to Flora Belle Surles, 29 July 1955, Flora Belle Surles Papers.

"In 1954, Wellington bought the 71 Ranch": Galt interview.

219   "the house Mother and I bought": JR to WR, 2 July 1938, WRP.

"Jeannette is debating": GRK to JR, 6 March 1944, JRP, SL.

"Sure, if she can get her money out": ibid.

"fix up the two places": Louise Rankin Galt to JR, 8 February 1968, JRP, SL.

"An inspection was made": Herbert B. Gloege to Louise Galt, 29 January 1968, JRP, SL.

"it would cost too much money": Louise Rankin Galt to JR, 8 February 1968, JRP, SL.

"companies that produced modern weapons": Wilson, "Her Lifework as a Pacifist," 52.

220 "wouldn't think of charging you": Louise Rankin Galt to JR, 5 February 1969, JRP, SL.

"Montana Flour Dividend check": Louise Rankin to JR, 12 March 1965, JRP, SL.

"paper from the Equitable Assurance Company": ibid., 28 September 1965.

"watching Boeing and United go up": ibid., 29 September 1965.

"will keep you informed": ibid., 28 October 1965.

"dividends [from] Montana Flour Mills": ibid., 14 March 1966.

"dividend check from Fairchild Hiller": ibid., 1 March 1967.

"willing to buy the Rim Rock oil wells": ibid., 7 June 1967.

"ninety shares of United Aircraft": Arthur P. Acher to JR, 9 July 1968, JRP, SL.

"checks [for] Social Security": Louise Rankin Galt to JR, 10 December 1968, JRP, SL.

"Big West Oil people": ibid., 24 November 1971.

"You have 1,180 shares": ibid., 26 December 1968.

"check for the 1,180 shares": ibid., 15 January 1969.

selling the Weiglow Ranch: DMB to George Thorngate, Sr., 20 December 1973, JRP, SL.

vigorous protest by Edna: ERM to Hannah Josephson, 27 August 1973, ERMP.

221 "charitable foundation": JR's will, JRP, SL.

"dumbest will I could imagine": ERM to Virginia Ronhovde, 18 March 1976, ERMP.

"fit, fought, bled, and died": DMB to ERM, 1 August 1977, ERMP.

they had angered Jeannette: ibid.

"leave everything to a peace organization": ibid.

9. EPILOGUE: A RANKIN FIRST

223 "eminently suited": Brownmiller, *New York Times Review of Books*, JRP, SL.

"include both public and private realms": Freedman, *No Turning Back*, 327.

Patricia Schroeder years later: ibid., 340.

224 "a large and powerful animal": Plato, *The Republic*, trans. H.D.P. Lee (New York: Penguin Books, 1962), 254.

"make the public his master": ibid., 255.

"poll-driven politics": see "The 'Feminization' Factor," *The Washington Post National Weekly Edition*, 22 March 1999.

"Government of the people by an elite": quoted in Maurice Duverger, *Political Parties* (New York: John Wiley & Sons, 1954), 426.

first African American woman elected to Congress: Mary Beth Rogers, *Barbara Jordan: American Hero* (New York: Bantam Books, 1998).

225 "stingy soul": confidential interview.

"felt close to her": ibid.

Selected Sources

MANUSCRIPT COLLECTIONS

Belle Fligelman Winestine Papers, Schlesinger Library, Radcliffe College.
Catharine Waugh McCulloch Papers, Schlesinger Library, Radcliffe College.
Edna Rankin McKinnon Papers, Montana Historical Society, Helena.
Edna Rankin McKinnon Papers, Schlesinger Library, Radcliffe College.
Flora Belle Surles Papers, Schlesinger Library, Radcliffe College.
Frances C. Elge Papers, Montana Historical Society, Helena.
Hannah Geffen Josephson Papers, Schlesinger Library, Radcliffe College.
Harriet Wright Burton Laidlaw Papers, Schlesinger Library, Radcliffe College.
Harriet Yarrow Papers, Schlesinger Library, Radcliffe College.
Inez Haynes Irwin Papers, Schlesinger Library, Radcliffe College.
Jeannette Rankin Papers, Montana Historical Society, Helena.
Jeannette Rankin Papers, Schlesinger Library, Radcliffe College.
Margaret Foley Papers, Schlesinger Library, Radcliffe College.
Mary Ware Dennett Papers, Schlesinger Library, Radcliffe College.
Norman and Belle Fligelman Winestine Papers, Montana Historical Society, Helena.

Wellington D. Rankin Papers, Montana Historical Society, Helena.

William F. Dunne Collection, Butte–Silver Bow County Archives, Butte.

INTERVIEWS

Crowley, William F. 28 November 2001. Interview by authors.

Galt, Louise Rankin. 25 April 2000. Interview by authors.

Haines, Tom. 8 July 1980. Interview by Helen Bonner. Transcript, University of Montana Library Archives.

Halinan, Vivian. 16 July 1980. Interview by Helen Bonner. Transcript, University of Montana Library Archives.

Jones, Daphne Bugbee. 13 September 2002. Interview by authors.

Page, Winfield. 9 July 1980. Interview by Helen Bonner. Transcript, University of Montana Library Archives.

Rankin, Jeannette. 29 August 1963. Interview by John C. Board. Audio recording, University of Montana Library Archives.

———. 1974. Interviews by Malca Chall and Hannah Josephson. Audio recordings and transcripts, Suffragists Oral History Project, Bancroft Library, University of California, Berkeley.

Smith, Norma. 3 July 1999. Interview by authors.

Winestine, Belle Fligelman. 14 July 1980. Interview by Helen Bonner. Audio recording, University of Montana Library Archives.

OTHER UNPUBLISHED SOURCES

Board, John C. "The Lady from Montana: Jeannette Rankin." 1964. M.A. thesis, University of Wyoming.

Bonner, Helen Louise Ward. "The Jeannette Rankin Story." 1982. Ph.D. dissertation, Ohio University.

Cheek, Katrina Rebecca. "The Rhetoric and Revolt of Jeannette Rankin." 1969. M.A. thesis, University of Georgia.

Goodkin, Susan Linda. "The Effect of the Ideologies of Carrie Chapman Catt and Jeannette Rankin on Women's Political Involvement in the Early Twentieth Century." 1980. B.A. thesis, Harvard University.

Harris, Ted C. "Jeannette Rankin: Suffragist, First Woman Elected to Congress, and Pacifist." 1972. Ph.D. dissertation, University of Georgia.

Hayden, Sara. "'House Beautiful': Media Responses to Jeannette Rankin's Election to Congress and Vote Against U.S. Entry into the First World War." Unpublished paper, University of Montana.

Hines, Richard K. "Wellington Duncan Rankin: The Man Behind the Myth." 1996. M.A. thesis, Washington State University.

Kahn, Alfred J. "Themes for a History: The First Hundred Years of the Columbia University School of Social Work." Accessed 21 August 2000. Available at www.columbia.edu/cu/ssw/events/ajkahn/.

Kirkley, John. "An Afternoon with Jeannette Rankin." Unpublished paper, Montana Historical Society.

———. "A Chapter in a Life." Unpublished paper, Montana Historical Society.

Murphy, Mary. "Women in the West Telling Their Stories." 5 March 1994. Audio recording, University of Montana Library.

Rankin, Jeannette. "How to Write to Your Congressman." 1972. Unpublished paper, Montana Historical Society.

Rankin, Jeannette, and John Kirkley. "Case for the Direct Preferential Vote for President." 1972. Unpublished paper, Montana Historical Society.

———. "Why I Voted Against War." Nd. Unpublished paper, Jeannette Rankin Papers, Montana Historical Society.

Schaffer, Ronald. "Jeannette Rankin: Progressive Isolationist." 1959. Ph.D. dissertation, Princeton University.

Smith, Norma. "Fighting Pacifist: Jeannette Rankin and Her Times." 1999. Unpublished manuscript, Bozeman, Montana.

Ward, Doris Buck. "Winning of Woman Suffrage in Montana." 1974. M.A. thesis, University of Montana.

Wilson, Joan Hoff. "Jeannette Rankin." 4 April 1977. Speech to the Montana History Conference, Helena. Audio recording, University of Montana Library.

———. "The Search for Jeannette Rankin's Past." 4 May 1979. Speech to the Montana Library Association, Bozeman. Montana Historical Society.

Winestine, Belle Fligelman. "Belle Fligelman Winestine: Feminist and Suffragette." 1976. Audio recording, University of Montana Library Archives.

———. "The First Woman in Congress." 8 July 1981. Speech to the Women's Resource Center, University of Montana. Audio recording, University of Montana Library Archives.

BOOKS AND ARTICLES

Alonso, Harriet Hyman. *Peace as a Woman's Issue: A History of the U.S. Movement for World Peace and Women's Rights.* Syracuse: Syracuse University Press, 1993.

Anderson, Kathryn. "Steps to Political Equality: Woman Suffrage and Electoral Politics in the Lives of Emily Newall Blair, Anne Hennrietta Martin, and Jeannette Rankin." *Frontiers* 18 (January–April 1997): 101–121.

Anthony, Katharine. "Our Gypsy Journey to Georgia." *Woman's Home Companion* 53 (July 1926): 14–15, 58, 60, 63.

———. "A Basket of Summer Fruit." *Woman's Home Companion* 53 (August 1926): 11–12, 50, 52.

————. "Living on the Front Porch." *Woman's Home Companion* 53 (September 1926): 32, 34, 83–84.

Brown, Mackey. "Montana's First Woman Politician: A Recollection of Jeannette Rankin Campaigning." *Montana Business Quarterly* 9 (autumn 1971): 23–26.

Calvert, Jerry. *The Gibraltar: Socialism and Labor in Butte, Montana, 1895–1920.* Helena: Montana Historical Society Press, 1988.

Chesterton, G. K. *St. Francis of Assisi.* New York: Image Books, 1957.

Cutter, Martha J. *Unruly Tongues: Identity and Voice in American Women's Writing, 1850–1930.* Jackson: University Press of Mississippi, 1999.

D'Emilio, John, and Estelle B. Freedman. *Intimate Matters: A History of Sexuality in America.* New York: Harper & Row, 1988.

Doig, Ivan. *This House of Sky: Landscapes of a Western Mind.* New York: Harcourt Brace & Company, 1978.

DuBois, Ellen Carol. *Woman Suffrage and Women's Rights.* New York: New York University Press, 1998.

Dykeman, Wilma. *Too Many People, Too Little Love.* New York: Holt, Rinehart, and Winston, 1974.

Emmons, David M. *The Butte Irish: Class and Ethnicity in an American Mining Town.* Urbana: University of Illinois Press, 1989.

Faderman, Lillian. *Odd Girls and Twilight Lovers: A History of Lesbian Life in Twentieth-Century America.* New York: Columbia University Press, 1991.

————. *Surpassing the Love of Men: Romantic Friendship and Love Between Women from the Renaissance to the Present.* New York: William Morrow, 1981.

Freedman, Estelle B. *No Turning Back: The History of Feminism and the Future of Women.* New York: Ballantine Books, 2002.

————. "Separatism as Strategy: Female Institution Building and American Feminism, 1870–1930." In *U.S. Women in Struggle: A Feminist Studies Anthology,* edited by Claire Goldberg Moses and Heidi Hartmann. Urbana: University of Illinois Press, 1995.

————. "Separatism Revisited: Women's Institutions, Social Reform, and the Career of Miriam Van Waters." In *U.S. History as Women's History,* edited by Linda K. Kerber and others. Chapel Hill: University of North Carolina Press, 1995.

Giles, Kevin J. *Flight of the Dove: The Story of Jeannette Rankin.* Beaverton, OR: Touchstone, 1980.

Goldmark, Josephine. *Impatient Crusader.* Urbana: University of Illinois Press, 1953.

Guinier, Lani. *The Tyranny of the Majority: Fundamental Fairness in Representative Democracy.* New York: The Free Press, 1994.

Harper, Ida Husted, ed. *The History of Woman Suffrage,* vol. 6. New York: National American Woman Suffrage Association, 1922.

Hinckle, Warren, and Marianne Hinckle. "A History of the Rise of the Unusual Movement for Women Power in the United States, 1961–1968." *Ramparts* (February 1968): 24–26.

Josephson, Hannah. *Jeannette Rankin: First Lady in Congress*. New York: Bobbs-Merrill, 1974.

Karlin, Jules. A. *Joseph M. Dixon of Montana, Part 1: Senator and Bull Moose Manager, 1867–1917*. Missoula: University of Montana Publications in History, 1974.

Kessler, Carol Farley, ed. *Daring to Dream: Utopian Fiction of United States Women Before 1950*, second edition. Syracuse: Syracuse University Press, 1995.

Kidd, Benjamin. *The Science of Power*. New York: G. P. Putnam Sons, 1918.

———. *Social Evolution*. New York: Macmillan Company, 1915.

Lasch, Christopher, ed. *The Social Thought of Jane Addams*. Indianapolis: Bobbs-Merrill, 1965.

Limerick, Patricia Nelson. *The Legacy of Conquest: The Unbroken Past of the American West*. New York: W. W. Norton, 1987.

MacKinnon, Catherine A. *Toward a Feminist Theory of the State*. Cambridge: Harvard University Press, 1989.

Malone, Michael P., and Richard B. Roeder. *Montana: A History of Two Centuries*. Seattle: University of Washington Press, 1978.

Malone, Michael P., Richard B. Roeder, and William L. Lang. *Montana: A History of Two Centuries*, revised edition. Seattle: University of Washington Press, 1991.

McGlen, Nancy E., Karen O'Connor, Laura van Assendelft, and Wendy Gunther-Canada. *Women, Politics, and American Society*, third edition. New York: Longman, 2002.

Moore, Sara J. "Making a Spectacle of Suffrage: The National Women Suffrage Pageant." *Journal of American Culture* 20 (spring 1997): 89–103.

Murphy, Mary. *Mining Cultures: Men, Women, and Leisure in Butte, 1914–1941*. Urbana: University of Illinois Press, 1997.

Richey, Elinor. *Eminent Women of the West*. Berkeley: Howell-North Books, 1975.

Rogers, Mary Beth. *Barbara Jordan: American Hero*. New York: Bantam Books, 1998.

Rupp, Leila J. *A Desired Past: A Short History of Same-Sex Love in America*. Chicago: University of Chicago Press, 1999.

Schaffer, Ronald. "The Montana Woman Suffrage Campaign, 1911–1914." *Pacific Northwest Quarterly* 54 (January 1964): 9–15.

Schwarz, Judith. *Radical Feminists of Heterodoxy: Greenwich Village, 1912–1940*, revised edition. Norwich, VT: New Victoria, 1986.

Sklar, Kathryn Kish. *Florence Kelley and the Nation's Work: The Rise of Women's Political Culture, 1830–1900*. New Haven: Yale University Press, 1995.

Smith, Norma. *Jeannette Rankin: America's Conscience*. Helena: Montana Historical Society Press, 2002.

————. "The Woman Who Said No to War: A Day in the Life of Jeannette Rankin." *Ms Magazine* 14 (March 1986): 86–88.

Smith-Rosenberg, Carroll. "Discourses of Sexuality and Subjectivity: The New Woman, 1870–1936." In *Hidden from History: Reclaiming the Gay and Lesbian Past,* edited by Martin Duberman et al. New York: New American Library, 1989.

————. *Disorderly Conduct: Visions of Gender in Victorian America.* New York: Alfred A. Knopf, 1985.

Steele, Volney. *Wellington Rankin: His Family, Life and Times.* Bozeman, MT: Bridger Creek Historical Press, 2002.

Waldron, Ellis, and Paul B. Wilson. *Atlas of Montana Elections, 1889–1976.* Missoula: University of Montana Publications in History, 1978.

Walter, Dave. "Rebel with a Cause." *Montana Magazine* (November–December 1991): 66–72.

Walzer, Michael. *Just and Unjust Wars: A Moral Argument with Historical Illustrations.* New York: Basic Books, 1977.

Ware, Susan. *Partner and I: Molly Dewson, Feminism, and New Deal Politics.* New Haven: Yale University Press, 1987.

West, Robin. "Jurisprudence and Gender." *University of Chicago Law Review* 55 (winter 1988): 1–72.

Wilson, Joan Hoff. "'Peace Is a Woman's Job . . .'—Jeannette Rankin and American Foreign Policy: The Origins of Her Pacifism." *Montana: The Magazine of Western History* 30 (winter 1980): 28–41.

————. "'Peace Is a Woman's Job . . .'—Jeannette Rankin and American Foreign Policy: Her Lifework as a Pacifist." *Montana: The Magazine of Western History* 30 (spring 1980): 38–53.

Winestine, Belle Fligelman. "Mother Was Shocked." *Montana: The Magazine of Western History* 24 (summer 1974): 70–79.

Witt, Linda, Karen M. Paget, and Glenna Matthews. *Running as a Woman: Gender and Power in American Politics.* New York: The Free Press, 1994.

Zinn, Howard. *LaGuardia in Congress.* Ithaca: Cornell University Press, 1959.

NEWSPAPERS

Anaconda Standard
Augusta Chronicle
Boston Traveler
Boulder Monitor
Bozeman Chronicle
Butte Miner
Butte Tribune-Review

Daily Missoulian
Denver Post
Great Falls Daily Tribune
Great Falls Tribune
Hardin Tribune
Helena Independent
Helena Independent Record
The Independent
Joint Strike Bulletin
Kalispell Times
Lewistown Democrat-News
Livingston Enterprise
Missoulian
Montana American
Montana Kaimen
Montana News
Montana Standard
The Nation
New York Times
New York World
Park County News
Portsmouth Times
Sanders County Signal
San Francisco Bulletin
San Francisco Sunday Chronicle
Seattle Times
Three Forks Herald
Washington Evening Star and Daily News
Washington Post
Washington Times
The Woman Citizen
Woman's Journal and Suffrage News

Index

MAR - - 2013